Ancient African Metallurgy

Ancient African Metallurgy

The Sociocultural Context

MICHAEL S. BISSON
S. TERRY CHILDS
PHILIP DE BARROS
AUGUSTIN F. C. HOLL

Edited and with a foreword by
JOSEPH O. VOGEL

ALTAMIRA
PRESS
A Division of
ROWMAN & LITTLEFIELD PUBLISHERS, INC.
Walnut Creek • Lanham • New York • Oxford

AltaMira Press
A Division of Rowman & Littlefield Publishers, Inc.
1630 North Main Street, #367
Walnut Creek, CA 94596
http://www.altamirapress.com

Rowman & Littlefield Publishers, Inc.
4720 Boston Way
Lanham, MD 20706

12 Hid's Copse Road
Cumnor Hill, Oxford OX2 9JJ, England

British Library Cataloguing in Publication Information Available

Library of Congress Cataloging-in-Publication Data

Ancient African metallurgy : the sociocultural context / Michael S. Bisson . . . [et al.] ; edited and with a foreword by Joseph O. Vogel.
p. cm.
Includes bibliographical references and indexes.
ISBN 0-7425-0260-0 (cloth : alk. paper)—ISBN 0-7425-0261-9 (pbk. : alk. paper)
1. Metal-work—Africa—History. 2. Metal-work, Prehistoric—Africa. 3. Copperwork—Africa—History. 4. Ironwork—Africa—History. 5. Ethnoarchaeology—Africa. 6. Africa—Antiquities. I. Bisson, Michael S. II. Vogel, Joseph O.

GN645.A52 2000
960′.1—dc21 00-036210

Printed in the United States of America

∞ ™The paper used in this publication meets the minimum requirements of American National Standard for Information Sciences—Permanence of Paper for Printed Library Materials, ANSI/NISO Z39.48–1992.

"Save the bellow, let the calf be hit."
"Wife of the smith does not know what brought her."
"Save the bellow, let the calf be hit."
"Child of the smith does not know how to walk aimlessly."
"Save the bellow, let the calf be hit."
"Wife of the smith does not know what brought her."
"Save the bellow, let the calf be hit."
"Child of the smith does not know what brought him/her."
"Save the bellow, let the calf be hit."
"White person of the hammer does not know what brought her."
To save the bellow—if it is put outside while the calves are feeding and the rain comes, you run to save the bellows and let the calves be beaten by rain.

Toro smithing song

Welcome in your search for charcoal,
chief ironworker, handsome ironworker.
All ironworkers are chiefs.
The beautiful woman, the handsome boy, the pretty house,
all are the work of the ironworker.
Strike the iron, but do not strike man.
If you are satisfied, thank the ironworker.
The ironworker is equivalent to the remedy against hunger,
the end of war, the antidote against disease.

Sabi-Monra (1991, 145), citing the Bariba praise singer Dama Guerra Orou

Contents

Tables, Figures, and Plates viii

Acknowledgments xi

Foreword, by Joseph O. Vogel xiii

1 Metals and Precolonial African Society 1
Augustin F. C. Holl

2 Precolonial Copper Metallurgy: Sociopolitical Context 83
Michael S. Bisson

3 Iron Metallurgy: Sociocultural Context 147
Philip de Barros

4 Traditional Iron Working: A Narrated Ethnoarchaeological Example 199
S. Terry Childs

References 255

Author Index 277

Subject Index 283

About the Authors 293

Tables, Figures, and Plates

CHAPTER 1

Table 1.1.	Distribution of archaeological sites according to morphographic units	29
Table 1.2.	Major characteristics of tested "neolithic" sites	33
Table 1.3.	Major characteristics of tested settlements with evidence of copper metallurgy	35
Table 1.4.	Major characteristics of tested settlements with evidence of iron metallurgy	36
Table 1.5.	General distribution of metal artifacts and slag	41
Table 1.6.	Diversity of recorded metal artifacts	42
Table 1.7.	Major characteristics of tested megalithic burial grounds	44
Table 1.8.	Hierarchy and regional spatial patterning of megalithic cemeteries	47
Table 1.9.	Settlement clusters and mound size in the Mema region	53
Table 1.10.	Settlement size through time in the Mema region	54
Table 1.11.	Major smelting sites in the southern forested region	64
Table 1.12.	Iron production sites of the Ndop Plain Industry	70
Table 1.13.	Iron production sites of the Glazed Sherds Industry	73
Figure 1.1.	Chronology of the development of iron technology	11
Figure 1.2.	Socioeconomic model of metal production	22
Figure 1.3.	Distribution of Late Stone Age sites	28
Figure 1.4.	Distribution of settlements with evidence of copper metallurgy	30
Figure 1.5.	Distribution of settlements with evidence of iron metallurgy	31
Figure 1.6.	Distribution of recorded megalithic cemeteries	32
Figure 1.7.	Variants of early copper-smelting furnaces	38
Figure 1.8.	Variants of later copper-smelting furnaces	39

Figure 1.9. Variants of iron-smelting furnaces 40
Figure 1.10. Cemeteries and putative territorial entities, Eghazer basin 46
Figure 1.11. Late Stone Age sites in the Mema region 50
Figure 1.12. Early Assemblage sites and iron-smelting localities 52
Figure 1.13. Middle Assemblage sites 55
Figure 1.14. Iron-smelting sites 56
Figure 1.15. Settlement size through time 57
Figure 1.16. The southern forested area 60
Figure 1.17. The iron-smelting site of Pan Mangueda in the Matomb settlement group 63
Figure 1.18. The natural draft furnace from the iron-smelting site of Pan Nsas in the Matomb settlement cluster 65
Figure 1.19. Industrial traditions and settlements in the Western Grassfields 66
Figure 1.20. Furnace types of the Western Grassfields 68
Figure 1.21. Settlement pattern at the climax of the Ndop Plain Industry 69
Figure 1.22. Settlement pattern in the Glazed Sherds Industry cluster 71

CHAPTER 2

Table 2.1. Radiocarbon dates from Kansanshi mine and smelting area 137
Plate 2.1. African mining at Dikuluwe, Democratic Republic of Congo 93
Plate 2.2. Kansanshi mine, Zambia 136
Plate 2.3. Kaonde refining furnace in operation, northwestern Zambia 138
Plate 2.4. Excavated base of Later Iron Age smelting furnace, Kansanshi mine, Zambia 142
Figure 2.1. Distribution of copper ore deposits in sub-Saharan Africa 86
Figure 2.2. Ancient mines and archaeological sites mentioned in the text 87
Figure 2.3. Early copper smelters from the Agadez region, Niger 90
Figure 2.4. Central African copper-smelting and -refining furnaces 96
Figure 2.5. Luba smelter 98
Figure 2.6. Smithing tools from southeastern Angola 104
Figure 2.7. Wire drawing tools from Ingombe Ilede, Zambia 106
Figure 2.8. "Roped pot" from Igbo Ukwu, Nigeria 108

Figure 2.9. *Manillas* 114
Figure 2.10. Ancient mines and archaeological sites in the south-central and southern African interior 116
Figure 2.11. Fourth- to twelfth-century ingots from Central Africa 117
Figure 2.12. Cruciform currency ingots from Central Africa 119
Figure 2.13. Ingot molds (clay) from Kipushi 120
Figure 2.14. Recent wire and bar currency from Central Africa 123
Figure 2.15 South African currency ingots 125
Figure 2.16. Trade routes for copper and other goods in central and southern Africa 127
Figure 2.17. The lower Congo River 129
Figure 2.18. Map of Kansanshi Hill showing location and scale of ancient workings 135
Figure 2.19. Kansanshi smelting area showing the location of components and excavations 139

CHAPTER 3

Figure 3.1. The Bassar industrial region showing specialist villages as they existed at contact in the 1880s 188
Figure 3.2. Smelting sites and production zones, Bassar region, with estimated slag volume 189
Figure 3a–h. Spatial organization of Bassar region smelting sites 193ff.

CHAPTER 4

Plate 4.1. Adyeri at old anvil stone 200
Plate 4.2. Preparing to put skin on a bellows 215
Plate 4.3. Adyeri's family hammers and clay tuyere 232
Plate 4.4. Toro smith working at his forge 236
Plate 4.5. Mining dance by Abachwamba clan 251

Acknowledgments

Michael Bisson:
I wish to thank Drs. Brian M. Fagan, David W. Phillipson, Joseph O. Vogel, and Nalumino Kantanekwa for their assistance during the fieldwork on which much of this study is based. Permission to work in Zambia was granted by the Commission for the Preservation of National and Historical Monuments and Relics. I am deeply grateful to Dr. Andrew Johnson and to Ann and Horst Matschke, avocational archaeologists without whom my work in Zambia would not have been possible. David Phiri and the Board of Directors of the Anglo American Corporation, Central Africa Ltd, granted permission to work at Kansanshi and provided generous logistical and financial assistance. I am also grateful to my wife, Marilyn Steely, who worked tirelessly in the field, and the many Zambians, particularly Axon Kanyakula and Benson Mutema, who conducted the excavations. Additional funding provided by the National Science Foundation and the Faculty of Graduate Studies and Research, McGill University, is also gratefully acknowledged. Many of the illustrations were drawn by Rosanna Chan and Jennifer Pamplin.

S. Terry Childs:
This project has benefited tremendously from the aid and support of a number of individuals and institutions. Peter Robertshaw provided financial assistance (NSF grant SBR-9320392) as well as important logistical and collegial support. Abwooli, or Charlotte Karungi, helped ensure the success of this project as my translator and friend during both field seasons. I wish to also thank the Uganda National Council for Science and Technology for research clearance; the Uganda Department of Antiquities and Museums, particularly Dr. Ephraim Kamuhangire, for its support; and the district executive secretary of Kaborole and his assistants for their help. Also, the British Institute of East Africa, particularly John Sutton and Justin Willis, provided use of a Land Rover during both field seasons. Finally, I owe my greatest appreciation to the wonderful people I met and interviewed in Toro, espe-

cially in the Butiiti area, such as Amooti Majiri, Sergeant Jane Kagura, the chief of Butiiti, and a number of ironworkers. I dedicate this chapter to the memory of Adyeri, or Mzee Ndunga, who tolerated my unending questions with both patience and love of the subject. I hope that by giving Adyeri full voice in this chapter, I will fulfill his dream of educating the world, especially Ugandans, about a soon-to-be-lost technology.

Foreword

Joseph O. Vogel

When the Africa Association first met in the 1780s, the gentlemen sitting at the St. Albans coffeehouse, in London's Pall Mall, were interested in the prospect of opening up new markets in Africa. In the preliminary stages of Europe's Industrial Revolution, capital sought the untapped African markets and products. Africa was then fairly unknown to westerners, who generally were still dependent on the geographic descriptions provided by Ptolemy, Leo Africanus, and other antique authorities. Nevertheless, they knew and were excited by more recent tales of Africa's processed metals and its products.

Merchantmen had long plied West African waters, bringing away slaves, ivory, gum, and especially gold. The prospect of a larger hoard in the interior had shone brightly ever since the incalculably wealthy king of Mali Mansa Musa made his *hajj* of 1324–25. Mansa Musa's retinue was reputed to have left sufficient quantities of gold in Cairo to deflate its value for some years thereafter. While we may speculate on the quality of the Cairene economy in the 1300s or the quantity of gold needed to disrupt it in so epic a fashion, we do know that Mansa Musa's golden cortege was impressive enough to keep its renown alive through the centuries.

Equally noteworthy is ancient Mali's center of commerce and Islamic learning, Tombouctou. Tombouctou and the Niger basin became objectives whose attainment consumed the gentlemen of the African Association, sponsors of a generation of adventurers willing to travel the unknown for an opportunity to find the source of West Africa's treasure. In time, the very name Tombouctou came to symbolize an African El Dorado replete with wealthy potentates and commercial opportunities. When Robert Adams—an involuntary traveler, having been shipwrecked in 1811, captured and enslaved in the town, and ransomed in 1813—returned to London, his account was disregarded as incredible. His descriptions of a commonplace Saharan market town simply failed to conform to the fabulous expectations of his listeners.

Europeans were more accustomed to accounts of the "silent trade" on the Senegal, conducted by merchants leading caravans from the Muslim north. Arriving after three weeks of arduous travel across the Sahara and unable to speak a common language with the local tribesmen, the merchants simply laid out separate piles of beads, salt, and manufactured goods on the ground. The local folk, who worked nearby strip mines for gold, examined the piles and placed beside each a heap of gold as a proposed payment. The local people then withdrew, and the traders returned to accept the offer or alter the size of their pile of goods. The silent trade proceeded in this way, with no face-to-face contact, as the price was arranged to the satisfaction of both parties. Only then were the different heaps of merchandise and gold taken up. Returning home, the Muslim traders once more faced a long, exhausting trip across the barren Sahara, driving their camels on anciently trafficked paths to transport the precious cargoes, which made the grueling journey worthwhile.

West African gold—mined and processed by indigenous miners and smiths and merchandised by African entrepreneurs—had been a staple of trans-Saharan commerce since time immemorial. It had underwritten Roman expansion, as it had Carthage. Not only the trans-Saharan caravans but Phoenician and later merchant captains as well bartered with local tradesmen at coastal entrepôts for the metal along with other goods from the interior. The African managers of this trade became overlords, able to govern large coalitions, or confederacies, of allied domestic stewards (lineagemates for the most part) with hereditary claims on natural resources and the labor needed to extract them. The empires of Ghana, Mali, and Songay, as well as a number of smaller descent-defined kingdoms, arose through the management of large-scale territorial assets while monopolizing these trade alliances. Similar trade alliances, statelike polities, and actual states emerged throughout the continent, drawing on control of natural resources, (e.g., copper and iron), the technologies needed to exploit them, and the means to market them and attract trading partners from near and far.

The indigenous smelting and smithing processes were refined crafts, and the means of attaining ore often were intricately conceived as well. In the 1870s, when Thomas Baines and other observers of African village life in the southeast described indigenous reduction of gold-bearing quartz (by crushing the ore in stone mortars before melting out the metal), members of the Royal Geographical Society argued that such methods were beyond the capabilities of traditional African metalworkers. Nevertheless, throughout the continent, local craftsmen were processing not only gold sands but also gold-bearing and other metallic ores and refining them for resale on world markets. Nor were African metalworkers solely dependent on surface finds.

Here and there, they opened mines, cutting narrow galleries, excavating along metal-rich seams, and extracting ore from deep underground. When the first European prospectors came to the mineralized territories of south-central Africa, they had little difficulty finding valuable deposits. They simply asked the local Africans, as George Grey did in order to "discover" Kanshansi mine in northern Zambia. In the late nineteenth century, W. F. Wilkinson, a mining engineer in present-day Zimbabwe, even published a map marking "ancient workings" that located precolonial gold-mining operations.

Where gold sands were plentiful, gold was extracted (as was copper) in clay crucibles at temperatures well within the range of indigenous ceramic manufacture. (In fact, in the early 1970s, we filmed Lunda men in northern Zambia smelting malachite into molten copper in clay pots.) However, this belies the fact that African smiths mastered a variety of refining methods, working at greater temperatures with metals that required further preparation to become usable. Most common was the production of bloomery iron, a frangible metallic material produced by melting iron out of the ore surrounding it. This process leaves much slag and a brittle bloom, which requires reheating and hardening at the forge in order to increase the metal's strength, and to produce a more malleable product. Technical skill beyond that required for the simple production of iron blooms was needed. Bloomery iron is usually quite soft, only slightly harder than pure copper, unless it is carburized over charcoal fires and refined with repeated forging, folding, quenching, and tempering. Smithing was an acquired skill that required training at the side of a master smith. It was always an arcane skill, evidenced by the "medicine holes" and single large smelting settlements found in the village aggregates of the Victorian Falls region, dated as early as the seventh century.

Though Rider Haggard altered the product of King Solomon's mines to diamonds, his literary predecessor, Hugh Walmsley, and legend had it that the king of Israel clothed his temple in gold from Ophir. In the nineteenth century, Ophir was popularly believed to be somewhere in the interior of eastern Africa. In the middle decades of the nineteenth century, travelers of an adventurous or a scholarly nature believed that a short trek inland from the shores of the Indian Ocean would be rewarded by discovery of the legendary mines said to have been visited by seamen sailing under the aegis of the Tyrean and Israelite kings. However, it was only in the theater of the mind—lamentably misrepresenting the ruins of Great Zimbabwe and other massive African-built towns—that European infatuations with the ancient golden trove of Africa could be fully played out.

The effect of African smiths went far beyond their ability to produce gold for the silent trade and to fuel European imaginations. Throughout tropical Africa, many generations of metalworkers refined valued commodities for local markets as well as for those far from their shores. Africa and its metalworkers appear always to have been part of a world system. Western Africa nurtured a number of progressively larger states that managed long-distance trade, communicating with the world touched by the Atlantic, and that exchanged gold and other natural products from the hinterlands for manufactured goods. If south-central Africa was not ancient Ophir, it was home to remarkable indigenous kingdoms in which metals again had a notable influence. Along with the gold sought by Portuguese conquistadores, copper was prominent in the rich flow of value underwriting the rise of maShona descent group stewards as the principal mediators of their societies.

Among the Luba-speaking people, on the divide at the head of the Zambezi and Congo Rivers, control of copper sources gave access to a worldwide bazaar of imported goods and underwrote the formation of states and social hierarchies. The copper processed in the Luba–Lunda kingdoms and molded into wire bars and cross-shaped ingots was carried toward the mouth of the Congo, to Swahili entrepôts on Lake Tanganyika, and down to the middle Zambezi. It passed through the hands of baTonga middlemen to the outposts of the "Empire of Monomatapa" to market towns such as Ingombe Ilede in the Gwembe valley. From there, Shona entrepreneurs and Swahili traders negotiated the copper's final passage to merchant cities on the Swahili coast.

The copper found ready markets on the Swahili coast, where coteries of merchant towns initially developed, apparently by satisfying market demand for high-quality iron produced by local smiths. East Africa's highly steeled product was so favored by smiths in the Indian subcontinent that it became a staple of the Indian Ocean trading network, helping to subsidize the conversion of coastal subsistence settlements with small-scale exchange alliances into important commercial centers. In time, the flow of traffic through the coastal merchant towns gave rise to prosperous city-states, such as Mombassa, Lamu, and Kilwa. These towns managed substantial reciprocal flows of value from their hinterlands that reached not only into Zambezia but also up to the indigenous states of the Great Lakes region and the Nile valley outward to markets in the Middle East, the Indian subcontinent, and beyond to the Far East.

The role of metals in the growth of trading networks is self-evident, as is the fact that trade was a principal influence on the emergence of indigenous states in Africa. However, the role of metals and metalworkers in the emergence of social complexity is a point that needs discussion since they seem to have had different effects at various times and places. That different metals took the fore in different parts of the continent is particularly interesting because it demonstrates both the capabilities of indigenous smiths and the versatility of the continent's entrepreneurs who seized on the commercial opportunities available to them.

Suggesting the influence of metals on African culture and history overlooks more integral arrangements arising out of the actual processes and management of locating and transporting ores as well as the manner or difficulty of reducing ore to metal and the organization of production and distribution. These appear mere matters of economics and technological knowledge, but in a noncapital environment they required enterprising social organization as well. They required a system capable of husbanding information and obligating labor. The physical processes of reducing ore into metal interest us not only for the basic chemistry and smithing operations, which vary from metal to metal, but also because African smiths coped with these physical intricacies while enshrouding technical understanding in an arcane veil. The concentration of knowledge—of the magical skills necessary to transforming stones into a valuable product—gave smiths the aura of power, of an ability beyond those of ordinary men. In an animistic world of finite good, a world inhabited by witches, such unmediated "power" could be viewed as threatening. In some places, the smiths had a lowly status, but more often they allied their social ambitions with those of their descent group stewards, acting as brokers of "transmutation" and transforming community leaders into semidivine "chiefs." The practice of metallurgy in Africa had not only obvious economic and technical aspects but social, ideological, aesthetic, and quite possibly psychological ones as well.

Though we have not exhausted the story of metallurgy and its role in crystallizing African society, we can look beyond its influences to questions such as how the knowledge of metallurgy arose in Africa in the first place and how came it to displace previously established technologies. The hotly debated question of diffusion from foreign sources or independent autochthonous invention is not easily resolved, but we can suggest some new signposts pointing to possible conclusions. At one time, many analysts believed that all iron-working technology was devised on the Anatolian plateau and diffused from there fully fledged by various routes until it reached tropical Africa. The usual routes associated with this diffusion scenario included those passing through Carthaginian settlements in the north and down along the ancient chariot routes across the Sahara or, alternately, along trade routes up the Nile valley to Meröe in the Sudan. It is thought that iron working that was nurtured in this indigenous African state, whose capital is replete with smelting debris and therefore may have been the site of intensive iron production, passed to other folk living in sub-Saharan Africa and gave rise to an "Iron Age."

This "Iron Age" was envisioned as a time when Bantu-speaking farmers used iron and fire to spread south and east colonizing the savannas of southern Africa. Though this picture lately has become more complex, it is evident that the earliest farming peoples on the southern savanna used iron. In my experience, related sets of village-communities in the Victoria Falls region each had a single associated smelter site and a wide inventory of iron tools;

however, only the kinds of iron tools (axes and hoes) that we recognize as principal to social transactions were buried alongside burials of these early farmers. These villagers also possessed copper, which they had traded for from some distant place and made into objects of bodily adornment. One of the very few early copper ingots came from among these settlements, even though the Victoria Falls region is far from the nearest copper mines. Obviously, trade in the commodity was established early in networks that stretched over hundreds of miles of open savanna. Though we may be led to construe too much from these limited observations, we can posit that metal working was already, in the sixth century, as well established and as integral a part of traditional village life in the continent as it would be in more complexly structured or metropolitan societies of indigenous Africa.

Given the obvious importance of the metallic thread woven into the elaborate tapestry of African culture, it seems appropriate to offer the four chapters presented here. Chapter 1 advises us of the processes by which myriad traditional African cultures received, assimilated, and diffused, as well as experimented with, metal-working technologies. As important, it reminds us that even if new technologies are perceived, they are not always immediately accepted and that new technological systems take a long while to be fully assimilated; the more complex they are, the longer they take to "take root" and the greater the effect on the intermeshed social fabric. A third point, arising from this observation, is the manner in which new technologies affect older, well-established cultural systems. Chapters 2 and 3 examine, respectively, the substance of African metallurgical knowledge and the societies that developed to exploit the potentials of metal usage. Chapter 4 gives a Ugandan metalworker an opportunity to tell his story, preserving and explaining his view of the metalworker's task.

1

Metals and Precolonial African Society

Augustin F. C. Holl

TOWARD AN ARCHAEOLOGY OF INNOVATION, PROCESS, AND TRANSFORMATION

Considered from a geological point of view, Africa is rich in metals. Metals of many kinds are found everywhere throughout the continent. Uranium, cobalt, manganese, bauxite, copper, gold, iron, tin, and the like occur in many different geological settings. Some of them were exploited in the past, giving rise to impressive indigenous African states, while others have been utilized only recently, as participants in the modernization and industrialization of a handful of countries at the southern end of the continent. The intensively worked copper belt of the Shaba province of the Congo and the adjacent district of Zambia, along with the gold fields of South Africa and Zimbabwe, represent spectacular examples of modern commercial exploitation of older workings, mined by Africans in precolonial times.

In precolonial times, traditional gold working took place in eastern Cameroon and the western Central African Republic as well as in the Poura region in Burkina-Faso (Kiethega 1983); tin mining was conducted on the Bauchi plateau. Reopening these mines led to the discovery of the renowned Nok Culture. Gold mines from the Red Sea hills and Nubia were exploited during the Pharaonic, Kushite, and later periods (Welsby 1998). West African gold fields at Bure, Galam, Sanakalan, and Bambuk were instrumental to the wealth and fame of the kings of Ghana and Mali. Early gold mining, the gold trade, and changing patterns of production in Zimbabwe were instrumental to the rise of the Zambezian states early in the second millennium A.D. (Swan 1995).

More widespread is the evidence for iron and copper working. This is found almost everywhere in the western, central, eastern, and southern parts of the continent. Archaeological, historical, and ethnohistorical information all suggest that the exploitation of these metals was an integral part of the fabric of African societies in the past. How far in the past? Where? How did they affect these social systems? These are some of the questions currently addressed by a burgeoning specialty within Africanist studies.

Over the past three decades, archaeological investigation throughout intertropical Africa has unearthed a varied and extensive evidence of early iron production. The data accumulated so far escape any simple and straightforward typological or chronological ordering. Former opinions on the processes of expansion of iron technology throughout the continent are being reconsidered in the light of more accurate contextual and empirical data. I will focus on the West African archaeological record, aiming to provide a broad social, political, and economic framework for comprehending the production and use of metals, the introduction of technological innovation, and the emergence of craft specialization. Copper, gold, and iron are, without doubt, the most important metals exploited and used in West Africa during the last two millennia. We can therefore view the archaeological record, with the help of carefully selected instances of West African metallurgy, and observe the effect of these metals on the indigenous cultures.

It is my further intention to attempt to go beyond a recitation of a time sequence for the appearance of metal here or there. I wish to indicate the cultural context and the effect on established social fabrics as well. As posited by Adams (1996, 13) summing up Braudel, "Taking a more inclusive view comes at the cost of correspondingly less rigorous methods and more ambiguous boundaries. Attention to the broad sweep of historically specific circumstances does not easily accommodate itself to formal, generalizable mathematical models." I suggest that by widening our focus, we can reflect on the many implications of current archaeological interests in early African metallurgy. To achieve such an aim, an abridged history of the debate with its contrasting principles will be discussed. It will be followed by my suggestion for an alternative way of looking at this evidence, one in which the dynamics of social systems play the major role.

Within the proposed model, it will be argued that a wider social and evolutionary framework is needed to make sense of the archaeological record. Different aspects of past social systems related to subsistence, socioeconomic, ideological, and symbolic systems may have sustained, inhibited, or otherwise amplified the aftereffect of innovation and technological change. As such, they may play a central role in the growth of culture. In order to test the strength and weakness of my proposal, three longitudinal studies will be described, with field data from (1) the In Gall–Teggida-n-Tesemt region in the Niger Republic, spanning a period of time from about 3000 B.C. at the early end to about 700 to 500 B.C. for the later determinations; (2) the Mema region in southwest Mali, with an archaeological sequence ranging in time from the fourth to the fifteenth century; and (3) two separate areas in southern Cameroon, situated within and along the northern edge of the equatorial forest, with a sequence of cultures dating from the sixth century B.C. to the early twentieth century A.D.

These places are spread over three separate biogeographical zones: (1) the Eghazer basin in the Sahara/Sahel zones in Niger, stretched from the Ténéré Desert in the east to Teggida-n-Tesemt in the west; (2) the Mema region in Mali, between Kumbi Saleh, the capital city of the ancient kingdom of Ghana (which flourished from the sixth through the thirteenth century), and the inland Niger delta located along the northern margins of the Sahel; and (3) southern Cameroon, comprising the settlement on the Yaoundé plateau and its periphery and the Western Grassfields stretched along its northwestern edge. From this interesting group of precolonial cultures, we can try to elicit answers to some of the questions that intrigue archaeologists about the adoption of new ideas into stable cultural systems.

FOR SAKE OF EFFICIENCY?

Human history may be characterized as a long-term exploration of technical expertise and the invention of increasingly efficient tools, with the taming of natural forces as the ultimate goal of our modern mythology. In archaeological systematics, past cultural periods are often divided into ages according to their technologies. In a general sense, this narrative is accurate, capturing the prevalent outcome of the evolution of technological systems. Technological systems are dealt with as if they are "self-driven autonomous" components. The overemphasis placed on technology and its products tends to obfuscate other relevant transformations, though Adams (1996, 277) stressed that "technology is best thought of, within this framework, not as an entity at all but as a field of interaction." Regarding African societies from 5,000 years ago to the present, evaluation of the impact of innovations is often no more than an intuitive assessment of the efficiency of the new materials—whether they granted a greater access to energy or decreased the energy needs of people while exacting an equal output, an improvement of productive capacity. As result, the capability to work iron has too often been conceived solely as a technical innovation with quasi-revolutionary consequences—that it revolutionized any society that developed or adopted an efficient new technology.

Van der Merwe (1980, 464) even suggested that in sub-Saharan Africa, the coming of iron was a catalyst that awoke half a continent from the slumber of the Stone Age and that had an immense impact on African culture. However, there are some assumptions embedded in this point of view that need to be challenged. First, it presumes that any efficiency gained from using iron tools was immediately perceived; second, that a radical new technology could easily be diffused between very different kinds of cultures; and third, that new tools were easily assimilated into established productive activities—that is, that the virtues of new technologies were immediately evident as vital substitutes for critical time-tested social and cultural behaviors. Such a presumption is debatable at best. If compared with contemporary high-technology contexts, it seems most difficult to attribute such goings-on to the past (Latour 1993).

With very few exceptions, as Trigger (1993, 33) has pointed out, the accumulated evidence from the world's great early civilizations do not support such a view of humanity's acceptance of new technologies. If anything, cultures are basically conservative, hesitant to accept new ideas that have the potential to disturb existing sociocultural fabrics. He goes on to note,

> Agricultural tools generally remain primitive in the early civilizations. The Inkas, Aztecs, and Shang Chinese relied on wooden digging sticks equipped with foot-bars to turn the soil, while their cutting tools were made of stone. The Mesopotamians and Egyptians employed light, oxen-drawn plows to conserve soil moisture and prepare the soil for planting; Mesopotamian plows were also equipped with drills to plant seed. While Mesopotamians began to use copper hoes and sickles during the Early Dynastic Period, as late as the Middle Kingdom the Egyptians continued to edge their cutting tools with chipped flint.

Nor need we facilely assume that new technologies, which may later be found of general value, are readily understood and absorbed into daily utilitarian activities. As Welsby (1998, 170) demonstrates, initially they may have more restricted uses:

> The earliest evidence for the use of iron by Kushites for utilitarian objects dates to the earlier part of the sixth century B.C. An iron spearhead, found in the tomb of Taharqo, was originally wrapped in gold foil, indicating the very special nature of the object and suggesting the great value attached to it. In the early royal tombs iron is excessively rare and only appears in foundation deposits beneath the pyramids at Nuri at the time of Harsiyotef. That jewelry was made from iron does not appear to reflect its high value when it was still a scarce commodity, as the use of iron for jewelry continued throughout the Kushite period. In the later Kushite period iron became commonplace and was used for a wide range of artifacts.

Here, then, lies the quandary, in that cultures do change and accept new ideas, leading to even more change. In the first case, the acceptance was virtually nonexistent, and in the second acceptance was within only a narrow segment of society. We will have occasion to explore the agents and dynamics of change, but it is wise to remember that the mere presence of a technology, later found to be of value, is not necessarily a sign that it was in general use or that it was engaged a priori in a cultural dynamic that was observable by us only after the fact.

We all understand that metallurgy was important to the development of some African cultures. It is our job to determine that importance not from some a priori ideal of the value of metals but from a critical review of the record. The appearance of metals and metal-working technology is attested in the archaeological record by different kinds of evidence—artifacts made of metal and tools used to work it. Even the by-products of metal-working processes—the slag spread around smelter sites, the vitrified clay from the walls and tuyeres from the furnaces used to reduce ores, or remains of dwellings, to mention a few of those most accessible to direct archaeological observation—might suggest where metals were worked.

As this discussion focuses on the processes of change, it is important to outline the kinds of phenomena that may have triggered transformations of precolonial African societies and permitted the adoption of metallurgical technologies. While the formulation poses no theoretical problem, in practice it is not an easy exercise to distinguish between "Late Stone Age," "Neolithic," "Copper Age," and "Iron Age" sites within the same region relying solely on a few metal objects. It seems somewhat more important to consider a larger aggregate of parameters. According to Kense (1983, 12), an Iron Age culture is one having a working knowledge or familiarity with iron. The same thing holds for Copper Age cultures. In this perspective, a distinction should be made between metal producers, who mastered the whole system of metal production, and metal consumers, who obtained their metal from others. In archaeological contexts, keeping in mind the limited sample size found at most archaeological sites, the presence of furnaces, smelting debris, and forges, even in the absence of metal artifacts, can be regarded as evidence of metal-producing societies, while the absence of such things, even when many metal artifacts are present, should be considered as evidence only of metal consumption. This distinction may help to explain some strange facts in the history of iron metallurgy in Egypt. Items of personal adornment in nickel-rich meteoritic iron dating from as early as 4000 B.C. to as late as 1780 B.C. have been discovered in Nile valley settlements. However, these are not considered the product of true iron metallurgy, that is, the reduction of ores and fabrication from the smelted product but rather the working of a "naturally" produced metal. During the New Kingdom (about 1570 B.C.) iron objects are more numerous and diversified, though some may be Mitannian imports; others, from the time of Toutankhamon in the fourteenth century B.C., were definitely manufactured in Egypt (van der Merwe 1980, 465–471). One has to wait another half a millennium, until 800 B.C., before we find a more general use of iron metallurgy in Egypt. Such a late acceptance of a full-blown iron-based metallurgy in Pharaonic Egypt, when compared to the much earlier absorption of the technology by neighboring

Middle Eastern states, has usually been explained as result of the so-called conservatism of the Egyptian society. In sub-Saharan Africa, different and conflicting explanations for the late appearance of metal working have been offered.

THE ADVENT OF METALS IN AFRICA: AN ABRIDGED HISTORY OF THE DEBATE

For several reasons, the debate on the development of African metallurgies is one of the most interesting in the history of African archaeology (Haaland and Shinnie 1985; de Barros 1990; Holl 1990, 1993, 1997; Robertshaw 1990; Schmidt 1997). Copper metallurgy originated in Eurasia sometime between 7000 and 6000 B.C. At first, native copper was collected and melted in crucibles, and vitrification products from this process have sometimes been mistaken for smelting slag (Mellart 1967). Hammering and annealing were initially employed to shape native copper, and since a charcoal fire can reach a temperature of 1,100 degrees Celsius, which exceeds copper's melting point of 1,084 degrees Celsius, this may have led to the recognition that the metal could be melted.

The ultimate source of sub-Saharan metallurgy remains subject to debate. There is no conclusive evidence of a gradual and autochthonous invention of copper smelting south of the Sahara, suggesting that the independent invention of copper metallurgy in Africa is unlikely. In almost all known cases, iron either is the earliest metal found in an area or appears simultaneously with copper. With the exception of the poorly documented record from the southern Sahara, mining and smelting now appear as a fully developed repertoire in most areas south of the Sudanic belt (van der Merwe and Avery 1982; de Maret 1985b; Miller and van der Merwe 1994). Among the most likely purported sources of copper metallurgy into sub-Saharan Africa are Carthaginian settlements or southern Moroccan traders traversing the Sahara. Many of the same arguments are made for the inception of iron metallurgy as well.

Throughout the colonial period, sub-Saharan Africa was considered a "backward" continent, on the receiving end of technological innovations from more advanced civilizations (Mauny 1952, 1953, 1967; Huard 1960, 1964; Arkell et al. 1966; Shinnie 1971; Tylecote 1975; van der Merwe 1980; Treinen-Claustre 1982). Since the 1960s, with the political independence of the modern African, there has been a movement toward the investigation of more recent eras of the African past. The cultures antecedent to many modern ethnic groups seems to have begun within that period that archaeologists in southern Africa termed the Iron Age—a period of time when endemic African societies developed a capacity for food production. Pottery and metals were prominent attributes of these archaeological cultures. That is, these cultures demonstrated a capacity for reducing metal from ores and using it in their everyday as well as their commercial life. Though formally we should regard this a "culture complex," it is sometimes spoken of as a time period, although it is appropriate to regard the metal-using peoples as ancestral to the varied cultural identities of present-day populations. For some, it is even the true beginning of African history (Lhote 1952; Diop 1968; Schmidt 1978, 1983a; Rustad 1980; Echard 1983; Schmidt and Avery 1983; Phillipson 1985, 1993; Schmidt and Childs 1985; Childs and Killick 1993; Shaw et al. 1993; Wiesmuller 1996, 1997). That is, the "Iron Age" was not some ahistorical descriptive entity but rather a vital part of Africa's past.

Though there is a certain amount of dispute among scholars, discussion of the origins of African metallurgies can be split into two influential but conflicting schools of thought—one of which may be termed "monophyletic" and the other "polyphyletic." Each of these competing hypotheses is grounded on a relatively rigorous set of arguments (Holl 1993, 1997).

The set of hypotheses belonging to the monophyletic family are premised on the conviction of the uniqueness of the act of invention of iron metallurgy and that it occurred somewhere between Armenia and the Anatolian plateau during the first half of the second millennium B.C. (van Grunderbeek 1992, 72; Wertime and Muhly 1980). From this core area, knowledge of the technology diffused outward by various means to neighboring folk and through distant lands before finally reaching sub-Saharan Africa. The idea of parallel and independent invention somewhere else is usually discounted because, as Phillipson (1985, 149) has written, "the associated technology is so complex, and in earlier African societies no other process involved heating material to such high temperatures, we have to consider a northerly source of sub-Saharan iron-working knowledge rather than duplicate independent discovery." The substance of Phillipson's argument is similar to one offered by Mauny and others according to which "it seems impossible that an invention of iron technology independent from the Mediterranean zone occurred there. This technology is so complex that it could not have emerged from a context totally ignorant of metallurgy" (Mauny 1967, 533).

Copper could be melted at temperatures consonant with those of indigenous ceramic manufacture. The reasoning that dismisses an indigenous experimentation with iron production seems very correct though dependent on the idea that iron technology can be invented if and only if the actual societies have a prior knowledge of a very complex and high standard pyrotechnology involving the heating of material to high temperatures. In their estimation, sub-Saharan societies did not possess this capability, and nowhere had they mastered high standard pyrotechnological systems. Therefore, for iron technology to be present in sub-Saharan Africa, it had to be imported from elsewhere (van der Merwe 1980; Grébénart 1985, 1988; Kense

1985b). As a result, archaeological investigation has focused on the search for a center of dispersion, the place in time and space where the technology was first nurtured and then disseminated as a full-fledged iron-based technology. In Africa, this search includes identifying diffusion routes along which the technology was spread into and throughout the continent.

Two main areas of consolidation and diffusion were singled out: Meröe, located in the northeastern part of the continent in the upper Nile valley, and Carthaginian North Africa, on the Mediterranean, are, as we have seen, the usual suspects. The Meröe hypothesis has been reputably refuted by Trigger (1969) and Shinnie (1985). As a result, the Carthaginian hypothesis remains the most likely source for the transfer of metallurgical knowledge to the subcontinent. However, recent investigations of Carthaginian settlements in northern Africa have yet to provide substantive evidence supporting this idea, as neither a smelting furnace nor any other mark of iron production has been discovered in a context dating from the period between 1000 B.C. and 700 B.C. (van der Merwe 1980; Kense 1983; Phillipson 1985, 1993; Holl 1988a, 1988b, 1990, 1991, 1993, 1997), and iron items found there in burials come from a later time, mainly after the sixth century B.C. According to Kense (1983),

> Tombs of this period contain small-size iron implements such as knives, nails, finger rings, daggers, forceps, blades and signet rings. But no direct evidence of iron smelting has yet come to light. That iron production was carried out locally by the second century B.C. is indicated by an inscription from Dougga which refers to the smelters from the Numidian kingdom of that time. (74)

This apparent silence of the Carthaginian archaeological record regarding the presence of iron working does not, however, preclude wide-ranging speculations. Think about this statement by van der Merwe (1980, 477):

> They [the Carthaginians] must obviously have had iron and the knowledge to produce steel, since their roots in the Eastern Mediterranean were practically in the heartland of iron-working of the time. No direct evidence for metalworking has been found in Phoenician sites of the North African coast, but many references to iron and copper smelters occur on the stelae. Metal production probably took place elsewhere in the interior, the coastal towns having been sited for reasons other than a metal industry. Iron-working in this region is likely to have been of a utilitarian nature, with emphasis on the tools of war. The Phoenicians traded extensively with the Berbers, who in turn bartered with the Neolithic peoples south of the desert. To the existing trade of salt for West African gold and slaves the Berbers probably added Phoenician goods, including iron.

The conjectural history formulated by van der Merwe is a conflation of historical events spanning a nearly 2,000-year period. One problem is the suggested pattern of Phoenician settlements in North Africa and the resulting division of labor. If they were indeed the "city dwellers," living in coastal towns, people in the interior (Numidians) must be considered the true producers of the iron implements. The second problem with this characterization concerns the extent of the early trans-Saharan trade. The idea of a consistent flow of exchange between Carthaginian North Africa through the Sahara into West Africa is not particularly unthinkable. A Carthaginian-like stone statuette found in a stone tumulus at Djorf Torba (Lihoreau 1993) attests to the possibility of contact between that remote place in western Algeria and the Mediterranean coast. In general, however, hard evidence—different from rock art depicting chariots, stone tumuli burials, and the Libyco–Berber invasion narrative—has yet to document trans-Saharan trade at this time.

The development of the "classic" trans-Saharan trade took place during the first half of the first millennium A.D. (Garrard 1980, 1982), and exchange of Saharan salt and "Phoenician" iron implements for West African gold and slaves does not seem reliably chronicled for any time as early as the last millennium B.C. In the present state of our knowledge of early African metallurgy, the synchronous emergence of iron production technology in eastern as well as western Africa does not seem to be explicable within a hypothesis of a single center of origin.

The somewhat more heterogeneous set of polyphyletic hypotheses are based on the premise of local, autochthonous development (Lhote 1952, Diop 1968, Andah 1980). In its earliest stage, without substantive archaeological evidence, the argument approaches a kind of wishful thinking. Nevertheless, we can state the conditions underlying it. In the first place, iron ore sources are found widely distributed throughout the continent, and, second, there is an extraordinary diversity of African iron-producing traditions. The inference is that such diversity could not have arisen from a single source but that it is a product of a set of local experiments, causing a discontinuous distribution of traditional methods.

The discussion by Diop (1968, 37) is particularly significant. After a review of the debate on the origins of iron metallurgy in Africa, she concluded, "Today, it thus seems proven that in Africa, traditional iron metallurgy is very old, widespread and autochthonous; however, it is still needed to identify the cradles of this metallurgy, to date them more securely, and to highlight the hypothetical routes of iron throughout the continent." In other words, an early date for the emergence of African iron-working technology is suggested, and these early metallurgies were widespread and autochthonous. Their original cradles of innovation and subsequent routes of expansion are as yet unknown. In short, a hypothetical position has been posed as the basis for future inquiry.

The relative simplicity of ideas, concepts, and arguments mobilized in the debate on the development and origins of African metallurgical systems is misleading because the concepts are considered at a highly abstract and general level. Systems of metallurgical production are complex sets of interacting variables and factors, comprising the physical environment, human social systems, technical knowledge, social demand, or whatever else might affect the development, assimilation, or utilization of the processes. It is clear that in order to undertake a rigorous analysis of the advent of early African metal-working methods, investigations of metallurgical technologies need to be compartmentalized into different components (Rustad 1980, 232). Different components of metallurgical systems may have different origins and developmental trajectories. Each could have been articulated differently in diversified combinations. In this perspective, the question we must resolve is, Was iron technology developed elsewhere and diffused into African cultures, or was it autochthonously discovered by African craftsmen?

CHRONOLOGY AND GEOGRAPHIC DISTRIBUTION

During the past few decades, archaeological research into early African metallurgy has provided a challenging, diversified, and rich harvest of results. The reports available are changing our conception on the origins and diffusion of African metallurgies. Evidence for copper metallurgy has been found in two West African regions, in the locales of Akjoujt in Mauritania (Lambert 1975, 1983; Vernet 1986, 1993b) and In Gall–Teggida-n-Tesemt in the west of the Aïr mountain range in the Niger Republic (Grébénart 1979a, 1979b, 1983, 1985, 1988; Holl 1993, 1997).

In the Mauritanian region of Akjoujt or, more precisely, in the vicinity of Guelb Moghrein, evidence for copper mining by sometime between 850 B.C. and 300 B.C. have been uncovered (Fig. 1.1). It is important to note that two additional dates from Akjoujt, 2,700 ± 100 years ago (suggesting a probable range from 990 B.C. to 790 B.C.) and 2,776 ± 126 years ago (1100 B.C. to 810 B.C.), though published by Flight (1973) and Willet (1971), are rejected by them as being too old relative to the other materials from the site (Woodhouse 1998, 173).

Coppersmiths geared their activities toward the production of small implements; weapons such as spearheads and arrow tips; tools such as burins, borers, axes, needles, sticks, and palettes; and, significantly, items of personal adornment, such as finger rings and bangles. Several mining pits and smelting features, characterized as short furnaces with tuyeres, have been found along the Amatlich. Copper items made in the vicinity of Akjoujt have been discovered in sites as far afield as western Mauritania, to the north of Nouakchott, and further away to the southeast along the sandstone cliff of Dhar Tichitt-Walata (Vernet 1986, 36–37).

Figure 1.1 Chronology of the development of iron technology

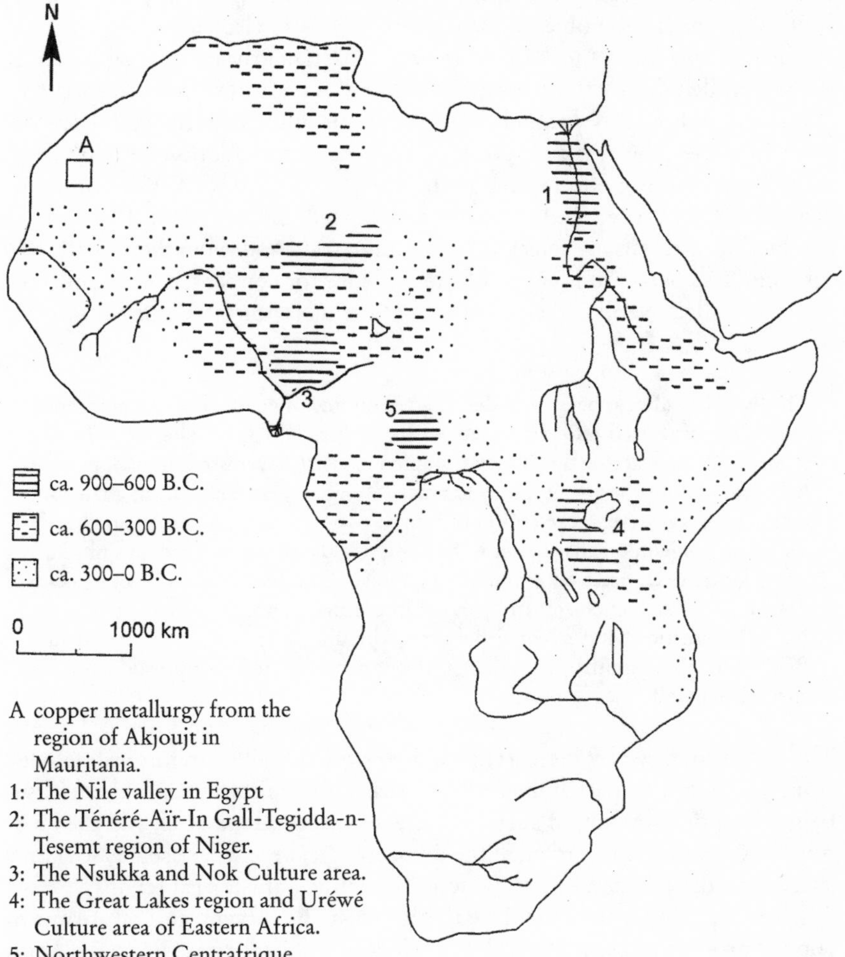

More recently, Vernet and associates (Bathily et al. 1992) excavated a dune site at Khatt Lemaiteg. In "habitation 2," dated to 3,310 ± 200 years ago (1890 B.C. to 1390 B.C.), they found copper artifacts consisting of projectile points, a copper bangle, and a stone bead attached to a wire loop. The objects are said to be "in the same style as objects found at Akjoujt" (Woodhouse 1998, 173), and the excavators considered them intrusive to the site. In the Akjoujt area and its peripheries, the development of copper metallurgy does not seem to have generated any remarkable change in the way of life of the people. It is worth noting that for some of those investigating Mauritanian copper metallurgy, "metallurgist folk from Akjoujt are unknown" (Vernet 1986, 37). That is, the objects must have come from elsewhere.

The example from the Akjoujt region is particularly interesting. Early in the last millennium B.C. or even earlier, new ways to produce copper were embraced without any parallel transformations in the material culture repertoire. However, the new craft created an extensive distribution network dedicated to supplying the region with manufactured goods, but sometime around 300 B.C., the whole structure collapsed and vanished. Beyond the production area stricto sensu, where mining pits and workshops with low furnaces have been found, most of the evidence for copper has been collected from so-called Neolithic contexts, as my translation of Vernet (1986, 37) documents:

> The finds had always been recorded in a Neolithic milieu: the rare copper implements are scattered and dispersed within lithic debris, potsherds, grinding stones and stone arrow tips. Copper implements are never predominant in their find spots. More specifically, they are often isolated or included in an alien context. There was never large concentration of people using copper. In an already arid environment, one has better to hypothesize the presence of groups of seminomadic herders, practicing some opportunistic rain fed agriculture along wadi drainages, mostly in closed and parallel interdunal depressions, oriented in the NE-SW direction, and situated between Akjoujt, the south of the Adrar and Boutilimit. Blacksmiths may thus have been a specialized group producing for specific demand.

The difficulty faced by interpreters in identifying the "metallurgical people" from Akjoujt is in part linked to the nature of the settlements themselves, being composed mainly of surface scatters of cultural material, and the taxonomic system used to organize the archaeological record, based as it is on a succession of ages: somewhat didactically defined ahistorical taxons.

It can, however, be considered that, with the advent and adoption of copper-producing technology, late Holocene pastoral nomadic societies inhabiting the Akjoujt region may have witnessed the development of a patterned division of labor—probably part-time craft specialization—geared to the production of highly valued copper goods that were channeled into far-flung markets through an extensive exchange network. The processes of ore procurement, smelting, forging, and distribution were probably deeply embedded within the structure of the socioeconomic systems of transhumant pastoralists. Therefore, it can be inferred that the procurement and smelting of copper ore took place during the seasonal sojourn in the Akjoujt and Bir Moghrein area, while forging and distribution were accomplished during the complementary round of seasonal moves from one camp to another. From this perspective, and regarding transhumant pastoralist societies in the last millennium B.C., the distinction between "metallurgist folk" and "Neolithic people" does not seem particularly relevant. They are different facets of the same culture.

The case of copper metallurgy from the region of In Gall–Tegidda-n-Tesemt in central Niger will be considered in more detail later. It is worth noting, however, that this tradition has been divided into two phases—Copper I, from about 2200 B.C. to nearly 1500 B.C., and Copper II, from about 850 B.C. to about 100 B.C. (Grébénart 1985). In the same region, there is another episode of copper production apart from this chronology. It is dated from about A.D. 900 to about 1500. It is one found in the "medieval" settlements of Marandet and Azelik (Bernus and Cressier 1991). Some doubt, though, has been cast on the emergence of early copper working in Niger. According to Killick et al. (1988, quoted in Vernet 1993a, 73):

> The only positive evidence for metallurgy in this region . . . is a single radiocarbon date of 1710 ± 110 B.C. (Gif 5176) for a copper-working furnace. . . . We suggest that this radiocarbon date be viewed with great caution until it can be corroborated by another method such as thermoluminescence dating of the fired lining of the furnace. . . . Until these are available, the evidence for metallurgy in Niger prior to 1000 B.C. remains in doubt.

The suggestion is reasonable, and this radiocarbon date must be rejected. However, there are other determinations as early, if not earlier, than the discarded one. The question of the antiquity of copper working in Niger remains open.

While awaiting further evidence, two equally relevant research methodologies seem possible: (1) we could begin by discarding all prior results on early metallurgy in Niger, a position favored by Killick et al., or (2) we could use the known data to derive some testable propositions that may be evaluated with new evidence and then and only then discard them as wrong. I prefer the second approach.

Regarding the origins of African metallurgies, the existence of early copper-producing traditions in Niger and Mauretania, tentatively dated from about 2200 B.C. to about 800 B.C. has shaken the foundation of diffusionist explanations. Explanations based on the presumed absence of advanced pyrotechnological knowledge in traditional African contexts are now much weakened (Holl 1988b, 1993, 1997; Wiesmuller 1996, 1997). However, this has not prevented new formulations of the diffusionist idea, as a new "Egyptian origins" diffusion scenario is being used to construe the puzzling new situation (Grébénart 1985, 410–412). As Kense (1985, 24) has written,

> It is not inconceivable that communication, however indirect and periodic, between the Nile valley and interior Sahara regions occurred over a long period and that the knowledge of working with metals (particularly copper) was passed

> along numerous routes to the west, southwest and south. Iron technology may have been introduced along similar networks by the turn of the first millennium B.C., although additional stimulus was provided by new links to the northern coast.

Nevertheless, if the early occurrences of copper working can be proved, then we will be able to posit that African metalworkers had an experience of an advanced pyrotechnical industry—albeit a simpler one operating at lesser temperatures than that implicit in the production of bloomery iron or the subsequent smithing of useful metal but still one that would have given them the background necessary to begin experimenting with these more plentiful metal sources.

Evidence for early iron working dated to the beginning of the first millennium B.C, if not earlier, has been found in Niger, at Do Dimmi in the Termit massif, Azelik, and Ekne wan Ataram in the region of In Gall–Tegidda-n-Tesemt (Grébénart 1983, 1985, 1988; Devisse and Vernet 1993). Fieldwork in the western Ténéré Desert focused on the Termit massif has produced a suite of twelve radiocarbon dates suggestive of a well-developed early iron metallurgy in the Termit-Egaro area during the second half of the second millennium B.C. (Paris et al. 1992, 58). Archaeological remains and charcoal are recorded from the following localities: Do-Dimmi, confirmed previous readings with three new ones (2,590 ± 120 years ago, 2,580 ± 120 years ago, and 2,500 ± 70 years ago), Termit-Ouest 8 and 95b, with three readings (2,924 ± 120 years ago and 2,880 ± 120 years ago for the former and 3,100 ± 100 years ago for the latter), and one dated sample each from Tchi Guiribe 127b (2,955 ± 100 years ago), Tchire Ouma 146 (3,230 ± 170 years ago), Gara Tchia Bo 48a (3,260 ± 100 years ago), and Gara Tchia Bo 48b (3,265 ± 100 years ago). Though these well-provenanced determinations are available (Paris et al. 1992, 58), the detailed site reports are not.

In Nigeria, first in the Nok Culture area around Taruga, then at Samum Dikuya, and recently in the Nsukka region on the fringe of the equatorial forest, early furnaces have been dated to around 750 B.C. (Okafor 1992, 1993). On the basis of these data, we may suggest that the practice of iron smelting was established there sometime between 800 B.C. and 500 B.C.

In Gabon, smelting furnaces from Otoumbi are dated to a period bracketed by 700 B.C. to 450 B.C. in the region of Moyen-Ogoué (Clist 1989; Jézégou and Clist 1991; Oslisly and Perrot 1993). Some interesting and exciting evidence of early African iron working comes from the Central African Republic (Zangato 1991, 1993, 1994, 1999). Zangato documents tightly knit settlements as well as an elaborate and complex system of iron production dating from the ninth or tenth century B.C.. The associated settlement grouping includes a smelting site set apart from the living site as part of a triad with a "megalithic monument."

In the Great Lakes region of eastern Africa, iron-producing sites date from around 1450 B.C. onward at Rwiyange I (radiocarbon determinations suggest dates of 3,180 ± 145 years ago and 2,855 ± 285 years ago), Mubuga V (3,160 ± 145 years ago), Kabacusi (2,815 ± 165 years ago), and Gasiza I and Mirama III in Rwanda and Burundi, respectively (van Grunderbeek 1992, 56; van Grunderbeek et al., 1982; Wiesmuller 1996, 169, 1997, 66), while those from the region of BuHaya in Tanzania are dated at Rugomora-Mahe from as early as 1740 B.C. (from a radiocarbon determination of 3,420 ± 120 years ago) to between 770 B.C. and 760 to 540 B.C. at KM3 (2,520 ± 100 years ago) and Rugomora-Mahe again (2,470 ± 110 years ago) (van Grunderbeeck 1992, 59; Schmidt 1978) (Fig. 1.1). It would appear that iron working was well established in the area by the middle of the last millennium B.C.

During the ensuing centuries, iron technology seems to have spread at a relatively fast rate in Niger and Nigeria in West Africa and in Rwanda and Tanzania in the eastern part of the continent. From around 600 B.C. to about 300 B.C., features of iron production appear in different parts of Africa, including equatorial Africa and within the forested area from southern Cameroon at sites such as Obobogo and Nkometou. Some apparently older estimates from Oliga, from around 900 and 800 B.C., have been rejected (Essomba 1987, 1992a; de Maret 1992), though they seem to pose several unexplained problems.

Early iron-producing sites have also been recorded in Gabon and Congo, in the province of Ogooué in the former, and in the regions of Pointe-Noire and Mayombe in the latter (Vansina 1990; Lanfranchi and Clist 1991). Beyond the Niger–Nigerian area in western Africa, the earliest evidence for iron technology is dated to the last four centuries B.C. in Mali at Nokara A and Jenne-Jeno (McIntosh and McIntosh 1980), in Ghana at Daboya (Kense 1985a, 1985b; Shinnie and Kense 1989), in Senegal at Tiekene Bassoura and Sintiou Bara in the Moyenne-vallée (Bocoum 1986, 1990), and in the Chad Republic and the Chad basin at Toungour, Zoui, Mdaga, and Amkoundjo (Lebeuf 1969, 1981; Lebeuf et al., 1980; Connah 1981; Treinen-Claustre 1982; Holl 1993, 1997).

In eastern Africa, material remains from the Urewe Culture, equated with what is usually referred to as the Early Iron Age, are attested to at numerous sites in the Great Lakes regions, in Rwanda, Burundi, Uganda, Tanzania, and Kenya (Phillipson 1985, 1993; van Grunderbeek 1992).

From this abridged survey of the early evidence of iron technology, it is certain that a case could be made suggesting that the synchronous development or adoption of this new set of techniques occurred independently in two different geographic zones: in the Great Lakes region as well as in the Termit-Aïr. Even discounting the likelihood that an independent discovery of iron working occurred in hundreds of places, it can still be inferred that some pioneer zones spread the knowledge of iron technology to neighboring territories through already existing interaction spheres. Whatever the ultimate resolution of this chronology, it is apparent that once iron working emerged on the continent, a great many different groups of people took advantage of it.

As stated earlier, stratigraphic sequences too often are spotty and fragmentary, giving us a skewed or partial picture of past processes. The archaeological sequence from Daboya, on the other hand, spans over 4,000 years, from 2000 B.C. to the present. Iron implements have been found in levels with datable pottery of a kind that the investigators designate Early Iron Age.

Despite the poor preservation of the iron, a number of pieces have been recovered from spits associated with pottery of Tradition II (E50, F135, P2, R, and V). This pottery has been dated from several spits in different units across the site to the middle of the first millennium B.C. and later. This evidence, along with the noticeable absence of any worked stone from those spits, has resulted in the designation of the Tradition II pottery as early Iron Age. Thus, although no piece of iron has been dated to a period earlier than the second century B.C., it seems that, on the basis of the pottery, the Early Iron Age at Daboya commenced several centuries earlier. This is significant, as it indicates an earlier age for the use of iron in northern Ghana than had been previously assumed (Shinnie and Kense 1989, 207–210).

To Shinnie and Kense, the occurrence of a distinctive kind of pottery suggests the presence of an iron-based technology, an equation that may be highly questionable since it is a typical assumption based on taxonomic arguments that an Iron Age cultural complex contains a specific "package of ingredients." After all, it is possible to suggest that changes in one technical domain (ceramics) may not be strictly connected to those in another (iron-working technology) or that one may have markedly preceded the other. Whatever the case, the importance of iron implements found at Daboya is suggested by their context. One-quarter of the iron finds were discovered in a cache containing four complete pots and 42 iron artifacts. This "treasure" was composed of items of personal adornment and a spearhead (Shinnie and Kense 1989, 201, 202–204). Four small-sized pieces of slag were collected as well, although there was no sign of a smelting or forging feature in the vicinity.

The very diversity of African metallurgical traditions escapes a purely taxonomic approach. The number of probable combinations of technical devices and technological knowledge is seemingly boundless. As seen in our short review of the chronology of early metal working, chronologies that appear to run counter to the prevailing idea of diffusion are often disregarded. The question is whether this rejection is based on a reasonable interpretation of the evidence at hand or is simply an unwillingness to accept evidence contradicting long-held ideas (Woodhouse 1998, 170).

METALLURGY: A SOCIOTECHNOLOGICAL APPROACH

Our discussion so far has dealt with the ordinary concerns of archaeology. We have established to some extent the *where* and *when* of early African metallurgical practices. We have explored an extensive, though still growing, body of temporal evidence. We have plotted the geographic provenience of these dates in order to determine where and when metallurgy first appeared in the various parts of the continent. We have even mentioned a cultural–stratigraphic unit, the Iron Age, a "portmanteau" concept that allows us to pack dates, places, and cultural things into an easily handled package. We even addressed an early Iron Age, when all of this began, but we are still unsatisfied.

Are we nearer to understanding not only the place of metals in African history but also the effect of this technology on African cultures? Do we understand the role of innovations any better? We have, in an ingenuous way, set our data into an acceptable space–time continuum, conveniently pigeonholing our evidence so that we can contrast one purported culture complex against others. I suggest that this is an insufficient way not only for comparing data from different times and places but also for exploring the ongoing sociocultural processes inherent in innovation and the kinds of change induced by the introduction of new ideas into already established cultures. We can, of course, steer our course along routes identified by classificatory mandate, or we can come to grips with the problem of understanding the makeup and processes inherent in the cultures we study. To this end, I suggest a greater adherence to a systemic analysis of culture, one that evaluates their structural cohesion and the ways in which altered relationships within them are affected.

Despite differences in methods, theories, and approaches, with the necessary and important debates on its nature, aims, and purposes, the ultimate ambition of archaeology is to generate genuine explanation and understanding of the past. My suggestion attempts to satisfy this ambition and thus to fuel debate. At the same time, it brings with it the supposition that investigators will carry into the field an intention to explore holistically the kinds of problem we are interested in. We are interested in more than the inception of metallurgy in Africa; we are interested also in the reception of metallurgy into stable lifeways and the development of cultures that embraced the technology. Ultimately, we will concern ourselves with the emergence of socially complex city dwellers from a fertile landscape filled with village farmers.

Over the past few decades, there has been a revolution in Africanist archaeology. One need only look through the journals to see the increased investigatory dedication to searching through the remains of the African past. As extensive as this effort appears, much of it has been uncoordinated. Investigators have not always concentrated their effort on solving problems related to metal working. As a result, metal artifacts have been collected here and there from many different sites for a variety of different reasons. Frequently, they are little more than a by-product of other research rather than being the object of a concerted attempt to resolve queries about the origins and growth of African metallurgy. Too many of the collections themselves are spotty, small samples or odd bits and pieces being haphazardly collected during areal surveys. While some artifacts were found in sites with important stratified sequences, many more were collected from surface scatter or unearthed from very shallow sites.

If we accept the idea that metallurgy is a significant component of African culture and that archaeology should be paying more attention to the organization of the cultures unearthed, then it will need to design its investigations in a more pointed way, screening the ashes of the past so as to detect more than cultural–stratigraphic units and to disclose the ways in which cultures develop and accepting or rejecting new things as internal imperatives dictate. I posit a sociotechnological approach, a vigorous analysis examining the role of technologies in the forging of society.

A rigorous analysis that allows sound comparisons between evidence from different contexts needs to distinguish between intrinsic and extrinsic properties of finds (Gardin 1979, 123). That is, such an analysis needs to differentiate the intrinsic properties of archaeological artifacts such as the *physical* properties of metal finds (Kense 1983; Tylecote 1983; Bocoum 1986; Okafor 1992, 1993). Within certain limits, recent advances in archaeometallurgical techniques allow in-depth study of the nature of ores used, the composition of alloys, and manufacturing techniques and the *geometric* properties, or the form of manufactured items and production apparatus. Regarding metal artifacts, the study of their shapes at different levels of archaeological stratigraphy—be it within strata, sites, or regions—can identify craft traditions within specific times and places and *semiologic* properties, or elements of style. It is generally understood that all such properties are culture dependent in that they are routinely used to delineate cultural contact and continuities. To this extent, they may support the idea of specific temporally or spatially delimited traditions, what are frequently viewed as "ethnic" zones.

The extrinsic criteria include *place* (or provenience), or where things are found, that is, the differently nested contextual levels of sites, strata, activity areas, or regions where relevant data are discovered; *time,* or the dating of finds and their associations; and *function,* or the organizing of finds into groups according to their primary use, though that use may vary over the "life" of any particular artifact (e.g., items of personal adornment, weaponry, tools, marks of religious or secular significance, status producing items or common items). The further extension of this is an assessment of the relative numbers of each group within the metals inventory at one site or another, at one time or another, or for one reason or another.

A research protocol employing such descriptive categories would allow us to make more accurate comparisons among different archaeological assemblages. We need to get beyond the recording and sorting of the minutiae unearthed. Instead, we must delve more deeply into the processes that operated to create them in the first place and that caused their general acceptance, distribution, and use. These things lie beyond the scope of classification. In order to circumvent prevalent limitations, our investigations must be fitted into a broader theoretical framework in which metal-based technologies are revealed within functioning socioeconomic systems.

For example, the inception of new technologies might be comprehended as an aspect of craft specialization or an aspect of the social division of labor that plays a part in larger movements toward social differentiation. In this light, we could study the rise of craft specialists, and the crafts they mastered, as a social dynamic permanently affecting, for example, the scheduling of critical activities or the allocating of strategic resources. Metallurgy would be evaluated in an evolutionary sense.

Granted, not all novelty has an evolutionary dynamic. However, in some developmental situations, craftsmen had the opportunity to dedicate themselves on a full-time basis to the marketing of their craft. Craftsmen did not create these opportunities, as a wealth of other social forces were at play, but specialization of craft activities is a sure sign of a society in a state of transformation. A critical shift in established arrangement, in this case creating social categories beyond those of age or sex, may, according to qualifying factors, create special categories within a class of social equals (horizontal divisions) or create ranks of social difference (vertical divisions). In either case, the prevailing structure is permanently changed, and a new equilibrium prevails.

In evolutionary terms, the mere accession of an innovation, albeit technological, economic, or social, that affects long-established rhythms of cultural life does not mean that it will be adopted (Lemonnier 1993). We have already noted the conservative, resistant nature of cultures. Here, we also distinguish between invention and innovation. Adams (1996, 19) has written that "the term invention is reserved for genuinely original acts of discovery, occurring under circumstances that are largely outside of and immune from economic processes. Innovations, on the other hand . . . involve the combination, modification, and application of themes drawn from an existing pool of knowledge."

Technological novelties may be trial-and-error propositions, and their effect will vary according to factors operating within the encompassing cultural environment. Some will nurture innovation, while vested interests in others realizing or repelled by novelty will reject it out of hand. The social and economic value of novel ideas is unpredictable, and we cannot decide a posteriori what held value for some bygone culture. As a result, we see innovation delayed for some time for some reason or another or rejected, ignored, or explored and then discarded. On the other hand, the new technology may be quickly mastered and widely embraced after a short period of trial and error.

The controlling factors are manifold, but the innovation can be termed *neutral* if it does not modify the general cultural format. Innovation can also trigger radical change, which has the potential to be either *positive,* causing further elaboration of the system, or *negative,* when the opposite effect occurs. These determinations of social value are also products of a posteriori decisions, twenty-twenty hindsight as it were. At some point, historians of past cultures need to use as the standard the perspective of the times in which the innovation first occurred. The future trajectory is interesting but does not always answer the question of why some new idea was acceptable in the first place. For this, we need to know the cultural environment into which it was introduced.

Technological systems of any kind are an integral part of their societies. The advent of new technologies may thereby create new and unsuspected social demands or satisfy preexisting ones. The inquiry into the emergence of metallurgy in Africa, and the specialist status of its practitioners, needs an appropriate research environment: a setting that takes into account physical environment, prevalent food-getting strategies, and trading partners and other bystander societies and that is critical of socioeconomic organizations. Of course, the new technology would never take root if it were not supported by sustained demand. In other words, any novelty has to make sense, or have what Lemonnier (1993, 17) calls "meaning," in a cultural context.

Metal products not only are utilitarian objects but also are part of far-ranging social tactics and strategies of identification and distinction (Bourdieu 1979). Consequently, to the usual archaeological question of *how*, one has to add *why,* not only as to some apparent function but also as to what ends an object intended. What, if anything, did it symbolize to the user or interested onlooker? I wish to avoid the usual taxonomic arguments, looking instead at relationships among ambient factors of the archaeological record. I see no need to posit a universally applicable classification, though I would attempt to appraise patterns of sameness or difference as way of determining kinds of cultural selection. Cultural selection surveys a universe of choices, preferring those that are most congruent with an existent social system, transmitted from one generation to the next. Other choices are ignored as aberrant, while others are culturally neutral, that is, something good to have around but neither essential or threatening.

Regarding metallurgy, in almost all instances of pristine development, it was initially dedicated to the manufacture of sumptuary goods; status-producing items such as weapons, scepters, or crowns; or items of personal adornment and the like (Levy and Holl 1988; Trigger 1993; Welsby 1998).

On the other hand, utilitarian goods—the tools of ordinary activities—are nonexistent or extremely rare during the initial stages. They result from a much later development, after the technology was "generalized" and became part of the common inventory (Trigger 1993). These are best thought of as by-products of historical circumstances, as emerging not as a technical adaptive response solving some preexisting cultural problem. Within a narrow social niche, metals had value, and the makers of it were able to benefit while bestowing prestige on those who fostered the practice. The step toward a rewarding craft specialization seems easily taken. The move toward social differentiation is also but a step away. The social impetus seems greater than any mundane or commercial one.

Though every technology has its specific physical and intellectual components that we can study separately, it should be regarded foremost as a social product (Lemonnier 1992). In this light, metal production should be thought of as a technological system with varied components in permanent and patterned interaction. The physical environment provides ores, fuel, and the materials needed to build furnaces and sets the scheduling and timing of production. The social environment sanctions specific kinds of labor apportionment as well as ways to recruit, train, organize, and purchase labor through domestic corporations, alliances, and friendships; it may also supply a social identity to craft practitioners as well as venues for competition, markets, raw materials, social prominence, and antagonisms arising from the same causes. Equally critical to the success and the continued vitality of any technology are sustained demand of its output (i.e., a way to meet changing patterns of consumption) and support for its distribution networks.

The potential stock of technological know-how is realized by the varied skills of differently capable craftsmen, leading to varied results and the appearance of altered style and innovation. As craftsmen became more specialized and market oriented and workshops labored to a more refined format, this kind of variation was minimized in comparison to cottage-industry practitioners. Such observations of behavior or the source of ores leads to a more precise perception, on our part, of the craftsmen's product and the society that engendered it. The production and consumption of metal items is divisible into seven principal activities, each with its own set of behaviors and material correlates (Fig. 1.2): procurement of raw materials; smelting processes of metallic ore in specially built furnaces; forging and manufacture of implements in workshops; dispersion of manufactured items and their consumption or use, maintenance, discard, or loss; and recycling of processed metal. Each step leaves behind a distinctive and identifiable archaeological residue amenable to systematic investigation. Regarding the mobilization of labor and the budgeting of time, the previously mentioned sequence of activities, inserted as they are within an operational chain of metal production, is generally integrated into the fabric of the whole social system and

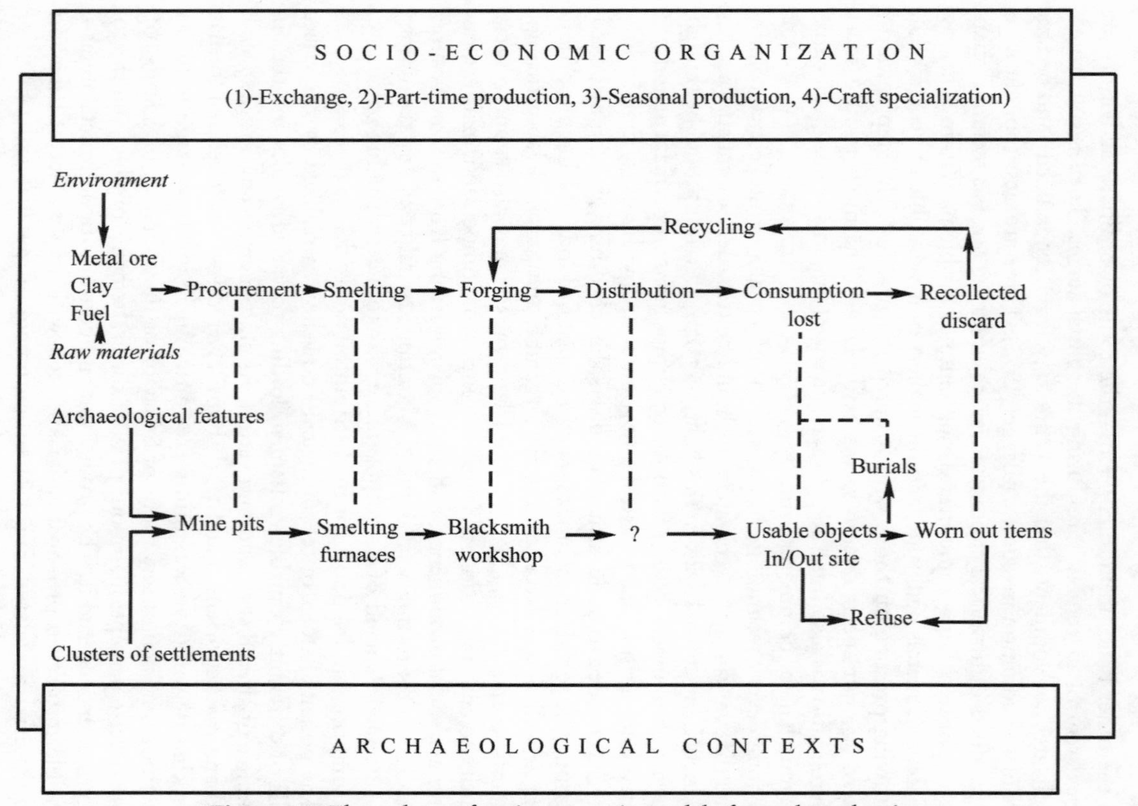

Figure 1.2 Flow-chart of socioeconomic model of metal production

structured around a few strategic operations that cannot be altered without serious damage to the whole production (Lemonnier 1992, 1993).

The interrelationships among ecosystem, technological knowledge, and social organization are far from simple. Depending on the circumstances, these three elements are permanently engaged in a multitude of feedback loops of differing intensity and effect, some amplifying parts of the system and others having a dampening effect (Renfrew 1984). Obviously, some will have wide-ranging consequences, while others will be quite trivial in their effect. For example, change in the quality of ores utilized, the fickleness of markets, or the manner of carburization or temperatures generated in furnace or forge will have a greater effect on the outcome of the process than will some change in the shape of arrowheads or bangles. Over time, change may invade the whole social system, drastically altering its nature. Others may disrupt and even collapse the social system (Tainter 1988). The creation of status-enhancing regalia may affect the political order, while a general dispersion throughout all levels of society may indicate a fall in prestige of a ruling class and a general diminution of the symbols of status. This is a purely technical difference since what we are observing is change, the effect of culture altering over a period of time. We tend to distinguish as positive those effects that enhance a given system and as negative those that disrupt it in palpable way. In reality, the social system has responded to the innovation by rejection, absorption, or alteration. It has somehow and in some way sustained a shock and settled into a new equilibrium. Within these bounds, most innovations are neutral, having little to no effect on the fabric of society. We must recognize not only new tools and techniques but also, as implied previously, new statuses and social roles caused by the development of some new technology.

The social status of metalworkers and how they are enfranchised as full-time practitioners are questions that have come to mind. Depending on the *worldview* and inherent patterns of social division of labor, metal producers may or may not be accorded a special social status (Echard 1983; Izard 1983, 1985; Monimo 1983; Schmidt 1983a, 1996c; David et al. 1989; Vansina 1990; Okafor 1992; Bernus and Echard 1992). Metal production may vary from one practiced full time, as in most complex societies, to one practiced as a part-time "cottage-industry," as in most other societies. In most "village societies," smiths practice other subsistence occupations through most of the year. The question then becomes one of constancy of demand if there is a steady market that gives smiths a special incentive to work at their craft year-round. Otherwise, it may be an activity carried out during the slack part of the year in order to fill immediate and local demand on a bespoke basis. That is, as societies become more complex, individuals who might otherwise be full-time farmers or herdsmen and part-time smiths are enabled to support themselves as full-time craft specialists building stocks of marketable goods.

The change is as much in the accounting of value as it is a social one. The perception of status and the ability to carve out an economic position derive less from the existence of the craft than from the demands of the social environment. It is the social environment that in the end mediates ongoing metallurgical traditions, setting not only the general direction of their development but also their effect on different social ranks: gold remains an elite commodity, and copper had a prominent role in social display, as did jewelry and iron, which began as an elite attribute and over time came into more general usage while retaining its unique status as a significant medium in social exchanges (e.g., bridewealth, death wealth, and burial furniture). In the end, the abilities of different social ranks to arbitrate access to the different metals and to license contact with other groups desiring the smiths' output affects the growth of African societies throughout the precolonial era.

SOME INSTANCES OF PRECOLONIAL METALLURGY AND THEIR CULTURAL CONTEXT

The Political Economy of Metal Production in the Eghazer Basin

The concept of political economy emphasizes the significance of social organization on production as well as the organization of production, allocation, and consumption of goods and services. Based on a sociotechnological model of production, this allows us to proceed beyond a strictly typological or chronological description of the evidence. To achieve such an aim, my analysis starts with a detailed discussion of the dynamics of the ecosystem from the In Gall–Tegidda-n-Tesemt region of Niger, an ecosystem that had a definite effect on settlement location. Different kinds of settlement and their inventory of metal objects will be discussed within a broader framework, attempting to identify the social demands and organization of metal production. The research protocol is intended to generate specific hypotheses within a more comprehensive model of change in In Gall–Tegidda-n-Tesemt societies.

The Ecosystem and Regional Distribution of Resources

The In Gall–Tegidda-n-Tesemt region is located in a basin ringed by the Aïr mountain range, the Tigidit cliff to the south, and the Azawagh headwater. It is watered by numerous seasonal streams, of which the Eghazer is the most important (Poncet 1983). The Programme Archéologique d'urgence surveyed an area over 51,000 square kilometers (Grébénart 1983, 1985, 1987; Poncet 1983; Bernus et al. 1984; Paris 1984; Bernus and Cressier 1991; Bernus and Echard 1992), dividing it into four sections: a large clayey depression watered by the Eghazer River at the center, the Aïr mountain range to the east, foothills of between 400 and 600 meters' elevation to the west, and the Tigidit cliff, which stretches over 200 kilometers east to west to the south. The Eghazer depression consists of the clayey zone along the Eghazer River drainage and sandy formations and areas of drifting sand along the Sekkiret valley. In the south, the Tigidit sandstone cliff on the southern limit of the Eghazer basin is a barren landscape with boulders and isolated hilltops.

Unfortunately, the Aïr range itself has been barely surveyed, though there are many valleys whose vegetation Poncet (1983, 26) described as congenial to herdsmen. The foothill zone on the Tadarast plateau and the *thalwegs* of water courses originating in the Aïr, like the Aïr mountain zone, is dotted with ponds during the rainy season. Some of these remain throughout the year and are attractive as dry-season camps for groups of transhumant pastoralists (Poncet 1983, 23).

The region's past climatic history is poorly understood, but examination of lake cores (Williams and Faure 1980; Pomel et al. 1991) make it appear that from over a 2,000-year period beginning around 4,000 years ago, the climate generally became increasingly more arid, though with noticeable local variations. The weather pattern may be described as a long dry season, followed by shorter wet one with stormy monsoon rains. Under these conditions, the ability of basin sediment to retain water played a crucial role in the rhythm of plant growth and the distribution of water and pasture throughout the region. Tranhumant pastoralists, dependent on these resources, developed complementary habits, seasonally moving their families and chattels from one subsistence opportunity to another, exploiting the most favorable combination of fodder and potable water.

Their task was a complicated one since water resources here may not always be fresh, and many sources are brackish. Fresh water is generally found in the east, while the brackish springs and ponds, needed for the health of their animals, are found in the center of the Eghazer basin. It is there, at Guélélé and Azelik wan Birni, that salt is found. High-quality pastures in clayey areas confined to terrain below 400 meters above sea level do not last very long. As Poncet (1983, 24) describes,

> In rainy seasons, brackish water ponds, considered as important for livestock health, are found almost everywhere in the clayey area; a dense and strong annual vegetation grows almost everywhere after rains, thus constituting rich pasture lands. The flooded areas of the Eghazer wan Agadez and its tributaries provide optimal conditions for the growth of annual species such as *Sorghum aethiopicum,* which constitute first order grazing lands.

The growing season is longer in areas with a sand matrix; though the grazing is of poorer quality and herds must be dispersed, it is available longer. In some places, it may last the whole dry season. The areas with the salt sources are famous for their influence on livestock health and are visited during the annual *cure salée* by pastoral folk (Bernus 1981; Bernus and Echard 1992) According to Schulz (1991), in years with moderate rain, the average harvest of wild *Sorghum aethiopicum* and *Panicum laetum* in the clayey depression of the Eghazer basin may amount to 250 kilograms per hectare, with an effective quantity of grain varying from 130 to 150 kilograms per hectare. Considering the quantity of natural grain available, it can be inferred that the drainage basin may have been a crucial area for pastoral societies of the last two millennia B.C.

Beyond sedimentary matrixes with their distribution into complementary sandy and clayey zones, the presence of saline sources, and the growth patterns of vegetation, which were crucial for the pastoral people living there, copper ore was present and used by the local people. The exact dating of the beginning of this exploitation is still a matter of debate. According to Grébénart (1985, 1988), a Copper I episode began about 4,000 years ago, while Killick et al. (1988) suggest that it is not older than 3,000 years ago. Whatever the case, "copper mineralization and even native copper are found in contact zones between the Agadez sandstone and the clayey formation from the Eghazer, or more specifically, in the faulted contact zones" (Poncet 1983, 16). The local copper sources are sedimentary, and traces of ancient utilization are not easy to identify because the miners did not leave behind ordinary mining pits. The layer with copper nodules (only some 20 to 40 centimeters thick) is sometimes exposed by erosion. The copper nodules may have been collected from the surface or taken from shallow pits 25 to 30 centimeters deep. Depending on the intensity of the exploitation, the exposed layers of copper ore may have been quickly exhausted. As a scarce and strategic resource, one expects prehistoric people to have devised some means to control or to gain preferential access to the copper zones.

Considering the whole complex of resources, soils, pasturage, salt, water, and copper, one can sanguinely expect site location to be geared toward timely and optimal utilization of the potential of the In Gall–Tegidda-n-Tesemt region. This practice, a kind of inherent procurement system, should have been arranged around a flexible schedule of seasonal moves from one resource area to another and marking control of these strategic areas and its resources, establishing primacy of tenure by such devices as the stone tumuli designating burial grounds, a practice consonant with territorial ancestral cults common in later times throughout sub-Saharan Africa. The descent groups became corporate landholders, warranting their title through the burial of their dead. Marking the locality and annual funerary commemorations reinforce the sanction.

Some places were occupied for only a short time, while others were reoccupied over and over again on a more or less regular schedule. An archaeologist working today must observe these past episodes as a palimpsest of these different settlement patterns, one settlement obscuring the next and both obscuring the interval between them. The site chronology does not always allow a precise reconstruction of the dynamics of the past social and economic landscape. The "layer cake" typochronological approach, with its "Saharan Neolithic" and "Sahelian Neolithic," "Copper I" and "Copper II," and "Early Iron Age" and "Late Iron Age" designations of past chapters in this story (Grébénart 1985, 1988), is seriously handicapped, even if it seems to make sense at first glance. It is severely limited because some of the patterns observed in the material culture residues crosscut the boundaries of the inferred chronological units.

Copper metallurgy is contemporaneous with both the Saharan Neolithic and the Sahelian Neolithic. Ceramics found in the Saharan Neolithic may also occur in Sahelian Neolithic contexts as well as in Copper I and II sites. Copper technology as well as Neolithic ceramic traditions seem to be different facets of the same phenomenon or, at least, of considerably overlapping entities, in that some settlements of each taxonomic period co-occur with settlements attributable to some other closely related archaeological period. That is, there is a basic cultural continuity evident, though not necessarily a chronological trajectory, and one did not necessarily follow the other. On the other hand, even though copper is still being produced, pottery from settlements demonstrating iron metallurgy is clearly different. At times, the typology may be a convenience, but to avoid these chronological difficulties, I suggest referring to a more flexible longitudinal analysis based on the dynamics of transhumant pastoral socioeconomic systems.

Settlement Patterns

With the exception of the poorly surveyed Aïr mountain range, evidence of human settlement has been found in the foothills, the Tigidit cliff, and the extensive depression of the Eghazer drainage basin. The chronology is far from satisfactory since few sites have been tested and dated. Many are dated by their associated cultural remains, which are often little more than surface finds.

Four categories of settlement will be considered in the following discussion: Late Stone Age sites, localities with evidence of copper production, settlements with evidence for iron working, and cemeteries. Most living sites are palimpsests of multiple episodes of occupation, congruent with the dynamics of nomadic pastoralists. The time span under consideration ranges over some 2,000 years, from some time nearly 4,000 years ago to about the beginning of the current era. Megalithic burials and cemeteries are gathered together with "pre-Islamic" monuments. Their chronology also begins about 4,000 years ago but extends until the end of the first millennium A.D.

Of the 148 Late Stone Age settlements known, 64 are located in the Eghazer depression, 10 in the foothills, and 74 along the Tigidit cliff (Fig. 1.3, Table 1.1). The highest concentrations are found in the sandy zone in the northwest and southwest, while 12 sites are located within the annual *cure salée* area. Three of the settlements—Afunfun 161 in the southeast, Chin Tafidet in the northwest, and Ikawaten in the north—had mortuary groups, which included humans and domestic animals, the latter appearing to be sacrificial offerings. These were not the only animal burials at these sites. Interments of cattle and dogs have been found at Chin Tafidet, those of cattle at Ikawaten, and those of sheep or goats at Afunfun 161. These three localities seem to have been the focal points of at least two kinds of pastoralist system once present in the In Gall–Tegidda-n-Tesemt region: the western variant, comprising two subvariants with an emphasis on cattle husbandry, termed "Saharan Neolithic" and an eastern one, with sheep or goats, called "Sahelian Neolithic." It is highly probable that these pastoralist groups moved into the central basin during the rainy season for the annual *cure salée* and the natural harvest of *Sorghum aethiopicum* and *Panicum laetum*, which seems

Figure 1.3 Spatial distribution of the recorded Late Stone Age sites

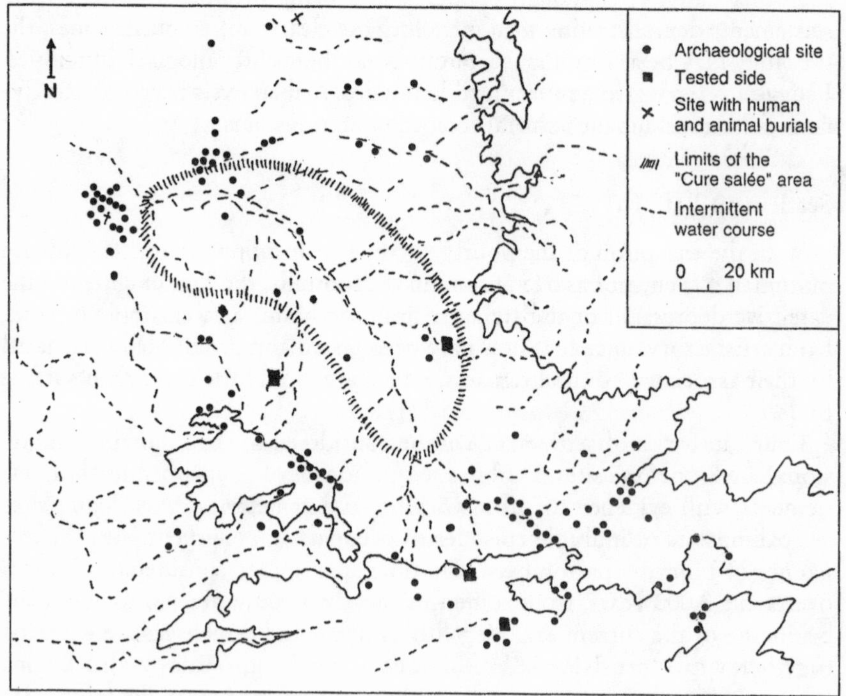

Table 1.1 Distribution of archaeological sites according to morphographic units

Morphographic Units	*Depression of the Eghazer*		*Foothills of the Aïr*		*Tigidit cliff*		*Total*
	Nb	*%*	*Nb*	*%*	*Nb*	*%*	
Neolithic sites	64	43,24	10	6,75	74	50	148
Sites with copper	15	57,69	3	11,53	8	30,76	26
Sites with iron	2	10,52	—	—	17	89,47	19
Undetermined	7	53,84	2	15,38	4	30,76	13
Megalithic cemeteries	48	46,60	32	31,06	33	32,03	103
TOTAL	136	44,01	47	15,21	136	44,01	309

to have been sufficient in most years to allow people to live without agriculture (Schulz 1991).

Compared to the number of pastoral Late Stone Age settlements, the sum of sites with evidence of copper metallurgy suggests a sharp decline in the density of occupation (Fig. 1.4, Table 1.1). Though this seems to be a particularly dramatic case of depopulation, this conclusion may be a causality of taxonomic error since only localities with positive evidence of copper have been mapped. The site data and radiocarbon determinations, on the other hand, suggest that copper metallurgy is but one facet of a more comprehensive socioeconomic system. Regarding the regional distribution of sites, it seems that 15 of them are in the central part of the Eghazer depression, being concentrated in the copper ore zone along the Guélélé–Azelik–Sekkiret anticline, while 3 are in the foothills and 8 along the Tigidit cliff. It can be inferred that during their annual visit to the depression, herdsmen obtained and processed copper ore along with the activities customary to nomadic pastoralists engaged in managing their livestock and the harvesting of naturally sown grain.

Settlements with evidence of iron metallurgy seem confined to the south limits of the region, with 17 of the 19 sites known along the Tigidit cliff (Fig. 1.5, Table 1.1). It is unlikely that the central part of the basin was not visited at this time. This skewed distribution seems to have more to do with the distribution of iron-bearing deposits than with any changes in the mobility patterns of local herdsmen. Once again, we must consider data reflecting economic opportunities within a rather comprehensive lifeway, which probably caused the herdsmen to visit many places not marked by the loss of iron artifacts.

Pre-Islamic burial grounds are more evenly distributed throughout the region. Forty-eight are in the Eghazeř depression, 32 in the foothills, and 33 along the Tigidit cliff (Fig. 1.6, Table 1.1). Thirty-nine of the 103 burial sites are found in the central area of the annual *cure salée*. The large cemetery of

Figure 1.4 Spatial distribution of the recorded settlements with evidence of copper metallurgy

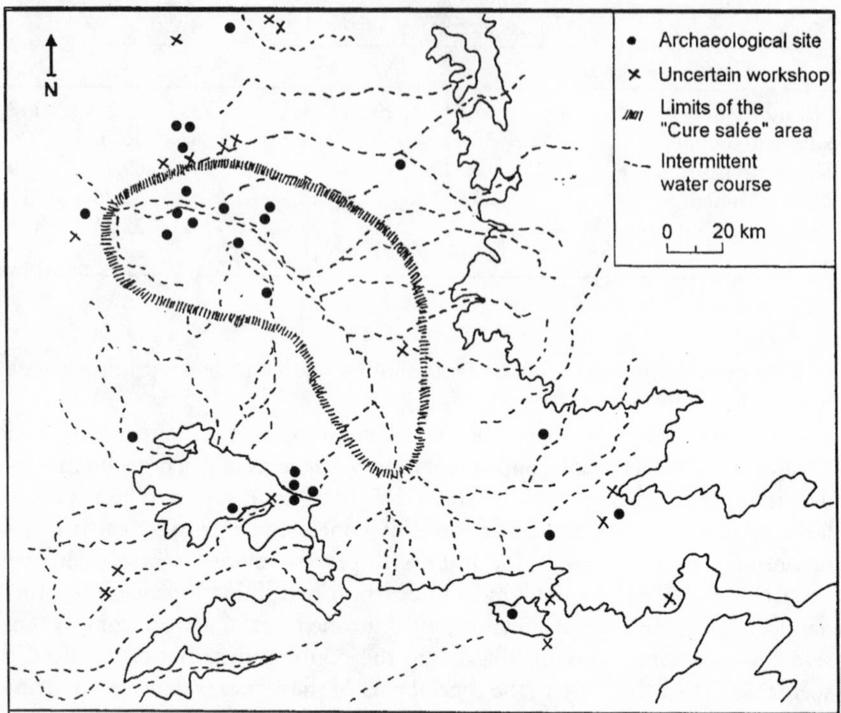

Asaquru is thought to be 5,400 years old, suggesting that traditional formal mortuary activities have a lengthy history. As was suggested earlier, ancestral cults are a traditional way of ensuring corporate title, marking the holdings of one descent group or another. It may well be that the earliest megalithic burial grounds were territorial markers supporting or emphasizing descent group claims on valuable strategic resources.

In all, 136 archaeological localities are known in the Eghazer depression and along the Tigidit cliff, while another 47 have been recorded in the foothills. The most striking feature of the regional settlement pattern is the contrast in the number and density of living sites relative to those devoted to mortuary activity. Since the burial locations with megalithic tombs are fewer in number than the domestic settlements, they probably are dedicated not to a single residential group but rather to some larger kin-sanctioned comity. Megalithic burial sites are both highly visible and fairly permanent and, as such, seem well suited to convey symbolic messages, marking the appropriation of resources and validating corporate tenure. Such symbolic usage was

Figure 1.5 Spatial distribution of the recorded settlements with evidence of iron metallurgy

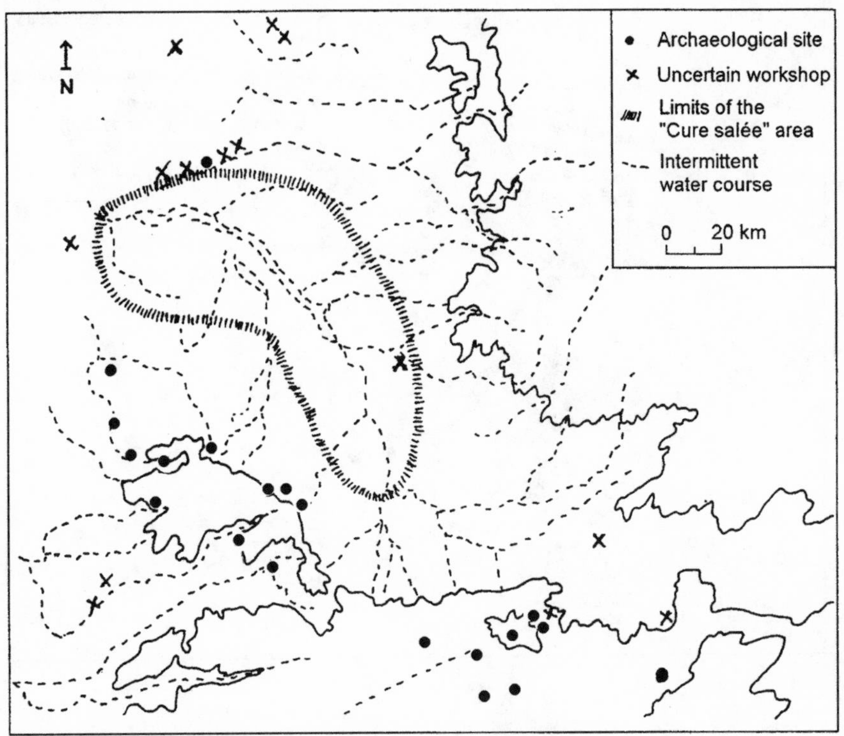

certainly crucial to the development of new social strategies; by staking their territorial claims, the pastoral nomads ensured themselves regular access to a full range of resources critical to their way of life. They also put themselves in a position to enhance and sustain metal production and the regulation of the metals trade with their less fortunate neighbors.

Living Sites

The Programme Archéologique d'Urgence discovered several hundred archaeological sites, but only a few of them have been tested. Of the 13 Late Stone Age localities found, 10 had evidence of copper metallurgy and 9 of iron. Two of the Late Stone Age sites are in the Eghazer depression, Chin Tafidet in the western sandy zone, and Anyokan in the central clayey area. Tuluk 211, a stone axe workshop, is in the foothills zone. Another eight were found along the Tigidit cliff (Fig. 1.3, Table 1.2). The size of these settlements

Figure 1.6 Spatial distribution of the recorded megalithic cemeteries

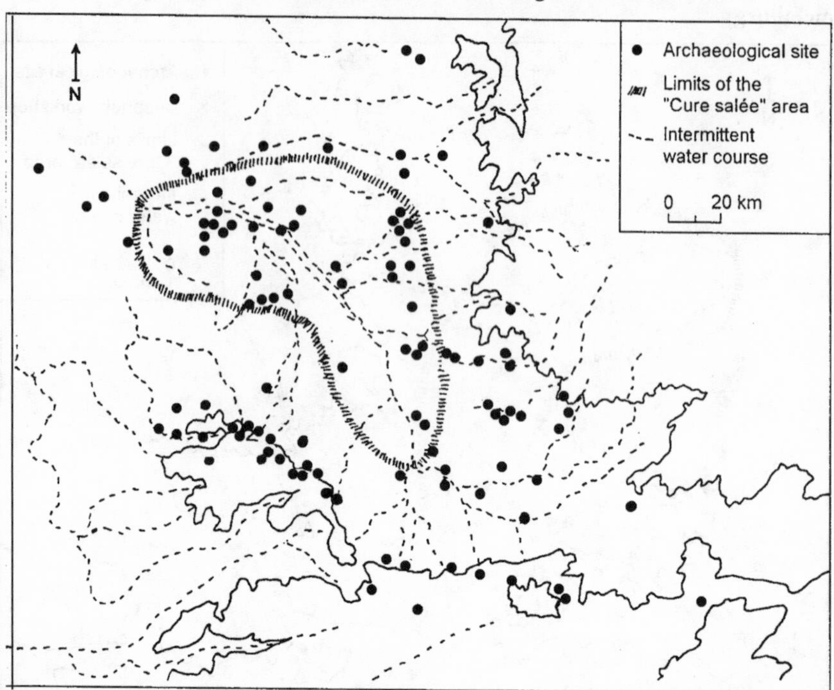

varies: the largest, Shin Wasararan, on the cliff plateau, covers 28.2 hectares, while the smallest ones, Afunfun 176, Afunfun 179, and Tama, are around 0.12 hectares each. No evidence of dwellings was found (Paris 1984; Grébénart 1985).

Thirteen complete or almost complete bovine skeletons, three of ovicaprines and two of the dogs used to aid managing the flocks, were recovered at Chin Tafidet, a site about 5,400 years old. Cut marks on the cervical vertebrae suggest that the animals, ranging in age from four to eight years old, were first sacrificed and then buried in association with humans. Only 12 of the 75 human burials from Chin Tafidet have been excavated, but we can describe a mortuary practice by which the dead were interred in groups, without grave goods, in graves containing both human and domestic animal remains. Four such groups have been identified: Cluster I, three humans arranged around a bovine skeleton; Cluster II, four humans placed around a bovine burial; Cluster III, two tombs, each with cattle burials; and Cluster IV, two sets of human burials, but neither with an companion animal burial.

It is worth noting that neither dogs nor ovicaprines (sheep and goats) were interred along with a human burial at Chin Tafidet. A similar pattern of hu-

Table 1.2 Major characteristics of the tested "neolithic" sites

Locality	*Situation*	*Surface (Ha)*	*Nature*	*Date B.P.*	*Peculiarities*
1—Afunfun 161	Cliff	2,00	Camp/Village	?	Humans & animals burials
2—Afunfun 176	Cliff	0,12	Village/camp	3000	Humans & animals burials
3—Afunfun 177	Cliff	1,50	Nécropole	?	—
4—Afunfun 179	Cliff	0,12	Village/Camp	?	—
5—Anyokan	Depression	12,5	Camp	?	—
6—Asaquru	Depression	+10	Cemetery	3400	Hundreds of tumulus
7—Chin Tafidet	Depression	2,36	Village/Camp	3400	Humans & animals burials
8—Efey Washaran	Cliff	0,19	Village/Camp	2900	—
9—Mio	Cliff	1,13	Village/Camp	3200	—
10—Orub	Cliff	2,16	Village/Camp	3400	—
11—Shin Wasararan	Cliff	28,2	Village/Camp	3200/2800	—
12—Tamat	Cliff	0,12	Camp	?	—
13—Tuluk 211	Foothills	1,75	Camp	?	Stone axes workship

mans accompanied by cattle burials occurs at Ikawaten. From these mortuary details, it can be inferred that the local herdsmen were accustomed to burying their dead in their dry-season camping area as part of a mortuary regimen meant to emphasize the strong connection between the people and their cattle.

At Afunfun 161 and Afunfun 177 in the southeastern part of the region and also dated to about 5,000 years ago, 4 burials out of 16 discovered at Afunfun 161 and 5 out of 25 at Afunfun 177 have been tested. At the first site, two burials had grave goods, mostly ceramics, while one of the deceased was buried with an infant sheep. In the other site, indications are that ceramics were included in 18 of the burials, but only one had the remains of a young sheep. In general, the grave goods were more varied, comprising ceramics, polished stone axes, a stone armband, and land-snail shells. The material part of the mortuary program in the Afunfun area suggests an emphasis on sheep or goat husbandry rather than cattle.

Settlements with evidence of copper metallurgy date from about 4,000 to 3,300 years ago. Four of the copper-producing sites are located in the Eghazer depression, two in the foothills zone, and four along the Tigidit cliff. They also vary in size from 20 to 0.03 hectares (Fig. 1.4, Table 1.3). Copper production is strongly attested to by a series of furnaces and slag heaps as well as by worn-out and lost copper artifacts. The principal copper smelting sites were located at Afunfun 162 and Afunfun 175, Eres-n-Enadan and Aghtauzu in the southeast, Azelik, the Sekkiret valley, and Ikawaten in the northwest, while smaller production centers were discovered in the foothills zone at Tuluk and Tyeral.

The nine localities with the earliest evidence of iron metallurgy, dated from as early as 4,600 years ago to nearly 4,100 years ago, are located along the Tigidit cliff, mostly on the plateau (Fig. 1.5, Table 1.4). Their size varies from 3 to 0.6 hectares, and it appears that the somewhat larger settlements are small villages within sedentary or semisedentary communities. The remains of iron smelting furnaces have been found at Ekwe wan Ataran, In Taylalen II 15, and Teguef N'Agar. The density and diversity of archaeological remains at these settlements are higher than those found at the transhumant encampments, a sign of prolonged occupation. A series of pits unconnected to iron production at In Taylalen II 15, Shin Ajeyn, and Teguef N'Agar (Grébénart 1985, 263–330) may have been used for storage, though no positive evidence of plant remains has been recovered. However, it would be seemly to suggest such features in villages occupied on a more or less permanent basis. These settlements may coincide with a decline or replacement of nomadic pastoralist socioeconomic systems and a shift toward more durable long-lasting villages.

Otherwise, camp sites were certainly visited several times for over hundreds or even thousands of years, leaving behind a very muddled archaeological

Table 1.3 Major characteristics of the tested settlements with evidence of copper metallurgy

Locality	*Situation*	*Surface (Ha)*	*Nature*	*Number of furnaces*	*Date B.P.*	*Peculiarities*
1—Afunfun 162	Cliff	12,00	Village?	44	2800/2500	clusters of furnaces
2—Afunfun 175	Cliff	20,00	Camp	100	4100/3100	clusters of furnaces
3—Afunfun 216	Cliff	?	Camp	1	?	—
4—Agtauzu 178	Cliff	12,56	Village?	10	2900	—
5—Azelik 210	Depression	8,00	Camp	?5	2500/2000	reworked
6—Eres n Enadan	Depression	17,66	Camp	—	—	—
7—Ikawaten	Depression	5,00	Camp	185	2200/1300	clusters of furnaces
8—Sekiret	Depression	?	Camp	+	3300/2900	clusters of furnaces
9—Tuluk	Foothills	0,03	Camp	?1	2350	—
10—Tyeral	Foothills	1,75	Camp	?2	2400	Tumulus

Table 1.4 Major characteristics of the tested settlements with evidence of iron metallurgy

Locality	*Situation*	*Surface (Ha)*	*Nature*	*number of furnaces*	*Date B.P.*	*Peculiarities*
1—Chin Oraghen 105	Cliff	1,75	Village	—	—	1 tumulus
2—Efey Washaran	Cliff	0,50	Village/camp	—	—	—
3—Ekne wan Ataram	Cliff	3,00	Village	Many	2450	—
4—In Taylalen II 15	Cliff	1,50	Village	Many	2200/2000	6 pits
5—Jibo 136	Cliff	0,50	Camp	—	—	—
6—Mio 169	Cliff	1,13	Village	—	—	—
7—Shin Ajeyn	Cliff	1,75	Village	—	—	1 pit
8—Tamat 157	Cliff	1,00	Camp	3	—	—
9—Teguef n'Agar	Cliff	0,78	Village	—	2100	10 pits

presence. At the same time, archaeological entities such as the Saharan Late Stone Age and Sahelian Late Stone Age are seemingly contemporaries of communities who had copper (i.e., Copper I and Copper II). This makes it difficult to distinguish between archaeological assemblages of one episode or another. Nevertheless, we can separate the late prehistoric occupations of the In Gall–Tegidda-n-Tesemt region into two principal periods. Period I, from about 4,000 years ago to about 2,600 years ago, is characterized by a transhumant pastoralist society. These societies can be further separated into those who herded cattle and those who kept sheep or goats. This period is also characterized by some indications of social differences and settlement patterns, appropriation of valuable resources, and sustained development of craft specialization geared to produce highly valued goods in copper.

Period II, on the other hand, began about 2,600 years ago and lasted until about 2,000 or 1,500 years ago. It featured a shift toward settlement of the southern portions of the region and was marked by more permanent settlements with storage features. This period with its altered settlement pattern saw a diminution of the numbers of transhumant pastoralists. It has been suggested that an influx of settlers from the north occurred at this time. We now may ask, How do the assemblages of metals items fit the model outlined previously?

Features of Metal Production

Evidence for metal production covers a broad spectrum of things—the procuring of ore and the manufacture of processing features, smelters and forges, ancillary equipment and their by-products, and the metal artifacts themselves. Before discussing artifacts, we should focus on production ancillaries (Bernus and Gouletquer 1976; Grébénart 1983, 1985, 1988; Bernus and Echard 1992; see Table 1.3).

In the copper-producing sites, smelting furnaces are arranged into groups and built to varying designs. Early copper furnaces from about 4,000 years ago to nearly 3,000 years ago are so different in their size and shape, as well as internal organization, that it can almost be said that each is unique. They can, however, be separated into four groups. The first, with two variants, comprises small, more or less cylindrically shaped furnaces with flat or curved bases and a single tuyere opening at the bottom (Fig. 1.7:1–2). The second kind includes larger furnaces averaging 2.00 meters in diameter, with many enigmatic conduits and enclosed pockets (Fig. 1.7:3). The third kind comprises complexly shaped furnaces with a subcylindrical body and a rectilinear extension (Fig. 1.7:4). The fourth kind seems to combine two cylindrical furnaces (Fig. 1.7:5).

Later copper-producing furnaces from between 3,000 years ago and 1,000 years ago are more uniform. They are all basically cylindrical, with variants

Figure 1.7 Variants of early copper-smelting furnaces

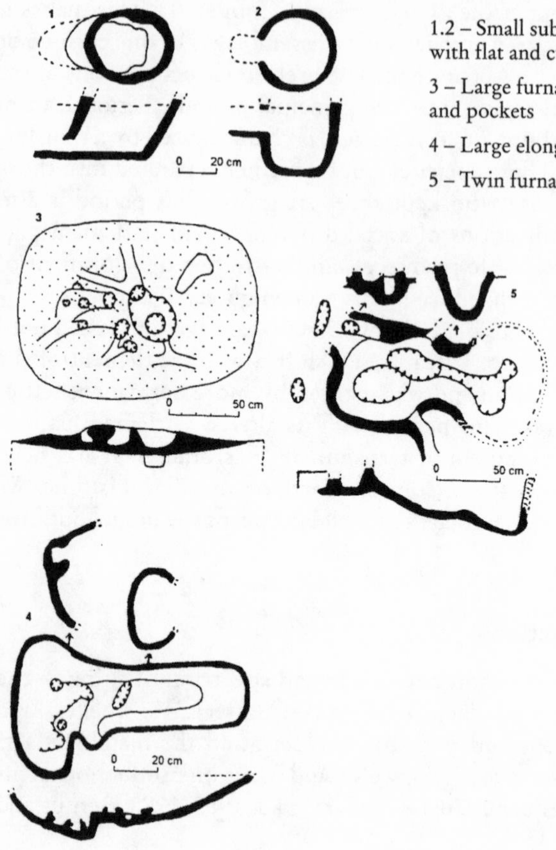

1.2 – Small sub-cylindrical shaped furnaces with flat and curved bases

3 – Large furnace with "enigmatic" conducts and pockets

4 – Large elongated furnace

5 – Twin furnace with two cylindrical shafts

distinguishable by the angle of their sidewalls and characteristics of the base (Fig. 1.8). The same cylindrical shape characterizes iron smelters as well, with some variation (Fig. 1.9). Some copper smelters, as well as some of the iron-smelting furnaces, have a small pit built into the bottom. This feature is reminiscent of "medicine" pots—for the ritual materials used by smiths to ensure the success of the smelt—found elsewhere in Africa (Essomba 1993; Schmidt 1997; Schmidt and Mapunda 1997). It may be that even at this early date, smiths were engaged in arcane practices that protected their monopoly of technical knowledge and secured their social importance.

The very variety of furnace types from this "pioneer" phase of copper production is puzzling but explainable. It is explainable if we suggest that

Figure 1.8 Variants of later copper-smelting furnaces

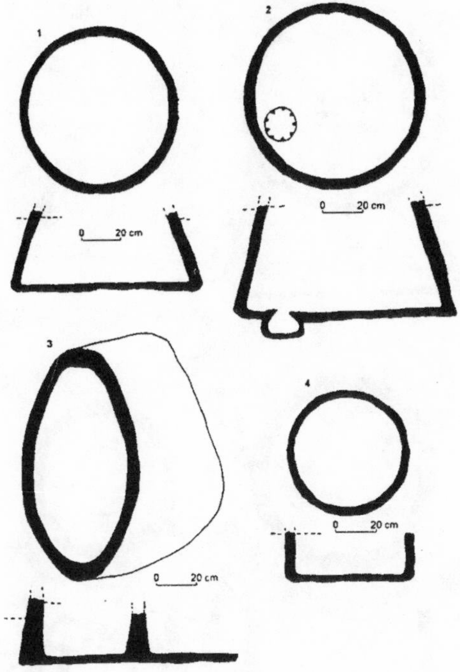

the methods for reducing ore were derived from many experiments rather than from a single source. It suggests variety as a by-product of trial and error, with each copper producer building and testing different devices until they came to comprehend the nature, quality, and quantities of ore and fuel (Bernus and Gouletquer 1976). It is far from certain that all these attempts to produce a useful product were successful. The small quantities of slag found at these smelter sites suggests only small-scale production, a "cottage industry" pursued to meet rather parochial needs (Table 1.5). After the phase of experimentation, the smiths seem to have come up with adequate technical solutions, smelting locally available ores to produce metal on a regular, if limited, basis.

Patterns Perceived in the Inventory of Metal Artifacts

The metal artifacts recovered, be they copper or iron, can be divided into five categories: weapons, items of personal adornment, tools, ingots, and indeterminate pieces (Table 1.5). The category of weapons includes harpoons, spear and arrowheads, and knives and daggers. Items of personal adornment

Figure 1.9 Variants of iron-smelting furnaces

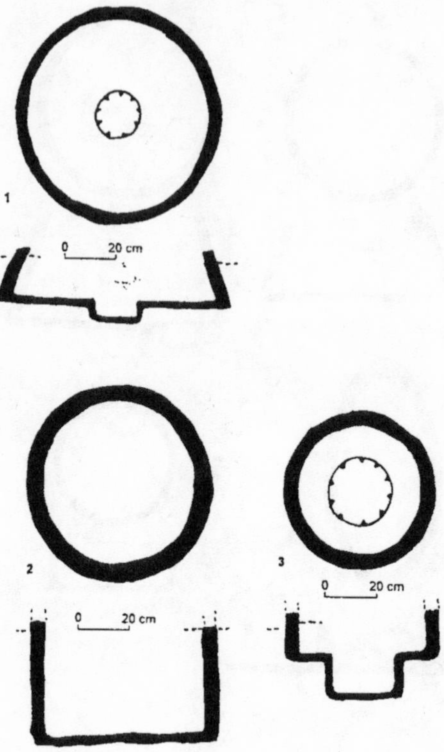

are more varied, including finger rings, bangles, plaques, foot rings, and pins. Among the tools, we find a few needles, burins, and awls, while the last category consists mainly of pieces of metal wire.

The inventories from sites with evidence for copper production include 38 copper artifacts and 58 iron ones. Twenty-nine out of a total of 38 ornaments are copper, while 40 out of a total of 58 weapons are iron (Table 1.5). The numbers of metal artifacts at each site varies from the 14 at Afunfun 162 to 2 each at Eres Anadan and Ikawaten 185 (Table 1.6). In collections from localities with evidence for iron production, 26 out of 28 items of personal adornments are in copper. Seventeen of these are from burials. Among the 43 iron artifacts, 11 are weapons, 17 ornaments, and 16 indeterminate. Three of the 17 iron items of personal adornment were from burials. Among metal objects collected from the six megalithic tomb sites tested, 10 are copper implements (3 items of personal adornment and 7 indeterminate pieces) and 4 are iron pieces (2 weapons and 2 ornaments. Table 1.6).

Table 1.5 **General distribution of metal artifacts and slag**

Locality	Slag	Copper artifacts			Iron artifacts			Total	
		W	O	Others	W	O	Others	Copper	Iron
Sites with copper evidence									
Afunfun 162	94,3 m³	3	4	15	5	8	26	23	39
Afunfun 175	Abundant	—	—	3	—	4	6	3	10
Aghtauzu 178	Present	—	—	+	+	+	+	+	+
Azelik	Present	—	—	6	1	—	8	6	9
Eres n Enadan	—	—	1	4	—	—	—	5	—
Ikawaten 185	32,5 m³	—	—	1	—	—	—	1	—
Tuluk	Present	—	—	—	—	—	—	—	—
Tyeral	Present	—	—	—	—	—	—	—	—
Sites with iron evidence									
Chin Oraghen 105	Present	—	3	1	3	—	1	4	4
Efey Washaran 151	—	—	3	—	—	—	—	3	—
	(Tomb)	—	10	—	—	—	—	10	—
Efey Washaran 183	(Tomb)	—	3	—	—	1	—	3	1
Ekne wan Ataram	Present	—	—	—	—	—	—	—	—
In Taylalen II 15	Present	—	—	—	1	—	—	—	1
Jibo 136	—	—	2	—	2	3	4	2	9
	(Tomb)	—	2	—	—	—	—	2	—
Mio 169	—	—	—	—	4	7	11	—	22
Tamat 157	Present	—	—	—	+	2	—	—	2
Teguef n'Agar	Present	—	—	—	1	—	—	—	1
Shin Ajeyn	Present	1	1	—	+	2	+	2	2
Shin Wasararan	(Tombs)	—	2	—	—	2	—	2	2
Megalithic burials									
Asaquru	Mon. D	—	1	—	1	1	—	1	2
Afunfun 8		—	—	—	—	1	—	—	1
Tegaza	Mon. 4	—	—	6	—	—	—	6	—
	Mon. 5	—	2	—	—	—	—	2	—
Tezzigart	Mon. 2	—	—	1	—	—	—	1	—
	Mon. 3	—	—	—	1	—	—	—	1

Key: W = weapons; O = Ornaments

Table 1.6 Diversity of the recorded metal artifacts

Locality	Iron artifacts				Copper artifacts				Number of classes
	O	*W*	*T*	*U*	*O*	*W*	*T*	*U*	
Sites with copper evidence									
Afunfun 162	4	3	—	1	2	1	1	3*	14
Afunfun 175	1	—	—	3	1	—	—	2*	7
Aghtauzu 178	—	2	1	1	+	+	+	+	>4
Azelik	—	1	1	1	—	—	—	1*	4
Eres Anadan	—	—	—	—	1	—	—	1	2
Ikawaten 185	1	1	—	—	—	—	—	—	2
Sites with iron evidence									
Chin Oraghen	1	2	—	1	1	—	—	1	6
Efey Washaran 151	—	—	—	—	2	—	—	—	2
Efey Washaran 183	1	—	—	—	1	—	—	—	2
In Taylalen II 15	—	1	—	—	—	—	—	—	1
Jibo 136	2	2	—	1	3	—	—	—	8
Mio 169	4	1	1	1	—	—	—	—	7
Tamat 157	1	1	—	1	—	—	—	—	3
Teguaef n'Agar	—	1	—	1	—	—	—	—	2
Shin Ajeyn	—	—	—	1	1	—	—	—	2
Shin Wasararan	—	—	—	—	1	—	—	—	2
Megalithic burials									
Afunfun 8	1	—	—	—	—	—	—	—	1
Asaquru	1	1	—	—	1	—	—	—	3
Tegaza	—	—	—	—	1	—	—	1	2
Tezzigart	—	1	—	—	—	—	—	1	2

**presence of ingots. Key: O = Ornaments; W = Weapons; T = Tools; U = Undetermined*

Granted that these are very small collections, it does appear that the range of metal artifacts collected from living and metal-producing areas is more varied than that found in the burial sites. At the same time, stone tools still played a prominent part in daily activities, even as metal artifacts were introduced into the cultural inventory. There are no metal tools for mundane domestic tasks. This absence is unambiguous, as such tools are usually valued highly enough to be used until heavily worn, at which time the metal would be recycled.

Whatever the case of individual applications, the metal implements recovered probably reflect a palimpsest of multiple uses, as would arise if metal were still a rare commodity. Objects collected from the burials comprise an even narrower range of artifact, consisting solely of items of personal adornment and weapons: the former mainly in copper and the latter in iron. The inventory of metal artifacts, since it is very narrowly ranged, suggests a consistent and long-lasting constellation of metal goods seemingly created and supported by underlying social demands. If there is in fact a socially determined selection process at work here, and I admit the data are still scant, then we can hypothesize that copper ornaments and iron weapons, whatever their other cultural uses, existed within a symbolic sphere endowing social prestige on their owners (Bourdieu 1979).

CEMETERIES AND PUTATIVE TERRITORIES

The burial evidence can be divided into three major categories: isolated tombs found at living sites, as at Efey Washaran 151 and 183, Jibo 136, and Shin Wasasaran; tomb groups, as at Chin Tafidet, Afunfun 161, and Afunfun 177 (Paris 1984); and hundreds of stone tumuli, some isolated, but more often than not grouped together in cemeteries, some of which are quite small, while the large ones are spread over several hectares. I will direct our attention to those burial grounds with stone tumuli, which we suspect marked discrete territories.

Several hundred burials in megalithic monuments, or stone tumuli of varying size, have been found in the In Gall–Tegidda-n-Tesemt region. They are found in varying concentrations in 116 different localities. Excavations have been carried out at 10 of these, with the number of burials varying from 8 at Shi Mumenin to 1 at Afunfun 8, Azelik, Tezzigart, and Tin Tegeis (Table 1.7). Five of these—Shin Wasadan, Asaquru, Azelik, Tegaza, and Tin Tegeis—are in the Eghazer depression; 3—Agadez, Imosaden, and Tezzigart—are in the foothills; and 2—Afunfun 8 and Shi Mumenin— are along the Tigidit cliff. Unfortunately, all are not reported with equal accuracy and consistency. From the available information, it appears that the cemeteries vary in size from 22.50 to 0.35 hectares and the number of burials from 4 to

Table 1.7 Major characteristics of tested megalithic burial grounds

Locality	*Situation*	*Surface (Ha)*	*Number of monuments*	*Number of excavated burials*	*Diversity*	*Date B.P.*
1—Afunfun 8	Cliff	?	?	1	?	?
2—Agadez	Foothills	0,35	77	6	1	—
3—Asaquri	Depression	+10	hundreds	7	Maximum	3350
4—Azelik	Depression	?	20	1	1	—
5—Imosaden	Foothills	?	31	2	?	—
6—Shi Mumenim	Cliff	?	8	2	?	730
7—Shin Wasadan	Depression	22,50	177	4	5	2450
8—Tegaza	Depression	7,00	25	5	5	—
9—Tezzigart	Foothills	?	?	1	7	—
10—Tin Tegeis	Depression	10	50	1	3	—

177 (Poncet 1983; Paris 1984). The megalithic monuments are extremely varied as well both within individual burial grounds and between different cemeteries. The megalithic structures may take the form of stone circles, quadrangular constructions, long rectilinear tumuli, and crescent-shaped (as well as tronconic) and disk-shaped monuments. The stone circles located in the foothills are early Berber burials. The quadrangular ones from the western part of the Tigidit cliff are quite late and date to the first millennium (Paris 1984). We need not concern ourselves with these or with the Berber grave sites.

The use of the same area for the burial of a community's dead over a long period of time is in itself an important social statement. By the same measure, the numbers of burials, the size of the cemetery, and the location of individual tombs one to another are equally significant. By the same token, even the geographic location of burial grounds one to another may be linked to some element of social dynamics and thought of as an element of some broader social design geared toward the demarcation of political space.

The cemeteries can be ranked by their size and the number of megalithic burials. Five of them—Anyokan, Asawas, Tuluk, Shin Wasadan, and Asaquru—are large cemeteries with more than 100 monuments each. A burial from Asaquru is dated to around 5,330 years ago, and another, Monument D, contained an iron spearhead and one copper and two iron items of personal adornment. At Shin Wasadan, a burial is dated to around 4,450 years ago. These five large cemeteries sited on the border of the *cure salée* zone appear to divide the Eghazer basin into five fairly equal territories. We should view them as critical nodes in the local political landscape, with the Eghazer River forming a kind of boundary, defining socially enfranchised areas that delimit the territorial range and annual routine of each group (Fig. 1.10).

Cemeteries with 20 to 100 monuments are unevenly distributed within these five territorial units, and as few as 4 to as many as 12 have been located (Table 1.8). They seem to have been burial grounds for the lower segments of the resident pastoral societies. The smallest cemeteries, with less than 20 monuments, may have been used by one or more descent groups of low status.

The cemeteries interest us particularly because there is evidence of at least two kinds of past behavior. The dead are "consumers" of prestige items produced by crafts specialists. As such, we get some insight into what might have been a mark of status in some ancient, now silent time. As we have seen, items of adornment or weaponry were preferred.

In order to build a large megalithic monument, a fairly large labor force is needed. As a result, the size and quality of furnishing of graves may indicate something about the organization of the community and the ranking of individuals or their corporate alliances. The status of the deceased and the ability

Figure 1.10 Cemeteries and putative territorial entities, Eghazer basin

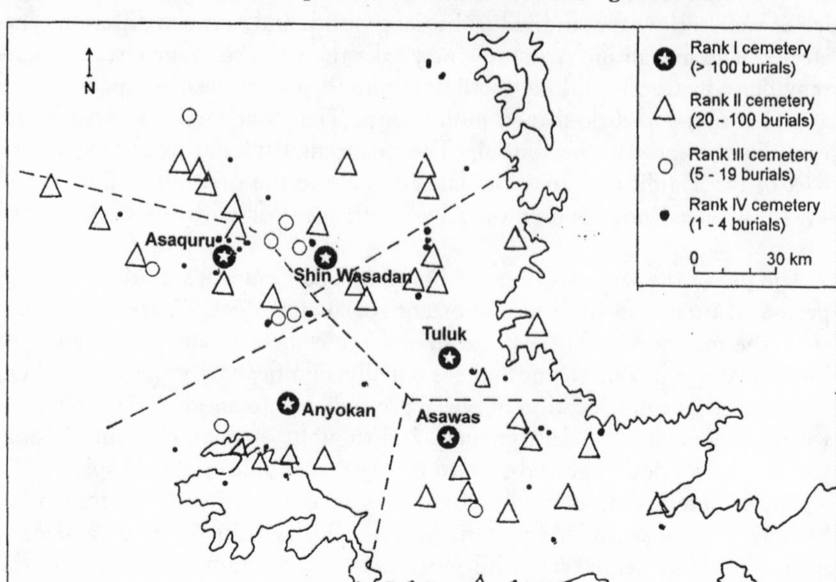

of his or her descent group to organize the necessary labor and accumulate the wherewithal required to support construction and the attendant burial and funerary celebration is often a mark of the social significance and status of the individual and his or her descent group. The marks of status may be read in the fittings and care attendant in the grave site. A large well-fitted-out grave suggests a more affluent situation than a poorly furnished one. By the same token, a variety of graves within a comparable mortuary format, or program, suggests elements of social difference and so forth.

Given the previously mentioned information, how would we characterize the nomadic pastoralists of this part of Niger? At the climax of their occupancy, the In Gall–Tegidda-n-Tesemt region seems to have been settled by five relatively large "tribal" units, each composed of a varying number of socially delineated blocs made up of particular descent groups acting as self-governing corporate entities. The number of domestic corporations in each tribe can only be suggested from the organization of the cemeteries, though it now appears that some social differentiation was present. Metal projected an element of social distinction that separated those who possessed it from those who did not. Metal producers provided their kinsmen with emblems of prestige and authority. How long this society lasted is unknown.

Table 1.8 Hierarchy and regional spatial patterning of megalithic cemeteries

Rank	*SW group*	*SE group*	*E. group*	*N. group*	*W. group*
I (>100)	Anyokan (IG 2)	Asawas (AG 31)	Tuluk (TTA 44)	Shin Wasadan (TTA 16)	Asaquru (TTS 48)
II (20–100)	4 (AG 30, IG 21, 23, 32)	12 (AG 32, 33, 34, 39, 62, 73, 75, 106, 108, 109, 117)	12 (TTA 25, 26, 28, 32, 33, 35, 40, 41, 42, 47, 51, 52)	8 (TTA 4, 7, 9, 15, TTS 9, 10, 11, 31)	6 (TTS 3, 38, 49, 53, 74, 88)
III (5–19)	1 (IG 27)	2 (AG 35, 53)	—	3 (TTS 2, 80, 82)	4 (TTS 75, 83, 92, 93)
IV (1–4)	10	8	7	5	5
TOTAL	16	22	20	17	16

On the face of it, the In Gall–Tegidda-n-Tesemt region in Niger does not give support to the hypothesis of *an increased efficiency of the productive equipment* as the primary reason for the adoption of metal production. Perhaps metal weapons can be deemed more efficient than stone ones. Though we do have evidence of violent contact between groups competing for the same resources, we have no evidence that metal-edged weapons were critical additions to the warrior's armory. Nor have we any evidence of a kind of warfare in which they would have made a difference. More to the point, the metal items found in different sites indicate a more palpable use of metal for bodily adornment. The status attached to the possession and display of metal objects—because of their rarity or the cost of their production and acquisition—argues that the real value of metal is ascribable to social rather than economic worth and that socially sanctioned demand for prestige and status items fostered the adoption of new technologies. The processing of local ores into prestige items seems to have reinforced an existent social order. To this extent, the acceptance of a metallurgical technology was not revolutionary but, rather, complementary of proven behaviors.

THE MEMA REGION: INTENSIFICATION AND DEVOLUTION

The Mema region is a place steeped in history. It is a vast, ancient floodplain located nearly 100 kilometers northwest of the inland Niger delta and southwest of the Lakes region (Togola 1993, 1996; McIntosh 1998). It was once neighbor to the renowned empire of Ghana, which flourished, during the sixth to thirteenth centuries, in southeastern Mauretania and western Mali. According to the medieval Arab traveler and geographer Ibn Battuta (in Levtzion and Hopkins 1981, 279–284), there was an important trade route through the region in the middle of the fourteenth century, when the area was part of the Mali Empire.

Regarding archaeological investigation, the area was visited in the 1950s and 1960s by Mauny, Monod, and Szumowski (Togola 1996, 96–97). Some controlled excavations have been carried out more recently as well. Haaland (1980) uncovered evidence for intensive iron production, dated to between A.D. 545 and 970 and between 1025 and 1225, at Sites B to E, south of the Boulel Ridge. This dated sequence fits marvelously with the "life span" of the Ghana Empire. Haaland traced the intensification of iron production to satisfying a booming market for weapons, tools, and objects of personal adornment within a growing local population. She suggested that the intensive production of iron exacted a heavy toll on the local hardwood forests, leading to an ecological crisis because of the extensive deforestation (Haaland 1980).

The upper levels of Kolima mound were dated to between 545 and 650 and between A.D. 1280 and 1310 by Togola (1996, 97), and Raimbault and Dutour investigated the Late Stone Age site of Kobadi. They uncovered several burials bracketed in a Late Stone Age occupation sequence ranging from 1600 B.C. to 350 B.C.

Togola (1993, 1996), in 1989 and 1990, surveyed an extensive area in the center of the region. Within this meticulously investigated area (nearly one-fifth of the Mema region), the Akumbu mounds—a group of settlement mounds formed by accumulating living debris—in the southwest were tested by excavation. The trenches dug at AK1 exposed a sequence dated to somewhere between A.D. 548 and 661 and 1274 and 1401. AK4 provided a radiocarbon date of between 1024 and 1183. AK3, at Akumbu B, exposed a sequence ranging in time from a period no earlier than between 342 and 442 to no later than between 780 and 1100. These mounds appear to have been occupied sometime between the fourth and the fifteenth century.

Many pottery fragments were found, as were 64 metal artifacts. Of these, 57 are iron, but nine-tenths of them are so heavily corroded that the original shape can no longer be determined. However, 4 ring fragments, 2 knife blades, and 18 miscellaneous iron artifacts were discerned (Togola 1993:,104). Seven pieces of copper, 2 of which were well-preserved bangles, were collected from an AK3 burial. In addition to bracelets, the tomb also contained a water jar, 13 cowry shells (*Cypraea moneta*), and 13 carnelian beads (Togola 1993, 80; 1996, 106–107). A glass bead was discovered in level 66 of AK1 and dated to the seventh century as well as 6 spindle-whorls in levels 34 (dated A.D. 985 to 1160) and 6 (dated 1274 to 1401). Iron metallurgy in the Mema region is attested to from around the fourth century onward and exotic imports from around the seventh century onward.

SETTLEMENT PATTERN AND THE INTENSIFICATION OF IRON PRODUCTION

The 137 known sites may be separated into distinct chronological units on the basis of a varied array of attributes. There are 27 Late Stone Age sites (Fig. 1.11). With two minor exceptions in the southeast, all the Late Stone Age sites are sited on degraded dunes and ancient water corridors. One hundred nine sites are Iron Age settlements, of which 94 are village mounds; 15 are smelting sites with slag concentrations, smelters, and broken tuyeres; and 2 are cemeteries with jar burials (Togola 1993, 41–42). Living sites appear organized into groups of mounds divisible into a time sequence as the Early, Middle, and Late Assemblages.

Early Assemblage Sites

During the first five centuries of the current era, the Mema region was occupied by small communities of fishermen, herdsmen, hunters, and

Figure 1.11 Distribution of Late Stone Age sites in the Mema region

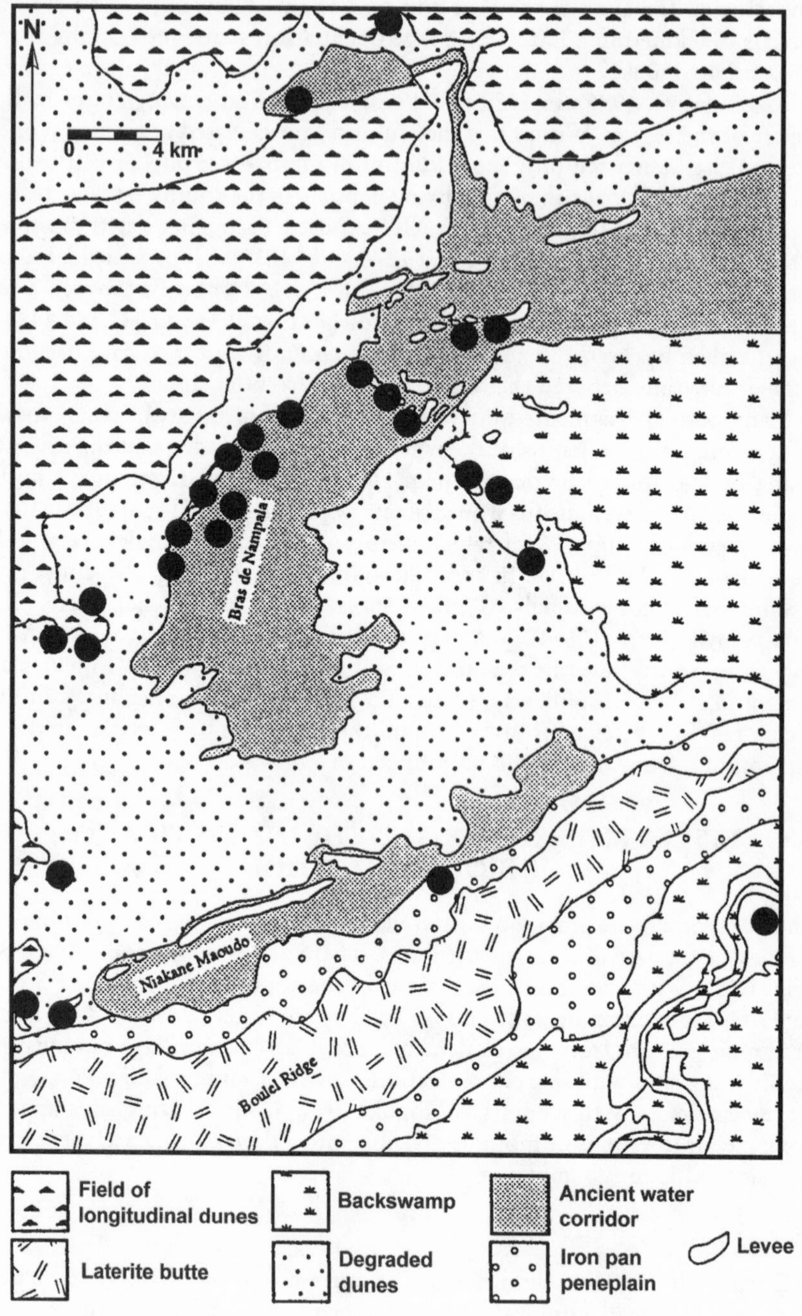

agriculturists (MacDonald and van Neer 1994; Togola 1996), and apparently very few of them practiced iron production, and that on a small scale. Forty-nine sites belonging to the Early Assemblage are dated to before 500. Three of them—Goudourou, Toule, and Kolima—are set apart, and the others form six groups of between 2 and 18 mounds (Fig. 1.12, Table 1.9). Thirty-six are within 2 kilometers of the Niakene Maoudo in the south, with 11 on the bank of the Nampala (Togola 1993, 53). Fourteen measure less than 1 hectare, while 13 are larger, though none is larger than 5 hectares (Table 1.10). Boundou Boubou North, with evidence of 18 settlements, and Boundou Boubou South, with 9, appear to have been favored as living sites at this time.

Middle Assemblage Sites

Twenty-five settlements belong to the Middle Assemblage. They range in time from the seventh to the thirteenth century. Though fewer in number than those of the earlier period, they are, on average, significantly larger (Table 1.10). Goundourou and Kolima each have two mounds. The largest at Akumbu has six mounds, but Bourgou Silatigui, Boundou Boubou North, and Boundou Boubou South have only a single mound each. Toladie and Akumbu are the largest and most important settlements of this period. Both were newly founded settlements, situated roughly 24 kilometers from each other (Fig. 1.13). However, Goundourou, Kolima, and Bourgou Silatigui had been occupied earlier and expanded at this time. At Goundourou, the single mound occupied earlier was supplemented by a second one, while at Kolima the number of settled mounds rose from one to three. On the other hand, one, Bourgou Silatigui, coalesced five small hamlets of less than 1 hectare into a single settlement of upward of 20 hectares. Toladie A, located in the central area, is nearly 80 hectares in area (Togola 1993, 48). The Akumbu mound group in the southwest comprises three living sites: Akumbu A, measuring 21 hectares and elevated nearly 7 meters above the floodplain; Akumbu B, 8 hectares in area and 7 to 8 meters high; and Akumbu C, a settlement mound of 3 hectares standing 7 meters high. There are two burial mounds a few hundred meters south of Akumbu A, and two small iron-smelting sites on the eastern and northern edge of the complex (Togola 1993, 66–67).

The chronology of the 15 known smelting sites (Fig. 1.14) is poorly understood. Therefore, it is not possible to distinguish those of the Early Assemblage from those of the Middle Assemblage. Akumbu and Kolima had two smelter areas each, while Boulel and Boundou Boubou had three each. Ndoupa, Bourgou Silatigui, Niakare Ndondi, and Goudourou in the north and northwest each had only a single smelting area in its vicinity. At Boundou Boubou, smelting Site 874-30 covered an area of over 1 hectare.

Figure 1.12 Distribution of Early Assemblage sites and iron-smelting localities

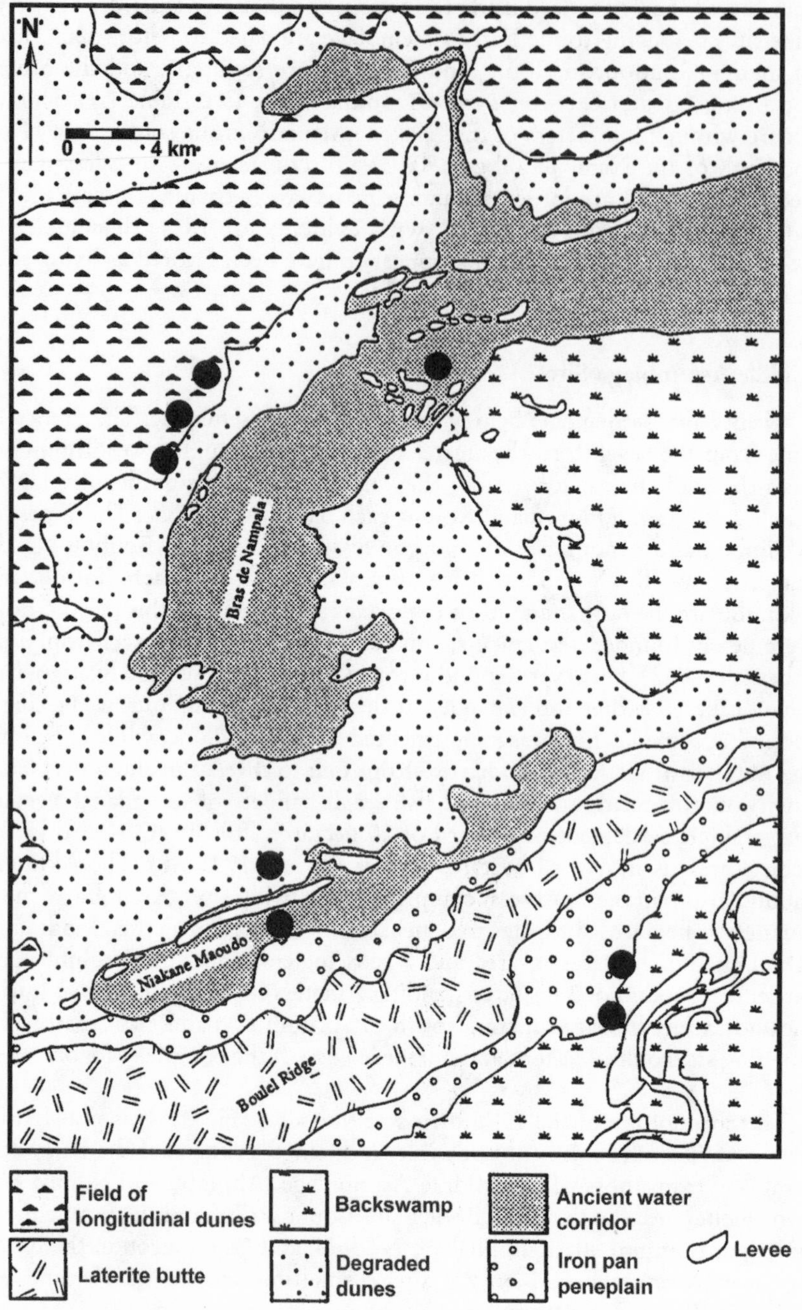

Table 1.9 Settlement clusters and mound size in the Mema region

Settlement cluster	< 1 ha	1–5 ha	6–10 ha	11–20 ha	>20 ha	Total
Early Assemblage Sites (300–500 AD)						
Akumbu	1	—	—	—	—	1
Boundou Boubou N	10	8	—	—	—	18
Boundou Boubou S	4	5	—	—	—	9
Bourgou Silatigui	5	—	—	—	—	5
Goudourou	1	—	—	—	—	1
Kolima	1	—	—	—	—	1
Niakare Dondi	2	2	—	—	—	4
Toule	—	1	—	—	—	1
Wiessouma	3	6	—	—	—	9
TOTAL	27	22	—	—	—	49
Middle Assemblage Sites (600–1200 AD)						
Akumbu	3	1	1	—	1	6
Beretouma	1	—	—	2	—	3
Boundou Boubou N	—	—	—	1	—	1
Boundou Boubou S	—	1	—	—	—	1
Bourgou Silatigui	—	—	—	1	—	1
Goudourou	—	2	—	—	—	2
Kolima	—	—	1	1	—	2
Toladie	1	—	2	1	1	5
Toule	—	4	—	—	—	4
TOTAL	5	8	4	6	2	25
Late Assemblage Sites (1200–1400 AD)						
Goudourou	—	—	—	1	—	1
Niakare Ndondi	—	1	—	—	—	1
Tiable Fame	—	2	—	—	—	2
TOTAL	—	3	—	1	—	4
Uncertain	—	—	—	—	—	8
TOTAL	32	33	4	7	2	86

Table 1.10 Settlement size through time in the Mema Region

Chronology	*<1 ha*		*1–5 ha*		*6–10 ha*		*11–20 ha*		*> 20 ha*		*TOTAL*	
	n	%	*n*	%	*n*	%	*n*	%	*n*	%	*n*	%
AD 300–500 Early Assemblage	27	56	22	44	—	—	—	—	—	—	49	57.47
AD 600–1200 Middle Assemblage	5	20	8	32	4	16	6	24	2	8	25	28.73
AD 1200–1400 Late Assemblage	—	—	3	75	—	—	1	25	—	—	4	4.59
Unknown	—	—	—	—	—	—	—	—	—	—	8	9.19
TOTAL	33	37.93	33	37.93	4	4.59	7	8.04	2	2.29	86	

Figure 1.13 Distribution of Middle Assemblage sites

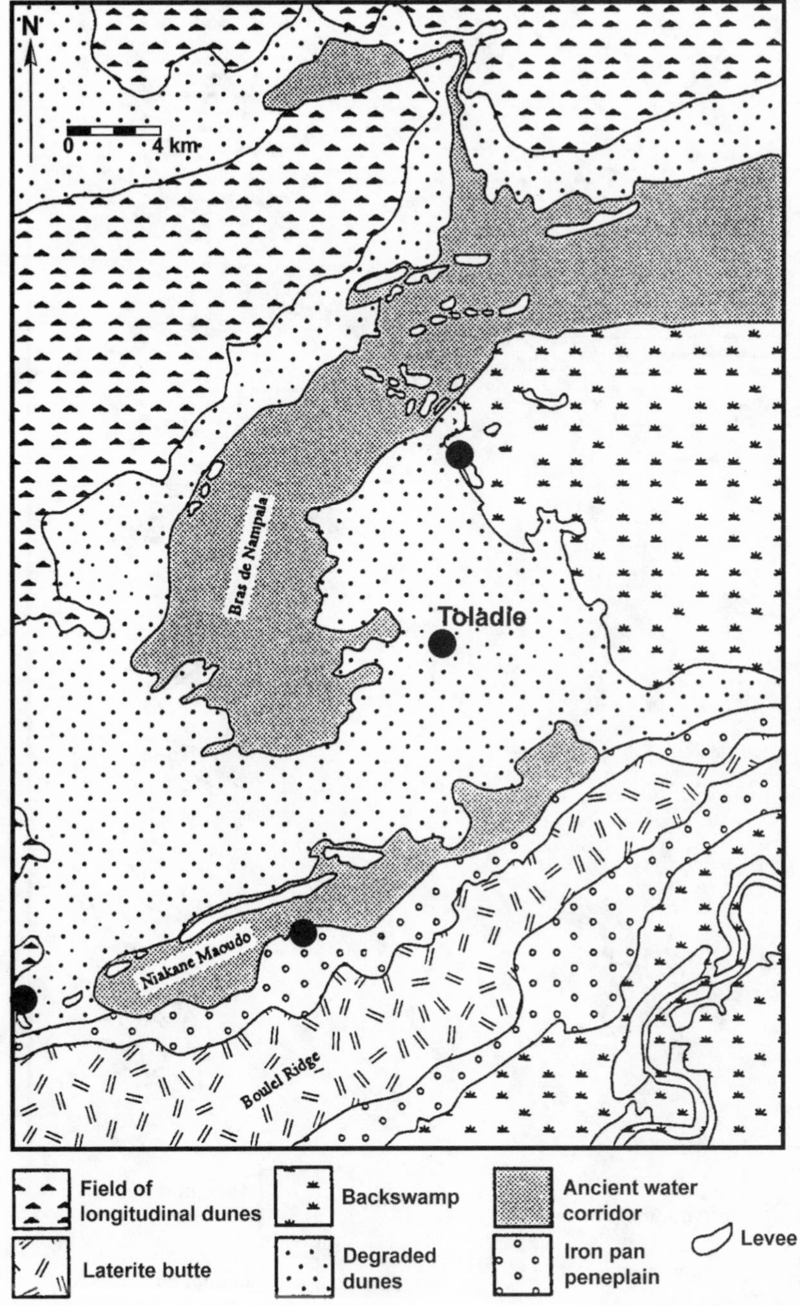

Figure 1.14 Distribution of iron-smelting sites

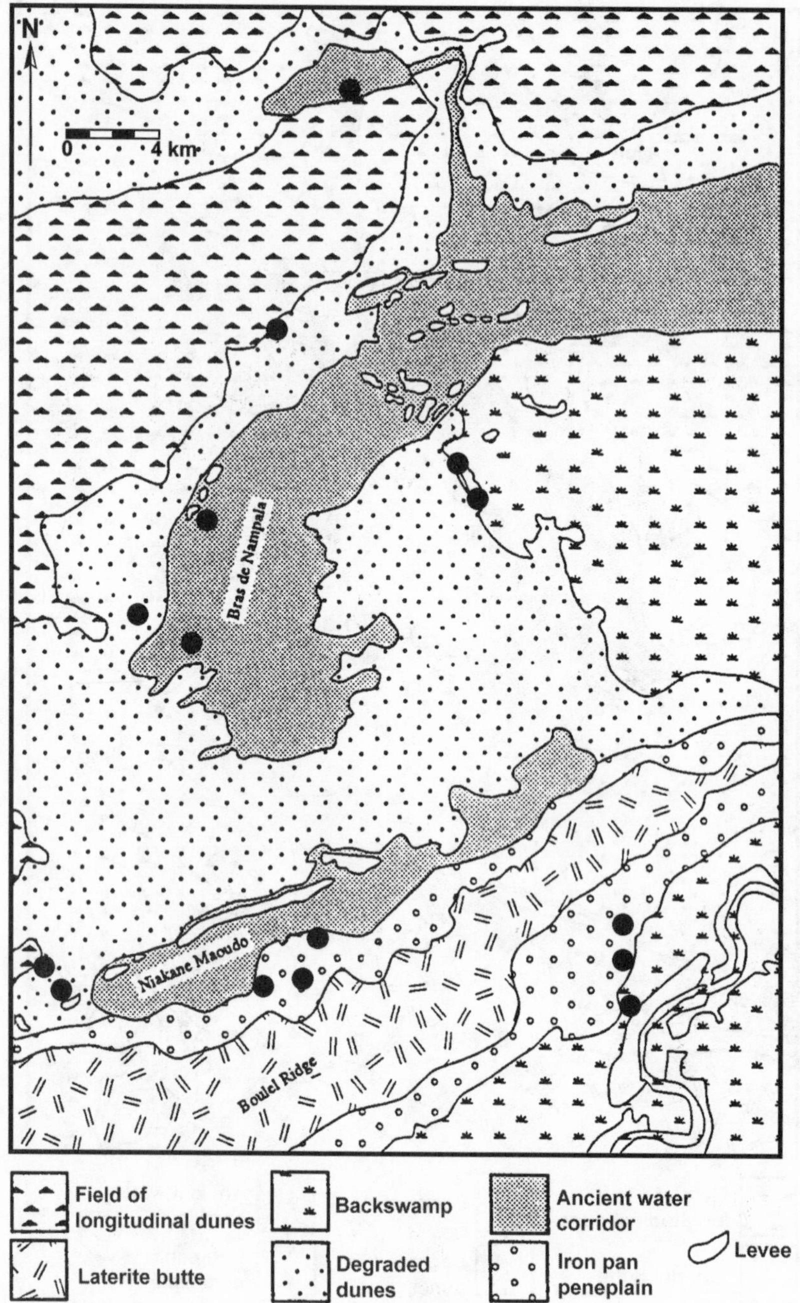

The one at Boulel, Site 913-1, measures 7 hectares and contains the remains of more than 100 furnaces, many of which are still visible (Togola 1993, 51).

The lack of any evidence of ore processing at Toladie is particularly striking. It is as if this centrally located, possibly dominant settlement was engaged in a different kind of relationship with its surrounding countryside. The distance between Toladie and the nearest processing sites varies from between 8 and 24 kilometers (Fig. 1.14). The Kolima smelters are 8 kilometers due north of it, and those at Nampala are 12 kilometers to the west. The northernmost smelting site, as well as those associated with Akumbu mound group in the south, is 24 kilometers away. Those associated with Boundou Boubou in the south, Boulel in the southeast, and the vicinity of Kobadie in the north-northwest are about 16 kilometers away. Toladie seems to have been in position to draw equally on the smelted production of these different communities.

The settlement pattern of the Middle Assemblage period is organized around six settlements of less than 20 hectares and two greater than 20 hectares. Five of them are found along a roughly southwest–northeast axis stretched from Akumbu to Kolima through Boundou Boubou North and Toladie (Fig. 1.15, Table 1.10). The distance between neighboring

Figure 1.15 Histogram of settlement size through time

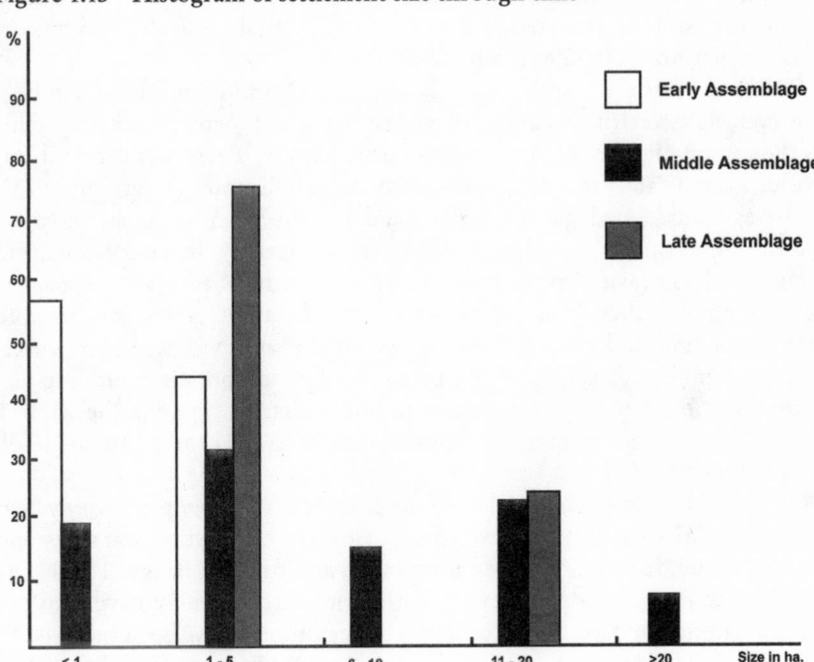

communities varies from 8 kilometers between Toladie and Kolima to 12 kilometers between Toladie and Boundou Boubou North. Toladie's central location and presumed primacy emerged as a consequence of changes in regional political decision making (Fig. 1.13).

Togola (1993, 53) considered the Boulel Ridge as the main source of iron ore because of the laterite and ferrugenous deposits located there. If this was the case, iron smelters from the central and northern parts of the Mema may have depended on folk from the south to supply them with raw materials.

INTENSIFICATION AND CHANGE

The appearance of imported objects at AK1 and AK3 indicate some involvement by the Mema region in West African long-distance trade networks during the second half of the first millennium. This was the time of the growth and fluorescence of the Ghana Empire, to which the region formed an integral part. Both Haaland (1980) and Togola (1993, 1996) suggest an intensified production of iron at this time. It is thought that the region came to specialize in high-volume iron production in order to supply markets in other parts of the middle Niger (Togola 1993, 53). Haaland (1980; Holl 1985) emphasized the interaction between the Mema region and the core of the Ghana Empire, whose capital, Kumbi Saleh, was located less than 50 kilometers to the northwest. Unfortunately, the process by which iron production was intensified has not been adequately investigated.

There are sufficient archaeological, historical, and ethnohistorical data, however, to assert the existence of diversified and dynamic market systems in the region connected to the trans-Saharan trade. There were several important towns and trading centers in the Ghana Empire (Levtzion 1973), with Tegdaoust (Awdaghost), Walata, and Kumbi Saleh being the most famous. Empires usually consist of a core area, an outlying tributary zone, and a more or less moving frontier on its peripheries. If "medieval" Ghana was such an empire, the Mema region would have been integrated into its core area at one time and part of the tributary zone at another stage of its development. Empires usually grow by progressively incorporating outlying territories through military conquest or political alliance, bringing these into a centralized political system of economic benefit to the center (Adams 1979, 59, in Hodge 1996, 19).

The issue here may be stated as follows: How was the empirewide system underwritten? One may suggest a range of taxes on markets, caravans and craft activities, labor corvées of various sort, and tribute (Trigger 1993). The intensification of iron production in the Mema region may have resulted from a tribute imposed by the center. The region may have been required to supply finished iron artifacts. Local "elites" would have organized the labor or, more likely, collected the product at some central locality, such as Toladie. From there it would be transshipped to the core of the empire. Tribute and exchange are not mutually exclusive, however, and the intensified production triggered by the exaction of tribute may have caused a concurrent increased output traded within the Mema region and beyond, as far east as the inland Niger delta.

There was a sharp decrease in the number of settlements during the period of the Late Assemblage, dated from the thirteenth to the fifteenth century. The Mema region was then part of the Mali Empire, and apparently there was a general depopulation accompanied by the abandonment of many established settlements throughout the middle Niger (Togola 1993, 90). Four sites are dated to this period. The largest, Goudourou, covered between 11 and 20 hectares, while the others, two settlements at Tiabel Fame and one at Niakare Ndondi, were some 1 to 5 hectares in extent (Table 1.10). Iron smelting was certainly still practiced, but the lack of excavated data precludes any further discussion of the issue. At this time, the trade routes shifted further northeast at Tombouctou, at the apex of the Niger bend, as the Mema region turned into a depopulated borderland of the Mali Empire.

THE NORTHERN EDGE OF THE EQUATORIAL RAIN FOREST

The Yaoundé plateau was occupied by food-producing communities by 6,000 years ago (de Maret 1992). Iron technology is attested in the area from sometime between 600 and 400 B.C., and investigations have focused on its emergence. Even if the currently available regional chronology is correct, recent work has broadened our knowledge of the areas settled within the southern forested zone, suggesting a situation more complex than generally thought (Atangana 1989, 1992; Ossah Mvondo 1990, 1991, 1992a, 1992b, 1993; Asombang et al. 1991; Mbida 1992a, 1992b).

Surveys conducted by Ossah-Mvondo (1993) in the southeastern part of the forest zone in the regions of Djoum and Mintom (Fig. 1.16) resulted in the discovery of six new settlements at Minko'o, Akontan, Akoafem, Alat Makay, Ze, and Ekom. Although they are not yet securely dated, they present an interesting range of archaeological data. Evidence for iron metallurgy and ceramics is present at all the sites.

In the southern province are two new groupings, one close to the small town of Zoetélé (Asombang et al. 1990) and the other comprising five localities—Ngulemelong, Avebe, Benelabot, Ngomessane, and Mengong—along the main road from Sangmélima to Ebolowa (Mbida 1992a, 1992b). No precise details are available for this second group, but there are indications of iron slag, pottery fragments, and pits.

Figure 1.16 The southern forested area with location of the studied regions

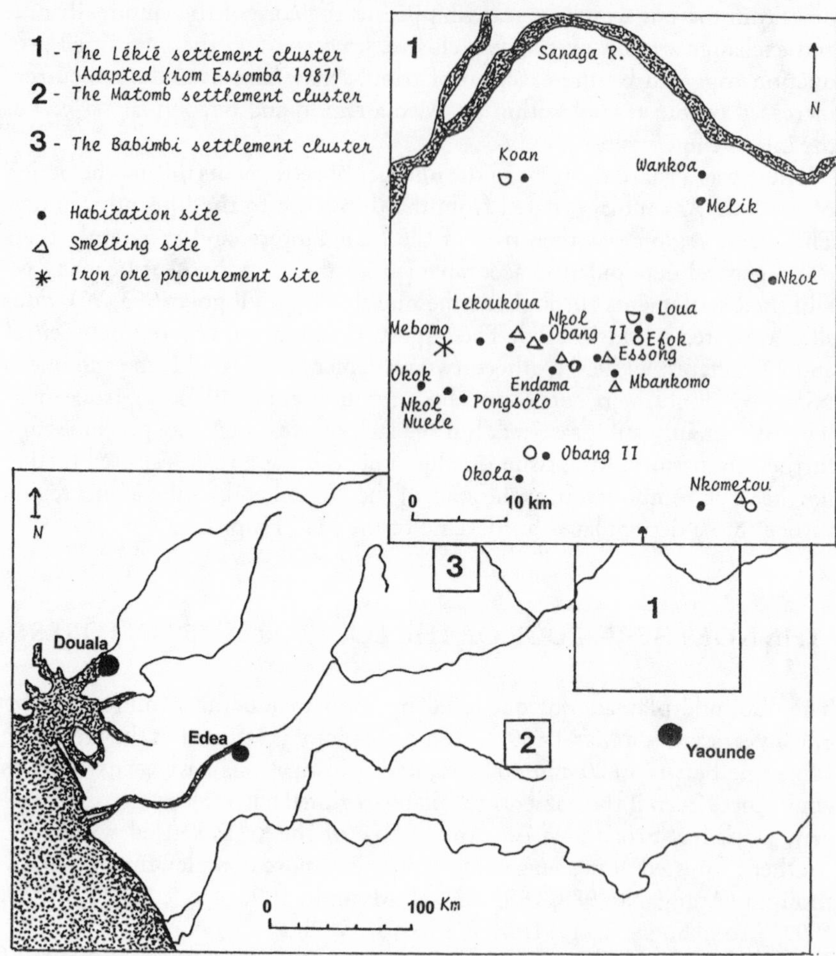

The Sanaga–Lékié Zone

More intensive research has been conducted in the Sanaga–Lékié zone (Fig. 1.16) in order to reconstruct the settlement pattern as well as the history of ethnic groups living there (Essomba 1985, 1986, 1987, 1992a, 1993; de Maret 1992; Mbida 1992a, 1992b). On the left bank of the Sanaga River, in the *département* of Lékié, is a relatively dense group of 16 settlements in an area measuring about 600 square kilometers (Fig. 1.15:1). These old settlement complexes seem to be organized into a living site, as well as adjacent smelting and smithing ones, the complex forming an integrated aggregate in which subsistence and living activities are joined with industrial ones. According to local informants, in precolonial times, iron ore was collected in the vicinity of Mebomo, where many mining pits have been found. It was then processed at the settlement aggregates. One smelting furnace at Pongsolo has been dated to sometime between 1500 and 1750. Another at Nkometou has been dated to between 1694 and 1728. That is, iron production was fairly general in the seventeenth and eighteenth centuries.

Unfortunately, very little is known about the kinds or variety of iron artifacts manufactured, their functions, or the pattern of their being discarded since few are left in the archaeological deposits. It is apparent, however, that iron production was carried out on consistent basis.

Nkometou (Essomba 1985, 1987, 1992a, 1993) is thought to be the first place reached by the Beti after their epic crossing the Sanaga River (Laburthe-Tolra 1981a, 1981b; Essomba 1992a). It seems to have been settled sometime around the fifth century B.C. by food-producing communities with some knowledge of iron working. The Beti migration hypothesis, on the other hand, focuses on a later occupation phase dating to the late seventeenth and early eighteenth centuries. According to Ngoa (1981), the name *Nkometou* is combination of two lexemes: *Nkom,* meaning "hill-rock," and *Otu,* from Otu Tamba, the name of the founding ancestor of the Beti.

A chronology based on Otu Tamba's genealogy suggests that his grandfather Essomba Nagbana settled at Nkometou after crossing the Sanaga River sometime in the early 1770s. Laburthe-Tolra (1981a, 1981b) thinks that this happened earlier, sometime closer to 1730, by different individuals belonging to another lineage. Other traditional histories assert that Nkometou was settled earlier yet, in 1689, by yet another group of individuals (Essomba 1986, 105–112). These differences, which appear puzzling at first glance, are an effect of each investigators relying on a different informant belonging to a different lineage. As we are aware, traditional history is frequently colored in order to ensure a political effect. This seems to be happening here. All we can say is that the only radiocarbon determination from Nkometou's later occupation agrees roughly with the chronology obtained from the traditional histories.

However, this consensus settles the case only of the latest inhabitants of the settlement, which otherwise has a history stretching 2,500 years into the past. Our interest is in the story of prehistoric iron technology in Lékié *département,* a history of various interaction spheres used for economic exchanges as well as important social transactions.

The Matomb–Babimbi Areas

Investigations in areas to the west of Yaoundé (Fig. 1.16:2, 3) suggest an interesting and unexpected picture of intensification of iron production. Two main settlement groupings have been investigated, one in the southwest within the administrative division of Matomb and one in the northwest in the area of Babimbi within the district of Ndom (Essomba 1985, 1986, 1987, 1993). Recently, a new site, which can be included in the Matomb ones, was discovered and tested at Mandoumba (Ossah-Mvondo 1992a).

At Mandoumba, located a few kilometers south of Matomb, three archaeological features, two smelting furnaces with slags, and an oval crucible have been exposed by erosion in the courtyard of the Presbyterian mission. Test trenching has shown that these features are remains of smelting furnaces still undated. About 10 kilometers north of Matomb are four sites: Mangwen I, a smithing site; Nkongteck, an iron ore mining site; and Pan-Manguenda and Pan-Nsas, two important smelting sites with impressive iron production features, located within 10 kilometers of each other. In each, there are the remains of three kinds of structure: two rectangular dwellings, heaps of smelting debris, and a large furnace set on the highest part of the site (Fig. 1.17, Table 1.11).

The smelting installation consists of a cylindrical furnace measuring 1.15 to 1.25 meters in diameter and 3.65 to 3.80 meters in height in a rectangular pit nearly 2 meters deep. The furnaces walls were built up with layers of clay coated with thin red fire-hardened bricks, similar to those used to pave the floor of the pit. At Pan-Nsas, there was a "medicine" pot in the floor of the pit (Fig. 1.18). These were natural draft furnaces durably built for long-term use. Their elevated location oriented to the northwest took full advantage of the dry season's predominant winds. The wind, being forced into the pit's cavity, was drawn upward through the furnace body into the load of burning charcoal and heated ore, giving forth a stream of molted metal. The most intensive period of iron production, during which the furnaces were built, occurred from the fifteenth to the seventeenth century (Table 1.11), a period coincident with the onset and fluorescence of the Atlantic trade—trade to coastal towns acting as middlemen to the commercial sailing vessels plying the Atlantic coast in search of western African commodities, minerals, and especially slaves to be transported to plantations across the Atlantic.

In the northwest, the Babimbi group in the vicinity of Ndom has not been excavated, but former blacksmiths dated it as belonging to "pre-German time." It shares strong similarities with the Matomb group. Similar large-scale smelting furnaces have been discovered at Nguilumlend, Nyeng, and Massangui II, some 35 to 40 kilometers to the north of Ndom (Essomba 1985, 3–4) in what appears to have been the principal ore procurement area (Table 1.11). Blacksmiths' workshops were located at Ngock and Nindje further south. According to informants, in "pre-German time" blacksmiths from Ngock and Nindje were provided with iron blooms produced in smelters from the Nguilumlend and Massangui areas. Their production was then distributed throughout the whole region of Babimbi, from Ndom to

Figure 1.17 Archaeological features from the iron-smelting site of Pan Mangueda in the Matomb settlement cluster

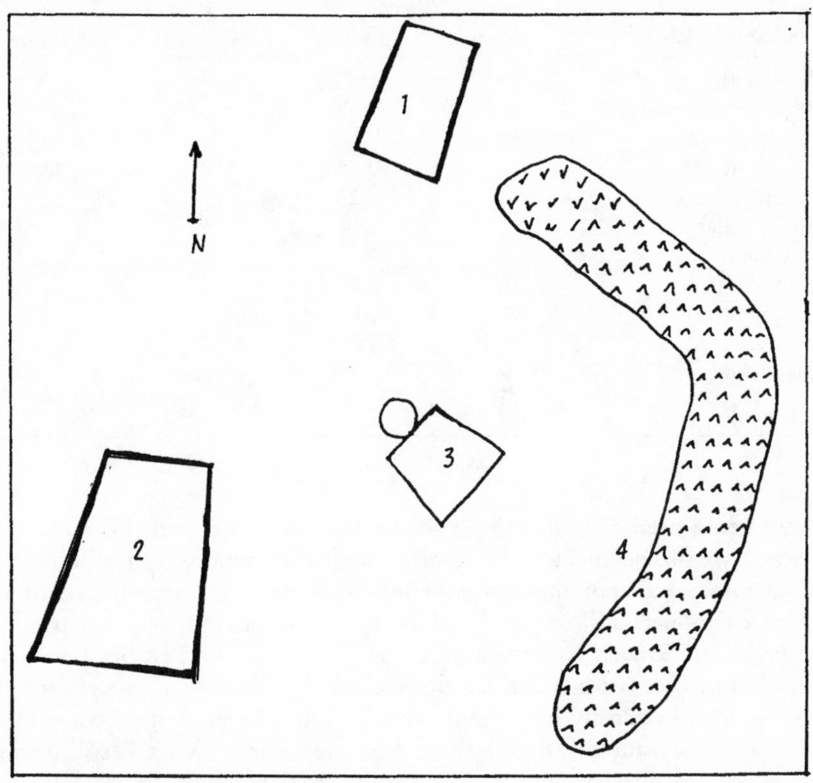

0 10 km

Key: 1 and 2 - quadrangular houses; 3 - Smelting furnace with a large quadrangular pit; 4 - Heap of smelting debris.

Ngambe and Edea (Essomba 1987, 57), though it would seem that iron produced in these smelters traveled farther along the Sanaga River valley toward the Atlantic coast. Because of the presence of falls, the locality of Edea played the role of an important market town that facilitated exchanges between the hinterland and the coast.

It would appear from the archaeological record that the Matomb and Ndom regions underwent a period of intensive iron production stretching from the sixteenth to the eighteenth century. This intensification seems due to a heightened demand caused by a combination of factors. Iron artifacts

Table 1.11 Major smelting sites in the southern forested regions

	Matomb		*Babimbi*	
Cluster Site	*Pan Magenda*	*Pan Nsas*	*Nguilumlend*	*Massangui II*
Surface (m²)	775	1572	?	?
Number of features	4	4	1	1
Smelting furnace	1	1	1	1
Height (m)	3.80	3.65	?	3.00
Diameter (m)	1;15	1.25	?	1.25
Rectangular pit	1	1	1	1
Length (m)	3.00	2.80	?	?
Width (m)	2.00	1.60	?	?
Depth (m)	120	2.00	?	?
Houses	2	2	?	?
Slag heaps	15 m³	Present	Present	Present
Chronology A.D.	1440–1750	1450–1700	1600–1700	1600–1800

were being used as tools in everyday activities, as weapons in warfare, as means for the payment of bride-price, and as currency. Iron tools were a vital commercial commodity participating in an interconnected set of exchange and mercantile networks of local, regional, and panregional extent.

From the Sanaga River valley to the Cameroon–Gabon border in the south, our ideas of cultural development in the equatorial forest area are being altered radically by current investigations. We no longer pass off this area as one unsuited for settlement. Although our evidence is still incomplete, it is adequate to suggest that iron-working technologies were well established there. The pattern of intensification observed in the Matomb and Babimbi regions is a testimony to changing socioeconomic circumstances between the fifteenth and eighteenth centuries.

The Western Grassfields

The Western Grassfields region (Fig. 1.19) is a high lava plateau with altitude varying from 500 to 2,000 meters above sea level. It is broken by volcanic peaks and flanked by a series of lower plains and valleys (Warnier and Fowler 1979; Warnier 1984, 1985). Formerly forested with a wide variety animal life, it has since been transformed into a high-altitude savanna following intensive clearing and burning by people over a very long period of time (Warnier 1984).

Recent archaeological surveys have brought to light many new sites (Ossah-Mwondo 1990; Schmidt and Asombang 1990b; de Crits 1992). In the Kom Culture area located in the subdivision of Fundong, there are 16 locali-

Figure 1.18 The natural draft furnace in the iron-smelting site of Pan Nsas in the Matomb settlement cluster

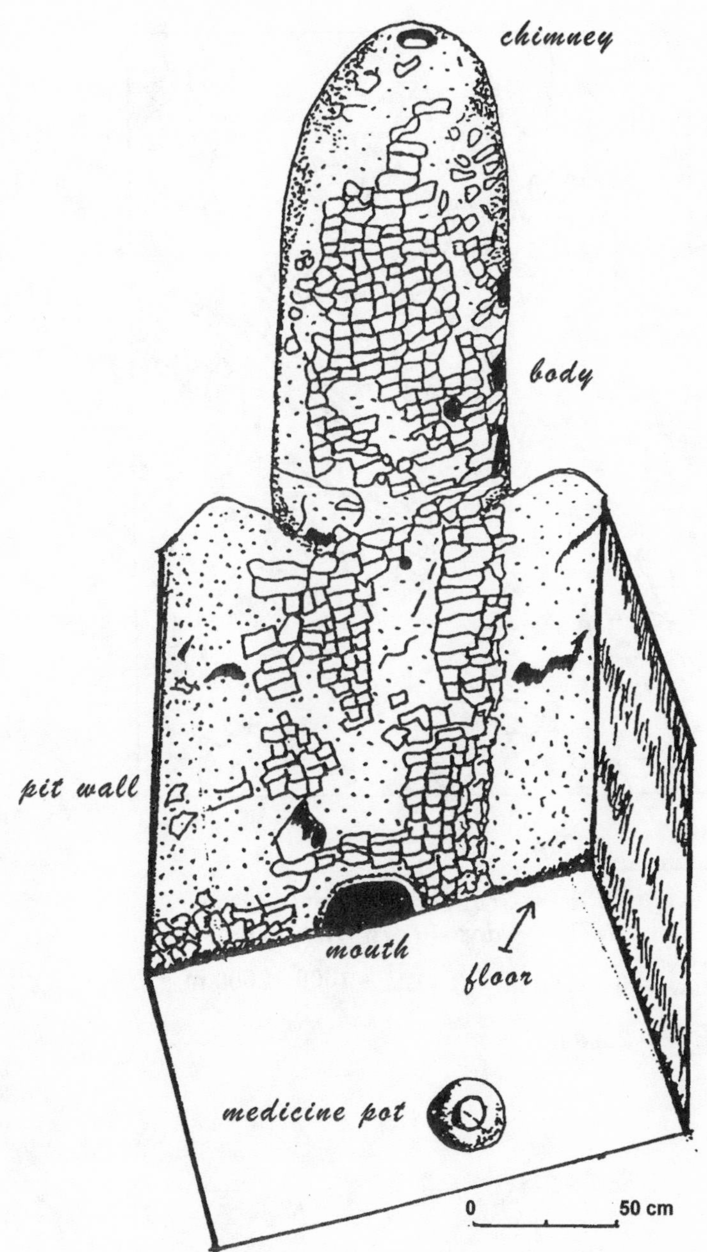

Figure 1.19 Distribution of industrial traditions and settlements in the Western Grassfields

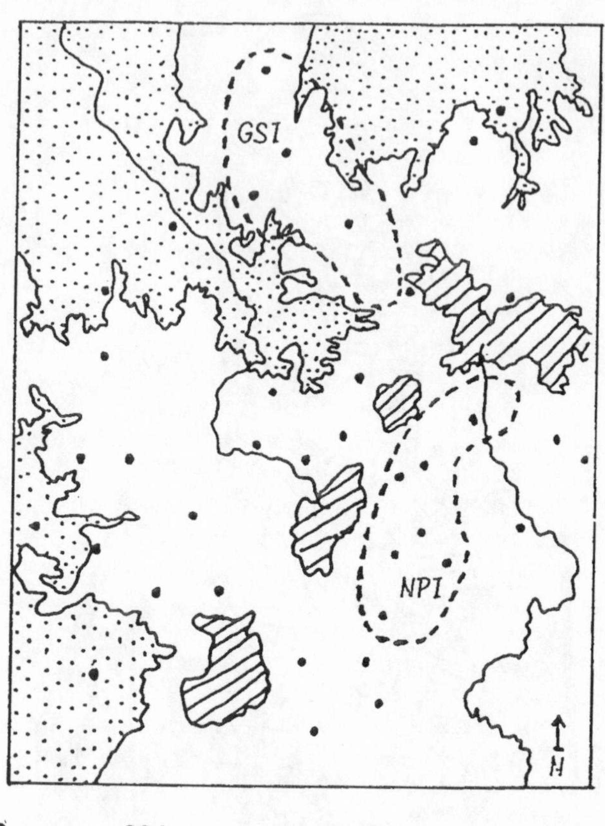

0 20 km

Key: GSI = Glazed Sherds Industry
NPI = Ndop Plain Industry

900 - 1000 m

> 1000 - 2000 m

> 2000 m

ties with ceramics separable into four groups. Though still undated, the associated ceramics suggest that they belong to the early ceramic phase (Schmidt and Asombang 1990b, 13). Evidence for iron metallurgy has been found at Banock in the *département* of Menoua on the eastern side of the Grassfields (de Crits 1992) and Mandja near Bagangte on the southeastern periphery (Mbida 1992a, 1992b).

On the eastern side of the Grassfields, at Banock in the *département* of Menoua, many pits are known to contain quantities of pottery (de Crits 1992), but information on their age is unavailable. On the southeastern periphery, at Mandja near Bangangté, pottery and iron slag have been found spread over on a surface of 6,000 square meters.

More is known about the transformation of iron metallurgy on the Bamenda plateau (Warnier and Fowler 1979; Warnier 1984, 1985, 1992; Ossah-Mvondo 1990; Rowlands and Warnier 1993), where the earliest evidence for iron production is dated to about 300. Three types of iron smelting furnaces are known. A low cylindrical furnace appears earliest and is the most widespread (Fig. 1.20:2), still being used in the 1940s in the northernmost part of the Grassfields (Rowlands 1986, 6). In the seventeenth century, a larger "clump furnace" was invented on the Ndop plain (Fig. 1.20:1), and during the last decades of the nineteenth century, a "small bowl furnace" was developed (Fig. 1.20:3).

Hundreds of iron-producing sites have been located (Warnier 1992; Rowlands and Warnier 1993) and sorted into two industrial traditions: the Ndop Plateau Industry found in the southern part of the study area and the Glazed Sherds Industry in the north (Fig. 1.18).

Within the Ndop Plateau Industry area, there are more than 274 smelting sites known and more than 228,000 cubic meters of iron production debris (Fig. 1.21, Table 1.12). The detailed chronology of this industrial tradition is not yet fully understood. However, with the help of traditional accounts, it appears that the intensification of iron production and the invention of the clump furnace started in the seventeenth century and reached its zenith in the late eighteenth century. The industry was finished by the first decades of the nineteenth century. It is also evident that this florescence was tied to the success of long-distance exchange networks. Some of the more important village chiefdoms, such as Babungo, Bamessing, Bafanji, and Bamenyan, became important providers of iron artifacts to the whole Grassfields and neighboring regions. Their product was even traded down to the Atlantic coast to Duala and Calabar (Warnier 1985; Rowlands 1986).

The clump furnace was labor-intensive but fuel-minimizing. Smelting could be profitably plied as a full-time activity for months on end, as alternating crews worked the furnaces. Though there are some small differences—such as the number and position of vents or the size of the furnaces—built by the four principal village chiefdoms (Warnier and Fowler 1979, 334),

Figure 1.20 Furnace types recorded in the Western Grassfields

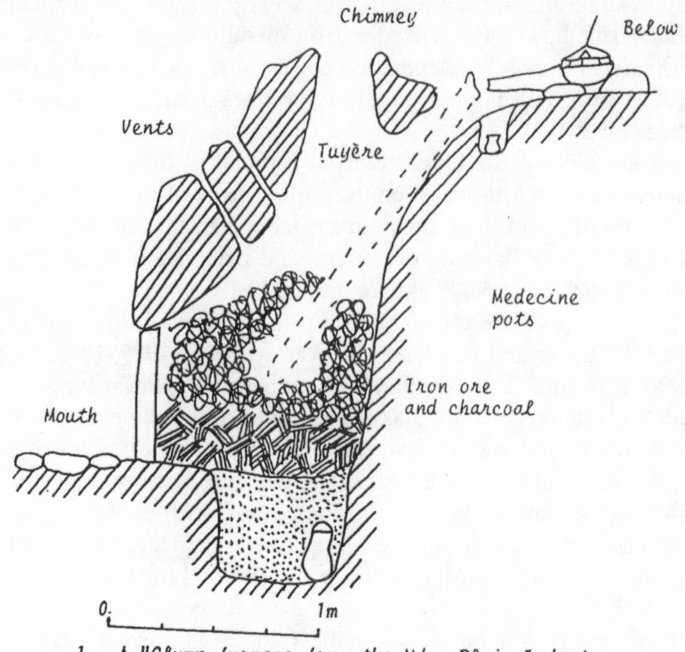

1 - A "Clump furnace from the Ndop Plain Industry

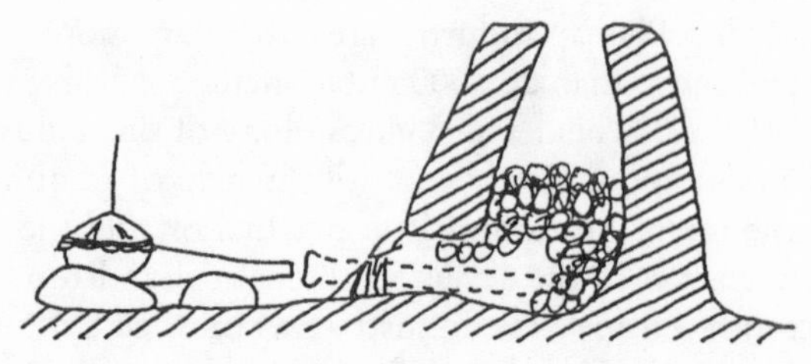

2 - A cylindrical furnace

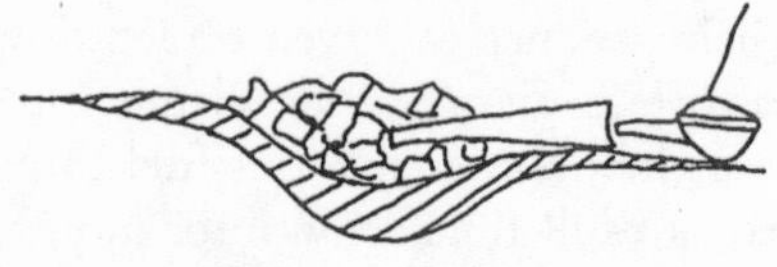

3 - A bowl furnace

Figure 1.21 Settlement pattern at the climax of the Ndop Plain Industry (NPI)

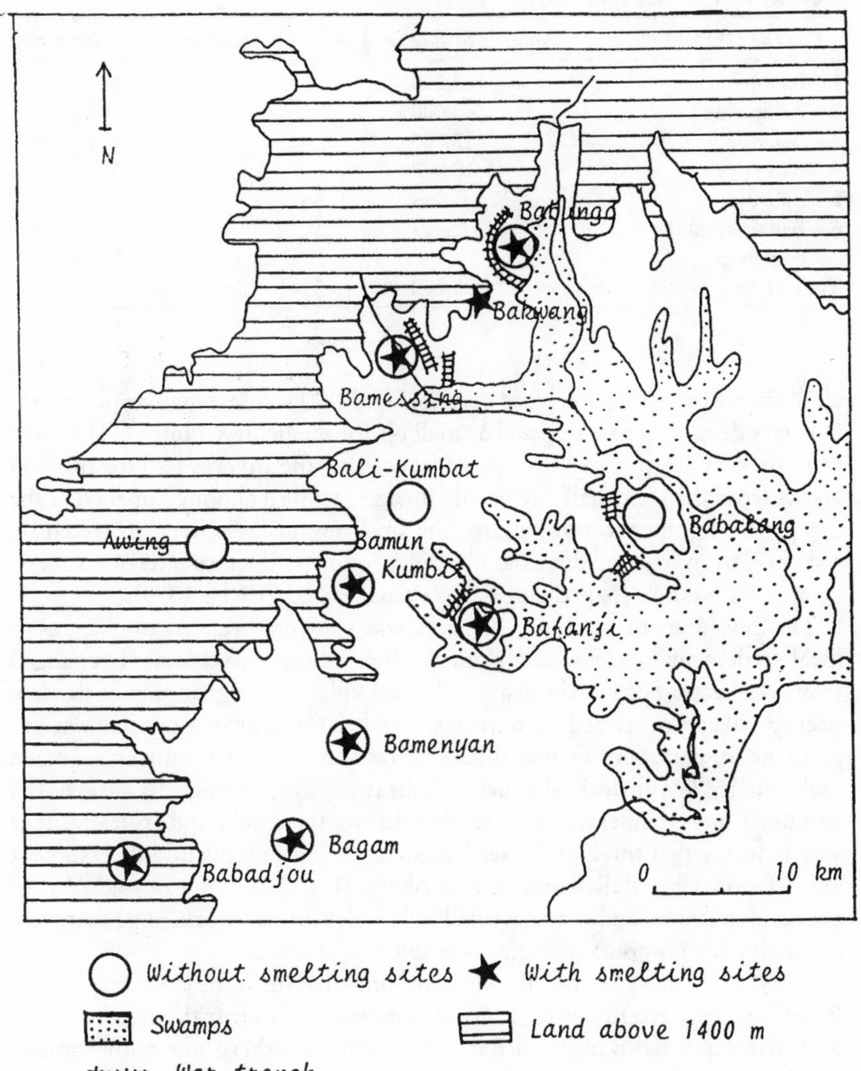

Table 1.12 Iron production sites of the Ndop Plain Industry (NPI) (source Warnier and Fowler 1979: 331).

CHIEFDOM	*Volume of slag* (m^3)	*Number of smelting sites*
1—Babungo	163,000	125
2—Bamessing	40,000	54
3—Bafanji	>15,000	25
4—Bamenyan	>10,000	>70
5—Babadjou	Traces	?
6—Bamenkumbit	Traces	?
7—Bagam	?	?
TOTAL	>228,000	>274

all of them share the same basic design (Fig. 1.20:1). A rectangular pit, nearly 2 meters deep, was first dug and a small pit for medicine set into it. The walls were then built up above the pit, and ducts for the tuyeres let into the wall across from the vents halfway up the furnace, while a chimney opened at the top providing the necessary draft. The smelting furnaces were protected by a shelter, from which debris was cleared, producing the characteristic subcircular or horseshoe-shaped slag heaps (Warnier and Fowler 1979).

The development of clump furnaces was somehow related to changes in local settlement patterns. Just prior to their adoption, settlements changed from a collection of widely dispersed small villages to a grouping of densely packed villages protected by trenches. The location of smelting sites was dependent, in part, on the availability of raw material. The smiths required high-quality kaolin to build furnaces, heat resistant enough to survive the sustained high temperatures generated during the smelt, and iron ore. It is worth noting that three of the settlement aggregates on the middle east–west axis—Bambalang, Bali-Kumbat, and Awing (Fig. 1.21)—are devoid of ore-processing centers and may have had only blacksmiths' workshops that were importing iron blooms that they worked into artifacts.

Away from these aggregates without smelting sites, the area may be divided into two groups of centralized settlement patterns: the northern one with Babungo, Bakwang, and Bamessing and a southern one with Bamunkumbit, Bafandji, Bamenyan, Bagam, and Babadjou. The most important of the iron-smelting polities, Babungo and Bamessing in the northern group, had 125 and 54 smelting sites and 163, 000 and 40,000 cubic meters of smelting debris, respectively. Bafandji (25 smelting sites with more than 15,000 cubic meters of smelting debris) and Bamenyan (more than 70 sites with more than 10,000 cubic meters) in the southern group are located about 10 kilometers from each other.

The highly compact spatial organization of the Ndop Plateau Industry sheds important light on the social dynamics of the economic system operating on that part of the Bamenda plateau during the last 500 years.

While the Ndop Plateau Industry is very compact, the Glazed Sherds Industry is characterized by its dispersal into small village chiefdoms (Warnier 1992; Rowlands and Warnier 1993). This industrial tradition has been recorded in an area extending from Fundong in the south to Isu in the north (Fig. 1.22); smelting sites are fairly evenly spread throughout this area, though apparently some places were more preferred than others. The 98 smelting sites known so far are separable into two broad groups. Some are

Figure 1.22 Settlement pattern in the Glazed Sherds Industry (GSI) cluster

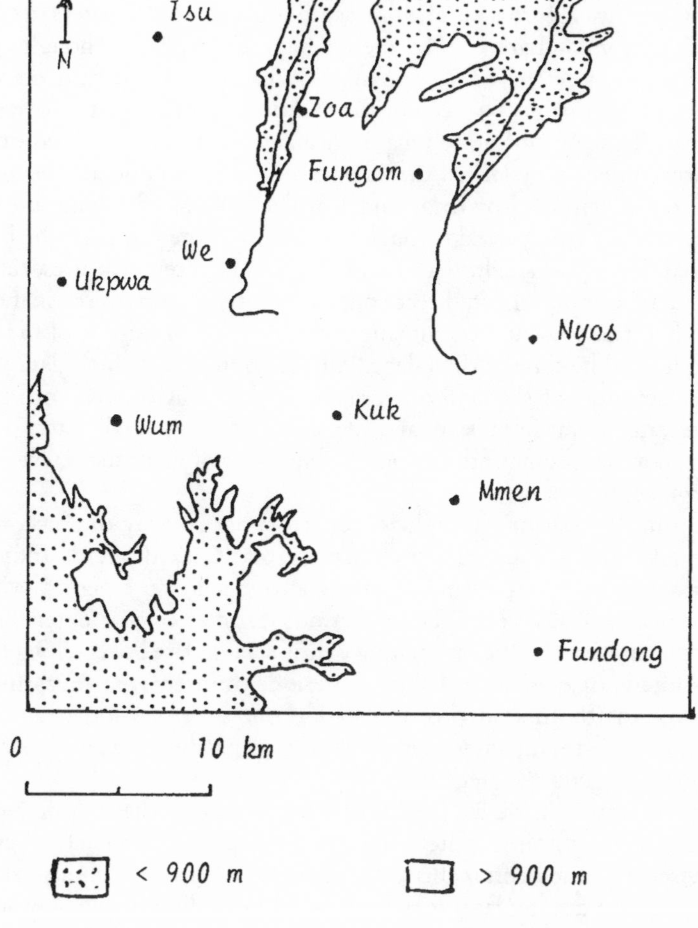

small, dispersed sites around Fundong (some 21 sites, each averaging about 6.44 cubic meters of smelting debris), and some are larger, concentrated within groups of settlements (77 sites, each with 12 to 330 cubic meters of smelting debris). Yet Rowlands and Warnier (1993, 515–516) report that the mass of smelting debris is heavily concentrated in the northwest, where two settlements—Wum and Ukpwa—produced fully three-quarters of all the smelting debris left by the whole industry.

The Glazed Sherds Industry owes its name to the recurrent presence of vitrified sherds on the smelting sites. Two radiocarbon determinations from smelting debris at Fundong suggest that it may date from as early as between 610 to 1260 and as late as between 1305 to1669, suggesting a millennium long *floruit* starting sometime after the seventh century that well lasted into the seventeenth. Traditional accounts carry that history up to modern times (Rowlands and Warnier 1993, 518, table 32.2). Iron production was accomplished in cylindrical furnaces. They measure some 0.7 to 1.5 meters in diameter at the bottom and are 1 to 1.5 meters high (Fig. 1.20:2). Though many of them have been destroyed, it is possible to discern that the furnaces were frequently built in pairs. Thirteen of the 98 known smelting sites have such twinned smelters. According to local informants, recent smiths used only a single furnace since they lacked the manpower needed to operate the workshop more extensively (Rowlands and Warnier 1993). In building the furnaces, the tuyeres were passed through the mouth of the furnace, which was then closed during the smelt. Because of the very high temperatures, the tuyeres and any clay pottery in direct contact with the bloom were vitrified.

It is difficult to present a convincing picture of the magnitude of the iron industry during the time of the Glazed Sherds Industry. At first glance, the very large amounts of slag and other smelting debris associated with these processing sites seems impressive and suggestive of a large-scale intensive effort to produce large amounts of iron, perhaps, as is often thought, even creating surpluses for export.

Such an interpretation, though somewhat supported by oral accounts, does not take into account the circumstance that Glazed Sherds Industry smiths processed varying quantities of ore into metal over a period of time spanning nearly 1,300 years. The question becomes one of determining whether the massive residue of smelting debris accumulated over a long time, as seems likely, or over several shorter periods of intensive processing. It seems to me that both scenarios occurred at one time or another and that this residue represents many generations of iron producers as well as some shorter spans of genuine intensification.

It is at this time that we have the first signs of polities that can be conveniently called chiefdoms. Chiefdoms are customarily a social covenant within descent groups enfranchised by redistribution in which a principal domestic steward accumulates social capital by collecting surplus output to inaugurate exchanges with corporate stewards of equal status. Prestige in chiefdoms accrues to descent group leaders able to mediate, through redistribution of the returns on his exchanges, the material needs of his adherents. Often this mediation extends far beyond the economic sphere, facilitating ideological as well as political goals. As collector–redistributors, chiefs are the focus of kin-chartered societies, managing procurement as well as production and allocation. The aptitude for profitably organizing surplus production lends prestige to the chiefly rank enhancing the status of all his associates, attracting even more clients, setting the chiefly class apart. The residues of production become an important clue to the growth of societal distinction and the metalworker's role in emergent social differentiation.

Lack of detailed and precisely dated archaeological material precludes a definitive evaluation of competing hypotheses about the meaning of the settlement pattern evidence. However, analysis of the way that settlements linked to the processing sites are spread about the countryside indicates that those village chiefdoms with the greatest concentrations of smelting debris—Wum, Ukpwa, and Isu—are found in the northwestern part of the area. (Fig. 1.22, Table 1.13). Those with a lower concentration of smelting debris (under 900 cubic meters) are associated with a greater number of smithing sites—Mmen (11 sites), We (13 sites), and Isu (9 sites)—and are found along a generally northwest–southeast axis extending from Fundong to Isu. It would appear that production was allocated to many more processing centers than was the case in the northwest. The village chiefdoms in the northeast—Fungom, Zoa, and Nyos—had the smallest volume of debris as well as only a handful of processing sites. Obviously, the volume of debris associated with each chiefdom is related to the number of centers it maintained for its

Table 1.13 Iron production sites of the Glazed Sherds Industry (GSI) (Source: Rowlands and Warnier 1993: 517).

CHIEFDOM	*Volume of slag (M^3)*	*Nb of smelting sites*	*Nb of smithing sites*
1—Fundong	135	21	—
2—Mmen	783	15	11
3—Nyos	?	3	1
4—Kuk	20	1	2
5—Fungom	25	2	5
6—Wum	3960	12	6
7—We	538	12	13
8—Zoa	150	2	1
9—Ukpwa	3152	19	—
10—Isu	902	11	9
TOTAL	9665	98	48

immediate needs. It can also be demonstrated that each of the village chiefdoms was organized in a patterned fashion, underscoring its affinity with its near neighbors and the intervening countryside. Three chiefdoms—Ukpwa to Wum, Isu to We to Kuk to Mmen to Fundong, and Zoa to Fungom to Nyos—consist of strings of fairly regularly spaced villages, the distance between neighbors varying from between 10 and 12 kilometers (Fig. 1.22).

This settlement pattern seems to suggest a coordination of iron production based on the mobilization of the manpower of domestic corporations. We may suggest further that this effort was geared primarily to meet local demand for iron implements needed in the daily run of domestic production—such things as hoes, cutlasses, knives, weapons, and the like. At the same time, this suggestion does not rule out the possibility that from time to time these locally oriented industries took advantage of an opportunity to participate in broader commercial arenas fitting them into the Hawsa-dominated trade network of West Africa and the Atlantic trade (Dillon 1981; Wilhelm 1981).

Neither living sites nor graveyards have been systematically investigated, and the narrow focus on iron processing tends to bias our picture of the development of Western Grassfields societies. Nevertheless, even with these limitations, the archaeological data available from the northern part of the Western Grassfields, like those from the southern forested zone, seem to suggest that the primarily domestic production of bloomery iron was from time to time deeply affected by the onset and later development of the Atlantic trade system and that domestic stewards, as the agents negotiating exchanges, achieved a new level of social prominence.

PROCESSES AND TRANSFORMATIONS

Some very interesting processual patterns emerged from our selective evaluation of the archaeological record. These patterns can be subsumed within four principal headings:

1. Population movement and settlement relocation
2. Development and elaboration of local, regional, and long-distance trading networks
3. Rise of craft specialization and intensified production
4. Progress toward social rank and unequal access to wealth and prestige within as well as between ethnic and cultural groups

The archaeological data at hand in each of these instances permits us to highlight the evolutionary pathways within this set of African prehistoric societies.

Population Movements and Settlement Relocation

Population movement and settlement relocation are among the most recurrent themes in traditional historical narratives (Tardits 1981a). In some cases, these oral accounts are supported by archaeology as well as the established historical record. In the Eghazer basin, long-standing pastoralist settlement patterns based on structured seasonal moves metamorphosed toward a more sedentary village-based model. This change coincided to some extent with the advent of iron technology. The Mema region, which was at first characterized by the settlement formats and densities typical of advanced transhumant foragers, saw its population density and settlement size increase. This trend crested in the Middle Assemblage period (between 600 and 1200), only to decrease sharply during the subsequent Late Assemblage period. Ultimately, this trend reached its nadir when the area was virtually depopulated during a period of serious ecological crisis. Looking at the size and placement of settlements suggests that, at its peak, the region was distinctly arranged into a settlement hierarchy of large central town and smaller satellite communities, suggesting a coincident social hierarchy as well.

Both this settlement and some very different settlement arrangements are observable in the materials described. These range all the way from the typical series of seasonal camps visited by transhumant pastoral groups (associated with cemeteries and metal processing sites and dispersed throughout the landscape in the Eghazer basin), to the more or less sedentary villages with iron-smelting facilities and burial grounds in the Mema region, to a system characterized by dispersed homesteads set up by the equatorial horticulturists residing in the southern forested area, and to the centralized villages protected by systems of ditches and earth embankments or walls in the Western Grassfields.

During much of the eighteenth century into the opening decades of the nineteenth, both the Western Grassfields and the southern forested zone appear to have witnessed population movements on a grand scale. It is not known how these various historical happenings are related, but the Chamba migration from the Tikar plain in the southern part of the western Adamaoua plateau resulted in founding the Bamun kingdom and the growth of the principal village kingdoms of the Western Grassfields (Tardits 1981b; Warnier 1985). This migration occurred at about the same time as the Beti one (Laburthe-Tolra 1981a; Essomba 1993). During the nineteenth century, the Vute, from the Adamoua plateau, expanded their territories toward the Sanaga River valley in the south (von Morgen 1982). It is almost as if these different ethnic and linguistic groups were pushing toward the Atlantic coast in order to take advantage of the new emerging trade opportunities. Generally, the movements of population and the relocation of settlements we have observed have tended to produce ever more extensive interaction spheres with overlapping social, economic, political, and ideological networks. In the end, these spheres of interaction between small-scale domestic stewards enlarged sufficiently to coalesce these exchange networks into the principal kingdoms of the region.

In brief summary, our survey of the prehistoric archaeology in these different parts of western Africa indicates a series of significant demographic changes through time as well as growing interaction spheres. The connection between the advent of metal-using technologies to these changes in village placement and population size and density or of the demographic changes to the advent and adoption of metallurgy is still to be decided.

Patterns of Exchange, Rank, and Hierarchy

Very little is known about organization of the exchange networks evident during the later prehistory of the In Gall–Tegidda-n-Tesemt region. For the moment, we are certain only that sometime between 4,000 and 1,500 years ago, carnelian beads were not only imported into the region but thought significant enough to be interred in human burials (Paris 1984).

At the same time, a copper spearhead, crafted in the In Gall–Tegidda-n-Tesemt copper-producing area, was found with an adult female burial in the cemetery of Iwelen (Paris 1996). Iwelen is located on the northwestern edge of the Ténéré Desert, nearly 500 to 600 kilometers north of the Eghazer basin. We understand that the ancient trading networks of Africa were not only very extensive but highly complex in the ways that goods were sent from place to place passing through many hands. This appears to be the case of the exchange networks we detect here as well. However construed, the Mema region clearly participated in the western Africa part of the trans-Saharan trade. This involvement is evident not only by the presence of carnelian beads but also by the region's connection to distant sources of cowry shells and glass by at least the seventh century (Togola 1996).

On the other hand, trade items are rarely found in the archaeological settlements of the southern forested area and the Western Grassfields. In part, this is a consequence of the investigators focus on discerning the evidence of iron-based technology. Very little is known of the regional exchange systems, past or present. Historical and ethnographic research (Dillon 1981; Tardits 1981b; Warnier 1981, 1985; von Morgen 1982) provide some important insights, demonstrating the wide range of goods, foodstuffs, drinks, and craft items involved in both short- and long-distance exchange in various parts of the Cameroons.

From the ethnohistorical information now available, it can be suggested that iron ore as well as artifacts were important commodities exchanged within local networks in the southern forested area (Essomba 1993). Smiths were highly esteemed individuals whose product formed an important component of the economic organization—being traded out of the region and exchanged within it. Iron artifacts had a symbolic as well as a real worth. They represented not only a kind of universal currency used in matrimonial transactions for the payment of bride-price but also domestic implements used to perform everyday activities as well as weapons of war granting a special status to their owners.

There is ample evidence for intensified iron production in the Western Grassfields with a proliferation of smelter types, suggesting an inquisitive and experimental cadre of smiths. The forms of smelter utilized included the clump furnace technology and the introduction of large natural draft furnaces in the Matomb and Ndom settlement groups seem congruent with radical changes in the associated societies and the development of some political format akin to the concept of "big man"—individuals who undertake to mediate their societies, arbitrating economic, social, and religious affairs of their descent groups and achieving status as redistributors of value (Godelier 1982; Vansina 1990). Access to status-producing goods, used for the display of achieved wealth and prestige, certainly played a crucial role in the aspirations of leaders, their descent group, clients, rivals, and even whole ethnic groups. Depending on the time, place, and access to significant trade alliances and producing areas, different "packages" of goods were involved in transacting interregional and long-distance trade coalitions. A prestigious leader, one accorded a high status, was an individual who successfully manipulated the system to the benefit of his following of kith and kin.

It is not surprising that we find the concurrent rise of prestigious leadership and the growth of the iron industry in western African societies. To get beyond the obvious economic explanations stipulating the influence of the value created by the smiths and manipulated by "big men," we need to interpolate backward through the ethnographic record. In the first instance, we have seen that, for the most part, iron metallurgy was a local and small-scale operation meeting the needs of a parochial clientele. It was not always wealth but power that the smiths and the newly enfranchised leaders represented. Smiths had the power to transmute, converting base stones into valuable metal. At the same time, they immersed their technical knowledge in an arcane experience, introducing ritual performance into an otherwise straightforward industrial process. Their aura was that of a magician, a "transmuter." In traditional African societies, investiture of leaders, be they chiefs or kings or whatever, is also a process of transmutation by which the paramount attains the aura of the semidivine. Smiths, almost everywhere, play a prominent role in the investiture process, sanctioning by their attainments as transmuters the elevation of society's principal mediators. Smiths and stewards found it convenient to mutually support the others' conceit, ensuring to each a significant role in the ideological life of the community. This scenario asks more of the information than do the familiar kinds of economic and technological arguments.

Whatever technological efficiencies smiths may have been brought into West African material culture, whatever the economic value of their effort, a principal motive for the spread and adoption of metallurgy was its effect on the sacerdotal and political life of emerging hierarchical communities, both sanctioning and creating the means for elite distinction. To this extent, the metalworkers' role in endorsing political change may have been more dynamic than any modifications they brought to the material inventories of their communities.

As rank society developed, other social dynamics came into play. In the Western Grassfields, there was a disruption of long-standing settlement patterns as people went about relocating and altering the layout of their settlements. This appears to be an effect of the emergence of competing peer polities or village chiefdoms. In the Atlantic trade zone, sea salt, brass *manillas*, glass beads, firearms, alcohol, tobacco, clothes, and the like were exchanged for ivory, game skins, and, in very large measure, slaves. The inland trade network was organized through chains of middlemen and two separate kinds of entrepreneurial distribution systems (Warnier 1985; Rowlands 1986). The first was a straightforward commercial enterprise, found in the centralized societies of the Western Grassfields and managed by local entrepreneurs—slave dealers with exclusive privilege to conduct the trade. These individuals were empowered by hereditary privilege to transact business with commercial interests in the coastal entrepôts of Calabar, Bimbia, Duala, and Malimba.

The second procurement system, managed by community stewards, was less rigidly formatted. Each of the descent groups involved had its own mercantile cadre who met and conducted business with traders of other communities. Business was negotiated in a border area separating neighboring ethnolinguistic groups. An example of this was Edea at the Sanaga Falls, where the Bassa conducted exchanges with the Malimba.

Entrepreneurs associated with the coastal communities also competed with one another. Competing descent groups marketed locally produced goods for necessities got from elsewhere. Such exchange networks had apparently existed from time immemorial, but now the flows of value exceeded subsistence necessity, and some of the entrepreneurs became wealthy. Successful entrepreneurial stewards used their central role in significant trade coalitions to attain the prestige of a "big man," elevating the status of their descent group and encouraging further production underwriting additional rounds of exchanges.

Long-distance trade as a cause of the emergence of complex polities has long been a tenet of those wishing to explain the motivation toward statelike formations. In the West African examples drawn here, the role of metals in these trading alliances seems to be of slight consequence. It was exchanged widely and used as a medium of wealth, but the trade in metals in western Africa does not seem to have had the dynamic effect that the copper trade did in northern Zambezia or the production of high-quality iron did on the East African coast. Processed metal was but one more line of goods employed by the emergent "big men" to cement their authority. In contrast, the countries producing gold had a prominence on world markets throughout recorded history, giving rise to the myth of the "gold-roofed" Tombouctou, where even the slaves wore gold. The "big men" of the middle Niger capitalized their own success as "kings" on this lucrative trade.

Other "big men" would one day be called kings as well, but many were not, strictly speaking, rulers of kingdoms (Bekombo-Priso 1981). They were stewards who, after "vesting" the excess output of their domestic corporations, profited socially from the trading and their dealings with other opportunistic entrepreneurial "big men." The reality was one in which ambitious domestic stewards, having no "capital" beside their personal reputation, invested and became indispensable intermediaries, accumulating the wherewithal necessary to satisfy the needs of their descent group as well as their clients. As successful entrepreneurs, they claimed the right to style themselves "leaders." Similar developments are observable in the post–sixteenth-century history of Congo and Loango (Vansina 1990) as well as elsewhere in the evolution of other precolonial states in sub-Saharan Africa.

The operation of the indigenous trading corporations of pre-colonial Africa is fairly well reported. For example, many Hawsa traders were active during the sojourn of von Morgen late in the nineteenth century, participating in an extensive exchange system. Exchanging cotton cloth, glass beads, and equestrian equipage, they received slaves and ivory in return. However, when the Germans entered the scene, they posed a challenge to the Hawsa trade alliance. As elsewhere, the foreign traders attempted to monopolize the trade. A village headman named Ngilla solved his problem by supplying the Germans with ivory and the Hawsa with slaves. The trade, nevertheless, became the cause of competitive stress as various trading coalitions strove to corner markets.

Conflicts and limited warfare between the Duala and Bassa early in the nineteenth century, as suggested in the epic poem *Les Fils de Hitong* (Ngijol 1980), was precipitated by their competition over access to and control of trading enterprises. In fact, the Atlantic trade throughout the nineteenth century caused some very peculiar patterns of interaction that can be likened to a domino-like effect emanating from the coastal towns to those of the hinterland. Factories were located so that trading partners achieved the greatest benefit. Coastal leaders from the Duala, Malimba, and Batanga offered protected venues that provided safety for commercial transactions. Some of these coastal leaders even became landholders, maintaining large maize and cassava plantations worked by their own slaves. This produce not only supported their own slaves but also was sold to feed the crews of ships plying the coasts of western Africa. Inland, the Mbo in the north, toward the Bamiléké plateau; the Bassa in the center, along the Sanaga River valley; and the Ngumba in the south, toward the land of the Beti, played the role of intermediaries expediting contact between the coastal entrepôts with suppliers and markets in the hinterland.

The availability of markets incited those able to exploit the situation. The Vute, for example, expanded their territory southward in search for ivory and slaves, a chief source of farm labor. Skilled manpower was free to engage in commercial production, and iron production was industrialized in a highly intensive fashion (von Morgen 1982, 252). In the village of Ngila, there were 12 workshops employing from five to seven blacksmiths, laboring daily from morning to night manufacturing weapons. No longer are we talking of a cottage industry intent on meeting the immediate needs of their kith and kin.

CONCLUSION

This chapter is an attempt to provide analyses of past social systems in three different and well-defined geographic areas. It focuses on the production and use of metals as well as the effect of metallurgy on society. As the reader has noted, our selection covers a broad range of social formations, subsistence and socioeconomic systems, and geoclimatic zones. In terms of settlement pattern, they ranged from the fluid seasonal transhumance of pastoralists passing in and out of territories on a scheduled basis (the Eghazer basin), to segmented descent groups in sedentary homestead-based systems (southern forested area), and to more complexly textured and centralized ranked chiefdoms and statelike societies (the Mema region within the Ghana Empire and the Western Grassfields).

I have not been able to directly address the questions of the origins and diffusion of metal-producing technologies in western Africa or in Africa generally. I have suggested that there is the appearance of multiple experimentation leading to a variety of systems of production coming into use at about the same time. Archaeological investigation is incomplete. Though the effort is ongoing, I believe that our ability to answer some of the larger questions may remain inadequate into the immediate future, when new data will, fortunately, create new riddles to investigate.

In the present state of our knowledge of African metallurgies, one thing is certain, namely, that the older explanatory models were too simple and misleading. Therefore, a new synthesis must be painfully worked out. To this end, I suggest that it is time to shift our emphasis from chronicling space–time systematics to the decipherment of local patterns of cultural and social transformation. Maybe then we will be in a better position to tackle the thorny issues of origins.

2

Precolonial Copper Metallurgy: Sociopolitical Context

Michael S. Bisson

> "In this land there seemed to us to be great quantities of copper which they wear on the legs, arms and twisted into their hair."
>
> —Vasco da Gama, 1498 (1962:13)

From the earliest European exploration of the African coast, it was evident that copper was being produced indigenously and traded widely in sub-Saharan Africa. Da Gama's note, probably written near the mouth of the Limpopo (Birmingham and Marks 1977), is among the first to record the metal's abundance. Although copper from the lower Congo was soon incorporated into the coastal trade, its other sources and how it was produced remained obscure. This was still the case three centuries later, when Dr. Francisco de Lacerda mounted the first major European expedition into the Central African interior in July 1798. His goal was to contact the kingdom of Kazembe, located on the Luapula River, and to gain access to and control of the production and trade in copper. The expedition failed. Lacerda did not survive, but his diary (Burton 1873) demonstrated to the outside world the vast mineral wealth of the Central African copperbelt and revealed the important role that copper played in many African societies.

Waves of explorers, missionaries, and prospectors followed in Lacerda's footsteps in the nineteenth and early twentieth centuries. Some, such as Fredrick Stanley Arnot (1899) and the Montseigneur de Hemptinne (1926), actually witnessed the large-scale mining and smelting of copper, and many others (e.g., Livingstone 1857, 1874) testified to the importance of copper as an item of trade and emblem of social status. Prospectors had only to inquire of local chiefs to be taken to large outcrops of ore already marked by extensive pits and shafts (Walker 1925; Bradley 1952; Summers 1969). Indeed, all significant surface deposits of copper ores in sub-Saharan Africa were discovered by African metallurgists (Bancroft 1961). One consequence of this impressive record is that few of the large precolonial mines have escaped obliteration by modern open-pit development.

Copper, along with its alloys, occupied a position that was significantly different from that of iron among the Niger-Congo–speaking peoples of western, central, and southern Africa. In contrast, East African peoples, particularly the pastoral groups, placed a much lower value on copper. In areas where it was in widespread use, copper can be considered an analogue to gold in the modern world (Herbert 1984). Throughout the continent, copper was only rarely employed to make utilitarian objects such as axes, hoes, and knives, for which iron was the preferred material. Instead, it was used to make personal adornments, decorative coverings or inlays, and objects used in ritual and ceremony. It also served as a means of exchange, sometimes in the subsistence economy but more frequently in social and political transactions, such as compensation for injury, taboo violation and bridewealth, or tribute to rulers. This dichotomy between the uses of copper and iron can be observed in even the earliest African Iron Age contexts, where the two metals occur together (Bisson 1976). Because of its long-standing role as a measure of wealth and prestige in Africa, the archaeological study of the mining, trade, and the uses made of copper can provide important insights into the socioeconomic and political evolution of African societies.

It is important to recognize the limitations of the data on copper metallurgy in Africa in comparison to the record for iron. Traditional iron smelting was practiced well into the twentieth century in many parts of the continent, and blacksmiths are still a fixture of village life. An abundant ethnographic literature exists on iron technology and the often complex roles played by ironworkers in African societies. The situation is dramatically different for copper. With the notable exceptions of the Yeke, Kaonde, Ngoyo, and Phalaborwa, indigenous copper production had ceased in Africa by the early decades of the twentieth century, and the only coppersmithing that survived is the lost-wax casting tradition still practiced widely in West Africa. Most of the extant descriptions of African copper metallurgy and its practitioners were made by missionaries, explorers, and geologists who were interested primarily in the technological processes of mining and smelting rather than the social context of these activities. Data collected by professional ethnographers on the social, political, and religious aspects of copper production are much more rare. The historical record is also less than ideal. Copper was an important commodity, and as such it received prominent mention in explorers' accounts, but in those areas where copper metallurgy was still active at the time of the first European penetration, Africans often deliberately kept the location of mines and metallurgical techniques secret from people they considered potential competitors (Volavka 1998). Although the indigenous production of copper had largely ceased by 1920, it continued to play an important role in many African societies. This was documented by Herbert (1984). Given these limitations, the study of African copper metallurgy must rely to a much greater degree on archaeology. This has the advantage of greater time depth and providing direct information on technological processes but the disadvantage of all the limitations inherent in a record that is sparse or nonexistent for many key areas and biased by research strategies that until recently were geared to discovery of culture-historical sequences rather than understanding of sociocultural change.

The inherent bias of the archaeological record accounts for the strong technological orientation of this chapter. It summarizes our current knowledge of the origin and development of copper metallurgy south of the Sahara and provides a comprehensive account of mining, smelting, and smithing techniques. The social, political, ritual, and economic uses of copper will be surveyed, stressing the important interactions between these spheres, followed by two instances from Central Africa that illustrate these relationships and complement the evidence for early copper exploitation in the In Gall–Tegidda-n-Tesemt region of Niger discussed by Holl in this volume.

DISTRIBUTION OF COPPER ORES

Unlike iron ore, copper mineralization is restricted to only a few areas of western, central, and southern Africa (Figs. 2.1, 2.2). These include some of the richest copper deposits in the world. The geological distribution and form of these ore bodies determined the location of ancient copper mining and the techniques employed. In West Africa, copper minerals occur primarily in the arid regions of the southern Sahara and Sahel. Relatively small ore bodies are found in the Sahel at Akjoujt in Mauretania, Nioro-Siracoro in northern Mali as well as bordering areas in southern Mauretania (Herbert 1984), the Aïr massif near Azelik and Agadez in Niger (Bernus and Gouletquer 1976; Bernus and Echard 1985), and Hufrat-en-Nahas in the Sudan (Bower 1927). No indigenous mines were thought to occur in tropical West Africa (Kun 1965), but recently a number of workings of both copper and lead have been discovered in the Benue Rift of southeastern Nigeria (Chikwendu and Umeji 1979; Chikwendu et al. 1989; Craddock et al. 1997). Copper mineralization in that area went unnoticed by European miners because it was associated with much larger deposits of lead and zinc (Craddock et al. 1993). Natural sources of copper are also virtually absent from East Africa with the exception of limited areas near Kilembe in Uganda (Bancroft 1961) and Rwanda, where small surface deposits occur.

The largest concentration of copper deposits, and thus ancient mines, in Africa occurs in a crescent-shaped geological structure called the Lufilian Arc. This is an 800-kilometer-long belt of later Precambrian rocks that extends from the Zambian copperbelt into southern Shaba province of the

Figure 2.1 Distribution of copper ore deposits in sub-Saharan Africa

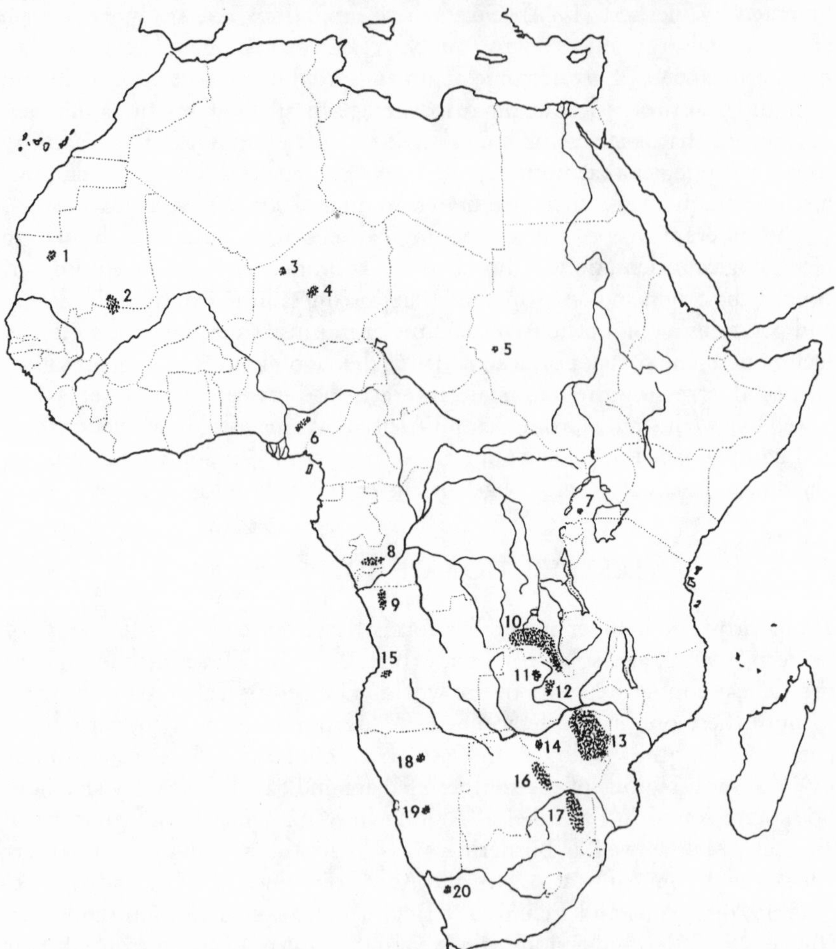

1 Akjoujt; 2 Nioro-Siracoro; 3 Azelik; 4 Agadez; 5 Hufrat-en-Nahas; 6 Benue Rift; 7 Kilembe; 8 Niari-Djoué; 9 Bembe; 10 Lufilian Arc; 11 Lunga Valley; 12 Kafue Hook; 13 Zimbabwe Highlands; 14 Huange; 15 Benguela; 16 Tati; 17 Transvaal; 18 Tsumeb; 19 Rehoboth; 20 Western Cape (Cline 1937; Bisson 1976; Chikwendu and Umeji 1979; Herbert 1984; Miller and Van der Merwe 1994).

Congo (Cahen and Snelling 1966). In the Congo, there are three main clusters of ancient mines. Beginning in the east, the first is situated near Lubumbashi and includes Etoile, perhaps the largest prehistoric mine in all of Africa, Ruashi and Kipushi (Walker 1927). The middle cluster is located near Likasi, 140 kilometers northwest of Lubumbashi. There are many more individual mining sites in this group, including extensive quarries at Likasi,

Figure 2.2 Ancient mines and archaeological sites mentioned in the text.

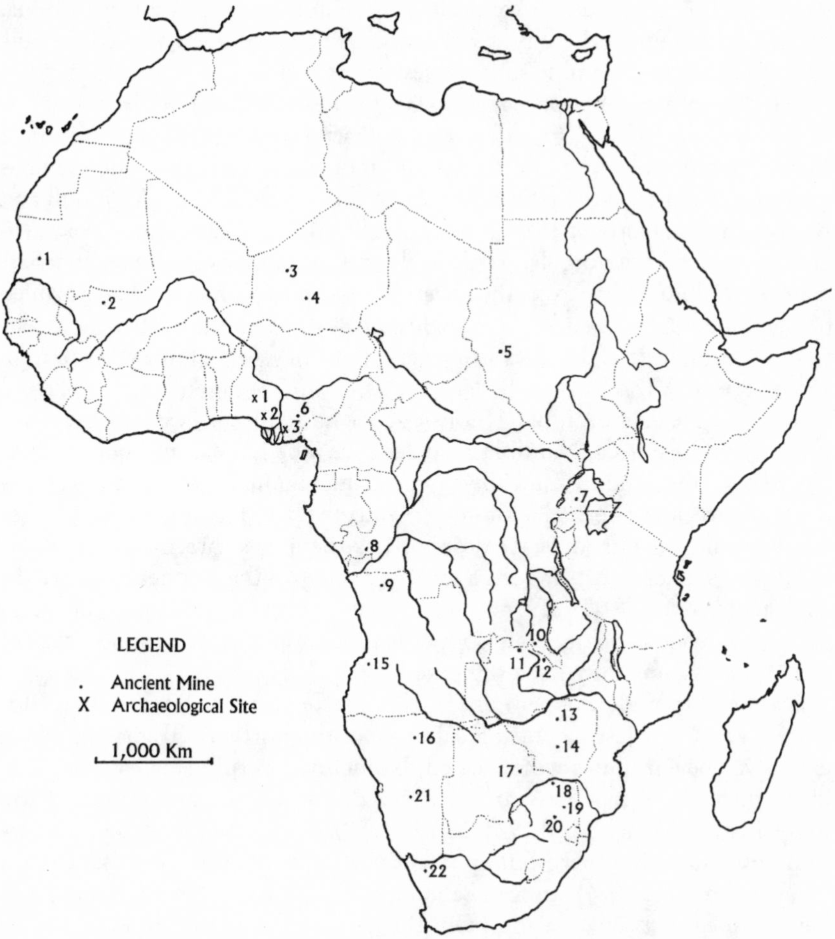

Mines: 1 Grotte aux Chauves-Souris; 2 Nioro; 3 Azelik and Afunfun; 4 Agadez; 5 Hufrat-en-Nahas; 6 Enyigba; 7 Kilembe; 8 Niari-Djoue; 9 Boko Songo and Mindouli; 10 Etoile; 11 Kansanshi; 12 Bwana Mukubwa; 13 Alaska; 14 Umkondo; 15 Benguela; 16 Tsumeb; 17 Thakadu; 18 Messina; 19 Phalaborwa; 20 Harmony; 21 Khuiseb; 22 O'Okiep. Archaeological Sites: 1 Ife; 2; Benin; 3 Igbo Ukwu.

Kambove, Kamatenge, Tenke-Fungurume, Luishia, and Kakanda. The westernmost cluster is at Kolwezi, 120 kilometers west of Likasi. The most important sites in this area are Musawi, Dikuluwe, Kolwezi, Ruwe, and Kamoto. Dikuluwe, and possibly Kolwezi, mines were being actively exploited by Africans as late as 1922 (de Hemptinne 1926). In Zambia, only four ancient mines were associated with the Lufilian Arc, of which only one, Bwana

Mkubwa near Ndola, was of significant size (Bancroft 1961). Copper deposits not part of the Lufilian Arc occur throughout much of western Zambia. By far, the largest of these is at Kansanshi Hill, 10 kilometers north of Solwezi, the capital of Zambia's Northwestern province.

Another important copper region is a north–south band of discontinuous ore deposits stretching from the Middle Niari River in the Congo Republic to northern Angola. The most important indigenous Congo Republic mines were associated with the rich Niari-Djoué mineral deposits at Mindouli and Boko Songho (Herbert 1984; Volavka 1998). Large-scale mines were also present in northern Angola, particularly in the vicinity of Bembe, approximately 190 kilometers from the coast. These mines, which were controlled by the kingdom of Kongo, were highly productive and attracted the attention of Portuguese authorities from the earliest days of colonization (Battell 1859; Pereira 1937).

South of the Zambezi, indigenous copper mines occur in Zimbabwe, Botswana, South Africa, Namibia, and Angola. The largest number of these (about 80) are found in Zimbabwe, where the two major concentrations are the Sinoia region, about 100 kilometers northwest of Harare, the location of Alaska mine, once incorrectly described as the largest precolonial working in Africa (Walker 1925), and the Sabi River valley in the southeast, where the largest ancient mine was at Umkondo. Although it was not among the major mines, evidence of indigenous copper exploitation was also found near the site of Great Zimbabwe itself (Summers 1969).

A zone of sporadic copper mineralization extends from Tati in eastern Botswana through Messina and Phalaborwa in the northern Transvaal, where extensive ancient mines were located. Numerous, mostly smaller, workings occur throughout the Transvaal, of which the largest was at Harmony Farm in the Letaba district (Steel 1974; Friede 1980). Copper was mined in association with tin at Rooiberg but apparently was not used to produce bronze (Friede and Steel 1976). In the Cape province of South Africa, copper was being mined in Namaqualand from the Orange River to O'Okiep, and in Namibia the large copper ore body at Tsumeb was exploited in prehistoric times (Herbert 1984), as were smaller deposits in the Khuiseb drainage (Kinahan and Vogel 1982).

THE ORIGIN OF COPPER METALLURGY IN AFRICA

The origin of copper metallurgy in Eurasia was briefly summarized elsewhere. Following a period of one or two millennia when native copper was exploited, the mining and smelting of copper ore appears to have arisen independently in Asia Minor, Eastern Europe, and Egypt between 5000 and 4000 B.C. Smelting and alloying may have been discovered during the production of kiln-fired ceramics painted with brightly colored copper ores (Craddock

1995). An alternative scenario sees the melting of heavily oxidized native copper leading to the recognition of copper ores. Throughout western Eurasia, smelted copper was widespread nearly 6,000 years ago (Tylecote 1992). Although there is no present consensus on the question of the origins of copper metallurgy in Africa, recent archaeological research in Mauretania (Lambert 1975, 1983; Vernet 1993a) and the Niger Republic (Grébénart 1983, 1987; Holl 1993, 1997) has found a wide range of variation in technological processes, suggesting that the first African metallurgists were flexible and innovative in adapting their methods to local geological and environmental conditions. This variability could be evidence for an indigenous origin of metallurgy, as suggested by Holl, but might also reflect the propensity of metallurgists to modify their methods to fit local circumstances. In the past two decades, our ideas of the transformation of foraging societies to metal-using agriculturist ones south of the Sahara have also become much more complex. Simple concepts of the diffusion of technologies or their spread in conjunction with expanding populations were an integral part of the culture-historical orientation of most pioneering archaeological research in Africa and may not be adequate to explain what actually occurred in the past. Today, metallurgy is also no longer considered to form a single technocomplex linked to the origin and spread of agriculture and, for example, should be considered independent of the "Bantu expansion" into central and southern Africa, a construct of historical linguists that is now recognized not to be evidence of a single expanding population (Vansina 1995).

The earliest archaeological evidence for copper mining and smelting in sub-Saharan West Africa appears roughly at the same time at Afunfun and Azelik in the In Gall–Teggida-n-Tesemt region near Agadez, Niger Republic, where copper has been found in both Late Stone Age and Iron Age contexts, and at Akjoujt, western Mauretania (Calvocoressi and David 1979). The Niger Republic sites, which may be slightly earlier, consist of irregular burned features that were initially interpreted as forges and copper-smelting furnaces with proposed ages as early as the second millennium B.C. (Grébénart, 1983, 1987), suggesting the existence of separate "Copper Ages" in Saharan West Africa (Mauny 1951) dating to between 2200 and 1500 B.C. for Copper I and 850 and 100 B.C. for Copper II (Grébénart 1985). Copper was also produced at the sites of Marandet and Azelik between 900 and 1500 B.C. (Bernus and Cressier 1991). Recent analysis has demonstrated that the earliest of these features are natural burned-out tree stumps, with only one being a real smelter (Fig. 2.3A). Its early radiocarbon date (1719 ±110 B.C. [GIF-5176]) reflects the use of the much earlier stumps as a source of charcoal. Although this date is suspect, there are many unambiguous furnaces at these sites that date to between 900 and 300 B.C. (Fig. 2.3B). The conclusion that these smelters represent the earliest securely dated copper working in West Africa (Killick et al. 1988) remains controversial.

Figure 2.3 Early copper smelters from the Agadez region, Niger

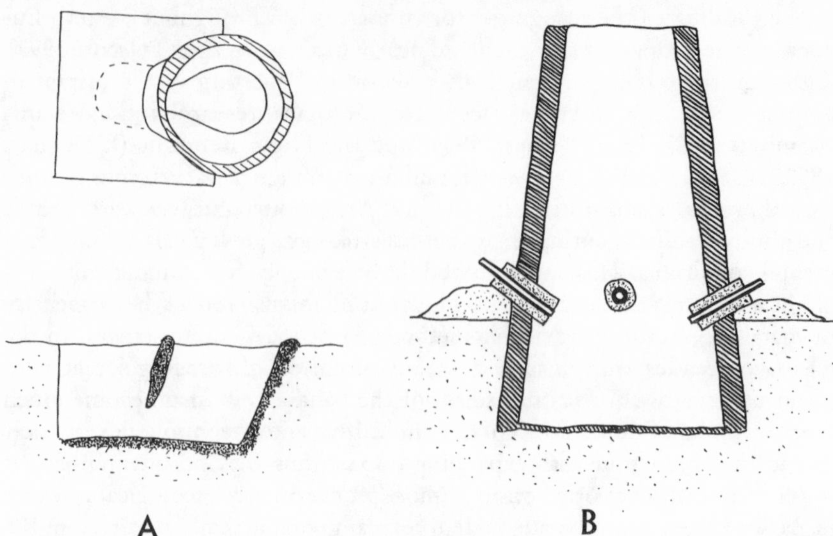

A. Afunfun Site 175, Furnace 8; B. Later Copper Age furnace from Eghazer basin (after Grébénart 1987).

Copper mining is now documented at Akjoujt in western Mauretania between 850 and 300 B.C. (Woodhouse 1998). Excavations in the Grotte aux Chauves-souris mine produced radiocarbon evidence of the mining and smelting of malachite as early as the fifth century B.C. Numerous copper artifacts collected from Neolithic sites in the region include arrow points, spearheads, chisels, awls, and plano-convex axes, along with a smaller number of bracelets beads and earrings (Vernet 1986). The dominance of utilitarian objects in this assemblage is in sharp contrast with most archaeological collections from farther south and also from the Niger Republic sites, where utilitarian copper artifacts are present but there is a greater frequency of ornaments, as demonstrated by Holl. Some of the Mauretanian copper implements are described as being stylistically similar to western European Early Bronze Age or Phoenician artifacts from North Africa, strengthening the case for a trans-Saharan origin for this technology (Lambert 1971). As Trigger (1993) has noted, in a situation of autochthonous development, the first metal artifacts are inevitably high-status items. Thus, the presence of more prosaic copper artifacts at the beginning of the Mauretanian sequence suggests that the technology may have its roots elsewhere. Whatever its origin, the development of copper metallurgy had potentially profound social consequences, for it represented the beginning of part-time craft specialization in these Neolithic societies of mobile pastoralists.

Dating the origins of copper mining in tropical Africa has been extremely difficult. No dates are available for the precolonial copper mines in Nigeria. The earliest direct date for copper smelting south of the equator (A.D. 345 ± 75) comes from smelting furnace debris at Naviundu springs near Lubumbashi in the Democratic Republic of the Congo (de Maret 1982). Kansanshi mine, Zambia, and Kipushi mine, DRC, produced similar evidence dating from the fifth to the twelfth century (Bisson 1976). In Zimbabwe, only Umkondo has been dated. A seventeenth-century reading obtained from a digging stick found in a mine shaft certainly reflects the most recent rather than the earliest mining in the area (Garlake 1970a). Thakadu mine in Botswana has recently been dated to between 1480 and 1680 (Huffman et al. 1995). In South Africa, archaeological research at Phalaborwa has demonstrated that copper mining began perhaps as early as the eighth and continued until the nineteenth century (van der Merwe and Scully 1971). Other major prehistoric mines in Botswana, Namibia, and South Africa remain undated.

INDIGENOUS MINING METHODS

The nature of an ore body exerted a determining influence on the methods and techniques used by precolonial Africans to exploit it. Thus, the geology of ore deposits is more important than historical or cultural influences in determining the precise form taken by a mine. Understanding the nature of the mineralization process and the transformations that ore bodies can undergo because of weathering can also aid our understanding of the mining process.

Most copper ore bodies begin as sulfides—compounds of copper, iron, and sulfur—of which chalcopyrite ($CuFeS_2$), and bornite (Cu_5FeS_4) are the most common. In deeply buried deposits, these minerals dominate. Ores that outcrop undergo chemical weathering, and the upper part of an ore body is often transformed into an oxidation zone that can vary from a few to hundreds of meters in depth. At the surface itself, all copper compounds may be leached away, leaving porous materials rich in iron oxides, known as gossan, to mark the position of the vein. Below the gossan in this zone, decomposition of sulfide ores creates carbonate and oxide ores, including the green carbonate malachite ($CuCO_3Cu(OH)_2$), the red oxide cuprite (Cu_2O), and the hydrated silicate chrysocolla ($CuSiO_32H_2O$) (Coghlan 1975). The carbonate and oxide ores are the easiest to reduce to metal, and it is these that were the focus of most early African mining activities. Sulfides require more complex multistage treatment before they could be reduced to metal and were generally avoided by African miners. Because the oxide zone contained the most desirable ores and was also structurally weakened by decomposition processes, elaborate deep-mining methods and specialized tools were unnecessary in almost all cases. Mining equipment was, for the most part, modifications of the axes and hoes that were the mainstay of African Iron Age agricultural technologies.

Copper mines were almost always open stopes or open stopes with shafts (Summers 1969). Open stopes are pits that are completely exposed at the surface as the miners dig following the distribution of the oxidation zone. If the ore is concentrated in a discrete, vertically dipping layer sandwiched between layers of harder country rock, open stopes can take the form of elongated trenches with abrupt vertical sides. However, in most cases they are irregular pits of varying size and form. Shafts are generally rare, although examples up to 6 meters in depth occur at Thakadu mine near Matsitama, Botswana (Huffman et al. 1995). Shafts with underground stopes (horizontal galleries) were employed at the mines near Kolwezi in the Congo (de Hemptinne 1926) and some of the lead and copper mines in Nigeria (Craddock et al. 1997). The most elaborate systems of shafts with underground stopes are found in the copper and tin mines of the Transvaal, which even included ventilation shafts (Evers 1974; Friede 1980).

Documentary sources supplemented by archaeology provide us with information on the methods used to mine copper. The two most comprehensive descriptions of African copper-mining techniques are those of the Monseigneur de Hemptinne (1926), who observed the Yeke tribe working at Dikuluwe mine (Plate 2.1) near Musonoi (Kolwezi district) as recently as 1924, and the geologist T. S. Carnahan, who saw other Yeke groups digging at what was probably the same site a few years earlier (Rickard 1927a). Both accounts are accompanied by photographs. As described by Hemptinne, Yeke mining began in the dry season and lasted until the first rains. The miners camped next to a river or stream close to the ore body so that millet could be planted by those not directly involved in mining itself. When mining began, women and children collected malachite from the surface of the ground while the men excavated large pits and shafts using iron picks. Fire setting was used to crack hard rock, and ore was transported to the surface using ladders and bark buckets. These mines averaged between 10 and 15 meters in depth and could have galleries up to 20 meters long. Ore was removed at a rate of about 1 meter per day, and in the deepest shafts (35 meters) wood beams were used to support the sides. Carnahan's account differs in that it was women instructed by a male foreman who did the underground mining using iron axes and hoes. Ore was sorted on the hillside and taken to a nearby stream for concentrating before smelting. At Dikuluwe, the male-to-female ratio of mining parties was about 1 to 15 (Rickard 1927a, 56).

Good descriptions of large-scale traditional African copper-mining methods outside the Congo are available for Zambia and the Transvaal, South Africa. The Zambian account was recorded in 1972 in an interview with a Kaonde chief, Simon Chibanza, whose immediate ancestors had operated Kansanshi mine up to the turn of the twentieth century (Bisson 1976). Like

Plate 2.1 African mining at Dikuluwe, Democratic Republic of Congo, circa 1920. The mining crew is described as being led by a woman.

the Yeke, the Kaonde mined copper only in the dry season but restricted their activities to about one month rather than the entire period between the rains. Also like the Yeke, territorial chiefs did not have exclusive mining rights, and anyone who wished to dig for copper could do if not opposed by the chief. A typical crew consisted of a mixed group of men and women, but only the men were allowed to mine. It was the women's duty to carry the ore. At Kansanshi, the ore was concentrated in vertical fissure-veins, and the mine took the form of deep trenches with vertical sides, making access difficult. The men used axes to break up the vein material—a mixture of quartz, malachite, and chrysocolla—and hoes and baskets to remove the ore. On the edge of the working, the ore was crushed, and the malachite and chrysocolla were separated from waste rock. To protect those working below, roofs of wood beams and branches were laid over the workings.

The Transvaal mines at Messina and Phalaborwa were being operated by the Venda well into the period of European contact, and a number of excellent descriptions are available (Stayt 1931; Van Warmelo 1940). The Venda dug shallow open stopes and inclined shafts to a maximum depth of nearly 27 meters, with some of these shafts having lateral passages following high-grade ore. Only men mined copper. The primary tools were hafted iron gads, chisels, and unhafted stone balls that served as hammers (Friede 1980). Particularly hard rock was loosened by fire setting. Stone hammers were used both with chisels and to crush rock in order to separate high-grade ore from the waste, which accumulated on the edge of the workings. The gads were mounted in the ends of heavy digging sticks. Euphorbia leaves or the pods of cassia bushes were burned to give light in deeper shafts, and access to the shafts was by ladders made of thongs with wooden rungs. Ore was concentrated by winnowing (van Warmelo 1940).

The available accounts suggest that all African mines operated on roughly the same technological level, which constrained the variety of techniques employed in the mining process. Variation appears to have been a consequence of slightly different geological circumstances at each site and the capabilities of the basic tool kit of indigenous African society. Although methods were simple, Africans succeeded in extracting large amounts of high-grade ore. There is no evidence to suggest that these techniques were introduced by Arabs or Europeans.

COPPER-SMELTING TECHNIQUES

There are many more descriptions of smelting techniques than there are of mining, and these can be supplemented with archaeological data. Observations and photographs were made of the smelting process in most of the major copper-producing areas. Although no accounts of smelting exist for West Africa, bronze and brass casting continued to the present and are very well documented (these are discussed in the section on smithing). Casting as it was practiced in other parts of Africa was an integral part of the smelting and refining processes described here.

In Africa, malachite is the most common copper mineral that was smelted, and hardwood charcoal was virtually the only fuel employed. The chemical composition of the simplest form of this carbonate ore is $Cu_2\,[(OH)_2/CO_3]$. This compound contains approximately 57 percent copper by weight (Kirsch 1968, 87). The reducing process by which the metal is extracted involves the following chemical reaction. As the furnace temperature rises to a minimum of 700° to 800° C, carbon in the charcoal combines with oxygen to form carbon monoxide:

$$2C + O_2 = 2CO$$

Sufficient oxygen must be present in the furnace, and this requires either a strong natural draught or a forced draught (Tylecote 1962). Once carbon monoxide is formed, the malachite is reduced:

$$Cu_2\,[(OH)_2/CO_3] + 2CO = 3CO_2 + H_2O + 2Cu$$

This process can occur in a "solid state," that is, without producing molten metal because of the difference between the temperature necessary to produce carbon monoxide and the higher melting point of copper (1084° C). Some of the weight of the ore is lost through the expulsion of carbon dioxide gas or water vapor. If sufficient temperatures are reached, the gangue (the usually siliceous nonmetallic component of the ore) fuses together to form a silicate slag that is lighter than copper and floats on its surface. Maintaining sufficient furnace temperatures and separating metal from slag were significant obstacles confronting all African metallurgists. Temperature was critical for other reasons as well. Many copper ores contain variable quantities of iron, and iron oxides were sometimes deliberately used as a flux. Iron is soluble in molten copper and hardens it, negatively effecting its malleability. Because higher temperatures are required to reduce iron, the ideal smelting temperature for copper was a delicate balance between attaining sufficient heat to produce molten copper and slag fluid enough to release the metal while at the same time minimizing the reduction and dissolution of iron (Rehder, n.d.).

Furnace temperature is a function primarily of airflow, and in most cases this was provided by bellows, an arrangement that allowed for greater temperature control than natural draught furnace designs. Separating metal from slag was more problematic, and a variety of techniques were employed. These included mechanical methods (primarily hammering), the use of fluxes such as iron oxides or lime in the form of shells to produce more fluid slag, furnaces that could be tapped to drain copper separately from slag, and in some cases separate smelting and refining procedures (Miller and van der Merwe 1994). Differing solutions to these two problems account for most of the variation in African smelting techniques.

The most important accounts of copper smelting in the Congo are those of de Hemptinne (1926) and Ladame (1921), and of these de Hemptinne's description of Yeke and Sanga smelting practices are the most complete. The traditional history of the Yeke states that the art of copper smelting was learned from the Sanga, who had occupied the area prior to the arrival of the Yeke in the nineteenth century. The Sanga produced copper in a furnace that is 1.75 meters high, with a diameter of 1 meter. This furnace was probably made of dried clay blocks or termitaria carved into bricklike form. De Hemptinne calls these building blocks baked bricks, but this probably refers to exposing them to fire to dry them rather than to full-scale baking, a process that was not employed in Central Africa. The furnace had a shallow depression at its base to collect the metal and openings for four pairs of bellows. Sanga furnaces were large enough to not require destruction to extract solidified copper.

The refining furnace used by the Sanga was as large as their smelting furnace and also fired by four pairs of bellows. However, it differed in that it was constructed on sloping ground, usually the flank of a large termite mound, and had at its base a layer of carefully compacted wood ash that could be broken to allow molten copper to flow out on the downslope side. A channel led from the opening to ash-lined clay cross molds that could produce large ingots weighing 12, 15, and 50 kilograms.

Yeke smelting appears to have been similar to the Sanga method, although at 40 centimeters in internal diameter and 75 centimeters in height, the size of the furnaces was reduced. The Yeke erected their smelters (Fig. 2.4A) on open ground, with as many as 20 or 30 being made at one time. Construction was carefully supervised by a master smelter who also performed rituals to ensure success of the operation. These rituals were considered essential to success but did not affect furnace design. There are no "medicine pits" built into the bases of these or other Central African copper smelters, as have been recorded in many iron smelters (Schmidt and Mapunda 1997). Three funnel-shaped tuyeres carved from the domed apexes of termitaria were placed at equal intervals around a circular depression, with the nozzles angled downward so that the air blast was directed at the base of the furnace. Walls were constructed of carved termitaria propped up with sticks, with gaps between the termitaria deliberately left open.

When construction was completed, a thin layer of hardwood charcoal made from wood of the *mobanga* tree (*Afrormosia angolensis*) was laid in the base, and this was covered with a densely packed layer of dry *mobanga* branches. Hot coals were introduced to ignite the fire, and once it was burning well and the fuel had been mostly consumed, another layer of charcoal was added. This was topped off with a charge of up to 50 kilograms of mala-

Figure 2.4 Central African copper-smelting (A) and -refining (B) furnaces

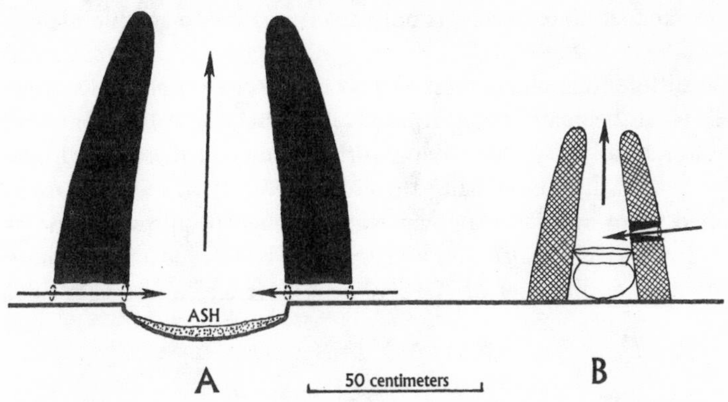

The smelting furnace is a non-pouring design that must be dismantled to extract the metal. These designs are common to the Sanga, Yeke, Lamba, and Kaonde.

chite broken into small lumps. For two and a half hours, the furnace was allowed to burn by natural draught, with air entering by the tuyeres and the small gaps between the termitaria that made up the walls. Wet clay was used to seal those gaps after the second charge of fuel was consumed. At the same time, the furnace was again filled with charcoal. The climax of the operation then began. Air was forced into the furnace for half an hour by a pair of bag bellows stationed at each tuyere. During this time, the malachite was reduced to molten copper and slag, both of which collected in the furnace base. When the chief smelter deemed the process finished, the walls of the furnace were quickly broken down, revealing a pool of copper from which charcoal and slag were quickly scraped away. After cooling, this was removed from the ground and broken into pieces with a large copper hammer for refining. Approximately 12 to 15 kilograms of metal were produced from the 50-kilogram charge (de Hemptinne 1926, 385–403). Cline (1937) noted that Yeke smelting was wasteful in that it did not employ a flux. Because malachite is over 55 percent copper, this caused a loss of between 40 and 50 percent of the metal because a flux is necessary to form a slag that was fluid enough to mechanically release more of the copper.

The Yeke refining furnace was smaller and different in design. Like the smelters, the walls were constructed of trimmed termitaria, but these surrounded a crucible made from an ordinary clay pot tightly packed with fine wood ashes (Fig. 2.4B). The entire furnace was only 40 centimeters high and 25 centimeters in diameter and was fired by a single pair of bag bellows. Charcoal and about 5 kilograms of copper lumps made up a normal charge, which was consumed after about half an hour of forced draught. The furnace was then demolished, the pot lifted out with the help of wet pads, and the copper poured into an ingot mold cut into the side of a termitarium and lined with ash. Large objects, such as a copper anvil or hammer, were cast in an appropriately shaped hole in the ground, again lined with ash (de Hemptinne 1926, 401).

A somewhat different smelting method was employed at Dikuluwe mine (Lekime 1966). It has been attributed to the Luba tribe (Cline 1937) but was probably common to all the groups living in the vicinity of Kolwezi. Unlike the Sanga and Yeke, a Luba smelting furnace (Fig. 2.5) was a permanent structure shaped from molded clay that was designed to allow casting as soon as the ore (exclusively malachite) was reduced. It was 40 to 50 centimeters high, with an inner diameter of 30 to 40 centimeters. On opposite sides

Figure 2.5 Luba smelter

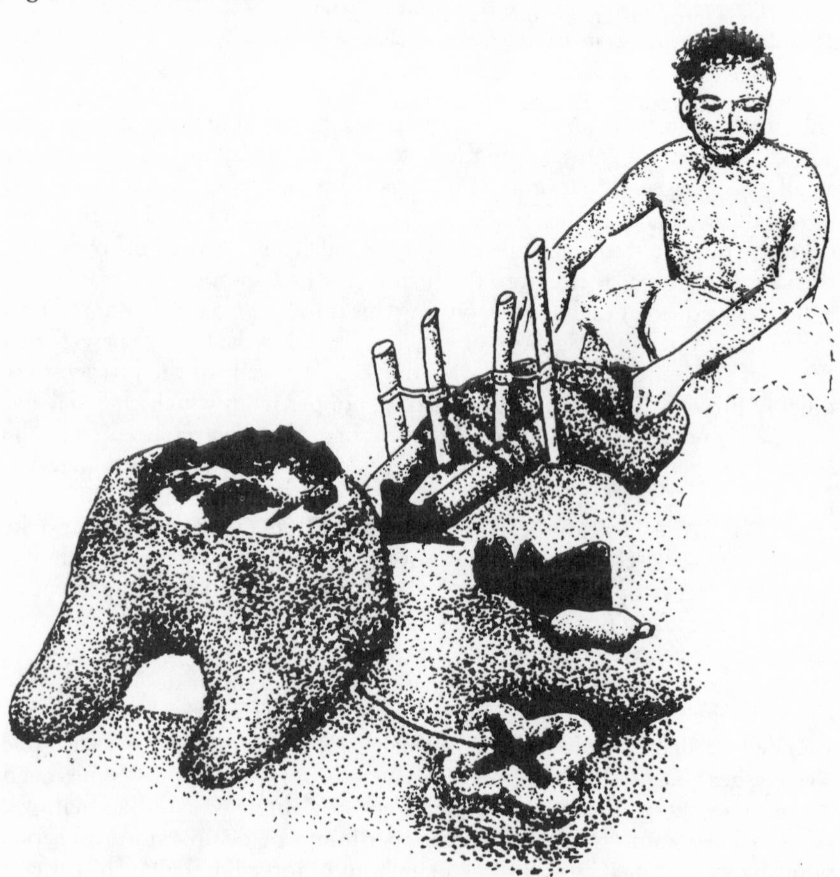

The nearest bellows and operator have been omitted to illustrate the furnace design (after Lekime 1966).

of the furnace were two arched holes, about 10 centimeters high, that admitted air. These holes were flanked by ridges of clay extending about 20 to 30 centimeters from the side wall of the furnace to channel the blast from the bellows. The whole structure was built on sloping ground. On the downhill side, midway between the two bellows holes, a small taphole was bored in the base of the furnace wall. This was carefully plugged with ashes and led to a channel that, in turn, emptied onto a flat clay surface. Either one or more shallow X-shaped molds of ashes mixed with clay were prepared on the surface, each with one arm terminating at the end of the channel. Roasted malachite was added to the furnace after the fire was hot, and the progress of the smelt was gauged by the color of the exhaust gases. When these signaled that the ore was reduced, the furnace was carefully tapped to allow the casting of a number of ingots, a stick being used to temporarily plug the hole after the release of an appropriate quantity of metal as assistants reoriented the channel to each mold and removed the solidified ingots to permit the molds to be reused. After all the copper (and presumably slag) had run out of the furnace, the hole was plugged and the process begun again. A large number of crosses could be cast in this way before the structure had to be rebuilt (Cline 1937).

In Zambia, only one group, the Kaonde people living near Kansanshi mine in Northwestern province, were still mining copper at the time of colonization. Traditional smelting of copper continued until about 1914. Although no longer producing metal for the indigenous economy, a Kaonde master smelter named Ndungu and two assistants frequently conducted demonstrations at agricultural shows and other exhibitions (Chaplin 1961; Bisson 1976; Miller 1994). What is noteworthy is that virtually all the smelting techniques observed in the Congo were at times employed by these Kaonde metallurgists. This variation in methods points to the potential problems of using only a single account to characterize a particular smelting technology. In the Kaonde case, it appears that the smelting method depended on the amount of metal that Ndungu wished to produce (Miller 1994), which in the past was probably influenced by the availability of ore. Copper smelting was an exclusively male activity. Prior to each smelt, the men were ritually purified and required to abstain from sexual activity the previous night. Women were prohibited from observing the smelting process, and their presence was sometimes invoked to explain failure.

The most frequent procedure is very similar to the two-step Yeke technique and was used to produce relatively small quantities of copper. In most of the demonstrations, pure malachite was the preferred ore. As the ore was being cleaned, a hole, 20 centimeters in diameter and 5 centimeters deep, was excavated on the flank of a large termite mound and filled with a layer of dry ashes. Walls and a single tuyere were constructed using termitaria and cemented with wet clay. To fire the smelter, a layer of charcoal was added until the furnace was filled to above the level of the tuyere. Burning embers were then tossed in, and when the fuel was fully ignited, a "few hand-fulls" (Chaplin 1961, 56) of malachite were added immediately above the tuyere vent. The furnace was filled with charcoal, and a pair of bag bellows was worked for three hours until a blue-green flame signaled that the copper was ready. The furnace was then dismantled to extract the metal, which was hammered to remove any adhering slag and charcoal in preparation for refining.

If a refining furnace was employed, it was virtually the same size as the smelter and differed from it only in possessing an ash-filled pot at its base, exactly as did the Yeke refiner. When melted, the metal was decanted into cruciform molds carved in termitaria and lined with ash (Chaplin 1961). Wet grass pads were used to handle the hot crucible. The necessity of employing presmelted copper for the use of crucible casting was made clear by the demonstrations conducted in 1971 (Bisson 1976). In those cases, a refining furnace was employed but charged with malachite. The resulting accumulation of slag at the mouth of the crucible prevented effective pouring of the copper, and no complete ingots were made, although sufficient metal had been produced. No flux was employed in any of the demonstrations; however, the Kaonde were earlier recorded as having used lime (Melland 1923).

Additional accounts of demonstrations in the 1950s by this same group of men have recently surfaced showing that they had a wide technical repertoire (Miller 1994). In most cases, ingot production was a one-step process, similar to that described for the Luba but with some differences in the design of the furnace. This was made of a single large termitarium carefully carved into a hollow cone 60 centimeters in basal diameter, tapering to nearly 25 centimeters in diameter at the top, approximately 50 centimeters high, and with a slight internal constriction approximately two-thirds of the way up from the base. The furnace was installed on sloping ground and placed on a carefully prepared clay floor that was slightly concave. A pair of tuyeres consisting of bamboo pipes covered by a thick layer of molded clay were set into a prepared clay support so that they entered the furnace on the upslope side approximately 5 centimeters above the floor. Bag bellows were attached to their exterior ends with leather thongs. A taphole was installed on the downslope side consisting of a 2-centimeter-diameter bamboo tube covered in clay directed toward a channel leading to the ingot molds. The ingot molds were symmetrical crosses cut into the ground and smoothed with a lining of wet clay and were dried and heated before use.

Once the furnace was charged with burning charcoal, malachite and additional charcoal were added throughout the duration of the smelt. When green smoke and slightly purple flame was observed, the bellows operator increased his pace to the rhythm of an incantation begun by the chief smelter. The entire smelting process took three-quarters of an hour, the taphole was opened with an iron spike, and the metal was poured out. In one case, an H-shaped ingot, described as being similar to those found at Ingombe Ilede and weighing 9 kilograms, was successfully cast. In other cases, smaller *handa-style* (see the following discussion) crosses were produced. In at least one reenactment, a pot was buried in the base of the furnace and employed as a crucible (Miller 1994).

As emphasized by Miller (1994), no single demonstration encompassed all the techniques available to Kaonde smelters, and it is clear that Ndungu and his team could modify their methods to fit the specific circumstances of terrain, the available material for furnace construction, the quantity of ore to be reduced, and the amount of copper desired. Although their technological repertoire certainly reflects indigenous knowledge, Miller notes that some subtle influences may have been exerted by the context of the demonstrations. The diversity of ingot forms produced may be an example. In 1961, the team spent one month doing demonstrations at the Maramba Craft Village, an exhibit of indigenous technologies near Victoria Falls that had informal connections to the Livingstone Museum. The furnaces made there were the crucible variety (Anonymous 1961) designed to produce small quantities of metal that was cast into crosses that were sold to tourists. The desire to maximize the number of items for sale, combined with what must have been a limited supply of malachite (since none was available locally), must have affected the types of ingots produced. At the same time, Ndungu and his team must have been taken to the Livingstone Museum to see Zambia's most spectacular hoard of ancient copper, the large crosses from the richly decorated burials of Ingombe Ilede, that had been discovered only one year earlier (Chaplin 1962). The production of an Ingombe Ilede–style cross by the same team shortly thereafter at Luanshya, where sufficient malachite could be easily obtained, more likely reflects a desire to demonstrate technical prowess to meet the expectations of the Europeans who were arranging for these demonstrations than it does the actual form of the ingots traditionally made by the Kaonde. There is no archaeological or ethnographic evidence that the Ingombe Ilede–style ingot was employed in Mwinilunga district, from which Mr. Ndungu's team came (Bisson 1976).

Ethnographic accounts of copper-smelting techniques from south of the Zambezi River are more limited because most of the mines had been abandoned prior to colonization, possibly as the result of the introduction of cheaper European trade goods in the 1850s (van der Merwe and Scully 1971). The best available record is for the Venda miners of Messina in the Transvaal (Stayt 1931, 64–66). As with other groups, the Venda began construction of their smelting furnace by making a shallow hole in the soil, 45 centimeters in diameter. This was lined with clay and ashes, and around it a circular wall of puddled clay reinforced with stones was built to a height of 45 centimeters. This wall was made of puddled clay and reinforced on the outside with stones. A single hole at the base permitted the bag bellow's nozzles to point into the furnace.

These smelters were operated exactly as those described previously, and the resulting mass of metal was cleaned by hammering. Refining was a simple process requiring no specialized furnace. Lumps of copper were remelted in an 18-centimeter-diameter potsherd that was placed over a hole in the ground filled with incandescent charcoal, with air blast provided by a bellows. Ingots were cast in molds made by pressing a 1- or 2-centimeter-diameter stick lengthwise into the soil. At one end of the mold, a small hollow was carved to create a small head, sometimes with short arms protruding from it. The rods produced by this method are known as *lerale* (Steel 1975). In some cases, the end of a larger stick was thrust into the ground, producing an oblong hole with straight sides and a flat bottom. The ends of smaller sticks were in turn pressed into the bottom of this hole to form a pattern of smaller holes, usually parallel lines. When filled to overflowing with copper, this mold produced a *musuku* ingot, a short cylinder with studs on one end and an irregular flange where the copper had spilled out of the top of the mold. This form was once thought to be a waste product, a casting sprue in which the studs were actually the remains of long, thin rods that were being cast as a first step in wire manufacture (Stanley 1929). However, experiments by Steel (1975) demonstrate that the studs are an intentional form of ornamentation. Among the Phalaborwa, rods were also reputedly cast in molds made of animal skins (van der Merwe and Scully 1971).

Perhaps the simplest form of African copper-smelting furnace has been reported from Thakadu mine, Botswana, which has been dated to the sixteenth to seventeenth century and is attributed to the Kalanga people. Excavations uncovered a group of four furnaces placed about 1 meter apart and oriented on an east–west axis, a characteristic that may have symbolic significance. The furnaces were oval pits, 40 centimeters in width and 50 to 60 centimeters in length, and 25 centimeters deep. At each end, a shallow trough indicated the placement of a tuyere. These pit furnaces apparently lacked a superstructure. The ore being smelted was primarily malachite but included some sulfide compounds, and the siliceous gangue did not require an additional flux. Fluxing was incomplete, indicating that furnace temperatures barely reached 1,200°C. The absence of crucible fragments suggests that the copper bloom produced in these furnaces was taken to villages for processing. The mine is thought to have been abandoned when the collapse of the Khami state isolated it from trade networks (Huffman et al. 1995).

CASTING AND SMITHING TECHNIQUES

As noted previously, in many cases copper was cast into the desired final form as part of the smelting or refining process. This is in part because its melting temperature is lower than that of iron and was routinely within the reach of traditional African technologists. A second important factor was the more limited role played by copper in African societies. Although the production of most ornaments required smithing, in almost all cases currency ingots were cast rather than forged. The creation of the desired number of simple open molds allowed smelters to produce the finished product with a minimum amount of additional effort. Open molds could be made of heat-resistant stone, such as steatite (Garlake 1973), clay (Bisson 1976; Anciaux de Faveaux and de Maret 1980), or ash (de Hemptinne 1926) or by pressing a template into either soil or sand (Steel 1975). Clay molds were often double, with mirror-image templates on opposing faces. Not only did this double the output from each mold, but the symmetrical cross section may have prevented cracks from developing as it dried prior to use or during casting. In many cases, these molds were preheated to prevent explosive breakage during the rapid temperature changes when the metal was poured and were lined with powdered ash to prevent the metal from adhering to the mold when it solidified. Although it is unrecorded in the ethnographic record, archaeological samples of some clay molds from Central Africa were fired like pottery and carefully burnished on the interior of the template (Bisson 1976).

With the exception of some wire drawing tools, the African coppersmith employed the same equipment as an ironworker. The primary technique used by smiths to shape copper was annealing, the alternate heating and hammering of metal. Because copper is more malleable than iron, cold hammering was also a viable option. In heating copper, especially very finely made ornaments, extreme care is required to prevent the metal from melting in the forge, and the success of African smiths in producing these ornaments is testimony to their high level of skill. The basic equipment of a forge consists of an iron hammer, anvil, tongs, bellows, and tuyeres (Fig. 2.6). Specialized items might include crucibles, which were often recycled small clay pots or conveniently shaped potsherds, iron chisels and wedges, perforated iron plates or balls for wire drawing, and other miscellaneous items. Hammers included a circular cross-section iron bar, blunted at one and tapering to a point at the other that was wielded by hand. Socketed or perforated iron hammers designed for hafting were less common. Anvils were made of either stone (massive, fine-grained igneous rocks such as granite) or iron. Stone hammers were generally only used for heavy-duty pounding (Cline 1937), and copper hammers were sometimes reserved for working only copper or copper ore (Bisson 1976). Although European trade goods had penetrated the interior of the continent early in the second millennium (Garlake 1973), it is unlikely that these contacts had a significant influence on smithing technology.

There are two basic forms of bellows employed by African metallurgists: "bag" and "drum." Bag bellows may represent the earliest development, as they can be found in almost all areas of sub-Saharan Africa where metal working is practiced, whereas drum bellows are restricted to the Congo, upper Zambezi, and upper Nile drainages as well as parts of West Africa (Frobenius et al. 1921). Bag bellows are essentially a sack of softened hide

Figure 2.6 Smithing tools from southeastern Angola

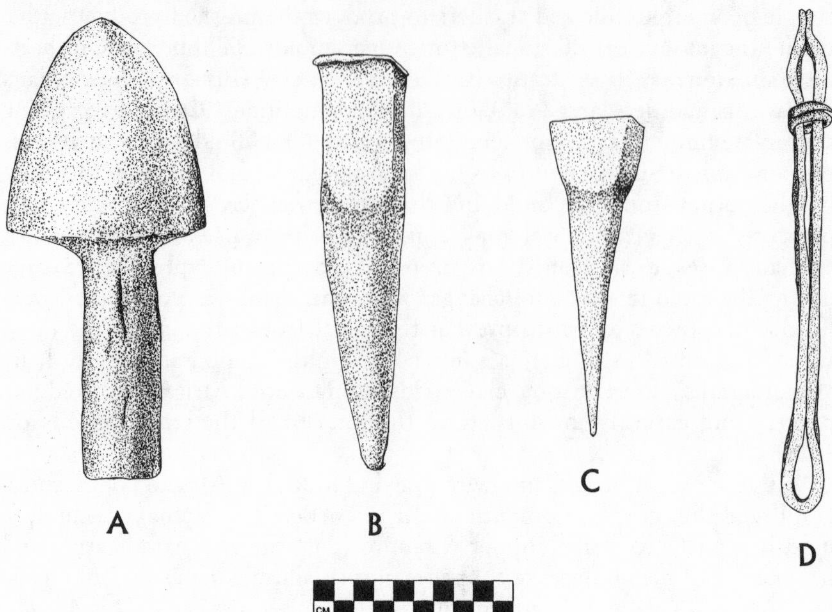

A, B hammers; C spike anvil; D bent bar tongs.

with a large opening at one end to admit cool air and a nozzle at the other from which the blast is forced. The nozzle and the bottom of the bag are tied to supports to hold the bellows in place and direct the blast into the fire. The intake valve is created by pair of wooden slats sewn across the opposite sides of the large opening, with loops on them to hold the fingers and thumb of the operator (Cline 1937). Bag bellows are normally used in pairs in order to maintain a continuous blast by filling one bag while expelling air with the other. A single bag may be all that is required to heat metal in a hearth for annealing.

Drum bellows vary in design but are essentially an attached pair of bowl-shaped chambers with an elongated, narrow air duct protruding from the base of each one and a loose diaphragm tightly fitted over the mouth of each chamber. Wooden sticks are usually tied to the center of each diaphragm to allow it to be raised and lowered, either drawing air into or expelling it from the chamber's single opening. The bellows could be carved from wood, in which case the nozzles were an integral part of the structure, or created from a combination of clay bowls with nozzles made of ceramic, wood, bamboo, or horn (Friede and Steel 1986). For these bellows to operate efficiently, the nozzles must point into a funnel-shaped tuyere. This prevents the intake phase from sucking incandescent charcoal into the bellows and causing it to burn. In addition, the gap between the tuyere mouth and the bellows nozzles permits greater volumes of air to be forced into the furnace through the Bernoulli effect (Bisson 1976). The volumes of air pumped by bag and drum bellows are approximately equal, but the drum design may have a slight edge in efficiency because it requires less skill to operate (Friede and Steel 1986).

WIRE DRAWING

Wire drawing was a difficult technique to execute and was not practiced everywhere. It occurred in eastern, east-central, and southern Africa (Cline 1937) but is not as well documented elsewhere (Herbert 1984) and appears not to have been done in the lower Congo basin (Volavka 1998). This distribution suggests that this technology was introduced into sub-Saharan by contacts along the east coast. Extremely fine gauge copper wire was an important constituent of the spirally wound bangles that explorers observed in widespread use during the nineteenth century (Livingstone 1857) and are abundant in central and southern African Later Iron Age sites (Bisson 1976).

Wire was drawn by pulling a thin hammered copper rod through a graded series of funnel-shaped holes in an iron plate or ball. Plates were rectangular cross-section bars with multiple holes, whereas balls had a single hole and required multiple tools to complete the process. A long tapering iron needle was employed to gauge the holes in the drawing plate (Cline 1937). To begin the process, a thin copper rod was created by hammering so that it was only slightly larger in diameter than the largest hole on the drawplate. One end of this was tapered to a point, forced through the appropriate hole, and gripped with a vicelike pair of tongs. The tongs are closed by hammering a coiled iron ring along the shaft until they are as tight as possible, and the ring is held in place with a wedge. The wire plate was fixed to a stand, often the crotch of two tree limbs, and in some cases a variety of levers; sometimes a simple form of windlass was used to pull the wire through the hole. The process was repeated through successively narrower holes until the desired gauge was achieved (Bisson 1976). Experiments have established that lubricating the wire with fat and heating it facilitated the process and decreased breakage (Steel 1975).

A complete selection of wire-drawing tools (Fig. 2.7) was recovered from the Ingombe Ilede burials in Zambia in direct association with X-shaped copper ingots, lumps of melted copper, a rough hammered copper bar, sheaves of hammered rectangular cross-section copper rod that represented the first stage of the wire production process, two spools of finished wire, and hundreds of spirally wound copper bangles (Fagan et al. 1969). Fagan (1972) has suggested that the lump of lead found in one of the burials was used in the creation of alloys to facilitate wire drawing. This is possible but has not yet been confirmed by metallographic analysis. The tool kit included

Figure 2.7 Wire drawing tools from Ingombe Ilede, Zambia

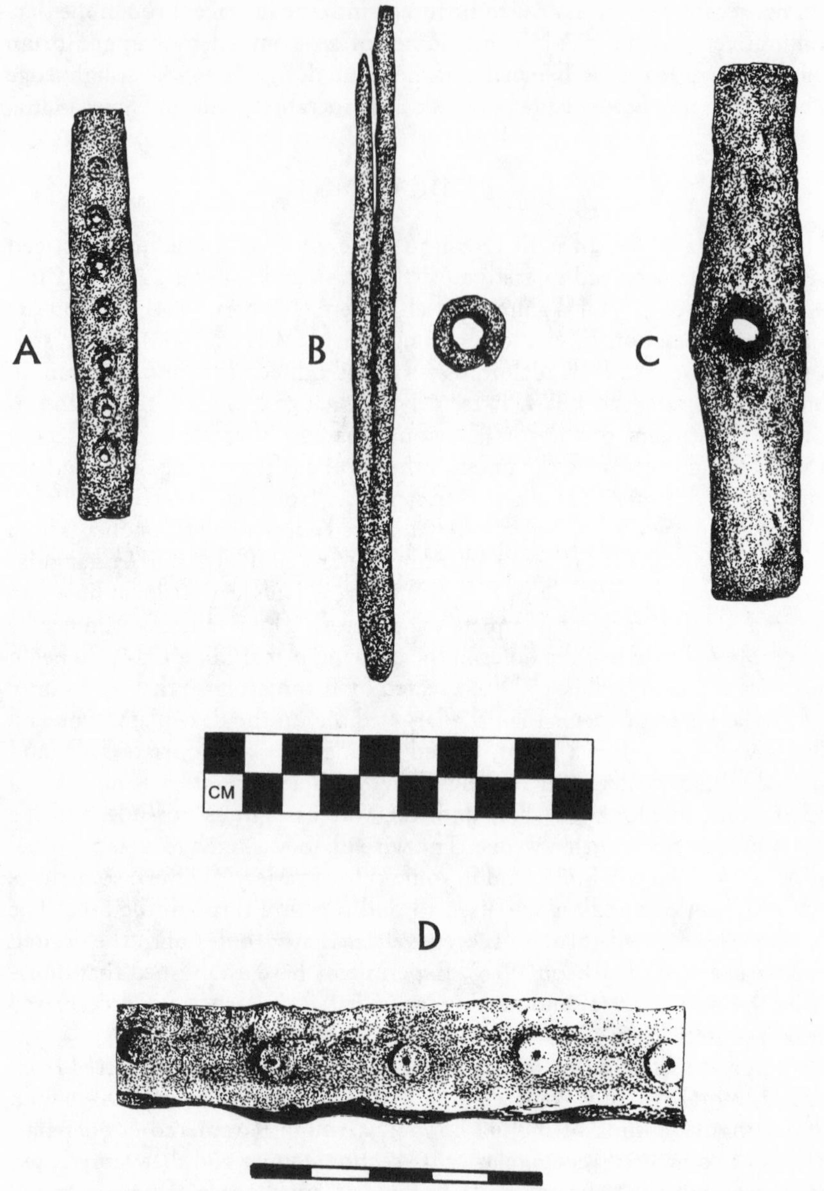

A drawing plate; B split-bar tongs; C hammer; D magnified view of drawing plate. (Drawn from photographs,. A–C burial 8; D burial 3. Coll. National Museum of Zambia)

six perforated hammers, six sets of tongs, and six iron drawplates. Four of the plates had at least one or both ends broken off at one of the holes, suggesting the considerable forces being applied to them during the wire-drawing process. The bars were rectangular in cross section, and the longest complete specimen measured 36 centimeters in length and was perforated with 14 drawing holes. Chemical removal of encrusted rust and sand from the four specimens that were not on public display revealed that the plates were in excellent condition and bore important traces of their manufacture.

Preparation of the wire-drawing holes was a three-stage annealing process well within the capabilities of indigenous blacksmiths. First, a circular flat-tipped punch, 7 to 10 millimeters in diameter, was employed to create a row of circular depressions, about half the thickness of the plate, and spaced at 1.5- to 2-centimeter intervals along its length. Working in the same direction, a sharp pointed punch was then used to perforate the bar at the center of each depression, creating the drawing holes. These were sized by turning the bar over and hammering the protruding nipple created by the punch until the hole closed to the desired diameter as determined by some form of gauge, probably a sizing needle. The diameter of the draw holes ranged from 3.5 millimeters to 1 millimeter. Although the copper wire of the bangles was heavily corroded, it appeared to correspond in diameter to the smallest of these holes.

LOST-WAX CASTING

Casting in a closed mold using the "lost wax" process was the most complex metallurgical process employed by Africans and was restricted to the southern Sudanic belt and tropical West Africa (Posnansky 1977). In this technique, an object is first sculpted in either solid wax or latex. In some cases, a clay model is covered with a thin layer of wax. One or more wax rods are attached to the surface of the sculpture that create channels or runners, called "sprues," through the walls of the mold, enabling the wax and gases to drain and molten metal to flow in without trapping air pockets. The entire structure is then dipped in liquid clay to cover it with the greatest possible fidelity, and when this is dry, the mold is encased in a thick clay jacket. After thorough drying, the mold is baked, during which time the wax or latex is eliminated, and while still hot, the void created is filled with molten metal. After cooling, the jacket is broken away, revealing the sculpture, which requires only removal of the casting sprues, cleaning, and polishing to be completed (Cline 1937). This technique first appeared in the western Sudan before the end of the first millennium and was eventually practiced from Lake Chad to Senegal (Posnansky 1977). As the superb castings from Igbo Ukwu, Nigeria (Fig. 2.8), attest, it reached a high state of technical competence as early as the ninth century (Shaw 1970). Other spectacular manifestations of

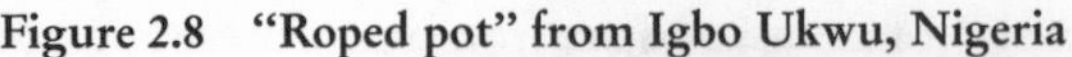

Figure 2.8 "Roped pot" from Igbo Ukwu, Nigeria

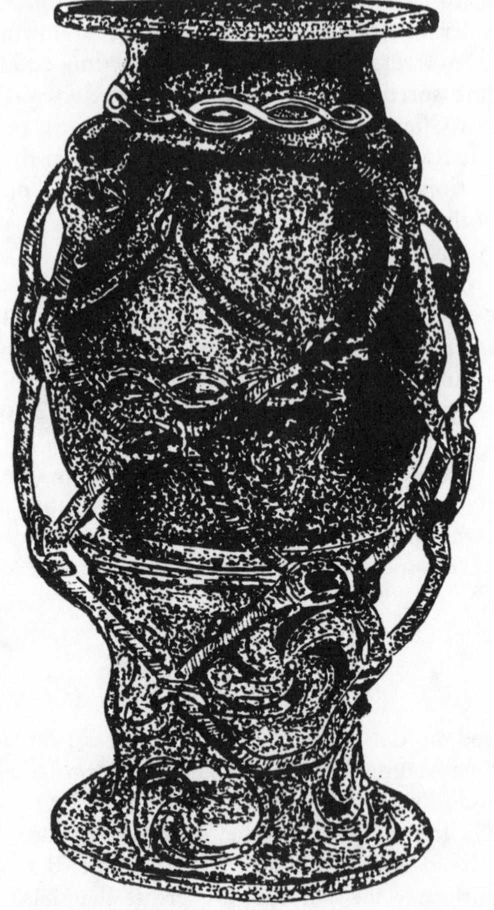

This bronze vessel, 32.2 cm high, was cast in a single piece, illustrating the technological mastery of the Igbo Ukwu metallurgists. (Drawn from photographs in Shaw 1970)

this technique occurred between the twelfth and fifteenth centuries at Ife, Nigeria, and between the fifteenth and nineteenth centuries at Benin (Willet 1967). The complexity and high technical quality of many of these castings, combined with incorrect estimates (ignoring the radiocarbon dates from Igbo Ukwu) that they all postdated the fourteenth century, led some art historians to conclude that this technique was introduced into West Africa in a fully developed form either as an offshoot of long-distance maritime trade with Europeans or by immigrant foreign craftsmen from the western Sudan in the seventeenth century. In this view, the technique first appeared in its most complex and well executed form and subsequently degenerated over time (Williams 1974). Although the antecedents of the Igbo Ukwu castings remain unknown, probably because of a lack of archaeological coverage in tropical Nigeria (Craddock et al. 1997), the consensus among archaeologists is that the lost-wax technique was probably introduced at a much earlier date, probably from North Africa, and was modified and transformed in various ways, depending on the local iconographic context, including terra-cottas and wood carving (Posnansky 1977). As Craddock et al. (1997) have argued, the innovative and highly skilled single-casting method of making thin-walled bowls with handles at Igbo Ukwu may be proof of indigenous origin since it shows that the makers were unaware of European hammering, riveting, or soldering techniques.

A related debate has surrounded the source and type of metal employed in West African lost-wax casting. Almost all cast objects have been characterized as "bronze" in both the art-historical (Williams 1974) and the archaeological literature (Willett 1967; Shaw 1970), and until recently it was assumed that this metal had to have been imported. In fact, the metal employed in the castings is highly variable and includes brass, an alloy of copper and zinc, and leaded copper as well as true bronze, which is an alloy of copper and tin (Posnansky 1977). A number of the Ife sculptures are cast of pure copper (Willett 1967). Alluvial tin could be easily obtained in northern Nigeria, and there is abundant evidence that it was exploited in the precolonial era (Calvert 1912). The recent discovery that numerous lead, zinc, and copper deposits in the Benue Rift of southeastern Nigeria were exploited by Africans (Craddock et al. 1993, 1997) provides additional proof that foreign imports were not necessary.

Because the most elaborate castings were not still being made in the twentieth century, there is no ethnographic documentation of how the extremely thin walls of the Ife heads or the open latticework of the "roped" pots from Igbo Ukwu were achieved. Simpler forms of lost-wax casting have continued to the present and have been thoroughly described in a number of areas (Neher 1964; Willett 1967; Fox 1986; Aremu 1993). It should be noted that in Africa the term *lost wax* should perhaps be *lost latex* since wax was less frequently used (Craddock et al. 1997). The most common natural latex employed in casting came from the *Euphorbia camerounica* tree, but the sap of *Detarium senegalense* was also used (Aremu 1993). Perhaps the most basic method was employed in the production of small geometric, zoomorphic and anthropomorphic brass "gold weights" by the Akan peoples of Ghana and the Ivory Coast from the sixteenth century onward. The earliest forms of these weights are biconical, cubes, or disks, decorated with incisions (Garrard 1973) and cast by simply shaping a block of beeswax and attaching one or two sprues. For the animal and human forms, a sausage of wax was cut to the appropriate length, limbs and other features were added using wax thread and buttons, and the figure was then sculpted, often with exquisite detail. In almost all cases, these castings were solid (Posnansky 1977). The common method for pouring the metal for the Akan as well as for peoples in northeastern Nigeria and Cameroon was to employ a "luted" crucible in which the crucible and mold were a single elongated piece with the mold at one end and the cup for the metal at the other. This was heated in a bellows-driven furnace to achieve the nearly 900°C melting point (depending on the proportions of the alloy) of brass, with care being taken to be no more than 70°C hotter to prevent flaws from developing on the surface of the metal as it cooled (Fox 1986). Pouring was accomplished by tipping the luted crucible to allow molten metal to flow into the mold.

Less ethnographic information is available for the creation of larger castings, and reconstructions of the techniques depend on the analysis of museum or archaeological specimens. For these pieces, one or more separate crucibles were necessary, as was a more elaborate system of vents to permit gas escape and to ensure that all parts of the mold were uniformly filled. A second problem with large castings was that the sculpture was almost always made over a clay core. This had two consequences. First, there was a danger that the core would shift after the wax or latex was drawn off, thereby spoiling the sculpture. Second, the introduction of molten metal might cause both uneven heating and expansion of gases in the core, which could either break the mold or bubble into the metal. In Benin, the solution to these problems was to embed a framework of metal rods in the mold to support the core and transmit heat evenly during the preheating phase, thus reducing the gas expansion problem (Herbert 1984). In Ife, one or more oval connections were made at the back of the sculpture between the core and the outer mold. These supported the core and permitted gas to escape. This system was exceedingly efficient at stabilizing the core and enabled the walls of some of the Ife figures to be only 1 millimeter thick. The large Ife heads also required a series of iron pegs to hold the core in place. The molds were designed with the face of the sculpture tilted downward, increasing the chance that it would be free of bubbles or flaws (Willett 1967).

COPPER IN AFRICAN SOCIAL, POLITICAL, AND RELIGIOUS SYSTEMS

To Europeans, copper was one of a number of commodities that might be obtained from Africans, and thus its trade features prominently in documentary accounts. However, the export trade of copper and its use as a currency is but a small and somewhat more recent facet of its overall role in many African societies. To understand this role, we must look past the Western conception of it as a utilitarian metal and understand how its physical properties were viewed within African cultural contexts. We must explore the "language of materials," the term that Herbert (1984) employs in her definitive study of the symbolic significance of copper in sub-Saharan Africa, which is summarized here. This language can be understood through both oral traditions and the nonmonetary uses made of copper. Of the latter, copper was used to decorate the human body, as a medium for sculpture (either cast or in the form of hammered sheets covering wooden sculptures), and as a means of decorating prosaic implements, such as knives and axes, in some cases transforming them for ceremonial functions. It is important to note that not only chiefly regalia but also weapons were among the implements frequently embellished with copper decoration. The great variety of artistic uses of copper cannot be summarized here, and readers should refer to Herbert for a comprehensive synthesis.

Why copper served as a highly valued decorative material cannot be explained solely by its scarcity or mechanical properties relative to iron, although these certainly must have been factors. Being both softer and more ductile, as well as having a lower melting temperature, copper could be shaped in a much greater variety of ways than could iron, given the available smithing technology. Nevertheless, gold shares these characteristics with copper and is rarer and easier to work, yet gold never attained the same status as copper in most African settings (for two of many examples, see dos Santos 1891 and Burton 1873) until its value was inflated by European demand (Herbert 1984). Copper often served as an important medium for storing wealth and exhibiting social status, but Herbert argues that it gained this significance because it symbolized power within the closely integrated "political, religious, social, economic and aesthetic spheres of African society" (1984, 242). This ultimately derived from three nonfunctional characteristics of the metal: its "redness, luminosity and sound" (277–282). The redness of the metal is often but not always associated with the life-giving power of blood, frequently specified as placental blood and the female force. As Turner (1967) observed among the Ndembu Lunda, red is also linked to social transitions. Thus, blood, power, heat, and the ambiguity of transitional states provide symbolic links between the redness of copper and political and social power in many African societies. The association of redness with transition would also account for the widespread use of copper in the investiture rituals of African states. The shiny surface of copper was also important, and ritual objects were usually kept highly polished to reflect sunlight. This ability to reflect light may also have suggested aggressiveness, power, and the liminal boundary between two states, again emphasizing the transformative powers of copper. The importance of the sound of copper is suggested by its frequent use in the manufacture of bells and rattles and to decorate drums or other musical instruments, thereby helping impart to them the power to summon spirits (Herbert 1984).

The ability of copper not only to embody power but also to create and transform it may account for its association with investiture regalia and burials of high-status individuals (Fagan et al. 1969) since both the assumption of power and death are important transitions. Because this pattern can be seen in some of the Classic Kisalian graves in the Lake Upemba basin, this role clearly pre-dates the widespread use of copper as a currency in the same area (de Maret 1977). Indeed, the archaeological record of copper throughout sub-Saharan Africa shows ornamental, ritual, and social-symbolic uses preceding its role as a currency.

Although much is known of the role of copper in African societies, the abandonment of indigenous copper mining and smelting by the first decades has meant that we have much less ethnographic evidence about the relationship of copper production to sociopolitical and religious beliefs, and most of this is restricted to Central Africa. As a prestige material, copper was of concern to politically powerful individuals, such as village headmen and chiefs, and among the Yeke, chiefs were the organizers and primary beneficiaries of mining activity (de Hemptinne 1926). Yet mining was not restricted to chiefs, although, as in the case of the Kaonde (Bisson 1976), it was normally conducted only with the permission of the local ruler. Although in some cases copper miners and smelters were distinct from smiths (see the Ngoyo case study at the end of this chapter), there is no evidence for smiths who specialized exclusively in copper. In most cases, the situation was probably one in which those who knew the art of smelting could produce either metal and were probably practicing smiths. However, not all smiths were capable of smelting metal.

The relationship between smithing and political power is discussed at length elsewhere in this book and is not repeated here, other than to emphasize that craft specialization such as smithing is an important part of a larger movement toward social differentiation (Trigger 1993) and that in Bantu-speaking Africa, blacksmiths were usually held in high esteem (de Maret 1980). How this relationship was expressed no doubt varied from one society to the next, but the Ingombe Ilede burials in Zambia exemplify how close the connection between the trade and smithing of copper and high social status could be. These graves contained copper ingots and the equipment to transform those ingots into wire bangles as well as abundant examples of all the stages of bangle manufacture, suggesting that the individuals interred with these tools were smiths. They were also people with high status and political power. The skeletons themselves were adorned with gold beads and thousands of copper bangles. Other grave goods included large iron ceremonial hoe blades and iron double gongs that in Central Africa are an important symbol of chiefly power (Fagan et al. 1969; Fagan 1972).

COPPER CURRENCY

Among the earliest European records of copper in the African interior were of its use as a currency (Livingstone 1874; Montiero 1875; Arnot 1899; Haddon 1908; Johnston 1908; Ibn Batutta 1929). This term, however, must be carefully applied. In the market-oriented industrial world from which these explorers came, the terms "currency" and "money" were essentially synonymous and referred to any standardized units of a valued substance that could be exchanged at agreed-on rates for all types of goods and services as well as to pay for social and legal obligations. That type of general-purpose currency may never have been widespread in sub-Saharan Africa (Bohannon 1959; Herbert 1984), and the known examples appear to have been relatively recent in date (Bisson 1975). Special-purpose currencies were much more common in Africa and served only some of the functions of a general-purpose currency. This was a consequence of the multicentric nature of many African economies, in which goods were exchanged within separated subsistence and prestige spheres, each having its own set of organizational principles and values. For example, virtually all precolonial African cultures were self-sufficient in terms of basic subsistence. Most households produced their own food through some combination of hunting, foraging, and agriculture. Trade was sometimes necessary to distribute foodstuffs or essentials such as salt, ceramics, or iron tools within a culture, but this usually involved simple barter and transport of materials only over short distances. The fact that some European explorers used copper bracelets to pay for food does not mean that this was the normal practice. Africans would certainly have taken advantage of the opportunity to obtain a prestigious substance for goods that within their cultural context were much less valuable. It is in the prestige sphere that copper objects were most frequently employed. This included marriage payments and the purchase of cattle or other animals whose ownership conferred social status. In some societies, special-purpose currencies were not interchangeable with currencies employed in the subsistence sphere (Bohannon 1959).

The role of copper currencies appears to have changed over time. Some of the earliest copper artifacts from Mauretania are utilitarian projectile points and knives (Lambert 1971), but that is the exception to the general rule that copper was normally employed either for ornaments or for ingots for exchange. Although archaeological coverage of Iron Age sites dating to before A.D. 1000 is uneven, the evidence available thus far is that copper was initially employed in personal adornments or as a decorative material. The most common types were bracelets made of hammered strip or wire, but not enough of these have been found to demonstrate that they were sufficiently standardized in size and form to be analogous to the *manilla* currency bracelets of West Africa or the wire bangles employed as currency in Mozambique in the nineteenth century. So few ingots dating to the Early Iron Age are known that we cannot presently assess their degree of standardization, which might be evidence for their use as a special-purpose currency. That role, however, cannot be ruled out a priori. In the second millennium A.D., unambiguous examples of copper currencies appear with increasing frequency in both the archaeological and the historical records (Bisson 1975).

In West Africa, the most common form of copper (or copper-alloy) currency was the *manilla,* a circular or oval cross-section metal bar with flaring ends that was bent into a bracelet-like ring (Fig. 2.9). These were extremely common as a traditional currency well into the twentieth century in the Niger delta (Johansson 1967) and their use extended southward into the lower Congo (Johnston 1908). The origin of *manillas* is not well documented. Historical accounts from the western Sudan mention rings as a medium of exchange as early as the eleventh century (Herbert 1984), and some archaeological discoveries from tropical West Africa include a few copper rings dating between the ninth and thirteenth centuries (Shaw 1970; Connah 1975). Documentary records of the trade in *manillas* concentrate on the vast number that were imported into West Africa from Europe during the slave and palm-oil trades. From these accounts, it is evident that *manillas* were used mainly for high-status purchases and served as a means of conserving wealth that could be readily converted into goods (Herbert 1984). The recent discovery of copper and lead mines in Nigeria (Chikwendu and Umeji 1979) increases the possibility that European brass, bronze, and even iron *manillas* were ultimately copies of indigenous copper-ring special-purpose currencies already in use in the coastal trade area.

Figure 2.9 ***Manillas*** **(Nigeria, coll. Redpath Museum)**

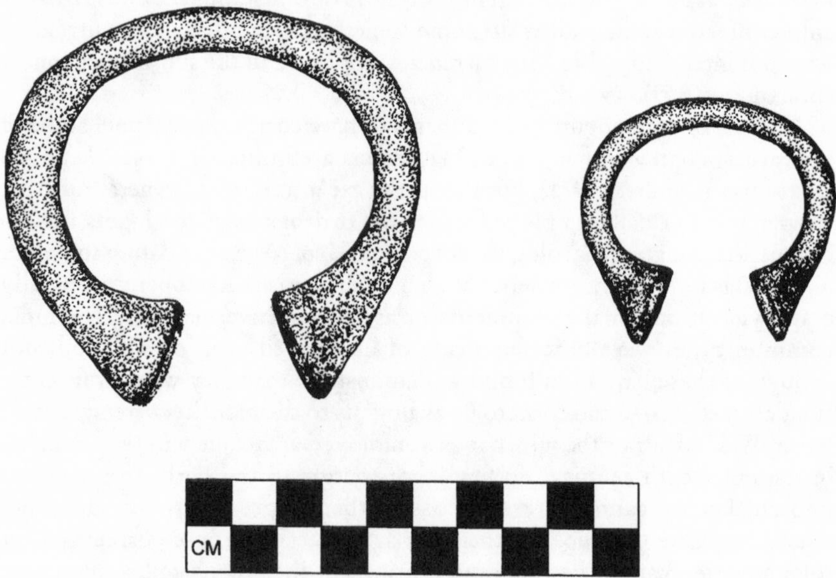

Other forms of copper currency in West Africa and along the west coast were more restricted in distribution. The *rotl*, a lump of copper weighing about 375 grams, was the standard monetary unit in the Sudanic kingdom of Bornu for many centuries. Foreign copper coins, including the United States penny, were exchanged in the coffee trade with Sao Tomé in the nineteenth century. "Neptunes," standardized copper basins imported from Europe, served as both a currency, primarily in marriage payments, and a utilitarian commodity in some parts of the Congo basin (Herbert 1984). Copper currencies found in the lower Congo basin are discussed in the kingdom of Ngoyo case study at the end of this chapter.

In the upper Congo (Lualaba) and Zambezi River drainages (Fig. 2.10), cruciform ingots were the most common form of currency. They were most prevalent in the upper Congo, where numerous ingot mold fragments have been found at Tenke-Fungurume and the mines around Lubumbashi (Bisson 1976; Anciaux de Faveaux and de Maret 1980). A long sequence of human burials containing ingots has been excavated at Sanga and other sites in the Lake Upemba basin (Nenquin 1963; Hiernaux, Longrée, and De Buyst 1971; de Maret 1977). The earliest evidence for copper working in Central Africa now comes from the Naviundu site in the Zambia–Congo border region that produced a radiocarbon date of A.D. 345 ± 75 (de Maret 1982). A buried crucible with associated copper slag with a calibrated radiocarbon date of A.D. 440 ± 90 was found near Kansanshi mine, Zambia (Bisson 1976). Copper artifacts are also found dating to the sixth century in the Early Iron Age Kamilambian culture of the Upemba basin (de Maret 1979). Although all these sites have evidence of the use of copper for ornaments, only one fragment of an Early Iron Age ingot has been recovered from this critical area. It nevertheless may be possible to trace the development of cruciform ingots using that specimen, a small number of early bars found in Zambia, and the large sample of second-millennium ingots from the Congo.

The Early Iron Age ingot mentioned previously was found in the Naviundu site, about 6 kilometers west of Lubumbashi and close to the Ruashi and Etoile ancient mines. This site yielded abundant evidence of copper smelting, including malachite; slag; broken pots, some of which had been used as crucibles; heavily vitrified and slag-encrusted tuyeres; fragments of smelting furnaces that had been made from termitaria; and one small refining furnace base lined with potsherds (Anciaux de Faveaux and de Maret 1984; for illustrations and microanalyses of these materials, along with an interesting introduction to her field observations of copper working, see Childs 1991c). Multiple radiocarbon samples confirmed the fourth century date for this site (de Maret 1982). No traces of clay ingot molds were found. The copper ingot fragment (Fig. 2.11A) was the rounded end of a relatively thick (13 millimeters) flat bar that was cast in an open mold. It was in the process of being converted into ornaments of which a solid, round cross-section brace-

Figure 2.10 Ancient mines and archaeological sites in the south-central and southern African interior

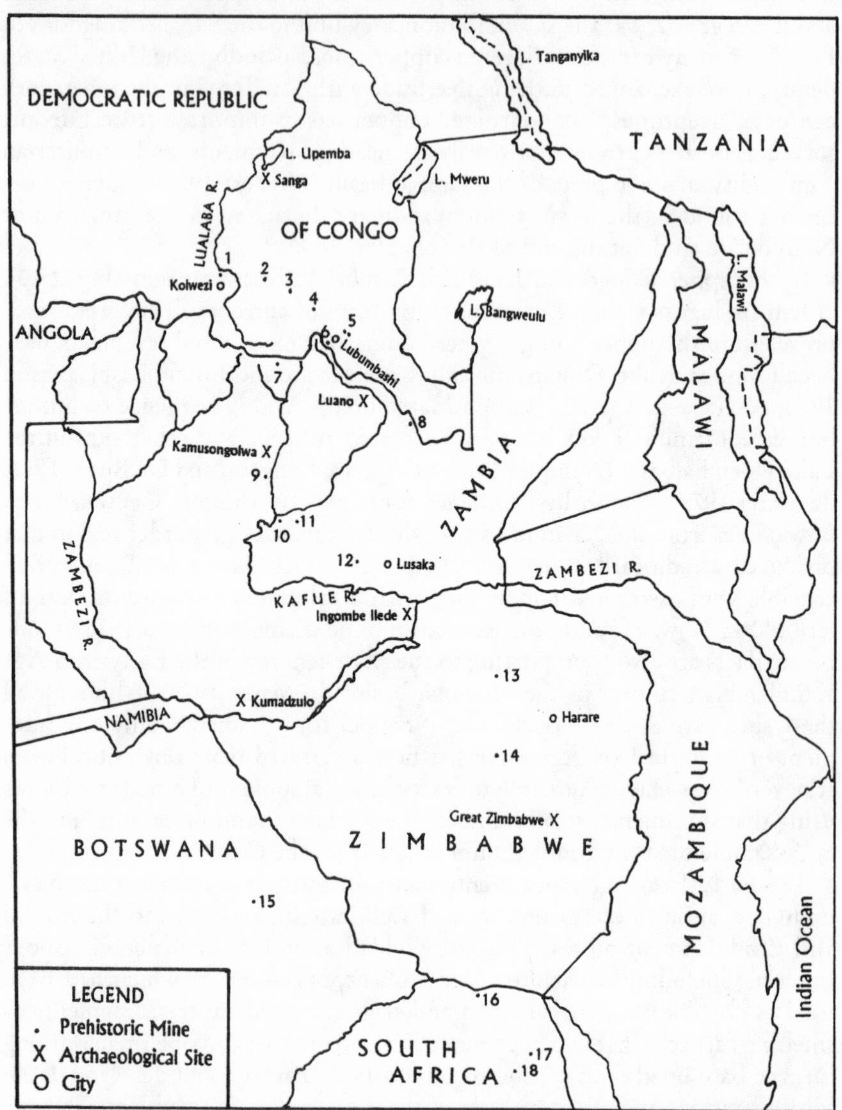

1 Dikuluwe, Musonoi; 2 Tenke-Fungurume; 3 Kambove; 4 Luishia; 5 Ruashi and Etoile, also the Naviundu and Luano Site A archaeological sites (Anciaux de Faveaux and Maret 1980, 1984); 6 Kipushi; 7 Kansanshi; 8 Bwana Mukubwa; 9 Chifumpa; 10 Hippo; 11 Silver King; 12 King Edward; 13 Alaska; 14 Umkondo; 15 Thakadu; 16 Messina; 17 Phalaborwa; 18 Harmony.

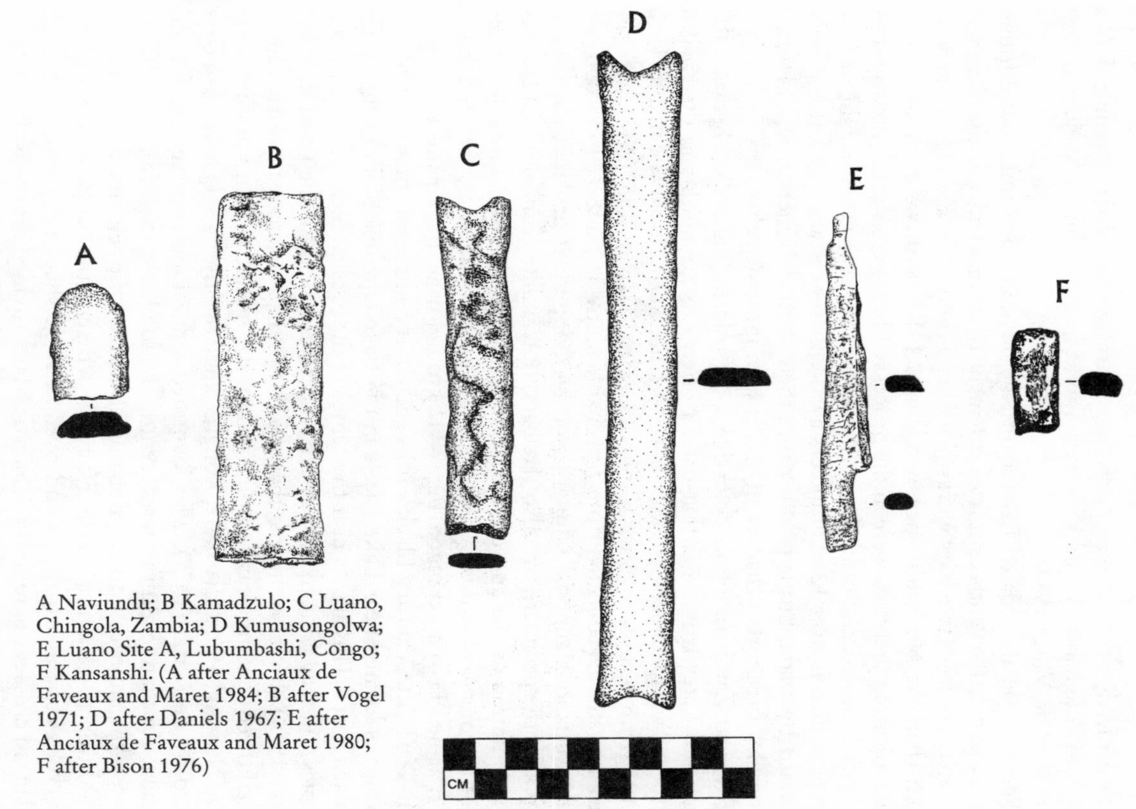

A Naviundu; B Kamadzulo; C Luano, Chingola, Zambia; D Kumusongolwa; E Luano Site A, Lubumbashi, Congo; F Kansanshi. (A after Anciaux de Faveaux and Maret 1984; B after Vogel 1971; D after Daniels 1967; E after Anciaux de Faveaux and Maret 1980; F after Bison 1976)

Figure 11: Fourth- to twelfth-century ingots from Central Africa

let decorated with a chevron design, a spirally wound strip bangle, and a length of rough-hammered wire were found in the vicinity (Anciaux de Faveaux and de Maret 1984).

The only securely dated Early Iron Age ingots from Zambia were found at the sixth- to seventh-century settlement of Kumadzulo in the Zambezi valley. These were two bars with squared ends and a cross section somewhat flatter than the Naviundu specimen (Fig. 2.11B). Both were broken at one end, indicating that they were in the process of being converted into the copper wire bracelets and beads found at the site (Vogel 1971). Since the nearest copper source is over 125 kilometers away, the ingots were almost certainly obtained by trade, but it is likely that their primary function was as a raw material source rather than as an object with intrinsic value.

The next Zambian ingots come from the transitional period between the Early and Later Iron Ages that dates to between the ninth and the twelfth century. Two specimens are known (Fig. 2.11C, D). One was dated to 1150 ± 100 from Kamusongolwa Kopje, Kasempa (Daniels 1967, 148), and another was surface collected from a probable ninth- to tenth-century component at Luano Main Site, Chingola, in the Copperbelt province (Bisson, in prep.). Both specimens are also flat bars, but, unlike Kumadzulo, each has an indentation at the end creating a "fishtail" appearance. The only other ingot fragment from this period is the broken arm of what was probably a short armed H-shaped ingot (Fig. 2.11F) found near the remains of an eleventh- to twelfth-century blacksmiths shelter at Kansanshi (Bisson 1976).

Sanga is located near Lake Kisale in the Lake Upemba basin of the upper Lualaba River. This area is near the center of the present distribution of Luba peoples and may contain evidence for the development of the Luba state (de Maret 1979). Initial estimates that the elaborately decorated burials represented three contemporary cultural groups dating to the eighth or ninth century (Nenquin 1963; Hiernaux, Longrée and De Buyst 1971) have been corrected by de Maret (1977), who identified a developmental sequence from Ancient Kisalian (eighth to tenth centuries), to Classic Kisalian (eleventh to fourteenth centuries), to the Kabambian (fifteenth to eighteenth centuries). In addition to ceramics, iron, and ivory artifacts, the Sanga graves yielded numerous copper ornaments and over 1,200 H-shaped ingots described as unflanged crosses or *croisettes,* which de Maret divided into four size categories: very small (648 between 5 and 15 millimeters in length); small (493 between 16 and 35 millimeters); medium (62 between 36 and 70 millimeters); and large (8 between 71 and 150 millimeters). Two crosses were also found that exceeded 150 millimeters (Fig. 2.12A–D). What is noteworthy about the Sanga sequence is that although copper ornaments are common in the Classic Kisalian, indicating the high value placed on that metal, ingots are not found until the succeeding Kabambian, and de Maret presents compelling evidence for temporal trends toward increasing standardization, decrease in

Figure 2.12 Cruciform currency ingots from Central Africa

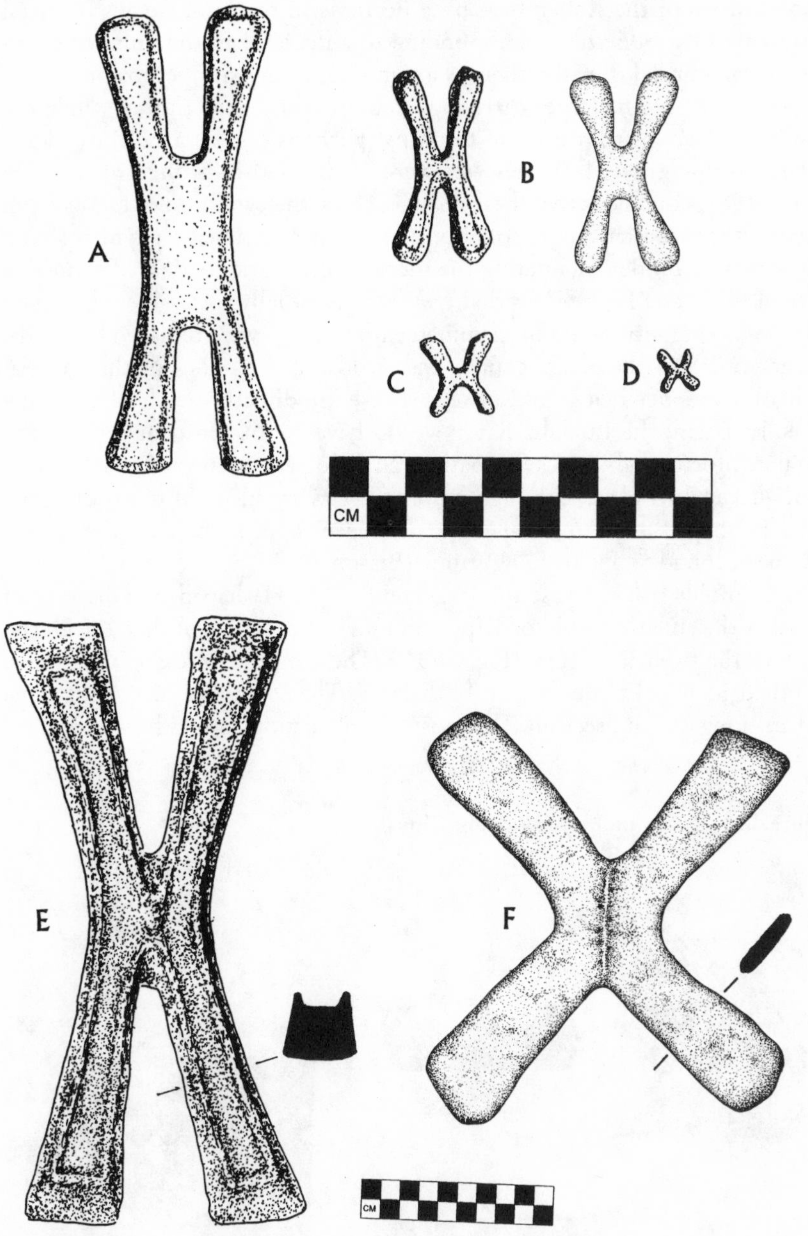

A large, B medium, C small, D very small ingots from Sanga (after Maret 1981); E flanged ingot from Ingombe Ilede (after Fagan, Phillipson and Daniels 1967); F *handa* from the Congo (coll. Redpath Museum).

size, and increase in the total number of *croisettes*. This is followed in the second phase of the Kabambian by a decrease in the total weight of metal represented by *croisettes*, corresponding to a decrease in the number of ingots in each burial. Finally, there is a temporal change in the positioning of ingots in graves. The larger early ingots are found on the thorax, while the smaller *croisettes* are found on the hips (perhaps tied to a belt) or in the hands. In one grave, 140 *croisettes* were found tied in groups of five. De Maret (1981) concludes that these changes show the evolution of ingots from a special-purpose currency possibly connected to marriage payments to a multipurpose money facilitating the increasingly market-oriented economy of the Luba state. He believes that *croisettes* eventually lost value when they became too numerous and in the nineteenth century were replaced by beads.

The source of the Sanga copper was probably the mines of the western Congolese copper belt near Kolwezi. These are directly south of the Lake Upemba basin; the Lualaba River would have facilitated transport of the metal. Unfortunately, no systematic archaeological studies of the Kolwezi mines have taken place, although numerous clay molds used to produce the small H-shaped *croisettes* that mark the recent end of the Sanga sequence have been found at Tenke-Fungurume (Bisson 1976).

Ingot molds used to cast the larger unflanged H-shaped bars have been found at the smelting area for Kipushi mine in a component dated from the ninth to the twelfth century (Fig. 2.13A). These molds were double; that is, they had identical templates on both faces. The templates had short arms and an elongated midsection. The most complete mold would have produced

Figure 2.13 Ingot molds (clay) from Kipushi

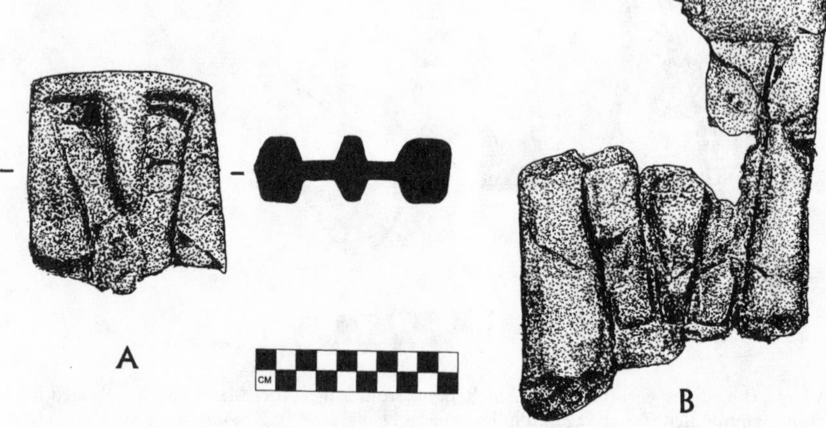

(A) Twelfth century; (B) fourteenth century

ingots measuring nearly 175 millimeters in length, with a maximum potential thickness of 10 to 12 millimeters (Bisson 1976). A similar mold, as well as fragments of two elongated-midsection ingots that had been cut longitudinally (Fig. 2.11E), presumably as a first stage in the production of hammered rods, was collected at the Luano Site A near Ruashi mine (Anciaux de Faveaux and de Maret 1980). Like many of the smelting locations in the region, this site is probably multicomponent, but the three potsherds illustrated with the mold and ingots are most similar to ceramics dating to the twelfth century at the Luano Main Site, Chingola, Zambia (Bisson 1989).

There is no archaeological evidence for the production of this type of H-shaped ingot after the twelfth century, although that possibility cannot be excluded. If they were a special-purpose currency as well as a source of metal for ornaments, they could have been in circulation for decades or even centuries before their incorporation into the archaeological record. For example, the only dated ingot of this type from Zambia was found in a nineteenth century burial at Sinde Mission near Livingstone (Inskeep 1962). Their almost complete absence in Zambia may mean that most were being traded north into the Congo (Bisson 1975), and the date for these molds suggests that demand for a standardized ingot form began somewhat earlier on the Zambezi–Congo watershed than it did at Sanga. Ingots of this type have also been reported from Great Zimbabwe, but not in a securely dated context. No identical ingot molds have been reported from that area, although the soapstone mold from Great Zimbabwe is roughly similar (Caton-Thompson 1931; Garlake 1973). A few similar bars have been reported from Mozambique (Bisson 1976). It would appear that this type of ingot was very widely distributed throughout the Central African interior beginning in the ninth through the thirteenth to fourteenth centuries and that regional differentiation in ingot forms, probably related to ethnic preferences, developed later as copper currencies came into more widespread use. A different ingot form was produced in the fourteenth century at Kipushi. A single slag pile among the over 30 Kipushi mine smelting sites found on the banks of the nearby Kafue River yielded fragments of two sizes of opposed-template ingot molds designed to produce the large, flanged X-shaped ingots (Fig. 2.12E) with long arms and a short midsection that are identical in size and shape to those found in a fifteenth-century context at Ingombe Ilede in southern Zambia (Fig. 2.13B). The single mold that could be reconstructed would have produced ingots approximately 34 centimeters in length (Bisson 1976). Molds identical in form but described (probably incorrectly) as "soapstone" have been found in undated contexts near Etoile mine (Walton 1957). At other sites near Lubumbashi (Luowoshi), this mold type is associated with pottery described as "recent" (Anciaux de Faveaux and de Maret 1980).

Although the only known source of these flanged ingots is the eastern group of mines along the Zambia–Congo border, no ingots of this type have been found in the Congo. In addition to the specimens from Ingombe Ilede

(Fagan et al. 1969), flanged ingots have been found in the Urungwe and Lomagunde districts of Zimbabwe, although these specimens appear to be shorter in length and somewhat thicker than the crosses made by the Kipushi templates. All the Zimbabwean specimens range from the fifteenth to the eighteenth century (Garlake 1970a), as does a single specimen found in southern Malawi. A cache of these crosses is also kept among the Bisa royal relics on Cisi Island, Lake Bangweolo, Zambia. This form was therefore traded strictly to the south and east of the mines and was not incorporated into the Luba and Lunda economies to the north and west.

The other well-known ingot type produced at the south-central African mines was the *handa,* often referred to by Europeans as a "St. Andrews Cross" (Fig. 2.12F). These were flat X-shaped ingots with wide arms of equal length intersecting at approximately right angles. It is likely that this ingot form is the most recent development of the cross shape. None are known from the archaeological record, although this may be a consequence of the almost complete lack of archaeological coverage of Later Iron Age sites in the southern Congo (Bisson 1976). The *handa* is also almost impossible to document at ancient smelting sites because it is made in a perishable ash or sand template.

Nineteenth-century accounts identify a number of other forms of cast and manufactured copper currencies in south-central Africa (Fig. 2.14). Forms of manufactured currency included heavy-gauge wire, bullets, hoe blades (ceremonial?), and even unrefined lumps of copper (Herbert 1984). The final major ingot type was the *mukuba wa matwi* made by the Sanga near Kolwezi. These were triangular cross-section bars that flared slightly at each end. They were the largest indigenous ingots produced in Africa and measured 90 centimeters or more in length, with weights in excess of 50 kilograms. De Hemptinne (1926) linked these ingots to the slave trade, and Livingstone (1874) observed their distribution to the south and east of the mines, where they were being converted into the ubiquitous spirally wound wire bangles used as both personal adornment and a currency. There is evidence that different mines produced ingots for particular markets. Arnot (1899) noted that within a single political unit (the "Garenganze" kingdom), some mines produced H-shaped ingots and others the *handa*. Smelting was controlled by lineages, and the ingots each group cast were extremely uniform in size. There may even be evidence that different ingot forms were produced at the same mine. The Kipushi mine smelting area included numerous discrete slag piles that, based on associated ceramics and the degree of weathering, appeared to be contemporary and postdate the fourteenth century. Yet only one contained the Ingombe Ilede–style ingot mold fragments, and most yielded no evidence of molds at all. Since the excavated furnaces at these sites had shallow bases and were designed to be tapped, this could mean that the *handa* was the type of ingot being made (Bisson 1976). This conclusion is

Figure 2.14 Recent wire and bar currency from Central Africa

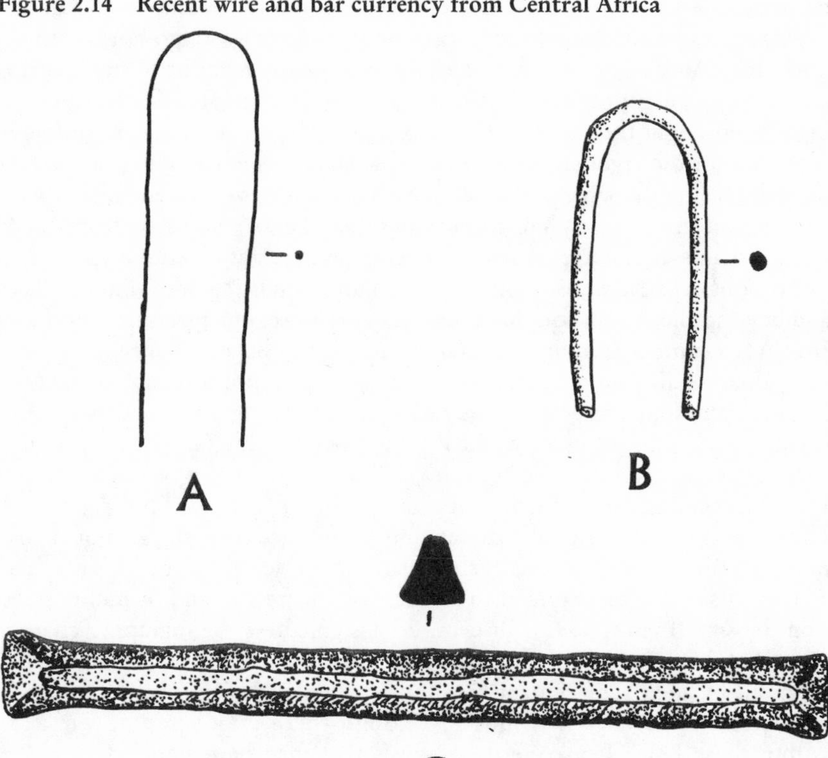

A, B light and heavy gauge currency from the Congo; C large *mukuba wa matwi* bar, c. 1 meter in length, Zambia (coll. Zambia National Museum [after Bisson 1975]).

supported in an interview with Lamba Chief Musaka, whose area included the Kipushi smelting sites. Without prompting, Chief Musaka accurately described the type of smelting furnace that had been discovered in the archaeological excavations, adding the detail that a tube of tree bark was used as the taphole of the furnace. He also stated that the *handa* was the usual ingot made and that these were traded to the Yeke for salt. He drew a sketch of a large X-shaped cross, which he said were occasionally made, but did not know where they were traded (interview by the author, August 12, 1972).

These ingots were not produced by a single archaeological culture, and the sequence outlined previously, progressing from simple bars to increasingly angular crosses, must not be seen as a unilineal development within one ethnic group but instead as one expression of a general trend toward angularity in the iconography of Central African Iron Age peoples. This trend is most clearly evident in decoration on ceramics. Although much work remains to be done, the pattern of temporal change in ceramic decoration motifs appears to parallel changes in ingot form on the Zambia–Congo border. In the Early Iron Age, ingots appear to have been primarily a means of transporting and storing metal until its transformation into ornaments. The form of the ingot itself might therefore be less important. The earliest bars are simple in form, and of the eight surviving examples, all but one have had portions removed. During the same period, ceramic decoration is elaborate, highly variable, and dominated by curvilinear designs. The societies that produced these artifacts do not appear to have been organized into hierarchically organized political structures. Iron Age population densities were initially low, and beyond the suggestion that there were broad regional traditions in Early Iron Age ceramics (Phillipson 1968b), there is too little evidence to identify individual ethnic groups. Moreover, there are some indications that variation in ceramic design was continuous rather than forming discrete clusters, implying that it was not used to signal group membership (Bisson, in prep).

Although migrations have been invoked to explain the appearance of Later Iron Age ceramics in parts of central and southern Africa (Phillipson 1974; Huffman 1989), the one fully documented sequence from the Zambian copper belt (Bisson 1989; in prep.) shows an in situ development of Later Iron Age motifs that corresponded to an increase in site size and overall population density (Bisson 1992). In ceramic design, these demographic changes correspond first to a simplification of the curvilinear Early Iron Age designs, followed by their replacement by simpler, angular designs that increasingly consisted of crosshatched lines. Although there is geographic variation within these Later Iron Age decorations that may have signaled ethnic or lineage membership (Phillipson 1974), a global trend toward increasing angularity and standardization is clear. The most extreme examples of standardized ceramic designs appear in the fourteenth or fifteenth century, a time when more rigid social hierarchies associated with chiefdoms or states had become widespread (Connah 1987). This is the same pattern we see in ingots during the Later Iron Age, where the more curved forms of the H-shaped bars are replaced by the rigid X shapes of the Ingombe Ilede and *handa* styles. Unfortunately, the meaning of the cruciform shape has not been recorded. It appears to have been viewed as "traditional," and those who saw the last copperworkers in action (the present author included) were remiss in not asking why a cross was the appropriate ingot form rather than a simple bar or ring.

Forms of copper currency were entirely different south of the Limpopo (Fig. 2.15). The largest and most unusual type was the Lemba *musuku* ingot, a subrectangular or cylindrical mass of metal with a wide brim at one end and a geometric pattern of studs projecting from the other (Stayt 1931). The smaller solid forms of this ingot were reported to have been used commercial transactions, while larger specimens with sand cores were ritual objects owned solely by chiefs. Few reliable estimates of the commercial value of the

Figure 2.15 South African currency ingots

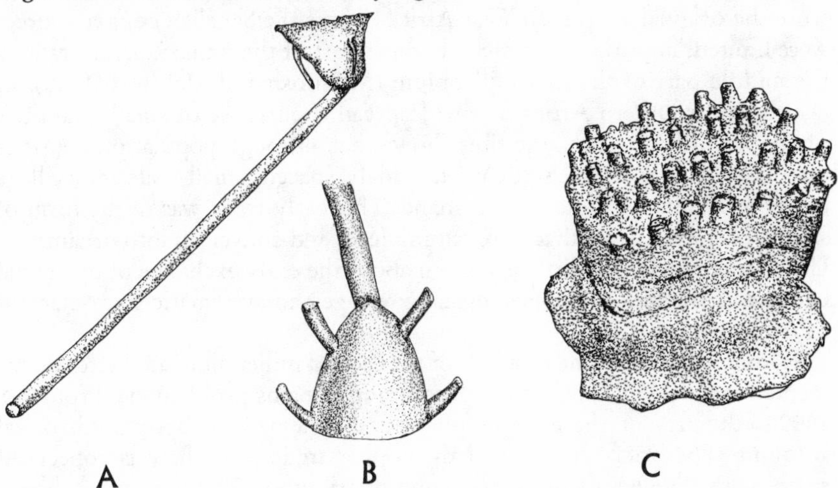

A *lerale;* B detail of *lerale* head; C *musuku* **with seams indicating three separate pours of metal in its manufacture. (Not to scale. Drawn from photographs. A after Lindblom 1926; B, C after Steel 1975)**

musuku are available, and so few specimens are now known that the degree of either size or weight standardization cannot be determined (Herbert 1984). A second type, the *lerale,* a long rod of about 50 centimeters with a funnel-shaped head bearing one or more elongated projections at one end, likewise appears to have been primarily a means of storing wealth since they were employed only in high-value transactions. Neither of these ingot types has been found in an archaeological context, suggesting that both are relatively recent forms (van der Merwe and Scully 1971). These copper ingots were often converted into bracelets or anklets, which could be more readily employed for small purchases (Herbert 1984). These standardized ingot forms were probably much less frequent than were hemispherical masses of copper (Friede and Steel 1975), which were bartered as a raw material to local blacksmiths.

TRADE

The distribution of indigenously produced copper provides clues to the exchange networks associated with each mining area. Beginning at about 500 B.C. in West Africa and in the first millennium A.D. in central and southern Africa, small quantities of copper passed through intervillage barter networks along with foodstuffs, iron tools, textiles, pottery, and salt (Fagan 1969). Although individual exchanges may have been between neighboring villages, the cumulative effect was the movement of copper long distances from the original source. In West Africa, where the Sahelian copper sources were limited, imports of the metal became part of the trans-Saharan trade in the middle part of the first millennium (McIntosh and McIntosh 1980). In central and southern Africa, the widespread occurrence of small quantities of copper in Early Iron Age sites shows that although population densities may have been low and settlements widely spaced, small-scale intervillage barter was sufficient to satisfy demand. This early trade was in the form of simple bars and ingots that were cut in pieces and converted into ornaments. Unfortunately, far too little is known about the early exchange of this metal because of the lack of archaeological coverage and systematic trace-element sourcing studies.

Trading patterns in the first half of the second millennium are better documented archaeologically, although sourcing remains problematic. From A.D. 1600 to the present, these are supplemented by a growing body of historical accounts. The brief summary of the copper trade given here is concerned solely with indigenous production and distribution. The import of copper and its alloys from Europe via the coast and to North Africa across the Sahara was an important part of the economy of some parts of Africa, but since these materials probably fed into preexisting trading networks (which they may have intensified), they are not discussed here. In West Africa, the investigation of the prehistoric copper mines of the Benue Rift is at too preliminary a stage to assess the contribution to those sources to the overall volume and direction of trade, although a link with Igbo Ukwu seems secure (Chikwendu et al. 1989).

The second-millennium trade of copper in central and southern Africa is better known, but the original trading patterns have probably been obscured by the part it played in the later long-distance trade of ivory, slaves, and gold. Copper has been recorded on most of the major historically documented trade routes (Fig. 2.16). In long-distance trade, copper was utilized not as much as an export commodity but as a means of obtaining provisions and things such as slaves and ivory, which in turn were used to obtain European or Asian imports. For example, Nyamwezi traders bought copper from the miners of Shaba with coastal imports and sold it in their own country for cattle and ivory, which was then transported to the coast (Gray and Birmingham 1970). Some copper from the far interior did ultimately reach the coasts, but its volume was small in relation to other commodities (Monteiro 1875; Oliver and Mathew 1963).

Ethnographic accounts provide useful information on how the internal trade of copper was organized. A case in point are the Lamba people who occupy the Zambia–Congo frontier near Kipushi mine. Among the Lamba, trading could take place anywhere, but it tended to concentrate in the chief's compound, where visiting traders would stay. Both parties to a transaction gave the chief a "present" for the privilege of trading, and in turn the chief

Figure 2.16 Historically documented trade routes for copper and other goods in central and southern Africa (after Gray and Birmingham 1970; Bisson 1976)

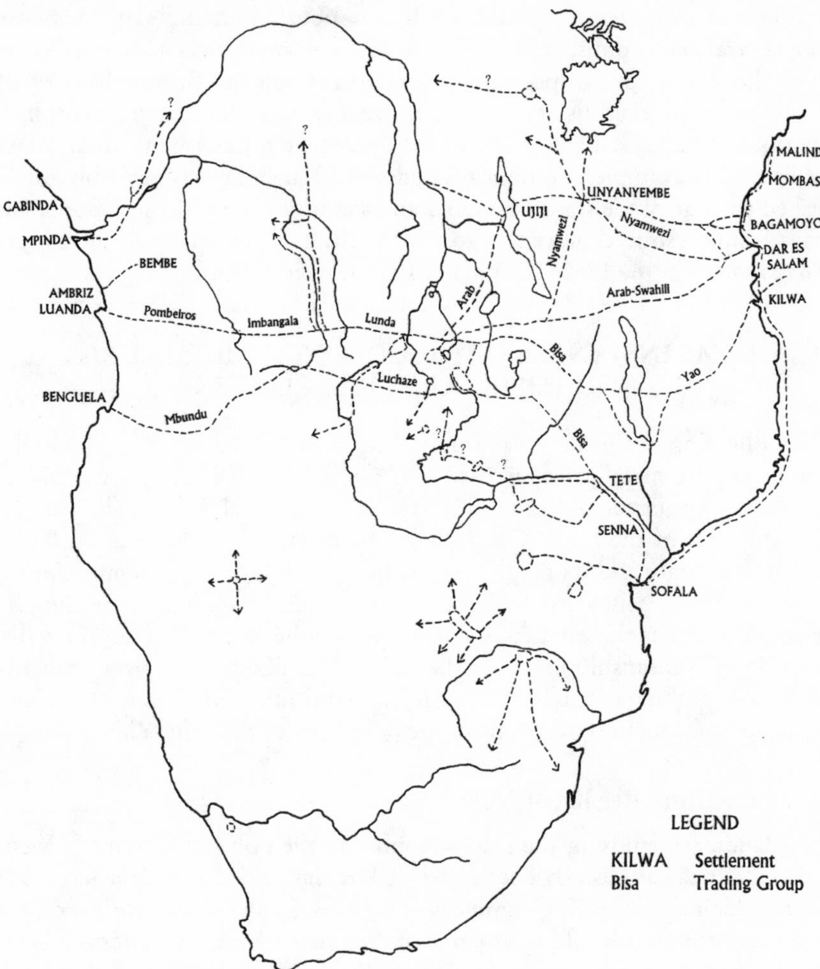

was expected to be generous to his people, reserving only the most prestigious items for himself (Miracle 1962, 203). At the time this was observed, cloth was the standard unit of value, but in the past, standardized units of copper could have served this purpose. It is easy to see how in this type of system copper could pass from one group to another and how much of it came under the control of chiefs.

The relationship between economic and political systems in south-central Africa was diverse. Some long-distance trading networks, but not all, were incorporated into centralized states. Those that were, such as the Lunda, Monomotapa, and Msiri's Yeke, traded either in slaves, which often required raiding, or in mineral products such as copper, gold, and salt. However, noncentralized groups, such as the Nyamwezi, were successful middlemen who did not control a specific resource area (Gray and Birmingham 1970). In most cases, long-distance trade was an expansion of existing trade networks, but once established, it exerted a powerful influence over indigenous politics. For example, the Lunda kingdom of Kazembe was probably established to control the trade of copper and salt in the upper Congo basin, and these same resources were the goal of Msiri in his conquest of the eastern Shaba mines in the 1860s (Cunnison 1959; Vansina 1966).

SOME INSTANCES OF PRECOLONIAL METALLURGY AND THEIR CULTURAL CONTEXT

The following two instances not only provide detailed descriptions of indigenous copper metallurgy but also illustrate the crucial role copper played in the sociopolitical and economic systems of Central Africa. The first, an investigation of the lower Congo River basin including the relationship of the Kongo state and its neighbors to the Niari-Djoué and Bembe mining areas, is based primarily on historical and ethnographic sources supplemented by the technical analysis of museum collections. The second, a discussion of Kansanshi mine near the Zambia–Congo border, uses primarily archaeological data to assess the political implications of changing patterns of copper production over time in the periphery of the Lunda kingdom.

The Investiture Regalia of Ngoyo

A landmark study of the role of copper in the political systems of west-central Africa has recently been published by the late Zdenka Volavka (1998), from which the following summary is derived. In 1976, Volavka discovered the investiture regalia of Ngoyo, one of the smaller Kongo kingdoms located north of the Congo River estuary (Fig. 2.17), misidentified as a "fishing basket" and other mundane objects in the collections of the Musée de l'Homme. This material consisted of a cap/crown, neckpiece, fragments of a belt, and a basket and associated lid, all woven from copper strip, and a set of iron objects including mining and smithing tools. These objects were not the normal court attire of the ruler of Ngoyo but instead were highly sacred symbols of the principle of kingship itself that were conserved in a shrine called Lusunsi and were donned by the elected king only during the final stages of an extremely elaborate multistage coronation process that emphasized the spiritual sanction behind his temporal authority. The Lusunsi shrine was considered sacred to many lower-Congo polities in addition to the Ngoyo, and

Figure 2.17 The lower Congo River (after Volavka 1998)

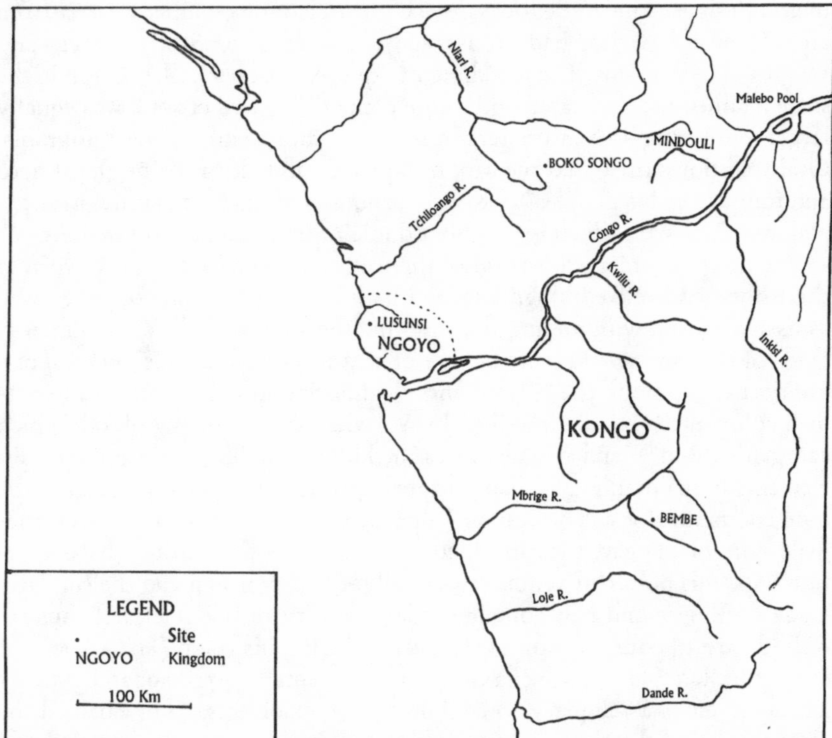

Volavka argues that rulers from a number of kingdoms were invested there. Based on an analysis of the symbolic referents of the various items contained in the regalia, she contends that they must derive from a prestate period (in the case of Ngoyo, probably before 1500) and represent the initial consolidation of political power in the hands of an association of blacksmiths. Her study of the interplay of metal working and ideology demonstrates how, in the Congo estuary, smiths symbolically made kings.

The Lusunsi hoard included 16 objects, many of them fragmentary. In addition to the woven copper cap/crown, neckpiece, and belt, all of which were made in superhuman proportions, there were the remains of a large basket and lid (also woven of copper), an iron double gong of the type traditionally associated with chieftainship in Central Africa, and various mining and smithing tools made of iron. Of these insignia, the most important was the cap/crown, a dome-shaped object with a hole at the apex that was made of coils of copper strip wound around thin, circular, copper rods. Its exterior was ornamented with a row of copper crescents, identified by informants as symbolizing leopard claws, and other rows of thin copper sheet cut in geometric designs. This piece, perhaps the most elaborate copper artifact from all of Central Africa, had an average diameter of 36.5 centimeters and weighed 11 kilograms. The matching neckpiece, a copper collar woven in the same manner and decorated with more copper "leopard claws," was equally large, measuring 45 centimeters in diameter and weighing 4.5 kilograms. Oral traditions attributed the cap, neckpiece, and belt to the mythical hero and founder of his people, Ne Kongo, who was of gigantic stature, thus explaining their size, which is roughly double normal human proportions.

The cap is an enlarged version of the traditional chief's cloth cap worn in the Kongo and related kingdoms, and its manufacture from copper as well as its association with mining and smithing tools attest to the central importance of the mining and manufacture of that metal to the consolidation of a political elite among the Ngoyo and neighboring kingdoms. Both the reddish color of the metal, described by Volavka as symbolizing blood (which can generate life), and female forces, including childbirth, were important elements in maintaining a balance of male and female that was crucial to the indigenous ideology. The copper leopard claws were also an important female symbol and gave the cap added power and prestige through its association with this powerful animal. Essentially, the cap/crown and the similarly made neckpiece and belt contained the authority of the chief and thus required careful conservation in the shrine during his reign. The associated copper basket and lid, which, although fragmentary, were apparently very large, served as a reliquary to contain the other objects. They enabled the consecration of the chief to take place by symbolizing the conservation and transfer of political power, just as a normal basket conserves and transports goods.

As noted previously, many of the iron objects in the shrine were conventional symbols of authority, but mining and smithing tools not normally considered to be chiefly regalia were also included. The inventory of metallurgists' tools in the shrine was actually larger than the surviving assemblage. The priest who collected the objects noted in his correspondence that a crucible was also present. Volavka concluded that these were objects specific to the investiture process itself, which in Ngoyo was a multistage ritual that could extend over many years. This association with smithing tools did not mean that the leader was himself a miner or smith. In fact, smiths were specifically excluded from that role. However, it does show an important relationship between priests and blacksmithing in that area. Oral traditions (Volavka 1998, 103) suggest that priests acting as symbolic smiths were the makers of leaders and that the Lusunsi shrine was the smithy where this took place.

Volavka also provides the first comprehensive account of the indigenous mining of both copper and lead in the Mindouli-Niari region of the lower

Congo basin. Her sources were primarily oral traditions, previously unpublished documents, and conventional histories (e.g., Monteiro 1875; Laman 1953–57) but were supplemented by extensive metallographic and trace-element analyses of provenienced objects from museum collections in order to trace trade patterns (Farquhar 1998; Franklin and Volavka 1998). Copper is known to have been an extremely important trade item among the various kingdoms of the lower Congo, and this study demonstrates that rather than the Teke and Kongo kingdoms themselves, it was local kin groups that controlled access to the Niari mines. Copper mineralization is widespread in the lower Congo, and by the turn of the century French explorers had noted over 100 working mines. The composition of these ore bodies is highly variable, and as a result, both mining and smelting technologies had to be flexible. The few descriptions of mines indicate that most were open stopes. At Mindouli, informants reported "horizontal caves" and deep mining (Volavka 1998, 183). The mines at Boko Songo, one of the most important producers for the nineteenth-century trade of copper, are reported to have been 10 meters deep covering an area of 100 by 250 meters. At Bembe, which was abandoned by Africans in the mid-nineteenth century, small ancient pits were found extending 1.6 kilometers along the length of the outcrop. In many of these areas, the oxidation zone was contained in a clay matrix, so the mining process was somewhat different from the hard-rock mining necessary in other parts of Africa. The only tools employed were simple hoes, a special form of knife used to loosen the clay, and baskets to transport material out of the mine. The miner simply dug a small circular hole, usually no more than a few meters deep. Because the pits tended to fill with water during the rains, mining was restricted to the dry season.

Unfortunately, the smelting process employed on malachite is not well recorded, but smelting combining malachite and lead received greater attention (Laman 1953–57; Volavka 1998). This was a multistage process that required first the production of metallic lead from cerrusite. Volavka observed this process on two occasions. She describes a lead-smelting furnace as a circular structure constructed on sloping ground. At the base was an excavated depression, 40 centimeters deep and 50 centimeters in diameter, surrounded by walls made of termitaria, adding about 25 centimeters to the height of the furnace. A hole in the walls allowed penetration of a single tuyere connected to bellows, and a taphole and channel on the downslope side permitted molten lead and slag to flow from the base. The process had to be carried out in the open air because of the noxious fumes it produced.

Copper production was a late-dry-season activity but could carry over into the early rains because the furnace was built in a shelter. Once the lead was obtained, an open a hearth with a semicircular back wall pierced by either one or two bellows was constructed with a crucible at the base. Lead was first melted in the crucible, and malachite gravel was added to the molten metal. The initial alloy created was light colored, resembling tin. This material was smelted a second time with a much larger charge of malachite. The metal was poured into clay or sand molds, producing cylindrical bar ingots. These brass bars were then roasted either on a porous stone or in a perforated crucible to release most of the lead. Local metallurgists were apparently very adept at controlling the lead content of their ingots and adjusted the quality of the metal depending on the supply of ore, the overall demand for metal, and indigenous cultural preferences for color and mechanical properties as well as the requirements of the export trade. Volavka notes that foreign traders were well aware of the variety of alloys produced by Africans, and seventeenth-century Dutch traders are recorded as complaining about being sold adulterated (leaded) copper (Volavka 1998, 191).

Transformation of copper was the job of smiths, not smelters, and smiths appear to have done little casting. Wire drawing was not practiced. Annealing was employed to make the copper sheet and strip wire that were used to decorate objects. The technical quality of hammer work was extremely high. The rectangular cross-section strip used to weave the Ngoyo cap/crown was precisely uniform in width over considerable lengths (Volavka 1998, 235–237).

One of the most interesting aspects of the Volavka study is the extensive information on the social context and symbolic meaning of copper mining, smelting, and smithing (Volavka 1998, 193–210, 218–222). Copper smelting was the exclusive domain of certain privileged kin groups, although mining could be done by both men and women of all social strata. The metallurgists and smiths were separate groups, with the latter having to obtain copper and lead through trade. Only men smelted copper and were a professional class (along with weavers) of freemen in an area where slavery was common. These men received payment from other kin groups to produce both copper and lead. The metal produced was shared by those who participated in the mining. Ingots, however, were highly prestigious and belonged only to the smelting kin group. Their distribution and introduction into trading networks was controlled by the group chief. These chiefs, as well as the rulers of the lower Congo states, took care to protect their mines. As early as 1536, attempts by the Portuguese and later the Dutch to visit the mines were deliberately rebuffed. As one, if not the most important, unifying element of the Kongo states, local kings had to carefully balance the benefits gained from the external trade in copper against the growing danger that foreign knowledge of the mines invited invasion. At times, Africans even ceased mining to prevent their discovery. Underlining the importance of the mines to the indigenous states, their conquest by Europeans was a major turning point in the collapse of the Kongo kingdoms. However, it must be remembered that the kings themselves did not own the mines, which always remained under the control of descent groups.

In the indigenous economy of the Kongo kingdoms, copper ingots did not serve as an all-purpose currency, that role being occupied by *oliva* shells. Currency ingots were present in many areas, but they did not have universal circulation. Their use was closely linked to the kinship system, and they were employed primarily in social or extremely high cost transactions, such as the purchase of a slave. Copper or copper alloy currency ingots included small, straight cylindrical bars (*mafeeki*) measuring 6 centimeters. in length and with a diameter of about 1 centimeter. Other forms of currency were open and closed rings (*milunga)* made of both pure and leaded copper cast in an open mold. A less well known form of copper currency was the *milàmbula* bar, which was made by annealing and hammering rather than casting and featured tapered ends with a rectangular cross section and an oval cross section in the middle. These appear to have been specifically employed as heirlooms kept with a kin groups treasures. This special purpose is further emphasized by the fact that these bars were not of a standard size. Lead ingots (*yéla*) were also in circulation. They were spherical, hemispherical, or smaller segments of spheres in form and came in standard three sizes. Iron currency was primarily in the form of iron hoe blades, but in some cases iron bars were used to make marriage and tribute payments. Imported European metal in the form of U-shaped strips of brass as well as the well-known brass *manillas* became a common medium of exchange from the mid-nineteenth century both in Kongo and in related kingdoms and farther inland along the Congo River. Some of the copper from the Niari plateau was apparently traded to the coast, recast into *manillas,* and traded back into the interior. Leaded copper was also traded along the coast, although there is no evidence linking it directly to the West African brass sculptures (Volavka 1998, 213–222), the metal for which may have been derived from both European and indigenous sources (Chikwendu and Umeji 1979; Chikwendu et al. 1989).

In the Kongo area, ingots were traded in formal, scheduled markets. These were often located near the original source of the metal. The Boko Songo market, for example, operated one day a week, and probably only during the early rains, when ingots were actually being made. In the Kongo kingdoms, trade contacts were regulated, and these markets were not open to all potential customers. In markets linked to the coast, copper and lead were exchanged for European goods, salt, and cloth. The common characteristic of these markets was that they were clearly special purpose and dealt with symbolically important, rare, or imported merchandise rather than mundane subsistence items. Smiths were often the purchasers of metal in these markets and became wealthy from transforming it into needed objects (Volavka 1998, 217–220).

Kansanshi Mine, Zambia

Because of modern mining, by the 1970s the only intact large ancient copper mine in Central Africa was Kansanshi in Zambia. This site was first inspected by J. D. Clark (1957) and briefly excavated in 1967 by Phillipson, who obtained an essentially modern radiocarbon date of A.D. 1870 ± 85 for charcoal found in the mine itself (1968a, 1970). Kansanshi was the subject of a more comprehensive archaeological study by the author in 1971–72 (Bisson 1976), shortly before it too was totally destroyed by open-cast development. This was followed by brief rescue excavations near the mine in 1978 (Bisson and Robertson 1979).

Kansanshi Hill was located 11 kilometers north of the Northwestern provincial capital of Solwezi. It was a roughly circular quartzite outcrop measuring roughly 320 meters in diameter and 34 meters in height. Four steeply inclined vein systems containing abundant malachite and chrysocolla crossed the hill in a north–south orientation. Ancient mining of these veins created deep trenches, the largest of which extended over 380 meters (Fig. 2.18). At the base of the hill, this vein was over 10 meters wide, but near its northern end it narrowed to an average of only 45 centimeters in width with a minimum of only 27 centimeters The maximum depth of the ancient quarrying could not be determined because centuries of weathering and some intentional backfilling during the mining process had partially refilled the trenches, but recent underground work intersected African excavations as deep as 30 meters below surface. A 5-meter portion of the narrow working was excavated (Plate 2.2) to a depth of 9.15 meters below the surface, where the vein became so narrow that it was impossible to continue following the ancient excavation. The undisturbed rubble filling the mine consisted of quartz tailings from the vein and slabs of the quartzite country rock that had been dislodged during the mining process. Charcoal and wood fragments yielded calibrated radiocarbon dates from the fifteenth through the early seventeenth century (Table 2.1) for the conclusion of mining in this particular part of the hill. No diagnostic artifacts that could identify the ancient miners were found in the excavation.

Kansanshi miners concentrated their activities on only the highest-grade ore and, unless it was absolutely necessary to expose a vein, left the extremely hard surrounding quartzite in place. Iron gads, one of which was discovered in the smelting area, were used to chop away the vein, probably starting on the downslope end of the exposure and initially working back into the hillside with an L-shaped cutting (Phillipson 1968a). To access deeper deposits, the cuttings were angled downward, and ramps were constructed using tailings. At the base of the hill, this pattern had to be modified by topographic circumstances because miners could not take advantage of the hill slope to gain depth quickly. Thus, they resorted to simple V-shaped quarries that followed the vein, and iron wedges were used to break the surrounding quartzite along natural cleavage planes. No evidence of fire setting was found. Preliminary concentration of ore took place beside the pit, probably by pounding it with iron and stone hammers. This created tailings that

Figure 2.18 Map of Kansanshi Hill showing location and scale of ancient workings (contour interval is 2 meters)

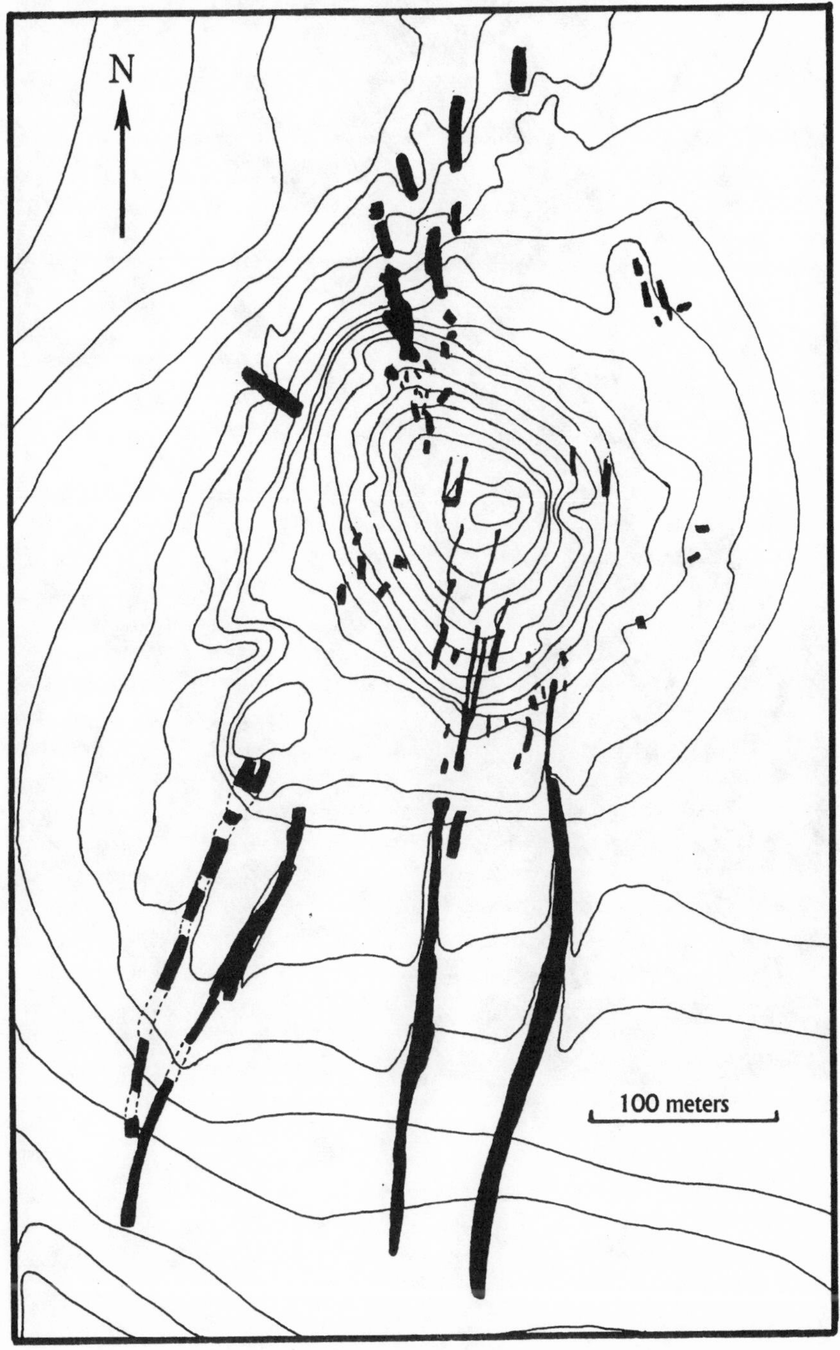

Plate 2.2 Kansanshi Mine, Zambia. High-grade oxidized ore has been removed, leaving the surrounding rock in place.

Table 2.1. Radiocarbon dates from Kansanshi mine and smelting area

Component	*Calibrated Date*	*Lab Number*	*Source*
	A.D. 1610 ± 150	RL1392	Component A, smelting furnace
LIA Phase II	A.D. 1515–1605 ± 85	N1281	Kansanshi mine
	A.D. 1460–1500 ± 85	N1282	Kansanshi mine
	A.D. 1420 ± 75	N1441	Component A, smelting furnace
	A.D. 1135 ± 90	N1606	Kansanshi West village site
LIA Phase I	A.D. 1110 ± 110	RL1393	Kansanshi West village site
	A.D. 1065 ± 60	N1434	Kansanshi West village site
	A.D. 1375 ± 75	N1440	Component B (contaminated?)
	A.D. 860 ± 120	RL1394	Component B
EIA Phase II	A.D. 770–790 ± 90	N1284	Component B
	A.D. 730 ± 90	N1607	Component B
	A.D. 710 ± 110	RL1389	Component C (refuse pit)
	A.D. 700 ± 110	RL1390	Component C (refuse pit)
EIA Phase I	A.D. 650 ± 85	N1283	Component C
	A.D. 480 ± 120	RL1391	Component C
	A.D. 440 ± 90	N1286	Refuse pit with copper slag
	B.C 440–460 ± 90	N1285	Component B (subsoil interface)

consisted of very small fragments of quartz as well as many tiny pieces of malachite that were lost during the process. The gender makeup of the miners could not be determined, but children must have been employed to excavate some of the narrowest portions on the hill.

Concentrated ore was carried to the banks of the nearest perennial water source, a dambo that was located 1 kilometer west of the hill where it was smelted. No other evidence of smelting was found within 10 kilometers of the mine. The smelting area (Fig. 2.19) measures 600 by 250 meters and is covered with a continuous blanket of copper slag, fragments of smelting furnaces, ore chips, and broken pottery. A stratified random sampling excavation strategy was employed to investigate this large area, with larger non-randomly placed excavations opened to uncover significant features. In addition to the smelting site, two Iron Age village sites were also encountered and excavated (Bisson 1976).

The smelting area was a multicomponent site with a relatively simple stratigraphy. The uppermost component was a dark black layer of densely packed smelting debris. The greatest depth of this stratum is 32 centimeters. It is thickest along the dambo and gradually decreases toward the other margins of the site. Two spatially separate components were found underneath this layer. One was a sparse scatter of smelting debris and pottery in the central area of the site, and another was a small hamlet, including remains of a few pole and mud houses, at the southern end of the site. The village site on the west side of the dambo had no concentrations of smelting debris.

Plate 2.3 Kaonde refining furnace in operation, Northwestern Zambia, 1972

Figure 2.19 Kansanshi melting area showing the location of components and excavations (Bisson 1976). Size of excavations not to scale.

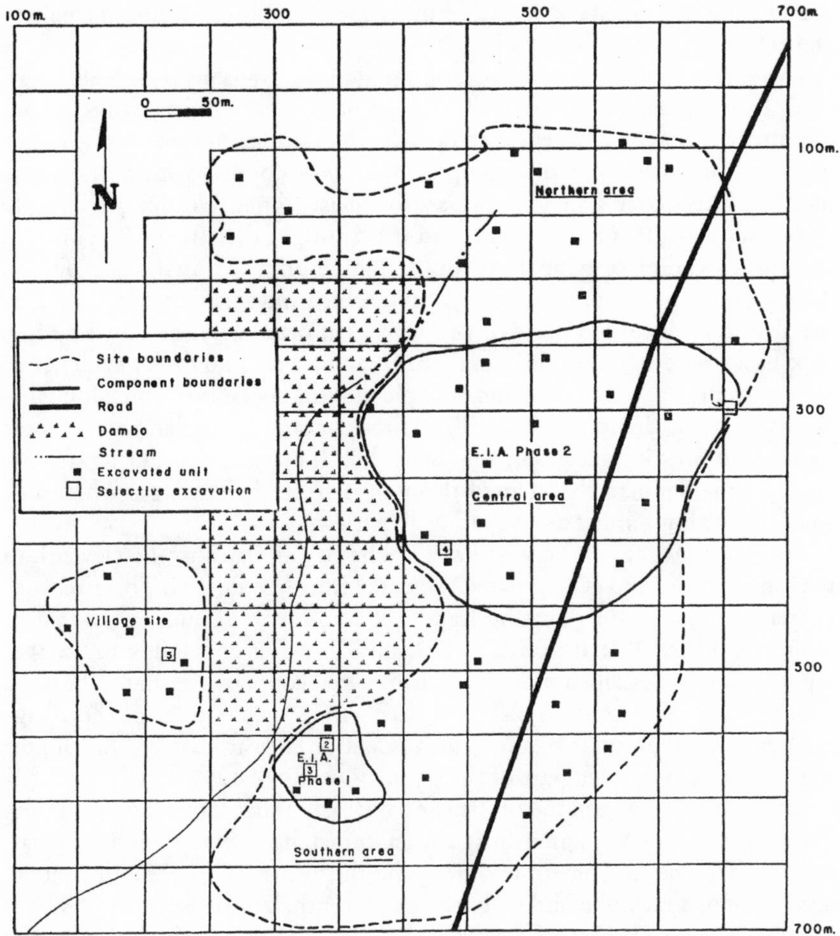

These four components range in radiocarbon age from perhaps the fourth to the eighteenth century. The earliest, designated the Kansanshi Early Iron Age (EIA) Phase I, is the hamlet at the southern end of the site. Although the ceramics from this component are relatively homogeneous in design, the spread of radiocarbon dates (Table 2.1) suggests that it may represent two occupation events: one in the fifth century and another sometime between the seventh and the early ninth century. An ancient pit feature containing fragments of a large crucible and 49.6 kilograms of copper slag dating to A.D. 440 ± 90 is associated with this component. No smelting furnace bases could be assigned to the EIA Phase I. Although the use of separate smelting and refining furnaces cannot be discounted, it is possible that a crucible surrounded by walls made of carved termitaria was employed for both smelting and refining during this period.

The second-oldest assemblage, designated the Kansanshi EIA Phase II, dates from the eighth to the early tenth century and consists of the scatter of pottery from 20 to 40 centimeters in depth in the central area of the smelting site. Ceramics from this component were decorated with a distinctive motif of interwoven bangle impressed or incised lines. No hut remains are associated with this component, and it is thought that the pots represent temporary camps of people visiting the mine on a seasonal basis. This is demonstrated by the presence of malachite chips and small quantities of copper slag in undisturbed parts of this layer. Unfortunately, no smelting furnace bases were found in this component, and there is no direct evidence of the use of pots as crucibles. These people did not necessarily come long distances to work the mine. Two village sites containing similar pottery were located within 7 kilometers of Kansanshi hill. It appears that during this period, people deliberately isolated themselves from their villages when they were engaged in mining and smelting activities.

The small village on the west bank of the stream dates to the eleventh to twelfth centuries and is designated the Later Iron Age Phase I. This site, with pottery similar to the contemporary collection from Kamusongolwa, Kasempa (Daniels 1967), included a blacksmith's shelter containing the copper ingot fragment described previously, hammered copper wire, and unfinished iron artifacts. The location of this shelter within the confines of the village boundaries corresponds to the general Central African pattern that smiths were not a marginalized part of the population (de Maret 1980).

After a break between the twelfth and the early thirteenth century, mining abruptly resumed at Kansanshi at a level unmatched by any previous occupations. This began sometime during the thirteenth or fourteenth century and continued until the middle of the seventeenth. The dense layer of smelting debris, designated the Later Iron Age Phase II, is a limited activity site containing little pottery, most of which resembled modern Kaonde designs. The seventeenth-century termination date of large-scale mining is in agreement with statements made by Kaonde elders, who indicated that only small-scale exploitation had been taking place at Kansanshi for about the past 200 years because surface deposits of malachite had been exhausted. By the nineteenth century, the only ore that could be collected was from the tailings of the ancient pits rather than exposures of in situ veins.

Two types of smelters were employed during this period at Kansanshi. One type was restricted to the central area of the site. These furnaces had molded clay bases and may have operated by natural draught. Using white clay obtained from the dambo, a circular, flat-bottomed floor was prepared in a shallow depression in the soil. Walls of unknown height and diameter were constructed from puddled dambo clay, with a series of holes at the bottom through which molded clay tuyeres were passed. A few termitaria fragments were also used in wall construction, probably as lintels for the tuyere openings. These furnaces could not be tapped and so had to be destroyed after each use. A mixture of copper and slag adhered to the floor, requiring it to be pried out of the ground and hammered to free the metal.

The second type of smelting furnace was also a nontapping design that appears to have been almost identical to the smelters employed by the Sanga and Yeke as described by de Hemptinne (1926) as well as the Kaonde (Bisson 1976; Miller 1994). These did not include large numbers of clay tuyeres and must have been operated by forced draught. They were constructed on flat ground and differed in design from the natural draught smelters in that the floor was a shallow (nearly 15 centimeters deep), circular depression made in the soil with a diameter averaging 60 centimeters. This depression was carefully packed with a layer of fine wood ash to prevent the metal from mixing with soil. For this reason, the floor of the furnace did not have to be destroyed to extract the copper and slag, and it is likely that the same base was used repeatedly because pronounced soil discolorations show that they were exposed to prolonged high temperatures. Walls of these furnaces were made of puddled clay a minimum of 20 centimeters thick. The wall was pierced at the original ground level by two opposed openings, each about 10 to 15 centimeters wide. Like the natural draught furnaces, the walls had to be demolished to extract the mass of copper, which was hammered to remove any adhering slag. Despite the vast quantity of smelting debris, not a single ingot mold fragment was found in this component. Since the most common furnaces could not be tapped, it is unlikely that the *handa* form was being made at this site. Fragments of crucibles were present, but in a much lower frequency than would be expected. It appears that although some refining was being done at Kansanshi, most secondary working of copper, including both refining and the casting of ingots, was taking place elsewhere.

One important goal of the Kansanshi project was the estimation of the amount of copper actually produced by the ancient mine during the different periods of its exploitation. Most previous attempts at estimating production (Trevor 1912a, 1912b, 1930; Dart 1924; Walker 1925, 1927) relied on intuitive guesses of the volume and metal content of material removed from mines. Only de Hemptinne (1926, 401–402) based his estimates on personal observations of smelting and interviews with surviving miners. For all the mines in the Dikuluwe group, Chief Nkuba's Yeke village produced a total of about 110 "masses" of unrefined copper per campaign. With each "mass" weighing 35 kilograms, this yields a total of about 3.850 kilograms. Nkuba directed 20 campaigns during his life, accounting for a total of 77,000 kilograms of cop-

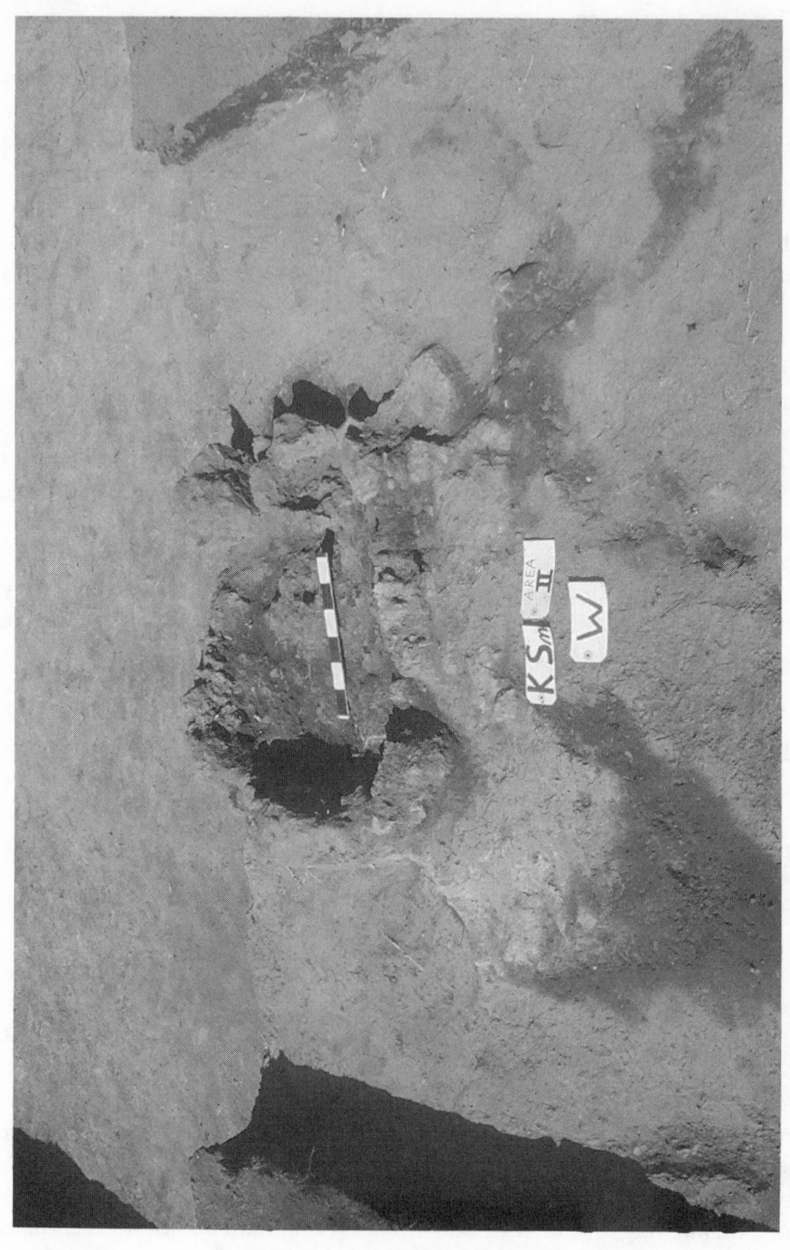

Plate 2.4 Excavated base of Later Iron Age smelting furnace, Kansanshi mine, Zambia

per. Because the Yeke area included six smelting villages like Nkuba's, this gave a total of 462,000, rounded to about 500 metric tons. An additional 200 metric tons were attributed to the Basanga, who lived in the same area. De Hemptinne thus estimated that the western and central Congolese mines produced a total of 700 metric tons of copper between 1850 and the arrival of Europeans.

A combination of experimental replication and sampling procedures was employed to estimate prehistoric production at Kansanshi (Bisson 1976). This method focused on the smelting area because it was the remains of actual metallurgical activity. Because slag is produced at a constant ratio to metal if all conditions of both ore and smelting technique remain the same, determination of the amount of slag in each component of the smelting site may be used to estimate copper output. To determine the ratio of slag to metal, experimental smelting operations were conducted in smaller replicas of the Kansanshi furnaces. In five trials, each beginning with 1 kilogram of malachite averaging 50 percent copper, a mass of metal was produced and separated from slag by hammering. The total amount of copper recovered (1,540 grams) represents only 62 percent of the available metal, a loss of 38 percent. De Hemptinne (1926, 392) observed similar losses of from 25 to 40 percent in the Yeke smelting process, probably caused by the absence of a flux. The five experiments yielded a copper-to-slag ratio of 1.09 to 1.

Estimation of the slag content of each component was accomplished by multiplying the total amount of slag recovered in a component by a conversion factor consisting of the ratio of actual slag per unit of sediment to the amount of slag per unit recovered in the excavations. The resulting number was divided by the total number of excavated units, and then multiplied by the total number of grid units (i.e., the area) of the component.

The conversion factor of excavated slag to actual slag content was necessary because hammering had reduced the slag to tiny fragments that fell through the screens. Fine screening of soil samples determined that the ratio of actual slag content to recovered was 2.44 to 1. Slag recovered from the Phase II component totaled 60.67 kilograms. The surface area of this component included 39,275 grid units, yielding an estimate of 129,333 kilograms with a confidence interval at the 95 percent probability level of ± 54,458 kg. For subsequent discussion, these figures are rounded to 130,000 ± 55,000 kilograms.

Modification of the estimation formula was necessary for the earliest iron-using phases because both the copper content and the total amount of slag were very low compared to the later stratum. The small quantity and uneven distribution of EIA slag forced the combination of data from both phases in the estimate. The total quantity of slag in the 13,750 grid units covering both EIA components was 37,889 kilograms, yielding an estimate (based on a copper-to-slag ratio of .72 to 1) of 27,280, rounded to 27,000 kilograms of copper. Given the great variance of the sample, computation of a confidence interval was useless.

These figures permitted estimation of annual copper production. For the LIA Phase II, the maximum difference between the range of radiocarbon dates at one standard deviation is 415 years, yielding a yearly average output of 313 ± 132 kg. If the difference between radiocarbon dates without standard deviations is used, the average output is 684 ± 289 kilograms. These figures are remarkably close to the annual production figures that can be extrapolated from de Hemptinne's (1926, 401–402) account of Dikuluwe mine. There, each campaign produced 45 masses of copper at 35 kilograms each, for a total of 1,575 kilograms. However, campaigns took place on average once every three years, so annual production figures were 525 kilograms. While this in itself does not prove the accuracy of the Kansanshi estimate, it does reduce the possibility that the experimental procedure was radically in error.

Average annual production during the EIA at Kansanshi was much lower. The greatest difference between the ranges of radiocarbon dates for both phases of this period is 630 years, yielding an annual production of 43 kilograms. If the 420 years separating the means of the earliest and latest radiocarbon dates is used, then the annual output is 64 kilograms. No attempts were made to estimate copper production during the LIA Phase I because no concentrations of smelting debris could be attributed to that period. Because a few copper artifacts were present in that period, it is likely that the low EIA production levels continued.

This history of copper production at Kansanshi, characterized by a long period of limited mining followed by an abrupt increase in metal output until all exploitable deposits were depleted, provides important clues to the development of sociopolitical complexity in that area. Like all other EIA occurrences in south-central Africa, there is no evidence for extremes of status differentiation or the production of surplus wealth in the first millennium. Copper was probably being distributed in small quantities through intervillage barter networks (Fagan 1969) and was not used as a currency. In northwestern Zambia, this situation appears to continue through the twelfth or thirteenth century (Bisson 1983). The abrupt rise in copper production may be correlated with the arrival of the Kaonde people into the area from the north, as is suggested by oral traditions (Melland 1923), but the archaeological record is not yet sufficiently clear to demonstrate that these events are contemporary.

The Kaonde are distinguished by their language. In the precolonial period, they did not form a single political entity but instead were governed by regional chiefs whose power and influence varied according to their individual personalities and ambition (Chibanza 1961). Thus, they were less politically centralized than the precolonial states (kingdoms) of the neighboring Lunda and Luba peoples of the upper Congo River drainage. Oral traditions state that during the reign of the southern Lunda paramount chief (*mwaant yaav*) Muteba, the Lunda regional chief Musokantanda established control over the Kaonde (Vansina 1966). The date that this occurred is unknown. It may have been accomplished militarily or by a deliberate decision by the Kaonde to form an alliance with their powerful northern neighbor. In either case, the result would have been the establishment of a tributary relationship in which some valued commodity would pass through a network of regional chiefs on up to the paramount. Interviews of elderly Kaonde village chiefs in 1971 confirmed that copper was among these commodities (Bisson 1976). Indeed, payment of tribute to paramount chiefs was "the outstanding characteristic of the Lunda empire" (Vansina 1966, 82).

It is likely that the explosion of mining activity at Kansanshi reflects the establishment of this tributary relationship as well as an increase in the number of status positions (village chiefs, territorial senior chiefs, officials in the paramounts court) requiring symbols such as copper to signify rank. The radiocarbon evidence that this took place as early as the fourteenth and certainly by the fifteenth century has important implications for our understanding of state formation in the Central African interior. This increase in output precedes the penetration of long-distance coastal trade networks into the area by at least one or two centuries (Bisson 1976), and although some Kansanshi copper may have been funneled into that trade, significant exports did not occur until the sixteenth and seventeenth centuries (Freeman-Grenville 1962; Birmingham 1966). If copper was not being exported, then it must have circulated internally, with the rise in production reflecting indigenous demand. This demand was apparently not local. The limited archaeological evidence that is available for the Iron Age of the Northwestern and Copperbelt provinces of Zambia shows no evidence of large settlements or the pronounced social hierarchies that would require as dramatic an increase in the production of a substance that circulated in the prestige sphere. Indeed, indigenous population density appears to have been low in this area because of the widely scattered nature of soils suitable for cultivation (Allan 1965). This was not the case to the north, where de Maret (1979) has noted the development of higher population densities and an associated rise in sociopolitical complexity as early as the late first millennium in the Lake Upemba basin. Kansanshi mine thus provides clear evidence of the expansion of the power of a centralized state that otherwise had what Connah (1987, 214) refers to as low "archaeological visibility" because it lacked permanent architectural remains. Without the evidence from copper, the extent and antiquity of these states might never be known.

3

Iron Metallurgy: Sociocultural Context

Philip de Barros

The advent of iron working was an important turning point in the history of the Old World, but nowhere was this more true than in sub-Saharan Africa. In much of Europe and Asia, Stone Age technology was gradually replaced by metal working focused first on copper and bronze and only later on iron. In sub-Saharan Africa, many stone-using cultures were brought directly into the "Metal Age," either by the adoption of iron-working (and copper-working) technology or by iron tools obtained through trade (Miller and van der Merwe 1994, 1). Scholars have suggested that this led to increased food production through more efficient bush clearance, weeding, and harvesting, causing higher population densities; larger and more stable village communities; increased specialization, trade, and social differentiation; and the appearance of a settlement hierarchy and more complex forms of political organization. A regional study of the Bassar iron-working industry of northern Togo has suggested that such demographic, social, and economic changes did in fact co-occur with the adoption and growth of iron metallurgy, though the degree of political centralization was often relatively modest, involving "big men" or small chiefdoms (de Barros 1985, 1986, 1988).

In other instances, the intensification of iron production is directly associated with the rise of a centralized state, such as the empire of Ghana (Haaland 1980; Togola 1993, 1996). Others have stressed the effects of the iron revolution on the African psyche and the difficult challenge posed by the integration of iron production into traditional society, suggesting that lineage stewards who exercised control over people would have resisted the development of a society based on control over production by a specialist class of ironworkers (Meillassoux 1978; Dupré 1981–82). The raw materials and technology of stone tool production could not be monopolized, whereas with iron working the production of key tools and weapons for food production, warfare, and the use of force was now in the hands of those privileged few who had access to the secrets of iron smelting and smithing and to its key resources: iron ores, clays for furnaces and tuyeres, and wood charcoal (Childs 1996, 311). This differential access to resources and the decline of particular industries resulting from the ecological devastation of eventual deforestation (Haaland 1980; Goucher 1981; Schmidt 1997) resulted in a complex and changing mosaic of iron-producing, -distributing, and -using societies. In this chapter, the impact of iron working on sub-Saharan African societies is examined in a variety of cultural contexts, including its place in myths of origin. Not surprisingly, much of the data comes from ethnographic and ethnoarchaeological studies, but archaeological contributions are increasingly important.

MYTHICAL ORIGINS

Nothing more dramatically illustrates iron metallurgy's impact than the important role that it plays in origin myths. A major theme portrays the ironworker or ironsmith as a divine hero who made civilization possible (de Heusch 1982; de Maret 1985b, 74–79; Dewey and Roberts 1993, 7). In the Dogon (Mali) creation myth, the ancestral blacksmith descends from heaven bringing the raw materials of civilization, that is, fire, iron, and seeds (Herbert 1993, 110). This primordial being (Nommo) "stole a piece of the sun, carrying it as a lump of red-hot iron down the rainbow to earth" (Dewey and Roberts 1993, 13). In the Mande creation myth, the blacksmith descends from the sky and brings fertilizing water to a parched land (Dieterlen 1957, 127). In Bushong (Democratic Republic of Congo) creation mythology, Woot is the creator, culture hero, and father of the first divine king. One of the riddles asked of novices during Bushong initiation rites is "Which hoes did Woot forge first?"; the answer, "The feet of men" (Vansina 1955, 140, 151). In Yatenga (Burkina Faso), the *forgeron* was linked to the origin of life. A song relates how the ironworker liberated men from their natural condition but could not eliminate death, how he made the axe for the creation of the village, and how he made the razor that cuts the umbilical cord (Samtouna 1990, 146). Among the Bassar (Togo), a common origins story portrays the blacksmith descending from the sky with his stone hammer and encountering humans living without farming and without iron tools; by teaching them iron working, he liberates them from their savage state (Martinelli 1982). The epic oral literature of the Mvet among the Pahouin (Beti, Bulu, and Fang) of southern Cameroon portrays humanity as emerging from the mother-stone (*Nana Ngawgaw*), souvenir of the cosmic stone responsible for the creation of the world. The creation of the world and of life is also represented by the forging stone or anvil (*Ngawg-Si,* or fundamental stone) genealogically linked to the mother-stone. Iron provided the basis for civilization by providing hoes and weapons, yet there was a struggle between those who wished to get rid of iron (as dangerous) and those who saw the folly of returning men to savagery (Essomba 1992b, 465–470, citing Nkolo Foe 1985, 22, 105). Much of the Mvet celebrates the superiority of those who have mastered iron metallurgy and portrays iron as a symbol of force, power, resistance, and immortality, qualities inculcated during Pahouin initiation rites (Essomba 1992b, 473–476).

According to Larick (1991, 310), blacksmiths "play seminal roles in the origin myths of the herding and foraging components" of the Maa-speaking Lokop of north-central Kenya. Many Central African royal dynasties are also linked to mythical blacksmiths: The founder of Rwandese kingship, Gihanga, was a hunter and a blacksmith, and the Luba founding myth also involves a hunter and smiths (de Heusch 1982, 193; de Maret 1985b, 78). In East Africa, the oral traditions of the Buhaya (Tanzania) present the earliest social and political leaders as the first ironworkers and ironsmiths figure prominently in the myths of origin of Buhaya kingship (Schmidt 1978, 1997). According to Schmidt (1997, 43), the mythology of the Bunyoro Kingdom of Uganda explains the origin of iron as follows:

> In those days Heaven was quite close to earth, it was propped up with a fig tree, a Kirikiti (Erythrina) pole and a bar of iron. When it had been made quite secure Ruhanga commanded Nkya to remain on earth, while he would go to heaven to see how things were going on there. . . .
>
> The bar of iron . . . is . . . a pillar that links heaven and earth. Ruhanga departed earth in order to escape the corruptions that this creation had caused. "So Ruhanga and Nkya left the earth and in order to prevent any intercourse between themselves and mankind, they loosened the props that held heaven to earth, so that it departed upward and the iron bar fell; breaking into pieces, it was scattered all over the world and provided man with tools and bracelets." (Fisher 1970, 70, 75)

Finally, the value of iron to early African farming societies has been reported archaeologically in southeast Africa, where caches containing unworked lumps of iron bloom along with forged iron tools have been found (Vogel 1972, 1975).

SOCIOECONOMIC CONTEXT OF IRON WORKING

The advent and integration of iron metallurgy into sub-Saharan African societies provided a major impetus for the development of specialization, trade, and social differentiation (de Barros 1988) and placed the iron worker at the nexus of the majority of socioeconomic circuits (de Maret 1985b, 76; van der

Merwe and Avery 1987, 150). It also made him a man of relative wealth (and often prestige) as iron tools became the center of economic, political, and often ritual life.

African ironworkers produced key tools for farming (various types of hoes, axes, and knives, as well as machetes, sickles, and metal-ended digging and walking sticks); for hunting and warfare, including cavalry paraphernalia (arrow- and spearheads, traps, knives, daggers, lances, swords, archers' finger guards, chain mail, bits, stirrups, spurs, and portions of saddles and eventually gun shot and guns); for fishing (harpoons and fishhooks); for the smelting and smithing of both copper and iron (picks, pokers, hammers, adzes, hammer-chisels, and tongs); for woodcarving, boat making, leather working, weaving, and potting (adzes, punches, boring and hollowing tools, chisels, knives, scrapers, pulleys, and blackening tools); for raffia-palm tapping (adzes and borers); for domestic uses (door locks, fire starters, needles, extracting pliers, knives, razors, tweezers, and spoons and ladles); for slaves (neck chains, chains, and leg irons); for ornamentation (bracelets, anklets, necklets, hairpins, rings, earrings, and beads); for music (gongs, bells, noisemakers, finger cymbals, chimes, flutes, and parts of thumb pianos); for royal regalia and prestige goods (double gongs, symbolically decorated iron staffs, long pipes and ceremonial hammers, anvils, and axes and spears); for currency and bridewealth (iron bars, iron hoes or hoe blades, and weapons rendered in symbolic shapes); for initiation ceremonies (circumcision knife); for private and public lighting (simple and complex lamps); and for locator bells for dogs, cows, and children and even for iron cache-sexes (Dewey and Roberts 1993, 14). Some of these objects were also used in religious ritual, and, of course, the blacksmith repaired most of these objects.

However, it was the production of the major implements of farming, hunting, and warfare that made the ironworker an indispensable and respected member of society. It was this economic power, along with the awesome magical power that enabled him to transform ore to metal, that was responsible for the frequently ambivalent social and political status of the ironworker in sub-Saharan African society (see this chapter's sections on political, religious, and social contexts).

The rise of iron metallurgy provided a powerful stimulus for the rise of social differentiation because of the specialization of labor that it frequently entails. Hunting and gathering and even simple horticulture do not require the relatively complex levels of organization of skilled and unskilled labor often needed for iron working, particularly iron smelting (de Maret 1980, 269; Haaland 1985, 50). While some societies or ethnic groups did not practice iron working—or smelted but did not smith or smithed but did not smelt, such as the pastoralists and foragers of southern Africa (Derricourt 1977), or served as itinerant ironworkers for many groups (de Maret 1980, 269)—and while smelting and smithing were sometimes performed by the same master ironworker and his family (Haaland 1985, 56; Killick 1990, 100; Buleli 1993, 475; Herbert 1993, 13), a great many societies subdivided iron working into a variety of specialist tasks (Roscoe 1923a; Pole 1974; Haaland 1985; de Barros 1986; Dugast 1986; van der Merwe and Avery 1987; Fowler 1990; Killick 1990; Sabi-Monra 1991; Essomba 1992b; Herbert 1993; Schmidt 1997). Smelting required the prospecting, mining, transport, and preparation of ores; the selection, preparation, and transport of wood charcoal fuel; the selection, extraction, transport, and preparation of the proper clays for the construction of furnaces, tuyeres, and pot bellows; the building of the furnace and the making of tuyeres and bellows; and the building of the foundry shelter and ancillary work areas, including the thatching of its roof; the loading and lighting of the furnace, the operation of bellows, the supervision of the smelt, and the extraction and shingling of the iron bloom. In addition, a number of rituals involving medicines (which had to be gathered), prayers, and sacrifices were necessary along the way to ensure a successful smelt; workers had to be provided food and water; and music, song, and dance sometimes accompanied the smelting process (Pole 1974, 34; McNaughton 1988; David et al. 1989, 195; Schmidt 1997, 218–223). After the smelt, the bloom was broken up, reworked, purified, and forged into tool preforms, a task done by the smelter in some societies and by the smith in others (Goucher 1984; Dugast 1986; Fowler 1990; Killick 1990). Forging (smithing) required charcoal preparation; the selection, transport, and installation of a large stone anvil; the making of the smith's stone and iron hammers and other tools; the building of a small bowl or crucible furnace for reworking the bloom; the making of bellows and tuyeres; the construction of the smithy shelter; and the actual forging of tools and rituals that accompanied some of these steps.

Smelting and smithing were performed by men. Women and children were often used for labor-intensive tasks not directly associated with actual iron working: mining, ore, charcoal, and clay preparation and transport; the construction of pot bellows and crucibles for bloomery refining; and provision of food and drink, including its transport to sometimes distant smelting camps (Herbert 1993, 27–30, 123). In rare instances, women were allowed to pump the bellows, as among the Kwanyama (Angola) and the Barongo (Tanzania), and Kwanyama women helped conduct the smelt as well (Estermann 1976, 148; Herbert 1993, 29, cited in Schmidt 1996b, 89–90). While many of the unskilled tasks were performed by extended family members, the primary smelting and smithing tasks required years of apprenticeship and could be done only by specialists. Some societies saw the rise of specialists in smelting, smithing, charcoal making, tuyere and bellows construction, furnace building, and even roof thatching. Sometimes such specialization was at the village level. In the case of western Bassar (Togo), smelters were concentrated in villages near the rich hematite deposits near Bandjeli, smithing villages were located near good-quality anvil stone to the south near Bitchabe, and the charcoal-making village of Dimuri was near extant forests still further south (Kuevi 1975; de Barros 1986, 150). Such specialization was not just confined to large-scale producers, such as the Bassar and the Babungo chiefdom of the Cameroon Grassfields; it also included smaller-scale producers, such as the Pahouin of southern Cameroon, the Bagham chiefdom of the Ndop Plain and the Bassar before 1000 (de Barros 1988; Fowler 1990, 20, n. 51; Essomba 1992b, 353, 355). Specialization was sometimes divided between different ethnic and regional groups, such as in the Mandara region of northern Cameroon, where many montagnard villages or groups with access to good ores, such as the Sukur, the Mabas, and several Mafa villages, specialized in smelting, whereas the Muslim Wandala smiths of the plains focused primarily on forging iron bloom obtained from the montagnards (David and Robertson 1996, 132–133). Finally, those smiths who specialized in the refining of bloomery iron usually produced the heavier tools, such as hoes, axes, bells, and the like, whereas those who forged tools from iron preforms made lighter items, such as knives and jewelry (Roscoe 1923a, 217–225; de Maret 1980, 269–270; Dupré 1981–82, 196; Dugast 1986). This division of labor was often ethnically based, as was the case in northern Togo, where the Bassar and Kabiye forged heavy tools, whereas their respective neighbors, the Kotokoli and Nawda, focused on lighter items (Dugast 1986; Hahn 1997, 75). The differences in the type of forging and tools produced are reflected in differences in tool assemblages and bellows type and in the organization of production (cooperative workshop for the former vs. dispersed individuals for the latter; Dugast 1986; Hahn 1997).

Some centers, such as Bassar and Babungo and the Yatenga region of Burkina Faso (Samtouna 1990), became large-scale producers for regional and long-distance trade. Intensive iron production in the Matomb–Babimbi areas west of Yaounde (Cameroon) is also associated with regional and long-distance trade between the interior and the Atlantic coast. The intensification of production was often accomplished by expanding the lineage labor pool using slaves and even nonkin freemen in exchange for access to the foundry or smithy (Martinelli 1982; de Barros 1985; Fowler 1990). The rise of regional and long-distance trading networks sometimes led to specialists in the trade of iron bloom and/or ironware. This included both local smiths who organized trading expeditions, as among the Bassar (Togo), as well as trading specialists or middlemen, such as the Wanga (Lake Victoria region). Several chiefdoms of the Ndop Plain (Cameroon Grassfields) specialized as middlemen in the transport of iron and iron products (and other craft and prestige goods) without performing iron working themselves (Martinelli 1982; de Barros 1986, 1988; Fowler 1990). The rise of such regional and long-distance trade inevitably helped to stimulate the rise of weekly markets that encouraged the surplus production and trade of other goods (Dupré 1981–82, 204).

There was considerable variability in the efficiency of iron production from one society or chiefdom to the next even within a relatively small region such as the Ndop Plain; for example, Babungo iron production was twice as efficient as Oku's devolved technology based on slag recycling and eight times more efficient than iron working in the Weh chiefdom (Fowler 1990, 219–222). Interestingly enough, it was 40 times more efficient than the Haya iron industry of Tanzania (Fowler 1990, 19–20). Strikingly, Babungo's efficient technology did not diffuse across political boundaries because its secrets were closely guarded and protected by the chief (*Fon*) and the ruling advisory council (*Tifwan*) composed primarily of the heads of smelting lineages (Fowler 1990; Rowlands and Warnier 1993; McIntosh 1994, 176–177).

Iron production was primarily a dry-season activity in most iron-working societies because farming activities were less intensive and because rain and flooding did not interfere with the preparation of charcoal, the collection and transport of ore, the lighting of the furnace, and movement of clients and specialist trading partners (Martinelli 1982; Haaland 1985; van der Merwe and Avery 1987; Sabi-Monra 1991; Essomba 1992b; Buleli 1993; Barndon 1996). However, in the Ndop Plain of the Cameroon Grassfields and among the Maa-speaking pastoral societies of northern Kenya, the rainy or wet season was the preferred period (Warnier 1975; Larick 1986; Fowler 1990), in part because of cooler temperatures. Whether iron working was a part-time or a full-time profession depended on a number of factors: the size of the society, the intensity or scale of iron production, and the land's ability to produce food needed by artisans (de Maret 1980, 270; de Barros 1988; Fowler 1990). Generally, most African ironworkers were part-time professionals who devoted some time either to farming, especially bush clearing and weeding, and/or to other artisanal and societal activities (McNaughton 1988). However, in societies focused on intensive, large-scale production, nearly all able-bodied freemen were involved in either smelting or smithing, and most if not all of the farming was done by the ironworkers' wives, children, and slaves (Klose 1964; de Barros 1988; Fowler 1990). In addition, some ethnic groups or clans, such as the Tegue (Congo) and the Hungana (Democratic Republic of Congo), were trader smiths and/or itinerant ironworkers who produced and sold their goods to a wide range of ethnic groups, sometimes on a full-time basis (de Maret 1980, 269–270). Itinerant ironworkers have also been documented in Nigeria (Neaher 1979) and Niger (Echard 1983) as noted in Childs and Killick (1993, 329). Blacksmiths living in major cities or towns in highly centralized polities, such as the Hawsa state of Kano, among the Nupe, in some of the Yoruba city-states, and in Benin (Nigeria), were often full-time specialists organized in guilds or guildlike professional groups and were under the control of the state ((Nadel 1942, 257–274; Dark 1973, 45; Jaggar 1973; Cohen 1987, 81–82; Lloyd 1988). In northern Cameroon, the Muslim Wandala smiths of the town of Manouatchi are organized in a guild governed by their own hereditary chief (David and Robertson 1996, 131–132). City ironworkers included additional trading specialists, such as commission agents and dealers in iron- and metalware (Jaggar 1973, 17).

In small-scale acephalous societies and in many societies organized in a "big man" system or as simple chiefdoms, iron production was generally under the control of family compound or lineage heads (Martinelli 1982; de Barros 1985, 1988; Essomba 1992b, 480–481). However, in relatively centralized polities (complex chiefdoms, kingdoms, and states) with a developed political economy, iron production and distribution inevitably fell under the control of the central power (de Maret 1980, 271; Haaland 1985, 64–67).

Regardless of his actual status in society (see the following discussion), the ironworker was generally well rewarded. A dramatic example comes from data on the Samia blacksmiths of Kenya who once could expect to receive a goat or a sack of grain for a single hoe, a bull for three hoes, or a heifer for six hoes; if traded to more distant areas, he might receive three goats for one hoe or a heifer for two hoes (Were 1972, cited in Coy 1982). The Songo (Democratic Republic of Congo) used to make three to six times more than the average earnings of others in their society during precolonial times (de Beaucorps 1951, 20, cited in de Maret 1980, 272; see also van Beek 1987, 30–31). In discussing Barongo iron working in northwestern Tanzania in the 1920s, Schmidt (1996b, 81-82) describes a smelter who carried fifteen hoes on his head to trade in Burundi, which was virtually deforested. He could obtain a cow for ten hoes, a bull for five, or a goat for one. At home, he could sell a goat for three hoes, turning a 200 percent profit for the trip.

Ironworkers and associated specialists (e.g., bellow and tuyere makers) working in their native communities generally received much of their pay in food, especially meat or livestock, but could also be paid in metal (bloom or preforms) or special-purpose monies (cowry shells or iron bars) and occasionally by labor in his fields (de Maret 1980, 271; Sabi-Monra 1991, 122, 175; Essomba 1992b, 449-455). In Malawi and Tanzania, he might also barter for such goods as local cotton cloth, arrow poisons, or salt (Killick 1990, 88; Barndon 1996, 62). In many areas, the client provided the ironworker with ore, bloom, and/or charcoal. In areas such as the Ndop Plain in the Cameroon Grassfields, where most societies were organized in chiefdoms and integrated into both regional and long-distance exchange networks, iron bloom or preforms might be traded for cowries, palm oil, salt, goats, hoes, camwood, cloth, guns and gunpowder, ivory, slaves, and high-value beads, with prestigious double gongs sold for slaves, elite cloth for chiefs, and the most highly valued beads (Fowler 1990, 260–261). In areas with well-developed trade circuits, prices were often determined by the law of supply and demand, but in many areas prices were set by tradition, for example, among the Nande in the eastern Democratic Republic of Congo (de Maret 1980,

272). In relatively uncentralized pastoral societies, such as the Endo of the Kenya Rift Valley, conditions of intense competition led to the development a guildlike professional group that sought to control prices and restrict competition (Coy 1982).

The wealth earned by clan, lineage, or compound heads was first used to purchase regional necessities, such as palm oil or salt. Additional sums could then be invested in one or more of the following: in bridewealth (cattle, cowry shells, hoes, and iron bars) for junior members, in the political sphere for fees for membership and rank (titles) in male associations, and in the purchase of slaves and freeborn dependent males for work in iron production and/or female slaves to expand the compound's food base through farming and the subsistence labor base through additional children, as was done in Babungo and Bassar. In societies such as Babungo, where smiths' access to political power was blocked by the hereditary dominance of the smelting lineages, wealth was converted into social prestige through public display during festivals, feasts, and funerals organized by private associations or clubs. Finally, wealth accumulated from regional trade could be used to acquire prestige goods through long-distance trade (Klose 1964, 162, 166, 177, 180–181; Martinelli 1982, 78–97; de Barros 1985; Fowler 1990, 6–7, 312–313; Sabi-Monra 1991, 168–175; Essomba 1992b, 455–458; Herbert 1993, 112–113, 122–124; Barndon 1996, 64). Among the patrilineal MaShona (Zimbabwe), the patrilocal residence rule was sometimes modified to fit periodic production needs:

> Prominent master smelters sought to expand their influence and industrial productivity through kin networks, specifically using their daughters to attract neighboring men of different clans as smelting apprentices. Once a man fulfilled his apprenticeship and, hopefully, married a daughter of the head smelter (who bore him many children), he either specialized in an aspect of the technology and stayed in the area or moved away to establish his own operations.
>
> When a master smelter achieved prominence and attained a large labor force, he became the political leader of a new village or, possibly, a small chiefdom. This achievement meant that he had created a political and economic power base through the control of kinship ties and the productive economy. By regulating the production of hoes, he controlled the agricultural and human reproductive potential of his people. (Childs 1991a, 351)

In short, a smelting or smithing clan, lineage, or compound head was often in a position to become a "big man" within his society. Here, the term "big man" is being used in a generic sense. The classical "big man" society of Papua New Guinea, as described by Strathern (1971) in *The Rope of Moka*, where big men seek and maintain prestige through competitive feasting and the giving away of pigs, is not typical of sub-Saharan Africa. Nonetheless, many African societies do encourage competition, which leads to differential access to prestige, economic wealth, and often political power. The ironworker, with his specialized knowledge and skills, was in the position to become wealthier than his non–ironworker counterparts, and those clans or lineages with access to the better ores and/or clays would be in an even better position to accumulate wealth (see also Schmidt 1997, 17–18).

This brings us to the interesting question posed by Dupré (1981–82) and Meillassoux (1978) regarding those societies that are unable to come to terms with the full integration of iron working into their society, particularly once it surpasses a certain production level and must be organized into specialist activities no longer under the full control of the *maîtres de la terre* (earth priests). The potential for increased production levels leading to export through trade, the concurrent development of a class of "big men" ironworkers, and ultimately the rise of a more centralized political authority seeking to control this production were resisted by some societies (Dupré 1981–82, 208). Metallurgy demanded a different economic organization than that which is compatible with a political and religious system under the control of the *maîtres de la terre* (Dupré 1981–82, 216). Some societies, such as the Tio and Tsaayi of the Téké (Congo), ultimately rejected iron production that went beyond bare subsistence needs. Dupré's view has strong echoes in the Pahouin epic oral literature of the Mvet, which speaks of the struggle between those who wished to get rid of iron (as dangerous) and those who saw the folly of returning men to savagery (Nkolo Foe 1985; Essomba 1992b).

Finally, it is important to note that if iron working first appeared in sub-Saharan Africa during the early first millennium B.C., it took a considerable length of time for the technology and utilitarian use of iron to become integrated into the various societies of the continent. As Holl (in this volume) observes, the adoption of iron technology may not necessarily have been the result of a conscious strategy to solve a particular societal problem, and its value may not have been viewed solely in terms of its "efficiency." As noted previously, some societies may have been threatened by the sociopolitical changes it might bring. Other societies were perhaps unable to participate in active iron working because of the lack of technological knowledge and/or adequate ores. Some societies, particularly foraging societies, may have had little to offer to trade for iron products. Finally, Atherton (1984, 251) has noted that the forest peoples of the West Atlantic region (e.g., Sierra Leone and Liberia) adopted iron technology in the eighth century; obtaining few iron items through trade, they barely used iron tools for subsistence activities. He notes Laing's (1825, 102–104) observation at the beginning of the nineteenth century that the Temne (Sierra Leone) used only wooden farming tools and that iron working was unknown in the region. Atherton (1984, 256-257) also notes that the Limba of northern Sierra Leone used few tools of iron other than the adze, which may have often been fabricated in dolerite or other stone. At least 20 types of traps were used by the Limba, but all were made of wood. Clearly, in such societies the cultural context of iron would have been relatively unimportant.

POLITICAL CONTEXT OF IRON WORKING

The conversion from stone to iron created the potential for centralized control of the production of tools used for surplus food production, warfare, and the use of political force. What was the relationship between the scale of iron production and the degree of political centralization? Did political centralization require centralized control of iron production? What was the relationship between kingship and iron working in both its political and its symbolic aspects?

The archaeological, historical, ethnohistorical, and ethnographic record suggests there was not a one-to-one relationship between the intensity of iron production and the degree of political centralization, nor did all centralized polities control their own iron production. The data from Bassar and the Cameroon Grassfields are illustrative. The Bassar region was one of the most important iron production centers in West Africa from the late sixteenth through the early twentieth century (de Barros 1986). While the archaeological record indicates increases in population density and site size and the appearance of a low-level settlement hierarchy (village and satellite hamlets), political centralization was probably no greater than that found in "big man" societies or those divided into major village chiefdoms. The Bassar chiefdom encountered at contact did not develop until the late 1700s, and it never ruled over the richest and most specialized iron production area along the Bandjeli–Bitchabe axis to the west. Moreover, there is little evidence that such political centralization was linked to the direct control of iron production and trade. Instead, it appears to have arisen to deal with the defensive needs and the huge influx of refugees resulting from constant slave raiding by the Dagomba and Tyokossi (de Barros 1985, 1986, 1988; Dugast 1988). Examples of this sometimes rather loose control of political leaders over metallurgy is illustrated by Bisson's observation (in this volume) that the territorial chiefs of the Yeke (Congo) and Kaonde (Zambia) did not have full control over access to copper-mining operations.

The Cameroon Grassfields contained numerous chiefdoms of all sizes and degrees of political centralization (Warnier 1975, 32; Fowler 1990). Babungo, which was the largest known iron producer of the late eighteenth through the early twentieth century in all of sub-Saharan Africa (Warnier and Fowler 1979; de Barros 1986), was a relatively small chiefdom of less than 3,000 people. Iron production was controlled by the chief (*Fon*) and his advisory council (*Tifwan*) dominated by the hereditary senior title-set of smelters

(*Voetughau*). The *Tifwan* with the *Fon* had direct economic power to manage the material resource base of the chiefdom by setting the conditions of trade, setting production goals, managing competition between smelting and smithing specialists, and fixing the prices of subsistence foods such as maize (Fowler 1990, 309). Babungo smiths had their own guildlike council (*Voetueyoe*) but had no political authority in the *Tifwan* and produced prestige goods (double gongs) for the *Fon* (Fowler 1990, 195–196). Though iron production was centrally controlled, Babungo was neither an autocratic nor an expansionist chiefdom and was dwarfed by much larger, expansionist chiefdoms, such as Bamum (60,000 people) and Bafut (Warnier 1975, 74; Fowler 1990, 324). Yet Bamum, for example, imported most of its iron from Babungo in exchange for slaves (Fowler 1990, 269). To the south, the chiefdoms of Bafanji and Bamenyam participated in a symbiotic trade relationship in which the former specialized in smelting and the latter in smithing (Fowler 1990, 326). To the west on the Bamenda plateau, palm oil–producing chiefdoms, such as Mankon, produced little or no iron and depended on the sale of palm oil to purchase iron from the Babungo and Oku chiefdoms (Fowler 1990, 262–269).

What is clear, however, is that an expansionist polity must directly control either iron production or access to that production if it is going to continue to expand and/or maintain its superiority. The archaeological and ethnohistorical record clearly shows that the central polities of Ghana (at Mema), Mali (at Niani), and Kongo (Mbanza Kongo) had important smelting centers adjacent to their capitals or royal palaces or otherwise had control over iron production (Haaland 1980, 1985, 70; Dupré 1981–82, 198–199; Filipowiak 1985, 36–49; Togola 1993, 1996). Herbert (1993, 145–146) notes that the Kuba dynasty asserted control over iron production and fought wars with the Luba kingdom over the excellent iron ores near the Mwabe River (Vansina 1978). Control over both iron ore deposits and the iron trade was critical to the political economy of the Luba kingdom, which had become a mature state by at least the eighteenth century (de Maret 1979; Reefe 1981, cited in Childs and Dewey 1996, 149). McNaughton (1988, 126), speaking of the Mande (Mali), notes that "four towns of weapon-making blacksmiths are said to have circled the Segou state's capital" and "fields of smelting furnaces are said to have marked the gathering places of Sunjata's and Sumanguru's armies before their final battles." The centralized polities and states of Kanem, Nupe, Benin (Nigeria), Ouahigouya (Burkina Faso), and Nikki (Benin) also exercised direct control over the production of tools for farming and warfare (Nadel 1942; Dark 1973; Killick 1990; Samtouna 1990; Conte 1991; Sabi-Monra 1991, 144). This control sometimes took the form of tribute paid by ironworkers to the royal chiefs, as was the case among the Fipa of Tanzania (Barndon 1996, 64).

Those larger, often expansionist polities that did not fully control their own iron production often sought to do so by guile or by force. The late nineteenth-century king of Bamum sent treasures in vain to the *Fon* of Babungo to learn their iron-smelting secrets in a desperate attempt to reduce Bamum's dependency on Babungo iron (Rein-Wührmann 1925, cited in Fowler 1990, 122). The Kongo kingdom, which had continual difficulty maintaining control over its iron-producing province of Nsundi, sought to diversify its sources of iron with the arrival of the Portuguese (Dupré 1981–82, 199). The Dagomba kingdom of Ghana tried various strategies to ensure access to Bassar iron production, including a symbiotic relationship in times of peace, intimidation through slave raiding and occasional demands of tribute, and finally a three-year siege of the Bassar chiefdom's capital in the 1870s (de Barros 1985). However, the conquest of iron-producing regions often had the opposite effect of that intended. When Bamum conquered several iron-producing groups, the ironworkers simply fled after defeat (Fowler 1990, 329). When the Dagomba besieged the Bassar agglomeration, many Bassar ironworkers fled, and others took refuge and survived by farming on top of Mount Bassar. With the death of the Dagomba king, Ya Na 'Abdullah, the Dagomba retreated (Cornevin 1962, 57), resulting in less control over Bassar iron working than before. When the Ngoni conquered the southern Tumbuka (Malawi), they allowed them to retain much of their social and political organization and iron trade networks and generally left them alone because they depended on their iron production (Killick 1990, 88). The Hawsa city-state of Kano exercised direct control over its blacksmiths but appears to have left alone the indigenous non-Muslim smelters (Magauzawa) that they formerly drove to the periphery of the state some 80 to 100 kilometers outside the city (Jaggar 1973; Darling 1983). Finally, David and Robertson (1996, 137–138) describe how the Wandala smiths of northern Cameroon had fled after the conversion of the Wandala elite to Islam but were persuaded to return by the sultan, Aji Bukar. However, they settled in Manaouatchi at a distance (12 kilometers) from the Wandala capital (Seignobos 1986, 34), reflecting the "tension between the Wandala state apparatus and the smiths . . . whose profession was profoundly embedded in an autochthonous ideology" (David and Robertson 1996, 138). Interestingly enough, Bisson (in this volume) states that it was also the local descent groups who exercised control over the copper mines in Niari (lower Congo River), not the Teke and Kongo kingdoms.

Some authors have emphasized the close but sometimes ambivalent ties between ironworkers and dynasts (chiefs and kings) throughout most of sub-Saharan Africa. These ties, which vary in their nature and symbolism, are due to the ironworker's very real economic power (Coy 1982; de Maret 1985b; Herbert 1993) and his perceived abilities as a sorcerer that allow him to manipulate the power or occult forces (*nyama* in Mande) that animates the universe, thus permitting him to transform ore into iron (and iron into tools) (McNaughton 1988, 15–21). The ironworker's economic and magical power thus poses a real challenge to would-be or existing hereditary dynasts. The elder ironworker controls the means of production of iron tools that are key to food production and warfare and may even subject a group to his curse and refuse to serve them (Coy 1982). He is perceived to possess supernatural or magical power that rivals that of the divine king who draws on the same force to ensure the fertility and well-being of his kingdom, and he has the potential to obtain considerable wealth through the sale of his products, using the proceeds to expand his economic power and prestige by investing in wives and even slaves (Coy 1982; Fowler 1990, 350; Killick 1990, 136–137; Vansina 1990, 60; Herbert 1993, 114). He is thus in a position to directly challenge both the secular and the spiritual authority of the king if he so chooses. As a result, the founding or expanding dynast must find a way to either subordinate the ironworker or enter into a symbiotic relationship with him.

In West Africa, close links or alliances between ironworkers and emerging dynasts is a common theme in pan-Mande oral traditions (McIntosh and McIntosh 1988, 151). Mande leaders over much of the Sudan historically retained ironworkers as advisers and interpreters, and kings whispered their decisions at the royal court to a blacksmith who then stated them to the assembled gathering (McNaughton 1988, 66). The legendary Sundjata Keita, the founder of the Malian state, arose from his crippled state by leaning on the iron staff that he ordered from a smith. Although the new king was not an ironworker, traditions speak of how he relied on them as his allies in the wars against the Sosso ruler, Sumanguru Kanté, who was both king and ironworker (Herbert 1993, 150–151). Traditions of actual smith–kings have been recorded from the Baguirmi kingdom (Chad) (Paques1967, 188-190, cited in Herbert 1993, 148), and Vaughan (1970, 87) reports that the ironworkers were instrumental in the founding of Gulagu and other royal clans of the Mandara Marghi. According to Talmari (1991, 230), some Malinke chiefs married an ironworker's daughter shortly after their rise to power (Doumbia 1936, 337) despite the fact that they are part of the endogamous artisan caste (Schaffer and Cooper 1987, 62; McNaughton 1988, 3–4). Similarly, the oral traditions of the Bariba chiefdom of Nikki (Benin) state that the foreign Wasagari (Mande) princes married daughters of indigenous ironworkers to help create powerful links of friendship (Lombard 1957, 16, cited in Sabi-Monra 1991, 135). Despite prescriptive endogamy for ironworkers, intermarriage with the king's clan was also permitted among the Ader Hawsa (Herbert 1993, 149), and Marghi kings (northeastern Nigeria) were required to marry a blacksmith's daughter despite a strong rule of endogamy (Vaughan 1970, 87). Herbert (1993, 149) believes that such marriages between emerging dynasts and their successors and the daughters of ironworkers reflect the latter's control of an indispensable technology and his membership in an indigenous group, as was true for the Bariba, Hawsa, and Marghi cases. As Talmari (1991, 239–240) has noted, while foreign dynasties may "deprive another of political and military power, it is generally believed that one may never dispossess a group of its religious or magical prerogatives," such as those associated with indigenous earth priests (*maîtres de la terre*) and ironworkers. Finally, in some cases ironworkers play an important role in the rituals of royal investiture: among the Dagomba aristocracy of Ouahigouya in Yatenga (Samtouna 1990, 154) and among the Marghi (Vaughan 1970, 87). Herbert (1984, 242) notes the important role that copper also plays in many investiture rituals because of its reddish color (like blood), its luminosity, and its sound in copper bells and rattles.

Throughout a vast portion of Central Africa (Congo basin and northern Angola) and the interlacustrine region of eastern Africa, centralized political authority was often well developed, kingship and smithing were hereditary (though not endogamous), and oral traditions speak frequently of the "smith–king" (de Maret 1980, 1985b; Herbert 1993, 132–134). Such smith–kings are known in the Tio and Loango (Congo), Kongo (Angola), Luba and Kuba (Democratic Republic of Congo), and Rwanda and Burundi kingdoms (de Maret 1985b, 73–74). Schmidt (1997, 33) notes that the first king of the Burundi dynasty is linked to the introduction of iron working (Célis and Nzikobanyanka 1976) and that the same is true of the Buganda kingdom. In some of these cases, chiefs state that they were once ironworkers, and in others ironworkers say that they were once chiefs because of their wealth (de Maret 1980, 268). In many cases, the link may be primarily symbolic (de Maret 1985b, 73), reflecting the fusion or alliance of kingship and iron working. Fallers (1965, 30–31) states that oral traditions relate how the Baisengobi or bushbuck people are descended from the Bunyoro king, who was a blacksmith by trade, and how they originated the ruling dynasties of numerous pastoral aristocratic states in East Africa (Coy 1982). The origin of *ntemi* chiefships throughout much of Tanzania is also linked to blacksmiths (Davidson 1969, 51; Coy 1982). In the highly centralized pastoral societies of the interlacustrine region of East Africa, the ancient farmers and ironworkers were dominated by intrusive pastoralists. These pastoral leaders maintained direct control over iron technology and developed oral traditions that state that their chief invented or brought metallurgy to the region; the development of metallurgy is similarly linked to royalty among the Kuba, Luba, and Kongo (de Maret 1980, 268; Herbert 1993, 145). The importance of iron production led the king to "assert his ultimate dominion over the smith and his ability to appropriate his power, both tangible and intangible" (Herbert 1993, 134). This subordination was symbolized by the use of the smith's hammer and anvil (and other iron weapons, bracelets, or bells) as royal regalia and by the important role that the smith often played in royal investiture and funerals/burials (de Maret 1985b, 79–86; Herbert 1993, 135–143;

Schmidt 1997, 33–43). De Maret (1985b, 84–86) has reported on several excavated royal burials from Central and East Africa that contained smithing tools (hammers, anvils, and so on). The only ruler in West Africa associated with the smith's hammer was the *oba* of Benin (Nigeria). Such rituals legitimized royal authority over indigenous metalworkers while acknowledging their "ancient claims to political and religious authority" (Herbert 1993, 138).

Childs and Dewey (1996, 147–148) discuss "iron axes of unusual shape and decoration that were . . . noticeably similar to recent Luba ceremonial axes" (de Maret 1979, 1985b, 1992) recovered in archaeological contexts dating as far back as the eighth and ninth centuries. The Luba ceremonial axes almost always occur in high-status burials (de Maret 1982), and lab analyses by Childs (1991b) indicate they were very well made. In general, the evidence suggests that such axes may have been linked to political power and prestige (Dewey and Childs 1996, 158). Today, among the Luba, utilitarian axes are common, but specially shaped ceremonial axes can be used only in certain political and religious contexts by certain groups: the Luba king, titled elders, and local chiefs who can carry them at all times as a symbol of royal ancestral power and social status; the spirit mediums (Bwana Vidye) as chiefs of the ancestral world only when in a trance communicating with spirits; and the leaders of the secret Bambudye society, guardians of the Luba political system's ideological secrets, who may carry the axes when they are dancing as they communicate with the ancestors (Childs and Dewey 1996, 159).

Shona ceremonial axes from the Zimbabwe kingdom have also been recovered dating back to the thirteenth and fourteenth centuries, at which time the "elite legitimized their power through extensive rituals and use of numerous symbols (including specially shaped axes and spears) directed to the ancestral spirits" (Garlake 1973, 1982; Huffman 1986; Childs and Dewey 1996, 150). Among the Shona today, axes are still kept and displayed as symbols of chiefly authority, but their religious function appears to be the most important (Childs and Dewey 1996, 159).

In Buhaya in northwestern Tanzania, centralized authority has long been symbolized by an iron spear and a chopping knife (*muhoro*), both of which are used in royal and clan headship investiture rituals (Schmidt 1997, 36). Schmidt (1978, 1983a, 1990, 1997; cf. O'Neill et al. 1988) discusses at some length how the Bahinda and Babito cattle-keeping dynasties gained political control over the Bahaya kingdoms of Kyamutwara and Kiziba near Lake Victoria near the end of the seventeenth century by legitimizing their position through the manipulation of myth, symbolism, and ritual. This was partly accomplished by seizing and then identifying with the most important sacred sites, especially those associated with iron working. For the Bahinda dynasty in the Kyamutwara kingdom, power over sacred symbolic space marked a major change in the political economy. It also led to the use of ancient history and the sacred symbols associated with iron production to make new histories that directly linked the new dynasty with the past, conferred legitimacy on the new rulers, and opened a new path for central taxation and direct management of iron production (Schmidt 1997, 21). The Bahinda and Babito clans were not ironworkers prior to the creation of their dynasties in Buhaya. However, once they were in power, new rituals were introduced during which Haya kings were symbolically transformed into blacksmiths during their investiture (Schmidt 1997, 33). Petro Nyarubamba, the king of Kianja (formerly part of the Kyamutwara kingdom), comments on his own coronation in the late 1950s:

> On the 4th day of my coronation, very early at six A.M. the smiths had started to forge iron. I entered the forge to join them as ritual requires. I beat the bellows and hammered the iron. The people outside cheered. I had become king of Kianja kingdom. I was iron. (P. Nyarubamba, June 29,1984, cited in Schmidt 1997, 33)

This symbiotic relationship between king and smith is also noted by the Bakuma clan head of Kiziba:

> In the old days when a new king was installed on the throne, one of the important rituals during the installation ceremonies was a visit by the new king to the newly built hut of the blacksmiths in the palace compound. Once the hut was completed, he would enter it, ritually take the sticks of the bellows in hand and pump the bellows for the forging fire. This indicated that smithing was something all men could do, even the king. The ritual also symbolized the special relationship that existed between the king and the iron workers. It is like a smith who brings his youngest male child to the forge and makes him operate the bellows. (Mutaihwa Lubelwa, Bakuma clan head, August 3, 1976, in Kigarama, Kiziba, cited in Schmidt 1997, 34)

While the ritual in the smithing hut acknowledges the power and importance of ironworkers in relationship to the throne, it is enacted within the palace grounds of the king or Mukama. It is the latter that signifies the real relationship between smith and king—"the subordination of the ironworkers to the Bahinda and Babito dynasties, who came to have the control over the resources used by ironworkers, the power to levy special taxes on iron production and the power to require smiths to perform annual service in the royal court" (Schmidt 1997, 34). In some instances, however, dynast and ironworker came to terms of mutual interdependence rather than subordination, as was the case with the Fipa (Tanzania) (Wise 1958, 233, cited in Herbert 1993, 147; Willis 1981, 150).

There is a natural symbolic link between kingship and iron working, as both king and ironworker are symbols of the fecundity and transforming ability of magical power (de Maret 1985b, 79). Both ironworker and king must control this power to bring the transformation of ore to iron and iron to tools and to ensure the fertility and well-being of the kingdom (Herbert 1993, 155). Moreover, the very investiture process represents the transformation of a simple individual into a divine king, a process analogous to the transformations wrought by the ironworker (de Maret 1985b, 82; Herbert 1993, 132, 135). Schmidt (1997, 33) believes that the emphasis on blacksmiths and smithing in these relationships is because smelting is too profoundly transformational, too secret, and too esoteric, whereas the more accessible and public nature of smithing allow its symbols to be more easily appropriated by non–iron-working dynasts. However, Schmidt (1997, 210–215) later argues that the Bahinda incorporation of the sacred Kaiija shrine associated with iron working within the royal palace grounds and the manipulation of ancient ritual and symbols have a broader meaning linked with the mystical and transformational nature of iron smelting as opposed to smithing.

RELIGIOUS AND SYMBOLIC CONTEXTS

Van der Merwe and Avery (1987, 143–144) summarize three universal aspects of traditional iron working in sub-Saharan Africa: Smelters must be technical experts and a variety of supernatural forces must be conciliated using magical practices; iron smelters, especially those in the chief supervisory role, have mastered both the technical and the magical and thus have special status, or, conversely, they may be avoided/casted (see the section "Social Status and Roles"); and smelting is accompanied by sexual symbolism and taboos. Scholars have viewed the magical aspect of iron working from three perspectives: magic as superstition without technical impact and/or as a ritual that helps to maintain a trade monopoly; magic as technology in its own right; and magic as an organizational frame of reference for the proper execution of the technological process (van der Merwe and Avery 1987, 144). Studies of the past two decades have emphasized the value of the second approach, but in two different ways. Those interested in an analytical (etic) assessment of the role of magic or ritual in the technical/scientific process of transforming ore to iron have concluded that it plays no scientific role; however, they recognize that African smelters believe that it is essential to the process and cannot do without it (van der Merwe and Avery 1987, 144). Those interested in native (emic) categories of thought emphasize that the African does not make such distinctions and that both the "technical" and the "magical" are indispensable parts of the technique of transforming ore to iron (Collett 1993, 499; Rowlands and Warnier 1993, 537; see also Gell 1988; Schmidt 1996a, 1996b, 1997).

In the former group, there are those who believe that African iron smelters see ritual, as opposed to technical procedures, as the key to success (Gardi 1969, 33; Avery et al. 1988, 262; Hahn 1997, 146). These same authors have often found African ironworkers to be reluctant to discuss or to appreciate the technical necessity of many of the smelting procedures, often stating that this was simply the way it is done: "*C'est comme ça!*" (Gardi 1969, 33, cited in Hahn 1997, 146ff). Speaking of Bassar ironworkers, Hahn (1997, 146) states,

> The master smelters do not know or understand the technical necessity of most of the steps involved in the preparation of steel. Only tradition, the repetition of what their fathers and grandfathers had done, leads them to respect the necessity of building furnaces as they have always been built. In short, the construction of a furnace as well as the smelting procedure itself was much more a matter of remembering how it had been done in the past than a matter of asking oneself, for example, why the tuyères must penetrate into the interior of the furnace and so on. In African societies little influenced by European thought, the learning of this process that we consider from a European perspective to be a technical procedure, is rarely done because of an immediate interest in technical matters. In most cases, from the perspective of the master smelters, it is the ritual aspects and sacred acts that determine success or failure.

This passage illustrates a certain ethnocentrism about the importance of technology and the European view of it (see also Schmidt 1997, 2–11). It also recognizes but misrepresents key differences in worldview between industrial and traditional societies, particularly differences in the attributes of causality. Western science or philosophical naturalism focuses on natural causes and effects and does not accept supernatural causes. Traditional folk science or prescientific (if that is the right word) thought accepts both supernatural and natural causes and does not see them as opposites. However, in terms of actual methods of problem solving, Hahn (and the authors he cites) suggest a dichotomy between traditional and modern science that was, until relatively recently, more apparent than real. Both traditional non-Western science and much of early European science were often more a matter of trial and error and experimentation, and success was not necessarily achieved with a full understanding of why it had in fact occurred. Schmidt (1997, 119) notes that an honest appraisal of the history of Western science would show that intuition, beliefs, and even superstitions played a role in what was often a haphazard approach to scientific discovery.

Schmidt's (1996a, 1996b, 1997) attempts to get the Barongo and Buhaya to recover and replicate their traditional smelting practices led him to the concept of "bricolage," which he borrowed from Levi-Strauss (1966, 19). Schmidt (1997, 105) observed that both the Barongo and the Buhaya smelters tackle and solve "formidable problems in ritual matters, materials failure and work organization" by experimenting with various combinations of ritual and technological solutions to achieve a successful smelt. He insists that traditional African problem solving uses both ritual and technological responses (1997, 110) and that attempts to etically separate the two domains have no meaning (1997, 119). He notes that when Haya smelts were unsuccessful, they emphasized the need for sexual abstinence and built a spirit hut for Irungu, but at the same time they changed the clay used for the tuyeres and decreased the furnace bowl size (1997, 110). He believes that technological experimentation and ritual bricolage cannot be separated (1997, 245). The former is legitimated by the latter, which in turn "opens space for technological experiment to find solutions."

Childs (1991a) and Barndon (1996) have emphasized the importance of the cultural association of technology and ritual in terms of the concept of technological style (after Lechtman 1977). Childs (1991a, 332) defines technological style as "the formal integration of the behaviors performed during the manufacture and use of material culture which, in its entirety, expresses social information." A technological style may include conscious attempts at innovation coupled with the perpetuation of certain traditions. The key is understanding how and why the behaviors interrelate and what is being communicated to whom, which requires investigating the environmental and technical constraints of the industry as well as the cosmological and ideological context for the interpretation of symbols (Lechtman 1977,14; Hodder 1982, 1986, cited in Childs 1991a, 337). Barndon (1996, 60) uses the same concept of "technological style" emphasizing an associational rather than a cause-and-effect relationship between symbolism and technology.

Killick's (1990, 126–139) work in central Malawi found four basic reasons that explained a failed smelt: (1) a technical error involving the use of improper ores, fuels, or clays or errors in the technical process, such as failing to keep tuyeres free of slag; (2) a failure to perform the proper sacrifices to conciliate and honor the ancestors (*mizimu*); (3) a failure to respect sexual taboos, especially regarding sexual abstinence and the presence of fertile and especially menstruating women; or (4) the smelt's being a victim of sorcery due to greed, envy, or spite. Sorcery was usually given as the explanation for the failed smelt when successful technical procedures had been faithfully followed and there were no known prohibitions or taboos that had been violated. The motives most frequently noted or suspected involved disputes over property and/or envy and jealousy of the ironworker's wealthy status. The sorcery succeeded in disrupting the smelt because the protective medicines placed in a pot below the furnace were not successful in warding off such evil (see also Fowler 1990, 22, 137–139, 158). This fear of sorcery led to considerable variation in furnace design, smelting procedure, and great variety in types of medicines used because smelters rarely communicated these differences to other smelters (Killick 1990, 133, 267; Sabi-Monra 1991, 79;

see also Fowler 1990; Childs 1991a, 353). Herbert (1993, 80–81) found that failed smelts were most commonly blamed on violations of sexual taboos, with sorcery close behind. Childs (1991a, 326–327) emphasizes that ancestral displeasure was the key and that one of the major explanations for failure was ancestral anger due to violations of sexual or marital rules.

The rituals and taboos associated with iron working vary considerably from culture to culture in type, frequency, and extent. Smelting is usually highly ritualized, whereas bloom refining and the act of forging tools are generally far less so (Fowler 1990, 197, 226; Killick 1990, 153; Herbert 1993, 98; but see Roscoe 1923a, 217–225). The following discussion of the extent and nature of these rituals is derived primarily from Herbert (1993, 55–116) and Schmidt (1996b, 1997). Medicines (vegetal and animal products) are viewed as indispensable throughout sub-Saharan Africa for the successful construction and operation of the smelting furnace and the smith's anvil (van der Merwe and Avery 1987; Fowler 1990; Killick 1990; see also McNaughton 1988, 42–43; Schmidt 1997). In much of Bantu (central, eastern, and southern) Africa, such medicines, sometimes placed in a pot, were buried in a hole or depression directly beneath the furnace (de Maret 1980; Fowler 1990, 222; Essomba 1992b, 361–364; de Maret and Thiry 1996, 34; Schmidt 1997; Schmidt and Mapunda 1997). Ethnographic evidence for such practices is known for the Barongo and Bahaya of northwestern Tanzania; the Pangwa of southern Tanzania, who placed the medicines in a pot; the Chulu and Phoka of Malawi; at Misungati in Burundi; in the Grassfields and Ndop Plain of southwestern Cameroon; and among the Beti and Fang of southern Cameroon, where pots were also used (Célis and Nzikobanyanka 1976; van der Merwe and Avery 1987; Fowler 1990; Essomba 1992b, 360; Rowlands and Warnier 1993; Schmidt 1996b, 92, 1997, 225–242). De Maret and Thiry (1996, 34) also note the presence of such a practice in Kivu (eastern Democratic Republic of Congo) and among the Cewa and Sukuma as well as the Fang of Gabon.

Archaeological evidence of such practices has been uncovered at the Moubiri site in the Congo (eleventh to fourteenth centuries) (Manima-Moubouha 1987); at the Mbam site north of Yaounde, Cameroon (eleventh to fifteenth centuries) (de Maret and Thiry 1996, 34); at the Pan-Nsas site southwest of Yaounde (fifteenth to seventeenth centuries), where a buried pot was discovered (Essomba 1992b, 1993); at a historic Isu furnace in the Cameroon Grassfields and in a pot at a pre-1830 Bakwang furnace near Babungo in the Ndop Plain (Rowlands and Warnier 1993; Schmidt 1997, 246–248); at a number of early metal-using sites from different time periods in the Buhaya region of northwestern Tanzania (Schmidt and Childs 1985; Schmidt 1997, 253–258); and at the sixth-century site of Kabuye II in Rwanda, where a buried pot was recovered at the base of the furnace (Van Noten 1983; Schmidt 1997, 261). Finally, and of particular interest, is the discovery of small pits at the bottom of some copper and iron furnaces in the In Gall–Teggida-n-Tesemt region of Niger that date between 1000 B.C. and A.D. 1000 (Holl, in this volume). If these pits were used for medicines, it would mark the first time that they have been associated with a non-Bantu area.

According to Schmidt (1997, 244–245), ethnographic evidence from the Barongo and the Buhaya demonstrates that the medicine pit ritual is associated with three potential purposes or meanings: to protect the smelt from witchcraft, malevolent ancestors, and other evil influences; to fertilize the furnace (womb) to ensure proper gestation; and/or to help the furnace produce a strong, heavy product. The use of whole pots in conjunction with these pits appears to have been associated primarily with fertility rituals, but among some groups such pots were directed primarily toward evil influences (Schmidt 1997, 246).

Elsewhere medicines are placed at the base of the furnace or incorporated within or applied to the structure, for example, among the Bassar in Togo (Goucher and Herbert 1996; Hahn 1997), among the Fipa (Barndon 1996, 66), and in central Malawi (Killick 1990, 132). They may also be used during other phases of the smelting process, for example, among the Ekonda of Democratic Republic of Congo. Prayers and/or sacrifices of animals (chickens, dog, and goat) may also be made to ancestral spirits or iron-working divinities to ensure success during the construction of the furnace and foundry, the emplacement of the anvil, the forging of the iron hammer, and the prospecting and storage of iron ore (Roscoe 1923a; Pole 1974; Killick 1990; Sabi-Monra 1991, 154–158; Essomba 1992b; Herbert 1993). In Bassar, a ritual is performed that focuses on the commercial success of the upcoming smelt, asking the ancestors to ensure that buyers come from far and wide (Goucher and Herbert 1996, 44-45; Hahn 1997, 28). Words (speech or songs), music, and dance also played a role in ensuring a smooth working operation by enhancing the morale of the participants and, more important, in helping to attract the beneficial spiritual forces that would ensure success (David et al. 1989, 195; Herbert 1993, 65–69). Schmidt (1997, 218–223) discusses the role of Buhaya iron-working songs at some length. The smelting songs are full of sexual metaphor relating to human reproduction, the female sexuality of the furnace, the phallic nature of the tuyeres, and the inseminating action of the bellows. Charcoal-making songs speak of the prosperity resulting from iron smelting. One song sung during the making of tuyeres expresses a number of related themes: "the wealth and agricultural plenty that arise from iron smelting, the fertility that ensues, [and] the reproduction of wealth and of society" (Schmidt 1997, 222).

Sometimes diviners were consulted prior to a smelt to determine whether it would be successful (Essomba 1992b, 477–478; Schmidt 1997, 76). At other times, diviners were consulted to determine why a smelt failed (Schmidt 1997, 90). In general, the medicines (along with sacrifices, prayers, music, and dance) were designed to prevent any evil spirits or living sorcerers from interfering with a successful smelt, to ensure that no taboos were violated, and to ensure the production of a high-quality bloom. Medicines were the key to success in smelting (Fowler 1990, 22; Killick 1990, 133–134; Herbert 1993, 71). Some cultures had specific deities or divinities linked to iron production, such as Mosani among the Bariba (Sabi-Monra 1991, 154–155), Ogun among the Yoruba, and Irungu in the Bacwezi pantheon of northwestern Tanzania, the god of the wilderness and the "patron of hunting and iron smelting" (Schmidt 1997, 92) who controls the resources for iron smelting, such as charcoal and iron ore.

Sexual taboos were also widespread. With few exceptions (Pole 1974, 32; David et al. 1989, 187–188; Kiriama 1993, 494–497), women were excluded from smelting and smithing rituals, and sexually active females were sometimes forbidden to touch the ore and charcoal that went into the furnace (Herbert 1993, 80). Women were often allowed to bring food and drink to the smelting camp, but postmenopausal women or young girls were preferable, as fertile, and particularly menstruating, women were considered especially dangerous to a smelt. Male sexual abstinence was almost universally required just prior to and especially during smelting operations and sometimes extended to all phases of smelting, including mining and charcoal preparation (Fowler 1990, 157; Herbert 1993, 80–81).

The explanation for these sexual taboos is to be seen in the nature of the smelting (and to a lesser extent smithing) process itself. The transformation of ore to bloom (and to a lesser extent of bloom to tool) is seen as requiring the control of powerful magical or occult forces (or *nyama*) that animate the universe and that are released in massive quantities during smelting (Kuper 1988, 496; McNaughton 1988, 15–21; Sterner and David 1991, 358–359). In Africa, sexual activity is often viewed as diminishing one's vital energies, or *nyama* (Cissé 1964; Herbert 1993, 178), and sexual prohibitions are associated with other important activities besides iron working (e.g., hunting, warfare, and boat building). Most African societies also make an explicit analogy between the smelting process and the procreative process leading to the birth of a child (Killick 1990; Herbert 1993; Barndon 1996; Childs and Dewey 1996, 153). The furnace (which may have female attributes, such as breasts) is the pregnant woman who, with the help of her smelter husband, will give birth to bloom (the fetus). Smelters must therefore abstain from sexual relations, or in effect they would be committing adultery, which could lead to a failed smelt. Female menstruation was viewed as particularly dangerous because it was viewed as a failed conception. Sexually active women represented a temptation for smelters to break their sexual taboos. This was often the primary reason why smelting camps were generally located at some distance from the village, though other reasons may be given by informants (e.g., fire safety, guarding technological secrets, and access to fuel and ore) (Killick

1990, 128). Goucher and Herbert (1996, 54) and Schmidt (1988, 1997, 217) have suggested that the enforcement of sexual taboos was an effective way for male ironworkers to retain control over the secrets of iron production and to keep them safe within their clan or lineage in the face of exogamous marriage practices. However, Schmidt (1996, 14) correctly notes that casted West African smelting groups have similar taboos yet practice endogamous marriage.

Not all African peoples described the furnace in terms of the procreative process (Killick 1990, 124), and some authors (McNaughton 1988; Fowler 1990, 344; Collett 1993, 504; Rowland and Warnier 1993, 164, 541; see also Leach 1976, 35, 82; de Maret 1980, 273) believe that both procreation and smelting fall under a broader transformational paradigm associated with generally irreversible activities that involve an ambiguous period during which one does not know exactly what is happening and that often require the control of occult forces, such as hunting (the killing of an animal), farming (the transformation of seeds to plants), circumcision (the transformation of child to adult), funerals (the transformation of person to ancestor), chiefly investiture (the transformation of an individual to a divine king), pot making (transformation of clay to pots), and rainmaking (de Maret 1985b; Herbert 1993). Bisson (in this volume) discusses a similar association between copper and the assumption of power (investiture) and the passage from life to death.

In two recent books, Schmidt (1996, 1997) has taken issue with the generalization that sexual taboos, particularly against menstruating women, were virtually universal in sub-Saharan Africa. Schmidt (1996a, 11–15) fears that Western bias regarding menstruation as representing filth and pollution and a tendency to focus on a sterility/fertility dichotomy (see also Herbert 1993, 85–86; Goucher and Herbert 1996, 54), along with biased and generally incomplete observations by colonial observers that often overemphasized reproductive rituals and taboos, may be obscuring and distorting the role of menstruation in many iron-working cultures (Schmidt 1996b, 121). He notes that the Njanja (MaShona) of Zimbabwe in the late nineteenth century frequently employed women in the smelting process (Schimmin 1893; Herbert 1993), that the Koni of the Ivory Coast had no rituals or taboos during smelting activities, and that the Busanga of northern Ghana also did not prohibit women's participation in iron working (Eckert 1974, 174; Pole 1975, 34; Herbert 1993, 124–125; Schmidt 1996b, 122). With specific regard to menstruation, Schmidt (1996b) describes the Barongo (Tanzania) smelting process at length and emphasizes that there is no taboo against menstruating women. The Barongo do not link menstruation with sterility and failed conception; rather, they see it as simply one part of the entire reproductive cycle "which cleanses the womb prior to fertility" (Schmidt 1997, 217). He notes that the ritual medicines placed in a pit in the furnace floor contain elements that are "symbolic of menstrual blood" and that the placement of sacrificial blood on the furnace itself "signifies the menstrual phase of reproduction" (Schmidt 1997, 217). The Barongo industrial intent is to induce slag to flow through the furnace as part of the smelting process (Schmidt 1996b, 120), and he believes that there is evidence "that running slags are represented as menses, [and] among the Ekondo of Democratic Republic of Congo, slag is compared to menses" (Schmidt 1996b, 121). He also cites the Chokwe of Angola, which, like the Barongo, appear not to have a menstruation taboo and involve the smelter's wife in furnace fertility rites (Martins 1966; Herbert 1993; Schmidt 1996, 97, 1997, 119–120). Schmidt's perspective is an important one insofar as it highlights variation in the types of sexual taboos and emphasizes the need to deconstruct colonial texts and to guard against Western biases.

Childs (1991a), Barndon (1996), Childs and Dewey (1996), and Schmidt (1996a, 1996b, 1997) also emphasize the need to see the various rituals associated with iron working in a broader social context. Many of these rituals are drawn from "myth, agricultural ritual, marriage ritual, general taboos, rainmaking, healing practices and oral traditions about legendary figures associated with ironworking" (Schmidt 1996a, 12). Among the Fipa, Barndon (1996, 66–68) links furnace fertility rituals and songs, sexual taboos, furnace decorations, the names of furnace parts such as tuyere inlets, and the production of iron bloom to Fipa wedding ceremonies and Fipa concepts of adultery and childbirth. If a woman is threatened with a miscarriage, the midwives will insist that she confess her adultery and name the father. In Fipa thought, illness that results from contact with adulterers is very dangerous and may lead to death (Barndon 1966, 68).

In discussing the rituals associated with Barongo smelting, Schmidt (1996, 95–97, 100–102) emphasizes how the meaning of these rituals can often be understood by examining broader cultural rituals of the Barongo and of nearby Bantu-speaking peoples. During the smelting process, the head smelter spat on a mixture of salt and a root dug up near the iron mines and shoved them into the end of a tuyere. This was done to improve the smelt's yield. Schmidt (1996, 102) discovered that a first menstruation rite of the Nyakusa (southern Tanzania) uses similar materials to symbolize the pain of intercourse and menstruation and to ease the pain of both (Wilson 1957, 87, 102). Similarly, the burial of a piece of bark symbolizing menstrual blood under the furnace hearth by the Barongo is echoed in another Nyakusa menstruation ritual. Here menstruation is described as "the molten iron is discharged, the blood for bearing children has come," and the accompanying beer preparation is done in honor of her "iron" (menstrual blood) (Wilson 1957, 104, cited in Schmidt 1996, 102–102). From the perspective of the social, economic, and political organization of African societies, Schmidt (1997, 229–230) concludes that beliefs associated with iron smelting help to preserve a sexual division of labor and specialist knowledge, to maintain the control of certain social groups over the iron-working industry, and to perpetuate symbolic systems that legitimize access to key resources and political power.

Childs (1991a, 348–350) and Childs and Dewey (1996, 153–154) illustrate how the metaphors of Shona (Zimbabwe) smelting relate to human reproduction, kinship and social structure, and the power of the ancestors, particularly the link between "the achieved fertility of the ancestral spirit and his ability to control the fertility and productivity of the land" (Childs 1991a, 350). Iron working produced hoes for agriculture and contributed to bridewealth for marriage transactions. It was thus seen as linked to success in human procreation and farming, both under the control of the ancestors (Childs 1991a, 350–351). In fact, rituals directed toward the ancestors to ensure a successful smelt are widespread in sub-Saharan Africa. (For the Bassar of Togo, see Goucher and Herbert 1996; Hahn 1997. For the Barongo, see Schmidt 1996, 80, 95. More generally, see Herbert 1993, 34–36.) Finally, Childs (1991a, 352) notes how the significance of social and fertility relationships pervades MaShona society and is dramatically demonstrated by the use of patterns of furnace design in other areas of material culture. Granaries, which contain the fruits of the soil, are decorated with breasts and parallel lines of scarification. Drums, which are viewed as a life force and a way to contact the world of the spirits, exhibit similar decorative patterns. In short, the political and economic success of the MaShona are directly tied "to control over fertility and production" (Childs 1991a, 352). Bisson (in this volume) notes some analogous trends with copper ingots and ceramic designs in Central Africa.

While smithing also involved the transformation of bloom or preforms to iron tools, it generally was subject to much less ritualization and use of medicines than smelting. Rituals (including sexual taboos) were limited primarily to the creation of a new forge, including the selection and installation of the anvil and the making of the iron hammer. Among the Buhaya, the center post of the forge, located near the anvil, was the place where sacred blood sacrifices to Irungu took place (Schmidt 1997, 198). Among the Kabiye blacksmiths in Tcharé (Togo), the first working of newly smelted iron is subject to ritual. A white guinea hen is sacrificed and its blood spread over the anvil; the clay wall that surrounds the smithy and the bellows and feathers are attached to all these items (Hahn 1997, 68). Some societies in central and eastern Africa excluded women from the forge, and some did not; in fact, some required sexual intercourse with the smith's wife as part of the ritual incorporation of the anvil and hammer into the smithy, welcoming it like a second bride.(Roscoe 1923a; de Maret 1985b, 80; Childs and Killick 1993, 327; Herbert 1993, 98–101). The prohibition of sexual relations prior or during smithing was not common, but menstruating women were still seen as dangerous. The lower degree of ritualization is probably due to several factors: the public nature of smithing as opposed to the secretive isolation of the smelting camp (McNaughton 1988, 17–18), the nature of the transformation being perceived as less dangerous in terms of forces that needed to be controlled and less technically demanding in terms of the complexity and ambiguity of the processes involved, and a smaller risk of failure (Herbert 1993, 115–116). Smiths were involved in societal rituals, but they were focused more on protecting the chiefdom or society from foreign witches that might extract life essences and harm fecundity (Fowler 1990, 197; Herbert 1993, 98).

While smithing was less ritualized than smelting, Dewey's (1985, 1986) research among the Shona (cited in Childs 1991a, 350) indicates the important influence of ancestors over smithing. Many Shona artisans stated that they obtained their knowledge of smithing from spirit-inspired dreams or spirit possession (Dewey 1986, 66). Childs and Dewey (1996) also show how the steps in the fabrication of a Luba weapon in the forge are a metaphor for "the growth and maturation of the individual members of society and . . . the reproduction of society in general" (154). In both Shona and Luba cultures, decorations on ceremonial axes associated with political investiture are named after the word for female scarification during rites of passage (Childs and Dewey 1996, 157).

Given the importance of magic and ritual in African iron working, some authors have questioned whether it did not impede technological progress. To the extent that smelters were secretive about their medicines and to the extent that chiefdoms were secretive about the techniques used by their smelters, new technologies were often slow to diffuse across political boundaries (McIntosh 1994, 176–177). However, the large-scale production of the Bassar and Babungo iron industries clearly shows that magic or ritual need not be serious impediments. In the Bassar case, much ritual remained despite increased iron production levels, which were made possible by the use of female, slave, and child labor in work not directly associated with smelting itself (Herbert 1993, 122–124; Goucher and Herbert 1996; Hahn 1997; 28–54). In the Babungo case, smelting rituals, medicines, and taboos were concentrated primarily in two individuals: the foundry owner (*Tunaa*), who possessed the secret mix of medicines, and the foundry supervisor (*Woeniibuu*), who was condemned to long periods of sexual abstinence (Fowler 1990, 151, 156–157). Except for the creation of the anvil and hammer, smithing in Babungo was relatively devoid of ritual and taboos (Fowler 1990, 187–188). The major thrust toward increased iron production was due to innovations in furnace type and fuel sources, the successful recruitment and integration of nonkin labor, and the rise of a complex division of labor in both the production and the distribution of iron and ironware (Fowler 1990, 344–347; see also Okafor 1993, 439). In the Babungo case, Herbert (1993, 122) suggests a direct cause-and-effect relationship between economies of scale and reduced ritual. However, Schmidt (1996, 16) notes that, like Babungo, the Barongo of Tanzania openly recruited iron-smelting apprentices, but there is no oral or written evidence to document such reduction in ritual in either case. Herbert (1993, 108) also suspects that prohibitions against sexual relations for blacksmiths were probably relaxed for full-time craftsmen. Finally, given stressful conditions, such as the threat of unpredictable attacks from slave-raiding populations or enemy powers, ironworkers may even move smelting operations near to villages or royal quarters despite the increased danger of violation of sexual taboos (de Barros 1985, 1988; see also Fowler 1990; Filipowiak 1985).

SOCIAL STATUS AND ROLES

The literature on the status of sub-Saharan African ironworkers has perhaps been overly focused on the concept of caste. This has resulted in numerous articles attempting to determine which societies have true artisan castes, including ironworkers. Much of the earlier literature focused on emic statements about craftsmen made by noncraftsmen, often resulting in a one-sided, distorted picture of "despised artisan castes" that often does not reflect the reality of daily social relationships (Richter 1980, 52; Coy 1982, n.d., 6, 29–30, McNaughton 1988, 8, Sterner and David 1991, 355). In the Indian Hindu model, a caste system consists of divinely approved, hereditary, endogamous occupational groups, protected by concepts of pollution (Todd 1977, 401). Tuden and Plotnicov (1970, 16) provide a similar definition but do not emphasize divine approval. Other criteria, such as residential isolation and caste ranking or hierarchy, are also relevant (see Richter 1980). Using the Indian model with its divine approval, only a few societies in southern Ethiopia and eastern Africa would appear to meet the criteria (Todd 1977, 1985). If divine approval is dropped but pollution concepts are retained, a greater number of societies would perhaps qualify: some in southern Ethiopia, some of the pastoral peoples of the East African grasslands and the Sudan, and some peoples of the Mandara Highlands of Nigeria/Cameroon (Cline 1937; Vaughan 1970; Todd 1977, 1985; Coy 1982; Galaty 1982; Larick 1986; Sterner and David 1991); however, the oft-described ironworking castes of the West African Sudan would not qualify because pollution concepts are basically absent (McNaughton 1988, 159–160). McNaughton (1988, 159), borrowing from Vaughan (1970) and Wright (1989), uses a minimalist definition of caste that will be used in the following discussion: "a specialized endogamous group socially differentiated by prescribed behavior and genealogically inherited professional capacities."

In the West Africa Sudan, among the nuclear Mande (e.g., Soninke, Bozo, Bambara, and Malinke), Tukulor, Wolof, Senufo, Dogon, Songhay, Minianka, and much of the Tuareg, Moorish, and Fulani populations, ironworkers belong to hereditary occupational groups that observe relatively strict rules of endogamy, are seen as a separate race or group, and generally live in their own village quarters or villages (Schaffer and Cooper 1987; McNaughton 1988; Talmari 1991). These authors disagree regarding issues of ranking and whether artisans farmed. Speaking of the Mande, McNaughton (1988, 159–160) argues that the old view that artisans (including ironworkers) are a "despised" caste is not accurate. Ironworkers, in particular, are held in awe because they are seen as sorcerers who possess magical powers (*nyama*), partially inherited from their ancestors, that allow them to transform ore to bloom and bloom to iron (McNaughton 1988, 12). This, along with the economic importance of the tools (hoes and weapons) that they produce, results in their being viewed with an ambivalent mixture of fear and respect by non-craftsmen castes (the noble caste of farmers and political leaders and the now-extinct slave caste). He believes that this ambivalent attitude toward ironworkers is analogous to a "joking relationship" and does not constitute ranking, particularly in the absence of an ideological justification and purity–pollution concepts. He notes that farmers often enjoy the company of smiths (McNaughton 1988, 10). Talmari (1991, 225, 230) argues that most West African social scientists believe that social hierarchies are present, and Schaffer and Cooper (1987, 62–64) tend to agree, but it is not clear whether the ironworkers' viewpoint is well represented in these studies. As for occupational roles, both Talmari (1991, 225) and Schaffer and Cooper (1987, 64) agree that artisans have always been allowed to farm, whereas McNaughton (1988, 4) says that they did not farm prior to the colonial period.

According to McNaughton (1988, 3, 15), today's blacksmiths (smelting is no longer practiced) go to great lengths to nourish a belief in their special powers by behaving dramatically, playing with fire in public festivals, showing fits of public ill-temper, and stressing that they are born with such power. This helps maintain their corporate identity and its associated trade monopoly. Furthermore, many Mande blacksmiths do far more than work with iron. As craftsmen, they also tend to monopolize woodcarving, including the sculpting of masks for secret societies. Their perceived magical and fecund transformative powers lead many to develop skills as doctors, priests, rainmakers, diviners, and amulet makers, and they exercise a total monopoly in the practice of male circumcision, marking the transformation of a child to an adult. They are also frequently called on to act as political and social intermediaries, and the smithy is a place of asylum (McNaugton 1988).

Richter's (1980) study of the Senufo of the Ivory Coast , however, suggests that considerable variation is present from one cultural region to the next. Because Senufo ironworkers once had immigrant status and because they are relatively few in number, they often violate emic rules of endogamy for economic and political advantage, sometimes becoming village chiefs (Richter

1980, 46, 49–52). Although artisans (*fijembele*) are emically seen as nonfarmers, most do farm, some exclusively so (Richter 1980, 40). Senufo *fijembele*, including ironworkers, use the threat of supernatural sanctions to prevent Senufo farmers (*senambele*) from entering their professions or even their work areas, thus maintaining their trading monopolies. While they make up a distinct social category, ironworkers clearly are not outcasts or of lower status (Richter 1980, 40).

South of the Sudan, in the coastal Guinean zone, ironworkers generally have high status, and castes are generally absent (Vaughan 1970, 62–67). Examples include the Bassar of Togo, the Kpelle of Liberia, the Bariba of Borgu (Benin), and the peoples of the Cameroon Grassfields (Lombard 1957; Klose 1964; Gibbs, 1988; Martinelli 1982; de Barros 1985; Fowler 1990; Sabi-Monra 1991; Rowlands and Warnier 1993). Among the Bassar (Klose 1964; Martinelli 1982), there were no rules of endogamy, and master ironworkers often became "big men" by using their wealth to purchase wives, cattle, and slaves. Bassar ironworkers were highly respected and held in awe and even today are viewed as the most powerful sorcerers in all of Togo; yet, curiously, they do not serve as diviners, healers, mediators, gravediggers, or ritual leaders outside of iron working. While all Bassar families, regardless of occupational specialization, participated in farming, master ironworkers left the farming to their younger brothers, wives, and slaves. Among the Bariba of Benin, ironworkers readily took on nonsmith apprentices, and intermarriage between iron-working families was actually forbidden (Sabi-Monra 1991, 134–135). They had a privileged place in the social hierarchy with chiefly honors and were both feared and respected for their economic, technological, and supernatural power (Sabi-Monra 1991, 147–149). Occupational endogamy was only loosely practiced in the Cameroon Grassfields, as nonsmith apprenticeship was common (Fowler 1990; Rowlands and Warnier 1993).

The status of ironworkers in the Mandara Highlands of northeastern Nigeria and northwestern Cameroon varied considerably, including various caste arrangements and the absence of castes (Sterner and David 1991, 361–362). In the case of the Marghi of northeastern Nigeria, Vaughan (1970) notes that the nonfarming, endogamous artisan caste (*enkyagu*) includes smiths but not smelters. The relationship between Marghi farmers and smiths is marked by pollution concepts, and they do not eat together or share food. However, the *enkyagu* are not despised; rather, they are simply different and do not resent their status. The farmer/smith relationship is seen as symbiotic. The negative emic view of *enkyagu* by Marghi farmers creates a social distance that the *enkyagu* encourage to help maintain their corporate identity. Among the Mafa of northwestern Cameroon, the nonfarming, artisan class (*ngwazla*) bears a similar relationship to the farmer class (*vavay*); like Marghi *enkyagu*, Mafa *ngwazla* are viewed as "permissible deviants," people who neither farm nor go to war (Sterner and David 1991, 363). Sterner and David (1991) also argue that variations in gender relationships within Mandara Highland societies provide models for intercaste relations. As in the West African Sudan, both Marghi *enkyagu* and Mafa *ngwazla* perform a number of other important societal roles (funeral directors and gravediggers, diviners, doctors, and drummers), and the wives are generally potters (Vaughan 1970, 83–85; Sterner and David 1991, 357). Grave digging is seen as polluting among the Mafa but not among the Marghi. The political role of the Marghi *enkyagu* was discussed previously. In contrast to these casted iron-working groups, in the northern part of the Mandara Highlands, the Uldeme smiths (de Colombel 1986) and related montagnard groups are not casted. Although they belong to specific lineages, they are not subject to strict endogamous rules of marriage and do not usually perform the other important societal roles typical of the *enkyagu* and *ngwazla* (David and Robertson 1996, 130–131).

The casted status of blacksmiths in the eastern Sudan is summarized by Muhammed (1993, 461):

> Al-Tunisi (1845 and 1851) referred to blacksmiths in Darfur, Wadai and Bornu as a hereditary caste. He said they were dishonest and, living mostly confined to their own community, did not mix with non-smith members of society. No ordinary non-smith would make marital links with them and they were disliked by people in the region. Those of Darfur were traditional hunters who organized long-distance hunting groups for big game. . . .
>
> Nachtigal (1971) described smiths as despised groups confined to their caste in Bornu, Wadai and Darfur. He reported that smiths in Darfur and in Wadai were organized in 1873–4 under the Malik al-Hadaddin, minor officials who were responsible for all the smiths of these sultanates. They administered justice among them and collected taxes, in the form of iron tools.

This attitude of contempt toward blacksmiths may be due in part to an attitude of superiority on the part of the Muslim ruling hierarchy toward indigenous blacks (Browne 1799, 267, cited in Muhammed 1993, 461). To the extent that local rulers were also pastoralists, their general contempt of farming and iron-working populations may also have been a factor (see the following discussion of pastoralism).

In southern Ethiopia, research by Todd (1977, 1985) and Haaland (1985) indicates that ironworkers often belong to hereditary, strictly endogamous castes that may or may not be ranked or associated with concepts of pollution. Among the Gurage, who practice mixed farming, the Fuga blacksmiths are not permitted to own land, cultivate the staple food crop (*ensete*), or cross a field with *ensete* or cattle because it is feared that their powers of sorcery may damage the fertility of the soil, reduce the fecundity of the cattle, and change a cow's milk into blood or urine (Todd 1977, 402). Among the Dimi (Dime), who are slash-and-burn horticulturalists, the society is divided into seven divinely approved hereditary, endogamous castes, ranked along a purity–pollution continuum, much like in Hindu India, and ironworkers were considered polluted; they were therefore avoided and excluded from all farming rituals (Todd 1977, 404–410, 1985, 91).

De Maret (1980, 266) has observed that there are no true castes (professional, hierarchical endogamous groups) in Bantu central and eastern Africa. While ambivalence toward ironworkers is found to some degree all over Africa, Bantu ironworkers are generally highly regarded. In some cases, they are feared and honored (Kikuyu, Kamba, and Chaga of East Africa) or people are indifferent to them (Fang of Gabon); only Nilotic pastoral peoples (see the following discussion) have negative attitudes toward Bantu ironworkers (de Maret 1980, 267–268). While there are no strict rules of endogamy, ironworkers tend to come from iron-working families, and where iron working is strictly endogamous (among the Bira, Mbala, and Yaka), ironworkers are not distinct as a social group (de Maret 1980, 266). Generally, ironworkers are viewed primarily for their technological and magical prowess in producing and manipulating iron (de Maret 1985b, 77). As Childs (1991a, 338) notes, "This was a skill of creation and transformation which few people possessed and was eclipsed only by the reproductive powers of women." Some ironworkers act as dentists and as makers of wooden handles for tools and circumcisers, but they do not generally act as healers, diviners, and social intermediaries; wives are not necessarily potters, either (de Maret 1980, 266, 272). Most ironworkers are generally not part of professional associations, and most engage in farming. The role of smiths in royal investiture in parts of central and eastern Africa and in origin myths was discussed previously.

One interesting question related to the status and roles of ironworkers focuses on their wives. Throughout much of West Africa and in many parts of the rest of the continent, the wives of ironworkers are potters (McNaughton 1988; Sterner and David 1991). Even in areas where castes are not present, potters tend to be wives of ironworkers (Herbert 1993, 203). Why should this be so? Some possible answers suggest themselves. First, knowledge of clay deposits is important for both the ironworker and the potter. Clay is used to make tuyeres, portions of pot bellows, and the furnace itself (David et al. 1989; Sabri-Monra 1991, 80, 91–92). Both ironworker and potter share common knowledge not only about clays but also about the use of pyrotechnology to transform ore to bloom, bloom to iron tools, and clay to pots. Their principal work periods coincide during the dry season, facilitating their cooperation in work activities but often making it impossible to participate effectively in farming; in short, the scheduling of their work makes them a natural pair (Sterner and David 1991, 363). Finally, at a symbolic level, both are involved in the irreversible transformation of products of the earth (ore to bloom and clay to pot) involving the use of heat (Collett 1993, 505; Herbert 1993, 200).

Up until now, the discussion has focused primarily on the status of ironworkers in sedentary farming societies. What about pastoral societies? Cline (1937, 140) noted that "despised smith castes and a lack of smelting ritual characterize the northern grasslands of East Africa . . . not so much by peoples who are ruled by pastoral aristocracies as among tribes who conventionally devote themselves to cattle, or who despise all forms of manual labor." Much more recently, Herbert (1993, 27) noted that "only among some pastoralists such as Tuareg and Masai do [blacksmiths] form a distinctly servile population." After surveying much of the literature (see Coy 1982), Coy (n.d., 4–5) notes,

> In much of East Africa, smiths have been identified by many as possessing the characteristics of an endogamous caste. Limited in their marriage possibilities, avoided in many cases and viewed with a certain notion of pollution, blacksmiths have been portrayed as marginal to much of social life. In addition . . . smiths have been widely described as being despised or at least as being held in low esteem. Related to this is a set of widespread notions, coloring the smith as a person without the benefits of a "normal" member of society; without cattle, without land.

Coy (1982, 1989) argues that this previous work tended to focus on the noncraftsman (pastoralist) perspective and has ignored the smith's major and positive economic role in society. Cline (1937, 114–115) described Maasai ironworkers as the "classic example of a despised smith caste" characterized by residential isolation (see also Larick 1986), strict hereditary occupational endogamy, and a polluted and impure status (and therefore avoided) because he makes weapons that can cause bloodshed. He is stigmatized because his need to remain near his furnace or forge separates him from typical Maasai life, that is, wandering in search of cattle pasture and periodic warfare (Cline 1937, 114). In a somewhat more balanced view, Galaty (1982, 10-11) notes that blacksmiths also keep cattle and are viewed as indispensable to Maasai life because they produce weapons of war and razors for the cutting of the umbilical cord and for circumcision. Larick (1986, 168) notes their role as leaders in the sacred ritual of circumcision (see also Spencer 1973). Their combined economic, ritual, and transformative (magical) powers set them apart, and they are viewed with ambivalence (see also Bonte and Galaty 1991, 24). Galaty (1982, 11) also notes that Maasai smiths refer to Maasai pastoralists as "despicable and contemptuous," indicating that the smiths do not consider themselves inferior.

Coy (1982, 1989, n.d.) studied blacksmiths (including apprenticing himself to one) among Kalenjin-speaking pastoralists of the Kenya Rift Valley that are similar in many ways to the Maa-speaking groups, such as the Maasai. His study of the relatively egalitarian Endo (Elgeyo–Marakwet district) and Tugen (Baringo district) led him to conclude that the view that smiths are a "despised caste" was the result of past studies focusing on the views of noncraftsmen about craftsmen (Coy, n.d., 29–30). Among both the Endo and the Tugen, he found that strict marital endogamy was not practiced, but marriages between smiths and nonsmiths were restricted for several reasons. The smiths themselves often resisted such marriages because of fear that it would lead to craft proliferation and increased competition. Moreover, nonsmiths were suspicious of the wealth and magical power of smiths, including their power to curse and withhold production, which might occur if affinal disputes were to develop. Finally, the immunity/neutrality of ironworkers during warfare/raiding (Larick 1986) and their peripheral involvement in generalized reciprocity exchanges (due to their role as both producer and distributor of material goods) made marriage to a blacksmith or his daughter relatively undesirable. Among the Endo, apprenticeship of nonsmiths did occur but could be restricted if it threatened to extend competition. Moreover, the Endo were organized into a guildlike professional group in which prices were fixed, kinsmen were required to sell in the local market and not at home, and clan elders could threaten uncooperative craftsmen with their curse. The Tugen allowed apprenticeship under their strict control and forbade apprentices from working within their trade zone. They also used secrecy and taboos to help perpetuate an effective craft monopoly. In general, Coy concludes that ironworkers are feared or disliked and respected but that they are not despised; in short, we see the ambivalent attitude toward smiths prevalent in much of Africa. Coy (n.d., 30) also stresses how ironworkers seek to preserve their trade monopolies by perpetuating the idea that the occupation is mystical, dangerous, and even despicable. In short, the ironworker appears to be willing to accept negative social status for the right to have monopoly control over the production of essential (iron) commodities.

Coy's (1982, n.d.) work among the Tugen, who are organized into both pastoral and farming groups according to variations in mountain versus lowland habitat, also showed that the status of ironworkers varied as a function of their control over the production of essential versus relatively less essential iron tools. Highland farmers generally feared and respected smiths because they so depended on their production of agricultural tools, whereas the lowland pastoralists depended less on iron tools for their subsistence and tended to dislike smiths and sometimes harassed them. Clément (1948) expressed a similar view, but we should perhaps not overgeneralize, given the cultural variation in Africa (de Maret 1980, 267). Finally, it is important to note that Cline (1937, 115–117) himself was aware of peoples similar to those described by Coy. He describes the Chaga of northeastern Tanzania in contrast to the Maasai: smiths are not despised but, rather, feared and honored;

nonsmiths associate frequently with smiths; strict endogamy is not practiced, but nonsmiths are ambivalent about marrying their daughters to smiths; smiths are neutral during warfare; and smiths exercise other important roles, such as diviners and healers. Cline (1937, 117) suggests that the higher status of smiths among the Chaga is due to the more tolerant attitude of the Chaga pastoralists toward nonpastoral pursuits.

Up until now, the discussion has focused on pastoral societies with relatively uncentralized polities. The picture is somewhat different if we focus on the pastoral aristocracies of the Interlacustrine district of East Africa and the Sahel. Cline (1937, 140) intimated that the status of ironworkers was generally higher in pastoral aristocracies. However, according to Roscoe (1923a, 105; 1923b, 8–9) and Cline (1937, 117–119), the pastoral people looked on farmers and artisans as serfs or slaves, and their manual labor was viewed as low and mean. Interestingly enough, a reading of Roscoe's (1923a, 1923b) descriptions of Banyankole and Bakitara (Bunyoro) origin myths, royal investiture, royal regalia, and royal funerals make little or no mention of roles played by ironworkers and iron tools (other than the royal spear). Schmidt (1990, 258), however, states that the sacred Bacwezi cult associated with iron working did play a role in Bunyoro rituals of royal installation. However, generally, chiefly authority among the Banyankole and Bakitara and its ideological and ritual links to divine kingship were mediated by symbolic and concrete links to cattle (Bonte and Galaty 1991, 23).

This is not the case with the pastoral aristocracies of Rwanda and Burundi or the with the Babito and Bahinda dynasties among the Bahaya in Tanzania (Schmidt 1978, 1983a, 1983b, 1990; de Heusch 1982; de Maret 1985b; Célis 1989), where the political, economic, and religious importance of indigenous iron-working clans has led to their playing important roles in dynastic origin myths and the rituals of royal investiture. The mythical ancestor of the royal dynasty of Rwanda, Gihanga, was supposed to have introduced metal working, fire, cattle, hunting, pottery, and woodworking as well as kingship; iron working, in particular, "mediates the passage from sterility to fecundity" in the Rwandese kingship origin myth (de Heusch 1982, 182, 185, 193; de Maret 1985b, 78). As found elsewhere in Central Africa, the hammer and anvil as royal regalia were the primary symbols of royal power in both Rwanda and Burundi (Herbert 1993, 134; see also Célis 1989, 26). In Burundi, royal regalia were made from copper (de Maret 1985b, 82). The kings (*bami*) of both kingdoms kept a hammer near their bed (d'Hertefelt and Coupez 1964, 308, cited in de Maret 1985b, 82–83; Célis and Nzikobanyanka 1976, 66, 79). While the Rwandan king could not forge himself as a member of the Tutsi aristocracy, "as king-elect he participated symbolically in the rituals in which the royal hoe was forged" (Herbert 1993, 134), and hammers were part of the royal regalia used during investiture (de Maret 1985b, 83). These rituals and regalia both emphasized the king's dominion over the ironworkers and recalled the myths that attribute the introduction of iron working to the dynasty's founder (Herbert 1993, 134). Finally, the tomb of the seventeenth- or eighteenth-century Rwandan Mwami Cyirima Rujugira contained two forged anvil/hammers serving as headrests (de Maret 1985b, 84). Hammers are also used during investiture rituals among the Nyanga in the eastern Democratic Republic of Congo (Herbert 1993, 134).

Among the Bahaya, whose iron industry originates in the first millennium B.C., oral traditions relate how the Babito and Bahinda pastoral dynasties imposed themselves on local iron-working clans, the Bacwezi, in the seventeenth century (Schmidt 1990, 258, 268; Herbert 1993, 146–147). In recognition of the Bacwezi's indigenous religious and political status, the Bacwezi played key roles in the investiture rituals of the Kiamutwara and Kiziba kingdoms in Buhaya, thereby legitimizing the new political system (Schmidt 1990, 258). Political power became closely tied to the myth, symbolism, and ritual associated with iron working, the base of the productive economy (Schmidt 1990, 268). In short, several of the pastoral aristocracies in the Interlacustrine region reached a political, ritual, and symbolic accommodation with local iron-working clans. It is therefore not surprising that the status of ironworkers in such societies was higher than those in which such accommodation did not occur.

Finally, Bonte and Galaty (1991, 24, 30) note that among some pastoral societies, "unequal statuses are codified as 'estates' within a stratified social system" (Bonte and Galaty 1991, 30), such as among the Tswana (Botswana), in Kanem (Chad), among Tuareg pastoralists in the Sahara, and among Moorish nomads. In nearly all cases, the hierarchy is based on the superior value of pastoral labor and livestock, and the status of ironworkers is relatively low. Here again, however, one must be careful not to confuse the emic view of ironworkers presented by the aristocratic warrior class with the reality of daily social relationships. Among the Tuareg of Niger, ironworkers are linked to chiefly lineages and warrior aristocracies for whom they made and repaired arms, jewelry, and objects of daily life (Bernus 1983, 239). They are part of hereditary, strictly endogamous castes, and the emic view of their patrons describes them as lazy liars and holds them in contempt and disgust, a view that ironworkers have internalized; however, an important Tuareg folktale stresses how the society would be in bad shape without them (Bernus 1983, 243). Their smiths' sense of corporate identity is very strong, including the use of a secret, pig-latin-like language (*tenet*) that only they can understand. In the stratified, centralized polity of Kanem, ironworkers provided the key tools of hoes and spears. As an imperial Islamic society gradually developed in these areas, the local hunter/smiths were politically, maritally, and ritually marginalized (Conte 1991, 226–227). Three social cleavages developed: "the first between cattle-owning 'people-of-the-spear' attributed 'noble descent' and the inferior 'people-of-the-bow', the hunters and smiths; the second between freemen and slaves; and the third between masters and dependents" (Conte 1991, 236). Barriers to the ownership of cattle by hunters and smiths were rigorously enforced (Conte 1991, 237).

WHY CASTES?

We conclude this focus on social status with a brief discussion of why ironworkers are often members of castes, as defined previously. Some have suggested that it is an adaptation that ensures that societies can retain a group of ironworkers to produce tools critical for survival, that castes help maintain strong technological traditions and stimulate cooperation among ironworkers, and that caste stigmatization helps keep people within the occupation and discourages others from joining (Vaughan 1970, 89; Haaland 1985, 58; David et al. 1989, 186; Sterner and David 1991, 361). While this view seems plausible, it does not explain why many iron-producing societies solve this problem without resorting to castes (de Maret 1980, 1985b; Sterner and David 1991, 361) and why other non–iron-producing societies simply import needed preforms and/or iron tools (e.g., the Luo, Lugbara, Bagesu, and Busoga; see Roscoe 1924, 20–21, 115; Were 1972; Middleton 1992, 2–13). Without referring specifically to castes, some authors have suggested that the status of ironworkers reflects primarily whether their clients are farmers or pastoralists (Cline 1937; Coy 1982); that is, farmers tend to fear and respect ironworkers who provide the key tools for their survival, whereas pastoralists in relatively uncentralized societies generally despise manual labor and are less dependent on ironworkers' services. As a result, farmers often have an ambivalent attitude toward ironworkers, whereas pastoralists tend to have more negative perceptions of them. Haaland (1985, 61) has suggested that castes are prevalent in societies with a long history of states and a complex civilization where the specialization of labor is well developed, such as in the Mali Empire and the kingdom of Ethiopia; however, this in part begs the question and explains nothing about casted pastoral societies. Hypotheses relating to Arab influence (Vaughan 1970) and the need to subordinate the authority of ironworkers to chiefly power (Talmari 1991) relate to Mande West Africa but cannot be generalized to Africa as a whole.

Another interesting set of hypotheses suggests that the introduction of iron working created a privileged and powerful class (ironworkers) whose economic and transformative powers incited envy, jealousy, and fear on the part of non–iron-working segments of traditional society. Ironworkers were feared for their powers of sorcery, their control of production and distribution of critical iron tools, and the wealth that such powers could bring them. Such wealth threatened traditional lines of power based on kinship and age as well as chiefly power, and therefore it had to be brought under control.

This power could be mitigated by labeling ironworkers as unsavory or polluted and dangerous, by using prescriptive endogamy to restrict the power of ironworkers to expand their political and economic control through the acquisition of wives, and generally by assigning them negative status (Meillassoux 1978; McNaughton 1988, 19–20, 158–160; Wright 1989; Samtouna 1990, 149; Sterner and David 1991, 364; Coy, n.d., 5). On the other hand, ironworkers often encourage noncraftsmen to hold them in awe and to view them in a negative light so as to maintain their corporate monopoly (Were 1972; Richter 1980, 37, 51; Coy 1982; McNaughton 1988, 15; Samtouna 1990, 150). Taken together, one may view it as an "unacknowledged conspiracy" in which the noncraftsmen (farmers or pastoralists) get a variety of needed services from the iron-working caste while simultaneously constraining the ironworker's social and political powers and in which ironworkers maintain their production and trading monopoly (Coy, 1982, n.d.; Sterner and David 1991). But, however intriguing and suggestive this interpretation may be, it still does not allow us to predict when castes will or will not develop. As de Maret (1980, 1985) cautions, human cultural solutions to similar problems are many, and one cannot always explain cultural variation in terms of deterministic probabilities.

IRON WORKING AND ETHNICITY

Earlier discussions noted that specialization within iron working was sometimes ethnic based (i.e., smelters vs. smiths or smiths converting bloom to heavy tools vs. those preparing lightweight tools and jewelry). An even more interesting question relates to the actual ethnic composition of particular iron-working groups, for example, the blacksmiths of the city of Kano, the Bassar smelters or smiths of Togo, and the Barongo ironworkers of northwestern Tanzania. Jaggar (1973, 13–14) describes the ethnic diversity of blacksmiths of Kano, who are mostly Kanuri and Kano Hawsa but some of whom are Katsina Fulani, Tripolitan Arab, and Tuareg serfs (Buzu) from Agades. He notes that although Kano blacksmiths are of mixed heritage, they have been more or less fully acculturated, primarily through intermarriage with the Hawsa. All speak Hawsa from birth, practice Hawsa customs, and refer to themselves as Kanawa (people of Kano) when asked by outsiders. However, if questioned closely, they will speak of their real ancestry.

The colonial administrator and historian Robert Cornevin recorded extensive data on the migration histories of Bassar iron-working populations. These histories indicate that many ironworkers migrated from the west, east, and north into Bassar during the eighteenth and nineteenth centuries (Cornevin 1962, 33–51; see also Martinelli 1982, 26–37; de Barros 1985, 416). My own interviews with various individuals and groups in the region confirmed these trends. It is clear that many ironworkers migrated from as far north as today's Burkina Faso, from Gonja territory in neighboring Ghana, and from nearby ethnic groups in Togo, such as the Kotokoli. The reasons for the migrations varied from the dislocation of populations resulting from slave raiding and war by populations such as the Tyokossi to the north (Mango), the decline of iron industries elsewhere due to local conflicts and/or deforestation, and the growing attraction of the Bassar iron-working region, with its nearly pure hematite ores and its location along a major Hawsa kola route (de Barros 1986, 166). These immigrant ironworkers were ultimately absorbed into existing villages, resulting in multiethnic smelting and smithing groups or clans. Like the multiethnic community of Kano blacksmiths, immigrant Bassar ironworkers have also been fully assimilated and speak of themselves as Bassar.

Schmidt (1996b, 123) notes a similar kind of multiethnic amalgamation for the Barongo ironworkers of northwestern Tanzania, except here they have taken on an identity of their own. They are not a tribe but rather a kind of work association or trade guild that uses a common technical language of specialized terms (*kirongo*) linked to iron working and its associated rituals. This gives them their identity as Barongo (Schmidt 1996b, 77–78). The Barongo (of Butengo) are a fusion of members of five ethnic groups or subgroups from west-central Tanzania, including the Bahaya. Plural origins and mixed marriages are typical of the Barongo. They describe themselves in ways similar to a Western craft association characterized by skilled workers of different grades (e.g., apprentices and master smelters); open membership without regard to ethnic group, family, or lineage; and the desire to preserve the craft and the trade of iron products only for the Barongo (Schmidt 1996b, 79). Schmidt (1996b, 80) attributes the rise of the Barongo as a "multiethnic work association" as a result of dislocations associated with the mid-nineteenth-century slave raiding and trading era south of Lake Victoria, including new commercial opportunities made possible by the east–west slave caravans between the interior and coast.

The development of multiethnic iron-working clans or lineages is essentially due to the highly specialized and transformative nature of their craft and the rise and fall (or dispersal and regrouping) of iron-working industries due to the disruption of civil war, conquest, or slave raiding and/or the gradual deforestation of a given region. Given the demand for iron for both hoes and weapons, there was always a market for the ironworker's craft. Given its highly specialized, ritualized, and often mystified nature and the sometimes casted or ambivalent status of the ironworker, it was perhaps natural that ironworkers would seek out other ironworkers; and, given their relative wealth, they would be seen as desirable spouses for other men's daughters.

Schmidt (1997, 265–288) presents archaeological, technological and ecological evidence that shows how thriving "Early Iron Age" communities in northwestern Tanzania eventually collapsed because of deforestation resulting from the use of wood charcoal to fuel smelting furnaces. By the seventh century, iron working had ceased in many areas and would not be reestablished until the thirteenth century, when the land had had a chance to regenerate itself. Schmidt (1997) also documents how the effects of such deforestation led to the use of poorer-quality wood charcoal and eventually the complementary use of charred swamp grass. Forest depletion eventually forced the Buhaya to become partly dependent on imported iron goods (Schmidt 1997, 22). In the case of the Bassar, gradually depleting forests led to the rise of villages specializing in charcoal making to the south of the main industrial zone and the importation of charcoal from other areas (Kuevi 1975; Goucher 1981; de Barros 1985; Hahn 1997). Elsewhere, it is likely that the iron-working industry of Mema situated within the empire of Ghana went into serious decline as a result of regional deforestation (Haaland 1985, 66). It is also likely that some iron-working areas of Burkina Faso sharply declined for the same reason. In short, throughout Africa, immigrant ironworkers were probably a relatively common phenomenon over the long term (McIntosh 1994, 177).

Finally, it is worth noting that ironworkers who traded finished tools often accommodated ethnic demands for stylistic differences in their products. The Bassar produced a large hoe for yam-mound building and a smaller hoe for weeding. The basic Bassar hoe was a circular disk, but Bassar blacksmiths produced three stylistic variations to accommodate varying village trademarks within their own region (de Barros 1985, 202). The neighboring Kotokoli blacksmiths who specialized in making light tools and jewelry also tailored their products to some degree according to the client (Dugast 1986). Larick (1991) discusses the role of stylistic variation in spear morphology among the Lokop of Kenya. He notes that Lokop blacksmiths must be sensitive to ethnic variations in weapon styles. He also discusses stylistic variation within an ethnic group and how it relates to differences in age grade and status (Larick 1991, 317, 326). Bisson (in this volume) observes that regional variations in the form of copper ingots reflecting ethnic differences developed as ingots were increasingly used as currency. He also notes that different mines produced ingots for particular markets.

THE SPATIAL ORGANIZATION OF IRON WORKING AND IRON-WORKING SOCIETIES

Holl (in this volume) discusses at some length some of the differences in societal organization for copper- and iron-working societies in Niger, Mema (Mali), and southern Cameroon. In the case of Mema, Holl traces the relationship between changing settlement patterns and the presumed growing centralization of politics and production in the region that was part of the empire of Ghana. Bisson (in this volume) discusses the importance of the mining, smelting, and working of copper to the power of the political elite among the Ngoyo and adjacent kingdoms. He also looks at the links between the increased political centralization of the Kaonde and the rapid expansion of copper production associated with the Kansanshi mine in Zambia. The results of a regional study of the Bassar iron-working region in northern Togo (de Barros 1985, 1986, 1988) revealed that the rise of large-scale iron production may indeed result in higher population densities, larger and more stable village communities, a settlement pattern aggregated in the ore zone, the rise of craft specialization at the village and regional levels, and increased regional trade. The data also suggested that even the introduction of a small-scale iron industry into a society may generate similar trends, though at more modest levels. However, in the Bassar case, neither small-scale nor large-scale production resulted in a significant increase in political centralization. In both cases, only a low-level settlement hierarchy consisting of a major village and associated hamlets developed in the vicinity of major ore bodies (de Barros 1988, 91).

There is considerable evidence to suggest that smelters and/or smiths often lived in separate residential areas. In addition to the rise of regional specialization in western Bassar (smelters near Bandjeli, smiths near Bitchabe, and charcoal makers at Dimuri), the villages associated with the Bassar chiefdom included such villages as Binaparba, which specialized in smithing, and Nangbani, which specialized in smelting (see Fig. 3.1). Four specialized potting villages were also present in the vicinity of Mount Bassar. In the Kabu chiefdom to the north, the chief resided in Kabu, but smelters and smiths resided in separate quarters in the nearby artisan village of Sara (de Barros 1985, 200). Sabi-Monra (1991, 110–111) notes that the Muga of Bagazi and Nassi-Conzi (Borgu region of northeastern Benin) had strict taboos against blacksmiths working near a smelting furnace or even within a smelting village. This was because the Muga smelters of these two villages possess a powerful deity or goddess of metal production for the entire region of Kalali. This mother deity of smelting could not tolerate the striking of her children (iron blooms) in her presence without reacting violently (Sabi-Monra 1991, 111).

Mbanza Kongo, the capital of the Kongo kingdom in Angola, had its own metal-working quarter (de Heusch 1975, 172, cited in Herbert 1993, 145), as did Awdaghost (Tegdaoust), the trading capital of the Ghana Empire (Vanacker 1979) and as did the eighteenth-century commercial town of Begho in west-central Ghana with its smithing quarter (Dwinfuor or Adwinfuo) and its smelting site (Dapaa) on the outskirts of the town (Posnansky 1973, 1975; Anquandah 1982, 98, 1993). Archaeological evidence from late first-millennium levels of the site of Jenne-Jeno (Mali) also suggests the "installa-

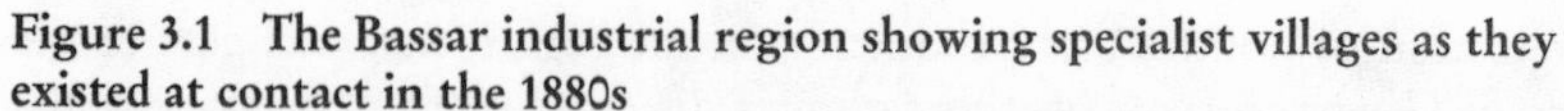

Figure 3.1 The Bassar industrial region showing specialist villages as they existed at contact in the 1880s

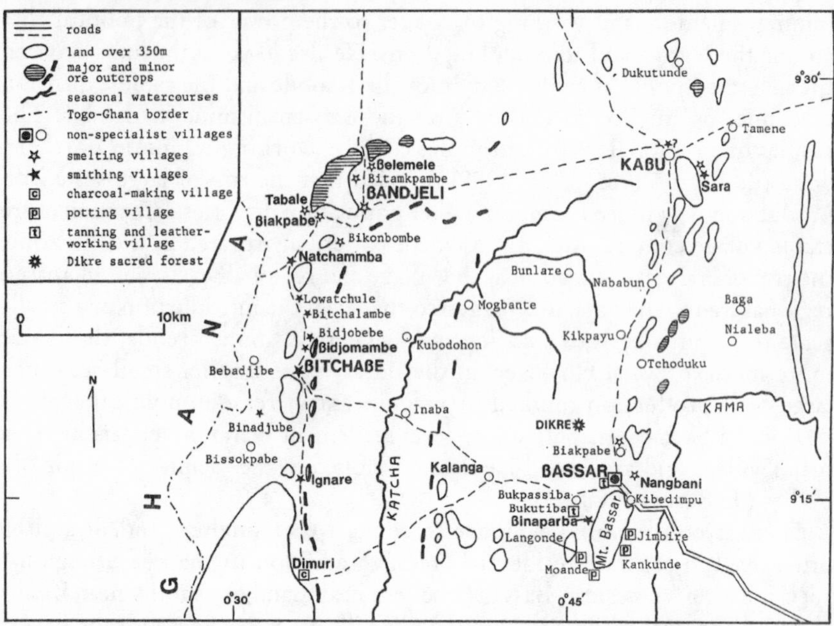

tion of smiths in specific locales or quartiers, probably as members of organized specialist-producer groups" (McIntosh 1993, 15). McNaughton (1988, 22) notes that Mande smiths sometimes congregated together in a special quarter (*numusokala*) or formed their own town or hamlet (*numudugu*), usually in close proximity to farming clan settlements. The same appears to have been true for blacksmiths in central Darfur (Sudan) (Muhammed 1993, 466). Survey data from the eastern part of the Bassar region also suggest the presence of specialist communities of blacksmiths in the late first millennium. On the other hand, there is no evidence for separate artisan quarters in the early first-millennium Akan town of Bono Manso (Anquandah 1993, 645). The presence of specialist artisan quarters or villages is probably correlated with one or more of the following factors: ethnic differentiation of iron-working groups from non–iron-working populations, as was apparently the case for the pastoralist Toutswe populations in eastern Botswana (Kiyaga-Mulindwa 1993); the casted nature and/or ambivalent status of many iron-working groups, especially in the western and eastern Sudan; and the special needs of occupational specialization in terms of resource procurement, work space, and the organization of labor.

Numerous factors affected the location of smelting sites themselves. Data from the Bassar region of Togo suggest that relative proximity to ore deposits was an important consideration, given the transport weight of iron ore (see Fig. 3.2). In Bassar, 50 percent (by volume) of all slag deposits recorded in the intensive survey zone are located within 1 kilometer of the nearest ore deposit (Bidjilib), and 57 percent of the smelting sites and 77 percent of the slag (by volume) are located within 2 kilometers. Finally, 85 percent of the sites and nearly all of the slag (97 percent) are found within 4 kilometers of the nearest ore (de Barros 1985, 195; 1986, 157). As Bassar became a major large-scale producer of iron in the late sixteenth century, settlements and smelting sites became heavily concentrated within less than 3 kilometers of the ore deposits (de Barros 1988, figure 6).

Aside from the relative proximity to iron ores, other major factors affecting the location of smelting sites include viable water sources (e.g., permanent springs) for furnace building and drinking, the avoidance of habitation areas, the availability of furnace clay and wood charcoal, and the avoidance of good agricultural lands (de Barros 1985, 135–137, 192–198). Data from Bassar informants and field surveys suggest that the proximity of the ore (especially during periods of large-scale production) and water were the key determinants. Furnace clay was available in many areas, and wood charcoal

Figure 3.2 Smelting sites and production zones, Bassar region, with estimated slag volume

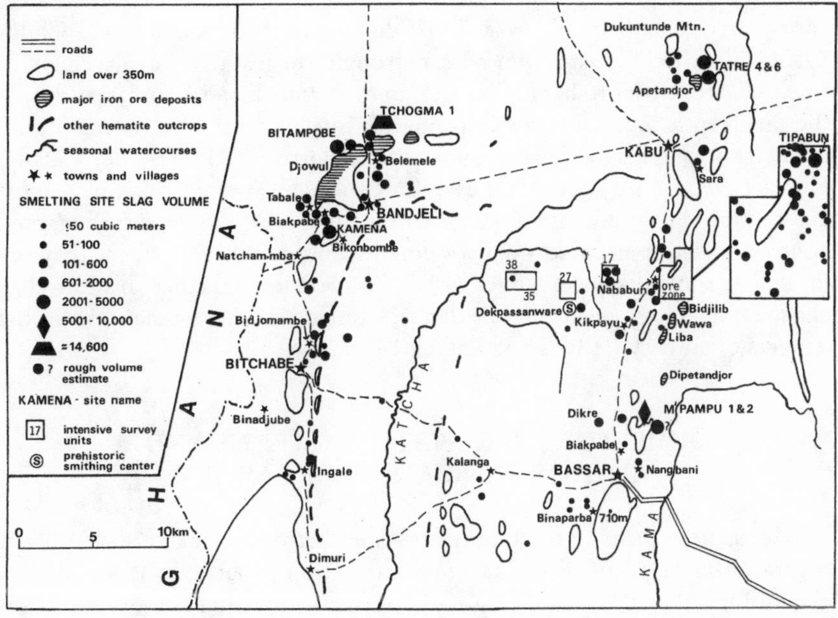

was frequently imported from some distance (de Barros 1985, 135–137). In the grassland savanna and sahel, the location of wood fuel may have been a more critical site location factor (McIntosh 1994,177, citing Echard 1992 and Bocoum 1987).

Previous studies suggest four principal reasons why smelting sites were generally kept away from habitation areas: to reduce the chance that sexual taboos against intercourse and the presence of fertile and menstruating women would be violated; to reduce the potential harm from witchcraft and other evil influences; to help protect the secrets of iron smelting from industrial espionage, particularly from in-marrying women of other clans or lineages; and to minimize the risk of fire (Sabi-Monra 1991, 78; Rowland and Warnier 1993, 519; Schmidt 1997, 191). The placement of smelting sites deep within the bush may have also helped add to the mystification of the transformational qualities of smelting and its association with the control of powerful forces (McNaughton 1988; Childs 1991a, 343; Essomba 1992b, 357). Furnaces may also have been located on ancient smelting sites to emphasize the link between success in iron working and ancestral spirits, as among the Ushi of Zambia (Barnes 1929, cited in Childs and Killick 1993, 328). Childs (1991a, 340–343) also discusses political and economic constraints associated with access to ore zones and the potential for group conflict, overexploitation or deforestation in certain areas, and the direction and force of the local winds (Sabi-Monra 1991, 112). There is plenty of archaeological and ethnographic evidence, however, to indicate that smelting sites were sometimes directly contiguous to habitation areas and that their proximity to such areas varied over time (Schmidt 1978, 1997; de Barros 1985; Schmidt and Childs 1985; Killick 1990). Data from Bassar strongly suggest that the placement of smelting sites closer to habitation sites in the Bandjeli and Kabu areas during the nineteenth century was due primarily to the threat of slave raiding by the neighboring Dagomba and Tyokossi (de Barros 1985, 693–707). Finally, Killick (1990, 76–77) notes that early smelting sites (before 1200) in Zambia and central Malawi are often located within villages and that this is in marked contrast to late nineteenth- and twentieth-century villages, where they are located at some distance. Killick (1990, 77) wonders whether this reflects a change in ideology regarding the danger of menstruating women and/or the dangers of sorcery (Childs and Killick 1993, 38).

SMELTING SITE SPATIAL PATTERNS AND THE ORGANIZATION OF LABOR

The focus now turns to the interrelationship between changes in the spatial organization of production and the organization of labor as revealed by a chronological analysis of changing patterns of smelting site organization from around 1300 to 1910 in the Bassar region of northern Togo. While some authors have discussed the spatial organization of smelting and smithing sites (Schmidt and Childs 1985; Fowler 1990; Killick 1990; Essomba 1992b; Schmidt 1997, 190–208), none of these studies examine changing spatial patterns as they may relate to changes in the organization of labor.

The Bassar iron-working industry began sometime between A.D. 500 and 750 with an emphasis on smithing as evidenced by a 15-hectare site named Dekpassanware (see Fig. 3.2) that contains five separate loci of smithing debris, including bedrock basins used to crush iron bloom prior to reworking it in the smithy (de Barros 1985, photo 19). If smelting took place in the Bassar region during this time (Period 1), production levels were apparently very low, as no slag mounds date to this period. Evidence for significant levels of iron smelting do not appear until around 1300 (Period 2). Large-scale production for regional and long-distance trade first appears between 1550 and 1600 (Period 3). Beginning sometime in the late eighteenth century (beginning of Period 4), the region was plagued by frequent slave raiding incursions by the Dagomba kingdom from the west and the Tyokossi chiefdom from the north. This led to the depopulation of the Bassar peneplain and the relocation of the industry close to major mountains areas. The Bassar chiefdom arose in response to these attacks and the flood of refugees they generated (Dugast 1988; de Barros 1997). The stability created by the Bassar chiefdom may have led to the growing importance of a Hawsa caravan route through Bassar heading toward the kola markets in Salaga and later Kete-Kratchi in the Middle Volta basin of Ghana. Iron production rose to new heights during the nineteenth century. It was interrupted by frequent Dagomba attacks, including the siege of the town of Bassar in the mid-1870s, but with German colonial rule after 1884 production reached new levels. The industry did not seriously decline until a flood of scrap iron associated with the new railroad and colonial vehicles made traditional smelting largely unprofitable after the 1920s. Relatively well dated smelting site spatial data are available for Periods 2 through 4 that suggest possible changing patterns of labor organization. The following summary of these data is taken from de Barros (1985, 220–239).

Period 2 (1300–1550/1600)

Throughout this sequence, there is a strong tendency for sites to be located near or within a network of water channels near the headwaters of small and large streams or near the confluence of two streams. Most smelting sites of this period are modest in size, usually containing 2 or 3 to up to 15 mounds that average about 80 centimeters high and are rarely higher than 1.5 meters. Mound lengths are typically 10 to 12 meters and rarely attain 20 meters. Total slag volume is typically in the 150- to 300-cubic-meter range, but some attain 500 cubic meters. Sites are typically composed of between one to four or five groups of mounds, with typically one furnace per group. The ratio of furnace emplacements to mounds lies between one to two and one to three. The layout of the sites suggests that two or more smelting teams often worked at the same location. Each group of mounds may correspond to the work of different extended families (*kinako*) (see Fig. 3.3A).

Period 3 (1550/1600–c. 1800)

While modest sites are still present, this period is characterized by large sites of 25 or more slag mounds, with the largest containing well over 100 mounds. Mound heights average over 1 meter, and at least 25 percent of the slag heaps are over 1.5 meters. At the largest site, Tchogma I, situated north of Bandjeli, many mounds are over 2 meters and some over 4 to 5 meters in height. Some mounds are 20 to 30 meters or more in length, and slag volume at the larger sites is close to 5,000 cubic meters. The largest site (Tchogma I) contains a staggering 14,583 cubic meters of slag in 184 mounds (see Fig. 3.2). The large-scale production of this period resulted in the heaping of large quantities of slag in large mounds that tended to take on crescent or horseshoe shapes; in some instances, additional contiguous slag mounds developed on the opposite side, creating a near circular pattern (see Fig. 3.3B). Generally, each crescent- or horseshoe-shaped mound cluster is associated with one or two furnace emplacements. The furnace to mound ratio is about two to three in the west (Bandjeli area) and about one to three in the eastern region (Bassar–Kabu axis). This is probably due to the lower-quality ores of the eastern region (30 to 50 percent iron), which required a larger furnace size to produce the standard 30-kilogram iron bloom produced near Bandjeli, which had access to nearly pure hematite ores (Hupfeld 1899; Koert 1906; Lawson 1972). The eastern furnaces are more durable in the face of erosion from tropical rains but take more labor to build. Ethnohistoric and ethnographic data (Hupfeld 1899, 181; Martinelli 1982, 47) indicate that smelting teams in the Bandjeli area were generally composed of three men, whereas a team of five was required for the eastern furnaces. Despite the large-scale production, the spatial organization of the large sites continues to suggest extended-family-level exploitation (which is confirmed by local oral traditions), but there is a tendency for large numbers of smelters to concentrate in the same area. Mounds again tend to form clusters at times, but these clusters are less distinct, as large sites tend to be relatively compact. Several descent groups, perhaps from more than one village, may have been involved.

Period 4 (c. 1800–c. 1920): Bandjeli Zone

Smelting sites vary extensively in size, but the very large sites of the previous period are absent, primarily because Dagomba and Tyokossi slave raid-

Figure 3.3 Spatial organization of Bassar region smelting sites

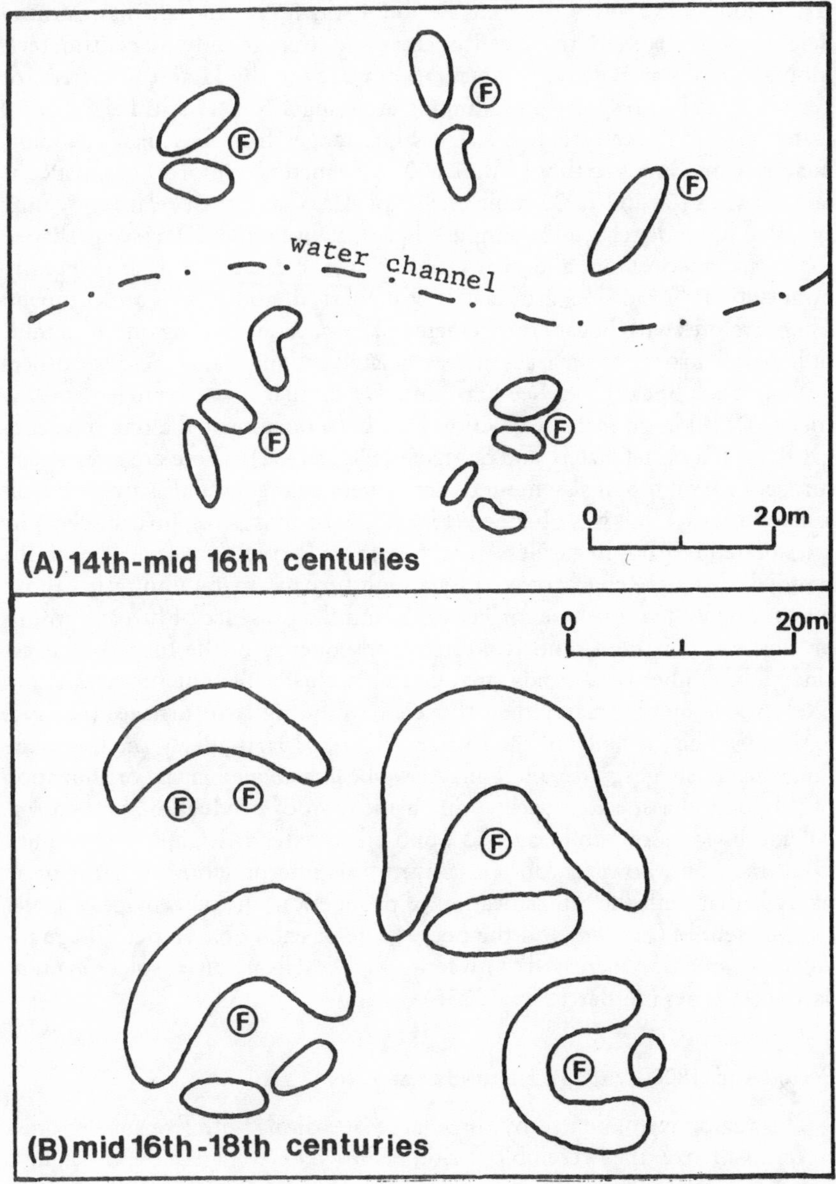

ing caused smelters to relocate in more protected areas. As a result, Period 3 lasted 200 to 250 years, whereas Period 4 was less than half that. Mound heights range from 40 to 80 centimeters and average only 60 centimeters. Mound lengths average only 7 meters, compared to the 11 and 10 meters for Periods 2 and 3, respectively. Mounds attaining 1.5 meters in height or 20 meters in length are rare. Site slag volume ranges from less than 100 cubic meters at small sites to those with 2,000 cubic meters or more, but most contain between 100 and 1,000 cubic meters of slag. Given their relatively young age, slag mounds tend to be simple ellipses, as in Period 2. Crescent-shaped forms are uncommon, and near circular or horseshoe forms are virtually nonexistent. Some sites are relatively dispersed, and others are compact. There are sites with linear arrangements of furnaces, including one with multiple parallel rows of furnaces and associated mounds, and there are others without such linear rows (see Fig. 3.3C, D). Similar linear arrangements associated with large-scale production have been documented along the Senegal River (Robert-Chaleix and Sognane 1983, 50–52). There are sites where furnaces are on top of slag mounds and others where mounds surround a pit where furnace earth was obtained (Fig. 3.3E). At most sites, furnace clay pits are situated nearby. Regardless of layout, most Period 4 smelting sites in the Bandjeli Zone are characterized by a high furnace-to-mound ratio (about one to one vs. two to three for Period 3) and the presence of furnace groups or clusters. This high ratio is a direct consequence of the furnace clusters since the number of mounds surrounding a cluster of four furnaces is not likely to be much greater than those surrounding two furnaces (see Fig. 3.3A–H). The presence of the furnace clusters, particularly the linear arrangements, suggests that there may have been a change in the organization of production associated with an intensification of production, perhaps involving lineages or sublineages as opposed to extended-family work units. Oral traditions, however, do not confirm this interpretation. What is more likely is that with the intensification of production, the percentage of males per household (*kinako*) and the percentage of each *kinako* per village involved in smelting increased, with fewer individuals involved solely in cultivation activities (de Barros 1985, 235).

Period 4 (c. 1800–c. 1905): Kabu–Bassar Axis

This region is dominated by three large sites along with five smaller ones. In terms of size, they resemble Period 3 sites. The average mound height is about 1.1 meters, and 30 percent have heights of 1.5 to 2 meters. Average mound lengths are generally longer (14 vs. 10 meters for Period 3), and the percentage of mounds greater than 20 meters (14 percent) surpasses other periods. In terms of site slag volume, the two large sites near the village of Nangbani near Bassar (M'pampu 1 and 2) are second only to Tchogma 1 near

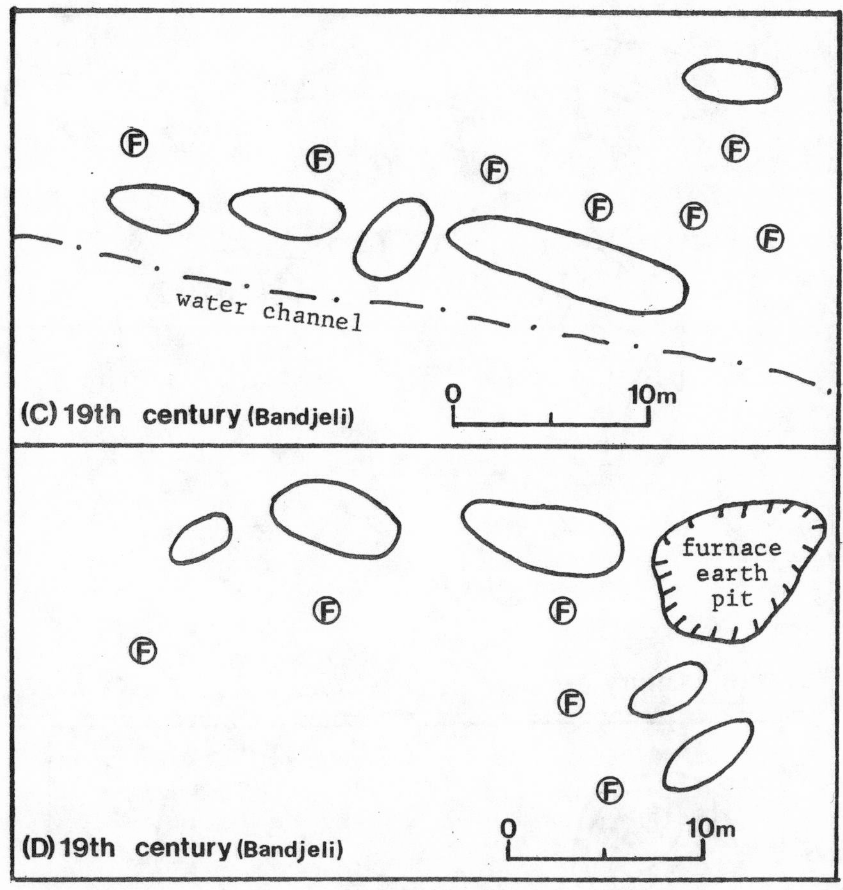

Bandjeli, with 7,381 and 5,500 cubic meters of slag, respectively. The spatial organization of the sites presents a more diverse set of patterns than in previous periods, just as we saw with Period 4 sites in the Bandjeli zone. In the Kabu–Sara region, the dominant pattern consists of near circular or circular mounds surrounding one or two furnace emplacements (see Fig. 3.3F). A similar circular pattern is present at the M'pampu 1 and 2 sites near Nangbani, but the circles are more discontinuous and at the same time more interlocking (see Fig. 3.3G, H). The result is a kind of cellular or maze pattern. M'pampu 2 is made up of 18 interlocking or rectangular cells containing a total of 59 furnace emplacements (Fig. 3.3G). Although the Kabu–Sara and M'pampu sites differ in size and spatial configuration, there are some important similarities. As in the Bandjeli zone, the furnace-to-mound ratio is higher than in Period 3 for this same region (two to three vs. one to three).

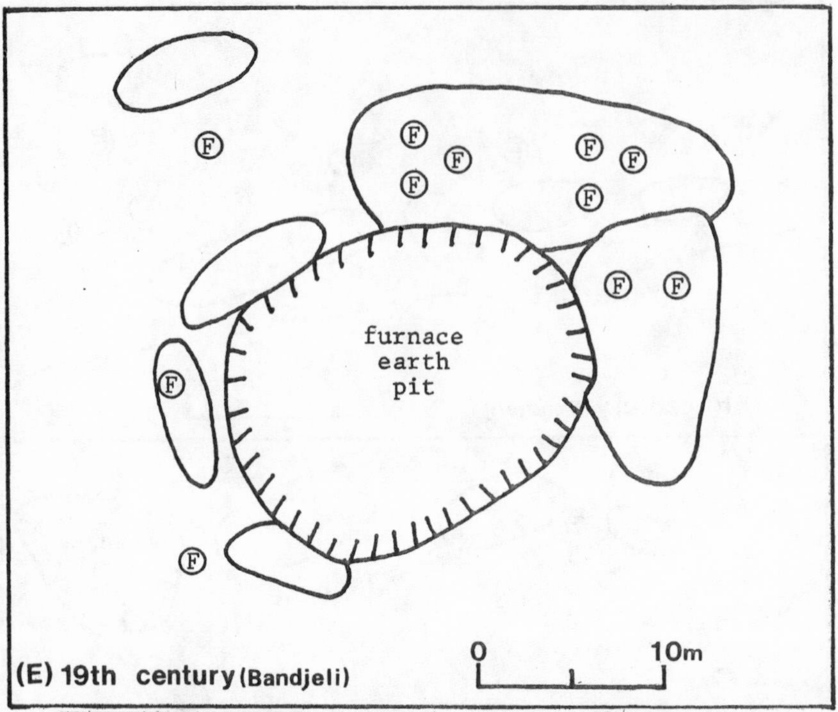

F
F
F
F
F
F
F
F
F
F
F
furnace
earth
pit
0
10m
(E) 19th century (Bandjeli)

F
F
F
F
F
F
0
20m
(F) 19th century (Kabu-Bassar)

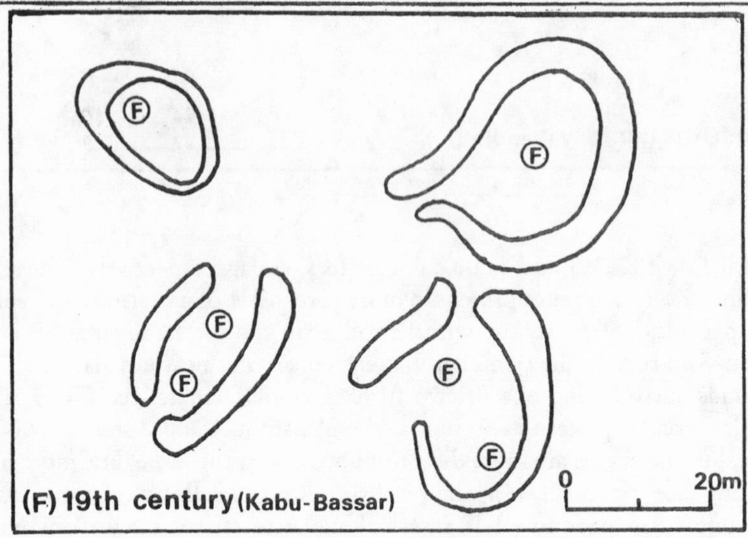

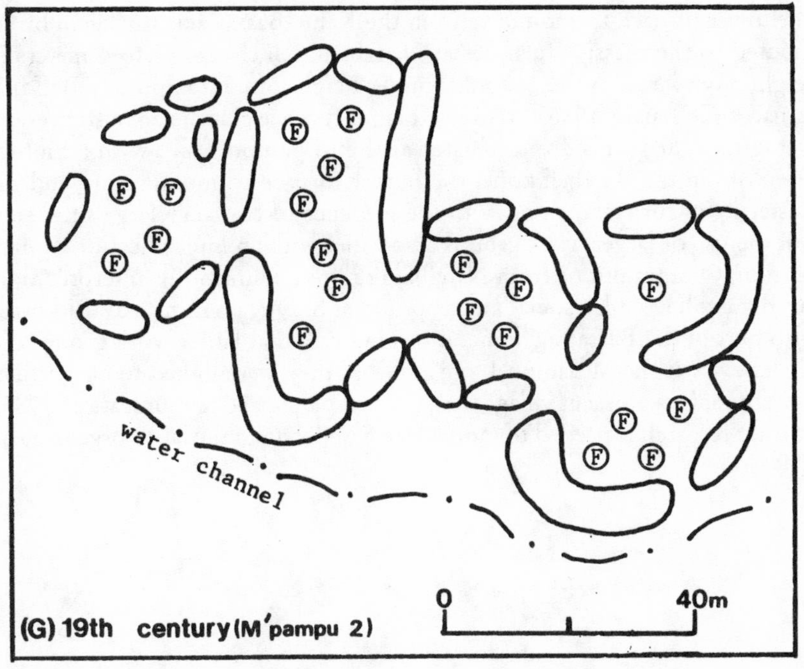
F
water channel
0
40m
(G) 19th century (M'pampu 2)

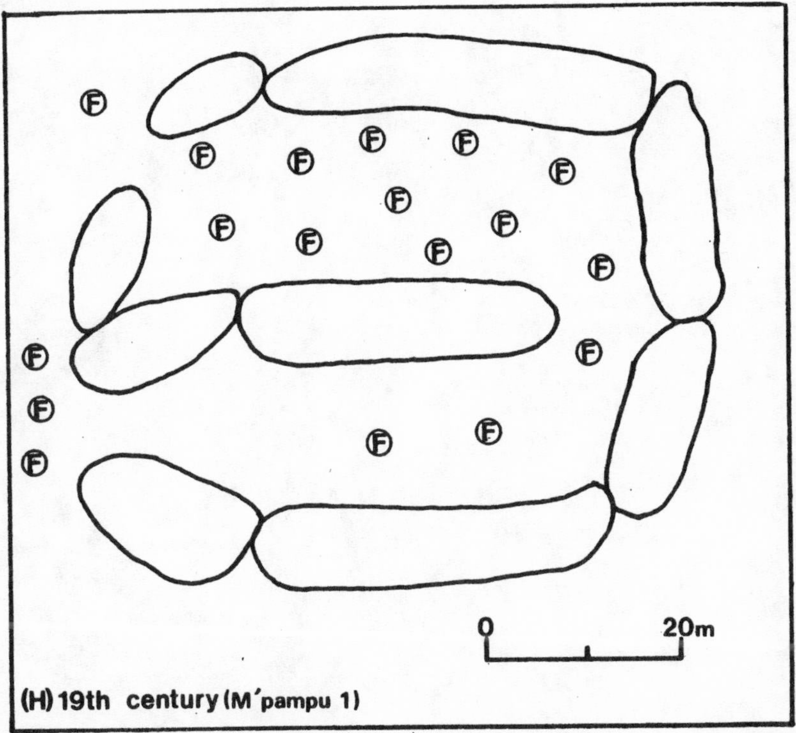
F
0
20m
(H) 19th century (M'pampu 1)

The lower furnace-to-mound ratio in the Kabu–Bassar axis can again be attributed to the massive furnaces at Nangbani, which are 3.5 to 4 meters in height, compared to the 2- to 2.5-meter height of contemporary Bandjeli furnaces (de Barros 1986, 151–154). Larger furnace clusters are also present, averaging four furnaces per cluster at the M'pampu 2 site with a high of seven. As in the Bandjeli zone, the higher furnace-to-mound ratio and the clustering of furnaces, along with the presence of two very large sites, suggest the use of larger work groups associated with an intensification of production. Oral traditions from Nangbani did not confirm this interpretation, but data collected by social anthropologist S. Dugast in nearby Bukutiba (also part of the Bassar agglomeration) indicate that larger work groups did in fact exist at the M'pampu 1 site and that they were linked to clan affiliations that often crosscut village ties (Dugast, personal communication, 1985). Further research is needed to more clearly understand the labor organization of Period 4.

4

Traditional Iron Working: A Narrated Ethnoarchaeological Example

S. Terry Childs

*Among the Toro of western Uganda, everyone has a pet name (*empāko*). My primary informant's pet name was Adyeri, and it is by that name I refer to him here. He gave me my pet name, Akiiki.*

I met Adyeri in July 1994 at the suggestion of my colleague Peter Robertshaw. He had met Adyeri in 1991 and found him to have a significant amount of knowledge about Toro iron working. This knowledge became very apparent to me after one afternoon with Adyeri, and so I ended up spending several weeks with him that year and visited him again for about two weeks in 1995.

All the time I worked with Adyeri, some of his clansmen, and others, I was accompanied by an interpreter, Charlotte Karungi (her pet name is Abwooli). Abwooli is Toro, speaks both Toro and English perfectly (as well as several other languages), and at the time was a graduate student in history at Makerere University in Kampala. When I met Abwooli, I was a bit concerned about two women attempting to interview male elders about iron working since sexually graphic topics could emerge in our discussions. In a very short time, however, Abwooli became the equivalent of a young relative of Adyeri's who was there to learn from him. He relished that role because he was afraid that the knowledge of early colonial iron working, including mining, smelting, and forging, would be completely lost when he and his colleagues died. He wanted that knowledge recorded and shared with others, particularly Ugandans.

Adyeri was born in 1914. His father and grandfathers before him were ironworkers. An unknown number of generations ago, his relatives came to the area from Ankole to the south and were both cattle keepers and ironworkers. As a boy and young man, Adyeri learned about the craft of iron working, including mining, smelting, and smithing, directly from his father

Plate 4.1 Adyeri at an old anvil stone

and his older brothers. The British developed a system of schools throughout the area, and Adyeri became a schoolteacher at the primary level. He continued to forge iron between school sessions to earn extra income. His father died in 1943, after mining and smelting had been banned from the area and forging was done using leaf springs of trucks.

Adyeri and his relatives are members of the Abachwamba clan [singular Omuchwamba]. Their totem is a cow called embazzi, *which has a white stripe from its nose to the back of its tail. The Abachwamba clan does not drink the milk of this cow. When it dies, they do not eat its meat. The* omuchwezi, *or spirit/god of the Abachwamba, is Ntogota.*

Adyeri passed away a few months after I left in 1995. He had been ill during the two seasons I spent time with him, although he began to perk up after I was able to bring him a wool blanket and some basic medicine, such as aspirin. It was because of his overall frailty that we did not attempt to mine or reconstruct a smelt, although we did visit some abandoned mines. We also visited several active smiths who forge scrap iron using traditional tools. Adyeri arranged a festive occasion with many Abachwamba clan members where they sang and danced many songs related to iron working.

The following discussion is primarily in Adyeri's words, as translated by Charlotte Karungi, to help fulfill his desire to document early colonial iron working among the Toro and especially the Abachwamba clan. (To see how I interpreted his words in other publications, see Childs 1998a, 1998b, 1999.) However, the discussion is not a continuous monologue or narration. I created the structure of the chapter using section headings. I then filled in the sections with Adyeri's statements about the topic from many different interviews over the two field seasons. Each paragraph is a complete remark, although I made some minor edits to his word flow and occasionally added comments in square brackets to help clarify a statement. I also include pertinent Toro words so that this dying vocabulary is documented.

We begin this personal narrative of Toro iron working by introducing a primary motivation for being an ironworker—wealth—and the principal players involved in various stages of the process. We then move into those stages—mining, smelting, and forging—that are punctuated with rituals, avoidances or taboos, celebrations, and other stages, such as the serving between smelting and forging.

OVERVIEW OF TORO IRON WORKING

Long ago, there was no job that brought in income—only that job [iron working] brought in income. If he was clever and he went to the mine and he got ore and he was also a craftsman [*fundi*] and took it for smelting and he was given iron, then he got it [iron] and he married. After all, it was only one hoe. So he took it to the girl's side and then they gave him a woman—"Take a woman."

At the ore, everybody [smelters] got cows, goats. That's where they got them from. Even a wife, when he smelted ore, he married a wife. He bought a cow; he bought a goat.

If you were a smith, you married many women because you had wealth. After all, a wife was only a hoe.

The Players

The discoverer [*omujumbuzi*] was the one the world knew. He's the one who discovered the ore. The whole hill. The whole hill, so he is the one who rules [*kulema*]. And he is the one who sacrificed [*ekyonzira*] at the mine. He would slaughter for the mine, do rituals, and all other things. What he does is to discover the mine and see that there is ore that others can mine. He is there as a leader. All those who get it will be getting it for him. If he did not know how to pound, how to smelt, how to prepare, he would take it to the ones who knew all those things very well.

If we had a smith in this village who was old/important, he would be known as *omuhēsi omukuru*. A smith's importance was his forge—where he forges from. If they are smelting, he has his smelt [*ejugutiro*], he would be the head. This smith does not lead like he has power—that is a county chief or a sub-county chief. He looks after his own forge. The iron [*ebyoma*] that comes to your forge—it is you who rules it. [I could not find a translation in the literature for *ejugutiro* but used the context to infer the translation provided here.]

Whichever smith died or if I died, they would cut a strip of a sheep's hide. That is all. He makes it a pillow [*kwesagura*]. It goes there. He makes it a pillow of the sheep that has wool.

They [smiths] did not come from the same clan. Some were from other clans and had their own gods [*abachwezi*]. The chief and god [*omuchwezi*] of any clan, for example where I am seated I am an Omuchwamba. All Omuchwamba clan members are looked after by Ntogota. Those from outside also have their own god.

Anything entering a home to spoil a home, to disturb a home, cannot be prevented. All of that is left to the spirit medium [*nyakatagara*]. That *nyakatagara* is the one who enters the home, she blows water on the walls, then all the trouble will be finished.

It is the *nyakatagara* to prevent it. Isn't it the *nyakatagara* who is the diviner [*embandwa*]? She is the god [*omuchwezi*] of the home. Things to destroy a home, she's the one to prevent them.

If disaster hit a home of a clansman, the *nyakatagara* would get up, get the horn, get a basket of millet, grind it, then put the horn in the basket. Then she goes to heal *[kutamba*] or prevent [*kutanga*].

The god enters the girl who is there if *Ntogota ya nkwale* is at the forging or when all the people sing the songs of the smith, dance, and hit the iron. It then climbs a girl who has not yet got married or has a wound. Then people see her falling there. "Someone has fallen. Call the *nyakatagara* to lift her from there." And whoever carried her away needed a lot of things. A person gave a lot of money to instruct the person because instructing was very expensive. That person was then taught how to dress and how to instruct others. That person is also taught how to sit on the wall and call the spirits of the dead [*emizimu*] and how to change the voice. That person who is instructing takes a lot of things. That is the *nyakatagara*. . . . The boys were not climbed by the god. It is girls. They are the ones who divine and become a *nyakatagara*. So if a god entered her, that was good luck and she was going to be taught.

A girl like that can be at the opening of a forge [*kukinguraho*]; she can be there. Isn't she important? Isn't she called to come and heal them? The forge is her house. If you have made things and they've become impossible, you go and call her again. Then she will repeat and make them good. If she finishes her work, she can go away. She can go to her other job. If she is married, she goes back to her work at home. She will have finished her job.

Ntogota is a god [*omuchwezi*]. Ntogota is the one who rules everything. If you are going to forge, Ntogota is there. Because he is the one who is going to help. His pet name is Adyeri. Without Adyeri, there is nothing that can be there. He is the one who pleads for you. [Many Toro men have the pet name Adyeri, including my informant and his god.]

Ntogota's goat stays in the home. It is called Defense [*Rutanga*]. That one and a big horn [*ihembe*] of a buffalo. . . . They look for a buffalo that has killed someone. It is the one that becomes Ntogota's horn in that house. They cut it out properly and that is how they got their god. It [the horn representing Ntogota] is given cowrie shells like we do in a church or mosque where we give money. So you throw cowrie shells in that open part and that is what is called to dress [*kusibika*] it. They would keep it in the shrine [*ihangiro*]. Then when you do not give birth, you go tell it, "I failed to give birth. I only give birth to girls. Can't you give me a son?" It's now like praying to St. Jude. The Basiita clan have their god. Every clan has its own. The Abachwamba have Ntogota. [The translation of *kusubika* comes from Davis (1938, 164).]

Together, the goat that is tied there, Rutanga, and the horn are Ntogota's. If Ntogota has made a mistake in the home, the *nyakatagara* goes to the goat and cuts off its ear, then uses the blood to sprinkle on the people and the doors. If there isn't a goat, she can have a chicken that is male [a cock]. She cuts off a piece of the crest [*orusunsu*], then blood comes from it, then they put it in the horn in the house of Ntogota.

MINING

Discovery of a Mine

A party would set out on an expedition to look for the ore in January, then in June to July. Since it was a source of income, many went to discover the mines. Since it was income, especially those who lived off smithing are the ones who went looking for the dung and the insect called an *ekijunjumira*. Its name was Kahinda. It has a white neck. This insect would find a place where a cow had left its droppings. It would dig in cow or buffalo dung or elephant droppings. When it dug, it had its own knowledge like all insects do. It would dig with its front legs and the back legs would clear the dug-up earth. When it dug, certain glittery small stones came up onto the earth's surface so when an expedition party came across them, they presumed there was ore below. The whole process of looking for the *ekijunjumira* is called to discover [*kujumbura*], to fall on suddenly. It is not easy to find the *ekijunjumira*. It is really luck to find it. It was very difficult to find it. When they went to discover, they walked for a long while before they came across any. [Davis (1938, 55) defines *kujumbura* as to "start prey from its lair; move, withdraw from ashes; take out quickly, forcibly."]

The person who discovered the stones called his friends to come and examine the stones on the surface. When they looked at them, they said, "Where there are these stones, beneath them there must be ore." They dug steps on each side of the pit to descend into the pit. They went down about 6 or 7 feet and the steps helped them to descend. Then they poked the earth and got the ore [*obutale*] that looked like what they had seen earlier on the surface. They tasted the stones. They were bitterish [not sweet, not sour]. The elder smiths [*abahēsi*] came to prove that there was ore there. They beat the stones so it would break/split up into very small pieces [*kusasanuka*]. If it had small stars that came out of it, they said, "Here, the things are there."

When they discovered that ore is there, the one who discovers the place says it is his mine [*enambo*]. If they have seen something profitable [*amagoba*], they can't go elsewhere. The discoverer would send a message to his wife, "Do not untie your belt."

Slaughter after the Discovery

The discoverer quickly slaughtered for the mine so that the ore comes out well. It is just a ritual. They may have wanted to eat but it was just a ritual.

They called it slaughtering for the mine [*kusāra enambo*]. If you sacrifice for something with blood, then it is called *omusaro*. They intended that the ore does not spoil [*kusisikara*] at the smelting stage [*kujuguta*]. They did all that in the name of Ntogota.

The discoverer would go to the *nyakatagara* after he had discovered the mine and said, "I have found a job. Please keep me well. Let the mine not kill people. Let me get wealth [*itungo*] from the mine. Let me get many profits from the mine. I get a woman. I get cows." He would then be pleading, kneeling in front of the *nyakatagara*. The *nyakatagara* would tell him, "Go, go with the king [*omukama*]." "Go with God [*Ruhanga*]." They used to call him Creator [*Nyamahanga*]. "Go with 'the one who gives.' "

The *nyakatagara* would cut a sheep while it was still alive and let its blood drip [*kutōnya*] or sprinkle it in the mine in the name of Ntogota, the ruler of everything. She would spit saliva on it there. So many things took place there [including dancing and singing]. They would even become possessed [*kubandwa*]. They also initiated [*kutendeka*] people from there.

All came when they were slaughtering, even women/wives. It was an offering to the ore.

The importance of why they had to slaughter a white sheep was because, if they did not, the ore would die. The ore wouldn't come out. They estimated that something that is white is what is good. The iron that will come out will be white. All that will come from that ore will be white. That is why they always slaughter white sheep.

Have you understood how the sheep has a lot of medicine? Don't you see it is the one they are slaughtering? The bellows—sheep. The hide—sheep. Its blood had to be used, otherwise you would fail to do anything.

Gentle person [*Kibonde*], if all things evil come, you are wearing medicine. So that thing can be soft [softening a situation]. All things will soften. Nothing will touch you. [Davis (1938, 66) defines *kibonde* as "a quiet gentle person or animal."]

And if they slaughtered it and it is white, they eat it all from there. They do not cook it. They get sticks and poke them into the sheep and roast it. They would throw it in the fire. Even the bones, they threw them in the fire where they are bellowing. It was not supposed to remain. It is a ritual for the mine.

After they finished the offering [*ekyonzira*], they then start mining.

Mining

The owner of the mine asked, "Who knows how to dig the ore," among those at the sacrifice. You see, people would never get lost. They would come because they heard there is work. Some were not Abachwamba, but if they knew the job they would all work and some would come from somewhere else of a different clan. You would make him work like your person. They've heard there is money so they come to get it. They hope that the discoverer would give them a small iron so that they can forge a knife [*entahirizo*] for cutting. The owner of the hill, if he does not get people to help him, then who will look after the ore? It is his mine that was first dug.

When the four or six workers identify themselves, they are told to dig. There was a hoe [*enfuka*] that was used to dig that pit. But even if all of them knew how to dig, there were only one or two who know how to identify [*kumanyirra*] the ore underground. He would know and identify that we have now reached the ore. And there would be someone up who would also say, "This is real ore."

No woman went to the mine when men were digging. They were bad luck. The men would tell them, "Tomorrow we are going our way and we are going to dig ore."

He would close his eyes because he cannot see. So the other two would answer [*kwanukura*]. When they answered—you see they wanted to have their work increase [*kukanyisa*] so that they didn't put many people to overcharge [*kusēra*] them. [Adyeri is referring to keeping the number of workers to a minimum so that the discoverer did not have to pay too many workers for their work.] So they would dry it, put it in a good place and dry it in that way. [Adyeri motions as though he is spreading out the ore.] They would then pick out their ore. They may get four baskets, but get one basket of ore. All they would take up is mud, but could get one basket of ore.

When the diggers [*abahaige*] go into the pit, they don't see outside. They would fill up the basket like a blind person. They can't speak and can't hear. They would put you in ropes and you'd start going down with long sticks. The people up would hold the rope. Then you go slowly. When you have entered down, you would shake the rope. Those who were answering the ore on top had a basket and a rope. After you found the ore and mined it, then they would send you a basket. After you put the ore in the basket, you would shake the rope so they know you have put in the ore. They pull the basket and you remain there. They would throw the basket back to you. It came with the rope. You then continue to poke for more. The tool used to dig was called thief [*omusŭma*]. They would use it to poke or worry [*kusondokora*] the ore. If ore wasn't there, then you would try on another side of the pit. You would make stations. Then when you finish, you put in more, and carry the basket on your head. They pulled the ropes and you climbed. You went with long sticks to climb with. If the mine broke, you couldn't come out.

They did not mine with clothes. They would leave their clothes. They would wrap a hide of a sheep over the shoulder [*kuhagatira*]. They mostly wore hides of a sheep. It is soft. And it had importance because it was like wearing medicine [*omubazi*]. It's the one that goes on the bellows. It is called *kibonde* [see previous reference]. If you were in things of ore, you would have worn medicine. They [Abachwamba] never wore charms [*ngisa*].

The people at the top called *abasagara* dried the ore. [I could not find a translation in the literature for *abasagara*.] They put it in a good place, spread it out, and picked out the mud so it could dry. Those who treated the ore, passed their hands through [*kurabyamu*] it. They sieved it to separate the mud from the stones. The mud remained and the bad stones also showed. The job of those outside was to pick out the bad stones and throw them away. So the iron was easily seen. Good ore does not split. It is just the stones that split—you hit them and they split. So they sorted the ore very well without the stones going in the ore. They removed them and said, "This is ore." They put them on the side. But they feared rain beating the ore, so if their homes were near, they would take them or cover them up. They would not allow the ore to be beaten by rain.

There was a tool they called the *omwangata* that is like the other hammers. It's the one they used at the top to beat and know that it was ore. It looks like a hammer but it is *omwangata*. It used to work at the forge and even at the ore it could work. [I could not find a translation for this word in the literature.]

When they dug the mine, they tried to dodge the rain when it rained. Another way of stopping the rain from getting into the pit was digging trenches around the mouth of the mine so the trenches trapped the rain. When they finished each day, they covered it with grass. When the rain was much, they built tracks in the pit.

To be able to dig that hole [*ekiina*], to reach underground, it took a long time. It couldn't take one day. Even tomorrow they would come back and come back also on another day. If they got tired and felt pain, they would stop.

If they got enough ore to smelt, they would get it and go. They would leave the mine there dead, like the ones we saw. So they would leave it there. They got their ore and went. After they sorted [*kusorora*] their ore, put it out to dry and it dried [*kwomya*]—after they sieved it and there are no stones, only ore—they would put the ore on their heads and look for where to smelt it. They never told them to smelt it from there. They had to take it where they wanted and smelt it there. They would go and make their furnace [*isăsa*] and smelt their ore. [The word *isăsa* seems to be used interchangeably for a smelting furnace and a forge.]

Payment to Miners

The discoverer knows his workers. The day he smelts he would pay them. He would give them their due salary. Someone would be paid according to what he did. You cannot give him more.

Before he dug the ore, the digger [*omuhaige*] came to an agreement with the owner of the mine and when they finished smelting he was given a piece of iron big enough to make a knife.

Those who know how to mine, the ones who mined the ore, were more important. They were more important because they had a lot of knowledge. When the mine broke [*kuchwa*], they were the ones who died.

Those ones who were up on the mine who dried and spread out the ore were not equal to the ones who were digging. The miners did more. If there were two or three, the discoverer would give them [those on top] a small iron—a very small salary.

The [piece the size of a] hoe was taken by the discoverer of the ore.

Deaths at the Mines

[*Kilembe, as it is referred to in the following, is the location of an international copper-mining operation of Uganda and England to the south of Toro. Many men went to work at Kilembe over the years, and many died there. Since the reign of Idi Amin and his successors, Kilembe mines have been hardly functional because of difficulties in maintaining the modern mining technologies. We visited the mines to investigate the archaeological potential of the area and determined that a systematic survey of a wide region was necessary to properly evaluate it.*]

Those big stones would come. People would die. If, for example, a big boulder split off the wall and it found someone, it would hit him and he'd die. If you twisted the rope and it acted like a bell into the mine and no basket came with it, then they knew the road was blocked. If they twisted the rope, twisted the rope, and there was no basket, then they would say that those people had dropped there. So they would condole/wail. "Oh they have been killed by the mine." They didn't blame anybody because they had gone to work. It is like in Kilembe; if a boulder hits someone, they don't ask, they say he had gone to work. It's an accident.

If someone was down there, saw small mud falling on him, then he would know it has beaten him. Then he started running out very quickly. He would shake the rope.

If they died, they never removed them. They would be buried there. Who would trouble himself by pulling up a corpse? They told their relatives that the mine killed their person or people; that the mine killed them. So they would mourn and put an heir.

They would know that it has rejected and, if that hill had ore, they would go to another spot and mine. They wouldn't go back.

If a mine grew old and it showed marks that it was going to fall, it fell and killed people. It was their failure to see. If they saw that it was old, they should leave it and go and dig elsewhere.

When a cow falls in a mine, you can't get it out.

Groups of Miners

It was their group [*ekitebe*]—the way they forged is the way they came. The way they forged and the way they smelted their ore is the way they came and worked together. Then they came to mine. They would make their shack. They would dig their mine until they got the ore.

If ore was discovered on that hill, the owner of the hill was the one who chose [where to dig] for them. He discovered the hill. When they came, he was the one who showed them. He was the one who ruled the whole hill. "You go and dig there." He was the one who showed them. "Oh, have you come? You go and dig there on the other side." It was not a problem. They would go. One would go and mine there, another one would mine far away—they all mined far away from each other because they were scared the world would turn upside down. If they dug 8 feet and found no ore, they wouldn't continue.

Don't you see, they hear that there is a hill where ore has been found. So people make themselves into a group and they come to work, to dig that ore. They do not have a leader [*omwebembezi*]. They just come and enter a mine to get ore. But if they got it, they would share it equally. When they share it, they all dig.

If the mine has got good ore, nepotism/favoritism [*tomunju*] will be there. [I could not find a translation of this word in the literature.] You may favor your clansman. That is what they call favoritism. You say, "You, do not come back in my mine." So you work putting in your house. Those who are mining say, "Here there's a lot of ore." But when you dig and go to the other side, there's no ore. So those people of that clan that you are favoring, you tell them, "Make your mine there." If they are your clansmen, you tell them, "There's more ore that side, but that other side, there is none." So you tell your people, who you are favoring, "You dig your mine here."

The [owner of the] hill, he was given ore. If they [the party of miners] didn't give him ore, they would give him an iron that could be enough for a hoe. It is called a payment to a smith [*omukīmba*]. So that owner of the hill takes it and forges a hoe. Why he does that is because all the rituals were finished by the owner of the hill. He's the one who did the offering. The god who came when they discovered that ore was his god.

Then he brought it to the *nyakatagara* and pleaded, "This iron, it came from so and so. He brought it to me as a payment for having mined at my mine, on my hill." Then the *nyakatagara* would say, "Where is it?" Then he would answer, "Here it is." Poo, poo, poo [the *nakatagara*'s spitting noises].

He will have given it to the *nyakatagara* to spit saliva on it—that iron from another home. "Go and forge your iron. It's a good iron." You prepare her a small meal of millet with mushroom, and the *nyakatagara* eats. She wasn't to be paid with cowrie shells [*ensimbi*]. She had her cowries to use for those jobs. They stayed there in the shrine.

If they came and mined in their mine, they would take him [the discoverer] a payment. They did not pay money/cowries, they brought payments like the one we talked about. They said, "Let us go. Let us go and forge our ore. If it comes out so well, we shall bring you your payment or your gift [*kisembo*]." They brought it later. They brought him an iron.

Entăbo

[*The Toro used two types of ore when they smelted.* Entăbo *is the second type. Although Adyeri considered it very important to the smelting process, he did not spend a lot of time discussing it. This is probably because he was never involved in mining it. We visited a place where it is still available and where smelting had occurred nearby in the past. Davis (1938, 133) defines it as "red clay; fertile soil."*]

Each had it own place. *Entăbo* was found in a separate place while the ore was in its own place. *Entăbo* was particularly from an area called Kigugu. They had to dig it up. It was down. It was like digging clay that they used to make pots. It doesn't go as deep as the ore.

It's those people of long ago who discovered the use of *entăbo*. You see long ago there was no other source of income and the smith was the only person who had a means of livelihood. It is he who was capable of buying cattle and marrying. When my mother got married, her dowry was one hoe. They never asked for anything else. They only asked to bring a hoe.

Entăbo looked like it glittered. The potters, after molding, they use some kind of earth to make the pots beautiful. It is reddish earth. *Entăbo* was only used in smelting.

They never performed any ceremony. What the owner did was to put it out and heap it there. He would pile it next to his ore.

He would say he discovered *entăbo* and whoever wanted some must come and negotiate. The owner of the *entăbo* would come to an agreement with the owner of the ore that, after smelting, he got a piece X. But that piece was small. The smiths were capable of making a sickle [*omuhoro*] from that small piece.

Entăbo was used to firmly join the ore [*kunywanisa*], to take hold of one another [*kukwatana*]. Without *entăbo*, iron could not stick together. They were just stones.

BEFORE A SMELT

Ore Preparation

Drying is a very big job. They dried when the sun shone in June or July, because they were careful. If they smelted it when it was wet, the ore died.

You still prepared another place for the *entăbo*.

He dried it at home because they would steal it if he did it at the mine. He made sure it was in his front yard [*muzigati*] as something that belonged to the owner of the home. He cleaned his compound very well, like where you put millet. That's where he put it. If it rained, they quickly put the ore in the basket and took them into the house. If it was sunshine, they dried them, then they mixed them with the *entăbo*.

They were dried by the owner of the house/husband [*nyineka*], the owner of the ore, or his wife [*nyinabwenge*] who was very, very trustworthy—the one who does not change.

That wife of the discoverer had many important roles to play. She never changed sides in bed. Immediately when the ore was discovered, you started embracing each other in bed. She had to sleep facing her husband until the smelting of the ore. She never turned away from her husband.

She could not cheat on her husband at all until they smelted and got the iron. Then she could cheat. Before the ore is discovered, you sleep how you want. A man can cheat on his wife, but when the ore is found, they don't part. The ore would die/spoil. It wouldn't come out. When you smelt, the ore becomes black, so it has died.

It was only at the ore time that they slept together with rules, so that she didn't spoil the ore. It didn't take a long time. It depended on when the ore dried, when they prepared it, and when the smiths came to remove the iron.

She had to be very careful. She had to ensure that people did not touch her shoulder like when they were talking and they touched her shoulder, or when they played with her in any way or even touched her [stomach or private parts]. It would be a crime. Her shoulder is a very crucial part. Even now if you met someone who touched your shoulder, you ululate [get angry and yell], "Why do you touch my shoulder? Do you want to leave me with all your bad luck?"

If she has children, she and her children and her husband are the only ones who can work on it [drying the ore]. But the children have to be careful. They are not supposed to touch her shoulder or private parts.

No outsider is supposed to come in. They [outsiders] might come to dry ore when they slept badly—no.

They first get the ore, dry it, then dry the *entăbo,* then pour the *entăbo* in the dried ore. They then mix them and make sure they dry. And at the time of smelting, they make sure that the *entăbo* is in the right proportions in the ore. They would estimate that for every three or four baskets of ore they would mix with one basket of *entăbo*. They used the same basket to measure. Then they start smelting.

Making the Tuyere and Bellows

He's the same person. He might be able to mold pots, to mold cooking pots, to mold bellows [*emijuba*] and also to mold tuyeres [*enkero*]. His name is potter [*rubumbi*]. It's only men who did it. A woman makes her cooking pots. Is she concerned with that?

He first molds a bellow. The clay is there. He would get it, strangle/squeeze it, and remove the bubbles, then he puts temper [*ensĭbo*] in the bellows and in the tuyere. *Ensĭbo*—when a cooking pot is old, one they used to cook from, or it broke, that is what they pound to get temper. They grind and grind and grind, then they beat the clay. They beat and beat and remove the stones. They then bring the temper, pour it in, and knead [*kutuga*] some more. Then they kick with their legs. It becomes soft and the stones are finished. The importance of the temper is to strengthen what has been molded, so that it does not burst [*kuhulika*]. If you don't add it and you put it in fire, "pop." It bursts.

They would sometimes put in slag but they feared it would burst the bellows and the tuyere in place of making them stronger.

After he beats it, he puts it on banana leaves.

Then he starts molding. He would mold it with a stick, then mold it with a stem of a banana plant. When it is cold, he would mold the bellows [pot] on. He molds the bellow, its hand [the pipe attached to the bellows pot], and he finishes. Then he pierces it. Then he puts a choke [*kaningo*] where they would wrap the hide and tie a rope, like the neck of a cooking pot. Then he gets the *orujerengo* and rubs it on when the clay is wet. [I could not find a translation of this word in the literature.] The *orujerengo* is made out of papyrus [used to make mats]. That papyrus is split and he ties it like a goat's rope. So when he has made a bellow, he dips the *orujerengo* in water and rolls it on the bellow while it is still wet. It is like how the man used to cut during Kabarega's regime [body scarification]; it's like the y-pattern. It gives it a design so it looks nice.

He dries it after which he gets reeds and burns it. You know when it is molded, they smoke it like the cooking pot so it remains like a cooking pot. When you heat a cooking pot, does it change size? If it isn't molded properly, it has air spaces in the clay. But if it doesn't have them and it burns properly, it can't break. Then he says, "Oh, that one is very nice." When he sees it is red, he knows it is ready. He removes it and keeps it, then he molds a tuyere. The bellows are two.

Then he prepares the tuyere. He uses the same clay. He molds it with a stick. Then he puts on a mouth slowly. You see tuyeres are different. There are those for smelting the ore and those for forging.

One smelt, one tuyere. Two bellows face the tuyere.

Payment for Bellows and Tuyeres

You buy one as you need it. There are times when there is an accident and the tuyere breaks—you know it doesn't break, it delivers [*kuzara*]. Such accidents, like cows walk in the furnace and step on it, then you need to replace it.

He'd set his own price for the two bellows the way he wanted. If one bellow delivered, you know it doesn't break, it delivers, the potter would then make him pay half the price. For example, 750 shillings as things stand today. But long ago, it wouldn't be that much. One needle and one hand knife is what was paid for two bellows.

If the female [bellows] got broken, they would say, "Mother of twins is sick," meaning there is a crack.

If he did not want money, he would ask for a hoe. But a hoe was a very expensive thing. Wasn't it the one that married a woman? They would give you a woman for a hoe. So he would be given a hand knife and a smaller knife [*entehirizo*]. Altogether today, a bellows would be 500 shillings. So two make 1,000 shillings or 1,500 shillings.

When he finished making his tuyere, you know those people of long ago never used money much. So he would probably be paid a knife. As things are today, he'd get 500 shillings then he'd be able to buy a tuyere.

Preparing the Bellows before the Smelt

I am going to give you a riddle: *Khoi khoikoi*? [Standard start to a riddle. No translation.] Two Europeans came in one shoe [*kilato*]. The answer is "bellows." So the two Europeans are two bellows. The shoe is the sheep's hide. The decoration used is for all bellows and whoever makes them decorates them the way they are supposed to be decorated. Their duty is to wear one shoe.

You'd be able to see one hide for the two bellows. He gets one hide, then gets two sticks—those sticks for pumping. When preparing the hide, if they know they are going to use it for wrapping the bellows, they cut very carefully to make two holes, stretch [*kubamba*] it properly, and then carefully shape the legs and hands. Those holes are for the sticks that have been wrapped. You wrap one stick with sheep's hide and tie it with a piece of cloth to make it tight and you also wrap the other stick with a sheep's hide and tie it with a piece of cloth. These are the ones you will hold when you are bellowing.

After that, they take the skin to make it nice and soft with other things. Then they smear it with *ghee* [fat] so that does not stiffen. They hold it very carefully because a sheep's skin is very soft. It is the fur that faces inside. It is the fur that fans [*kuhuha*] with strength. They used a sheepskin because it was soft. A sheep's hide is the softest of all hides.

If the sheep's hide was not there, they would use the civet cat [*entamujuguta*]. [Note that the word for "to bellow" is *kujuguta.*] It's a big animal. It has patches [*emibambabamba*]. It looks like a dog. During the moon, it is white. During the dark, it is black. It keeps changing itself. It stays in the bush. The wool is the one that brings the strength of the air. Its hide was more or less the same as for a sheep.

[An aside about the relationship of the sheep hide to the bellows.] If they are bringing something to that home, or a woman is getting married, or there's an important ceremony when they sing/dance to bring the *nyakatagara* to a smelting place, that is when they slaughter a sheep and remove its hide. That is when they know that they will be mediating some day soon. They remove the hide, stretch it. They eat the mutton there and then. That hide is what they will tie over the bellows—that new hide of the sheep they have eaten. It's the one they smear with fat to make it soft. Then they tie it to the bellow. The sheep is the ceremony; the one for the bellows. That is why the *nyakatagara* puts the horn [of Ntogota] in the sheep's skin. The sheep is a quiet animal that prevents bad things/evil.

The Gender of Bellows

There is one bellows [*omujuba*] that they made female and one they made male. On the bellow that was female, they would roll the *orujerengo*. They would decorate it up to where it faced the tuyere. It resembled that of a water pot so that it could be different. So that this is a female bellow and this is a male bellow.

There at the smelt the male is called "father of twins" [*esebarongo*] and the female they call "mother of twins" [*nyinabarongo*].

But people just imagined twins and made an equal example [like a metaphor]. They saw that if there are two things, one will always be male, another female. Even when they are molding it, you'll find a sign/pattern/example [*akokurorraho*]—a navel [*omukundi*]—and that is a male. They used to put it in front where it has grown fat/bulged [*kugomoka*]. They'd put it above the hand. The one that has *orujerengo* is female.

Those who made them would even put the male private parts [*obusaija*], then this one would be male and the other female. They made the male private parts out of clay and fixed it on the bellow. They would put it where the bellow faced. Then it would be facing the female's decoration so that you could see it dangling [*kujenlingera*].

Plate 4.2 Preparing to put skin on a bellows

It was the rule [*ekiragiro*] to show that it is a female bellow. They would then know that the one with the *orujerengo* was to be put on the left. Then the male they put on the right. That was the way of the past.

The female would also have a breast [*ibere*]. You can know a female from the breast. That is why they put a navel to show that one is male and the other one is female.

They are equal. They simply put [decorations] to make differences. They used two [bellows] because they want the fire to go with strength.

Father of the twins and mother of the twins. Producing is the job. This one is male, this one is female. Aren't the children the ones they forge? The iron they forge? And why they put two bellows is because, if they put one, it does not have strength. It sips [*kuhūta*] a little. So that's why they put two. And there they also put two so that it can sip with strength so that the ore can be cooked [*kuhya*] quickly. [Sipping refers to pulling in air by the bellows and then sending it out into the furnace.]

Father of the twins and mother of the twins—they say mother of twins when she has produced children. Why they say there should be bellows, mother and father of twins, is because they produce so many things. They are mother and father of twins because they produce wealth and many other things for people.

If there is no bellows, those things are not there. Children produced by the bellows—wealth. Wealth, a wife, a cow, a goat, many. Those are the twins born by the two bellows.

It produces good twins. Didn't you hear the way they sing? When a woman doesn't know the tuyere, she doesn't know what brought her. If it rains, she has to get the tuyere and put it in the house. If the bellow is beaten by the rain because you did not roof the furnace or forge well, it is very bad. So, save the bellow. Put it in a good place where rain can't beat it. If you have not roofed, you get it and keep it in the house. Don't let it be beaten by rain. It can burst and get spoiled. So the twins are the things the bellows produce—wealth and other things. Those are the ones and that is why they call it mother of twins because it produces many things.

You keep it [bellows] properly so it won't produce [break] after you use it to smelt or forge. You put it in the house. If it is in the house, then there's no problem. If you leave it there and a cow or a goat steps on it, it gets spoiled. Even the hide. After you have finished, you have to keep it. You remove the hide and you keep it alone. You also keep the bellows alone. If you don't have rats, you hang it [sheep hide] in the house. When the time comes to work, you get the bellows, take them to the smelt, and you start working.

That tuyere and bellows have a very big job. That's why you heard it in the songs we sang, "Save the bellows" [*Karokore emijuba*]. While the calves are tied there and the goats tied are there, the rain can beat the bellows. "Save the bellow. It shouldn't be beaten. Let the others be beaten." If they die, the bellow will replace them. A woman who does not know a tuyere, doesn't know what brought her. She doesn't know what brought her in the house. That is a tuyere and she looks after it very carefully. Before it is dry, it shouldn't be beaten by the rain. "Save the bellows, let the calf be beaten." That is it.

If the bellows is there, that home is very rich. Those bellows.

Gathering Charcoal

Charcoal is prepared from trees called *omuhakwa* and others called *omusoko*. [Davis (1938) defines *omuhakwa* as a "small tree with sprays of purple pea-flowers. Millettia spp." (182). He defines *omusoko* as "a common tree in Kibale Forest, Toro. The wood is yellow-white and scented. Warburgia ugandensis" (184).]

Omusoko is what you find in the big forest. It's the best. It's very hard wood. They go for it. Those who make charcoal go to the forest and cut it. Either *omusoko* or *omuhakwa,* they all work well. The *omuhakwa,* if its charcoal lights, it doesn't get used up quickly.

The *omusasa* come in because they know how to make iron ready properly [Davis (1938, 183) defines this tree as "a forest-edge tree with graceful drooping foliage, red tinted when getting old. Its wood is used for making charcoal. Sapium ellipticum."].

They would smelt with *omusasa*. They smelted with *omurongo*. [Davis (1938, 183) defines this tree as "with bi-pinnate leaves, pink flowers and flat pods. Albizzia grandibracteata. A. zygia."] They would smelt with *ekibirizi*. [Davis (1938, 181) defines this tree as "with very bitter leaves which are chewed to clean the mouth and used for rubbing inside beer pots."] They would smelt with *omuhakwa*. When they went to the forest, they would also smelt with *omusoko*.

If they knew how to make charcoal they would cut their trees and make a long raft [*orubaya*] full of charcoal. And they carry and take it. They are easy to find. He can see them in the forest; he can see *omuhakwa*. If he doesn't find *omuhakwa*, he uses others.

Or the charcoal owner would bring his charcoal and tell him [the smelter] that "for my charcoal that I have brought you, you will give me a piece of iron" and that piece of iron would make half a hoe. But the specialists [*abatezzi ba bamakara*] in burning charcoal would set their price. He would say, "I want *orusagwa*." So you know *orusagwa* is a piece of iron, but it can get a big thing out of it. [I could not find a translation of this word in the literature.]

It was the same charcoal they used. It would have remained from the smelt and the same charcoal would then be used at the forging to get irons [objects].

You would know that this volume of charcoal would prepare two baskets of ore. How did you measure the charcoal? Did you put it in a basket or a big bag [*ekigega*]? You would put it in a small basket [*akagega*] like the one that would be enough to prepare the ore.

The one [basket] for ore was smaller. The one for charcoal was slightly bigger.

SMELTING

Preparing the Furnace

The furnace [*ejugutiro*] looks like a nest.

They measured [*kulenga*] how much ore would go there—two or three baskets—and then dug.

The ones who are smelting—he might get his ore from a certain hill. Then he asks, "Where can we smelt this ore?" If there is a place he wants to smelt from, he makes his makeshift house just to stop the sunshine. They would get a good place and clear it. If the bellows and tuyere could fit there and all else required could fit, like where to sit, there was no problem. Then the smelters come and make sure the area is flat where they can bellow. Then they smelt. They bring those big foundation sticks [*omuganda*] [to build the furnace house]. You dig and plant [*kusimba*] a wet stick there and plant a stick there and plant a stick here. You plant four sticks and you tie up other sticks. They cut banana leaves and put them there to prevent the sun. They put a shade to stop the heat and the sweating.

If he went to a different place, he might make a long lasting one [furnace house]. If others have their ore and want to smelt it quickly, they simply tie up [*kusĭba*] a house and then roof it so that it [the rain or sun] doesn't beat them. Then he smelts his ore there. If the ore is ready he may transfer to another place.

You chose where it was flat. Assuming this is the hut, you dug the pit here. The pit where they bellowed from was 3 feet where they would pour the ore and the charcoal. That's how the pit went but it does not go far. Maybe 2 feet or one and a half [feet deep] where they knew that the ore would be ready. It was as wide as almost this table [about 3 feet].

Then you prepared where to put the male bellow and the female bellow. Then you prepare where the tuyere will go, but the tuyere does not go very deep. The tuyere is the one that kisses [*kunywegera*] the bellows. It's the one that blows the fire, then takes it to the ore. Its length is from the bellows to where the ore is. That is why we say it is 3 feet.

It [tuyere] would be straight to where you put the dried reeds [*efunga*]. Right in the middle of the dried reeds so that all the ore is cooked. It never went to the bottom of the pit and it ended where the ore stopped.

You have to bring the earth to cushion/pillow [*kusagura*] it [tuyere] so that it is right in the middle where the fire would come. Do not to let it fall or the air goes in the wrong direction. You put it in the middle.

They dug a small hole to enable the bellows to settle properly and to be on the same level. So you would dig here and dig there where to put them. So you put them to face the tuyere. You put the dirt to cushion the bellows so that they don't move. You know the strength with which they smelt can make them move. You put dirt so that it [tuyere and bellows] stays in line. So that the fire does not go astray [*kuhaba*].

You put the tuyere in before you make the fire. It is the air from the tuyere that lit the fire. Even if you brought fire from elsewhere and you poured it in, still the tuyere had to light it. You could see the tuyere in the charcoal. It's not supposed to disappear in there. You were careful to put it to target the bellows so that the smelter could see it and see if the air came out. So if the fire lit, aha!

After making the pit nice, you first put ash, so that if you put fire, it does not go out [*kuzima*]. You take ash from another cooking place, like where they cook from. You get it, bring it, and you put it there. You put a little just to cover the pit and under the tuyere to safeguard the tuyere so that it doesn't fall. You spread it out properly so that it [tuyere] does not protrude to the bottom [of the pit]. The ash is put there so that the earth doesn't rise to put out the fire.

Then he brings the dried reeds. You get a bundle, break it into pieces, then you put it in like this and this and this [demonstrates crossing layers of reeds]. Yes, so that the charcoal does not go through. If he brought one bunch, he put it all there. He never added more. When he set it out, he estimated that what was enough to cover the pit and be able to protect the charcoal. When the fire lit the dried reeds, the reeds lit the charcoal, which lit the ore.

The charcoal is put on the dried reeds. You put the charcoal, so that the ore does not go through the charcoal. Then they pour the ore there.

The water in the small pit [*ekijabago*, next to the furnace pit; it is common in forges] is a lot of water. It is not something to play about. They prepare that pit and put water and then they put in the grass sprinkler [*isiza*]. The sprinkler is so big. It is the one for dipping in the water and then sprinkling so that the dust does not rise and get to the people. It also helps the charcoal not to burn very fast, so that it all does not get finished very fast. It also helps very much so people don't sweat a lot.

For the ore, the one who is bellowing works so hard. When it [the ore] got fire, when it was ready, it would then slowly pour off [*kukenenuka*]. Then there would be a song.

After he smelts, he gets his iron and leaves the slag there. And he goes.

The "Prison"

Anybody would come, but if the ore wasn't ready, they wouldn't allow people to come there. There might be those who slept badly.

When they were smelting the ore, they would put a mark, one that stopped people, one that stopped people that here, there are smiths of ore. "Do not go there." People should not go there with a sick brain or who slept with someone or who might do anything that cannot be managed. So if a person sees a prison [*nkomo*] on the road, he will pass to the other side.

When they prepared to smelt that day, they refused someone who had slept outside. They planted this way and planted this way, then they put something like a customs [barrier]. Whoever saw it would not pass there. He would go back.

When we were making things for ceremonies, we put a prison. Nobody should come there. At the prison, they put a stick. That stick blocked the way. But if there was ore, they put a stick of *orusororo* [Davis (1938) defines this as "a shrub the twigs of which are used for cleaning teeth and as a broom" (153). He defines *kusorora* as "sort, separate, pick and choose, distinguish" (164).] Someone sees it and says, "Eh, they are smelting ore there. I won't go there. They can kill me." The smiths of ore used *orusororo*. Its meaning is "they have separated themselves." They do not want someone who has evil to go there. They planted their *orusororo* at the road. It is from the bush. They put the prison only where they smelted ore.

Both men and women came to see the smelt, but there were particular about those who slept badly, who were sleeping around.

The smith would tell them at a distance, before they arrived, "If you know that you slept badly or you are a prostitute, then don't come here." If he [ironworker] hides and does not speak out to them and someone bad comes, then he spoiled [the smelt] for others because the ore would die.

They would refuse a woman because she might have slept with a man or a man slept with a woman. They didn't like it. They would ask, "Did you pass the night well?" "Yes, I slept well."

If you were going to smelt, you did not sleep with a woman. You could sleep with a woman but you could not sleep on her. [Note that Adyeri says that the owner of ore must sleep with his wife until the smelt, then not after.]

Yes, they would refuse you because you'd go with a woman, sleep with her. The ore would die. The iron would get spoiled; it would become slag, not iron. And if someone slept with his girlfriend, then he shouldn't look at the ore—it will die.

There is no bad if a person who slept badly does not come there. Maybe he is a bachelor or he is a man who touched someone else. He is not supposed to come there. Or if he has a stomach discomfort and squats and passes gas from there, he is not allowed to come. The ore would die. If someone squats there during a smelt and passes gas, the ore will die. They feared that the gas enters the ore and kills it; spoils it. It would become black and wouldn't get ready.

The women were not allowed to go where they smelted. They would stand up there [a place removed from the smelting site] and say, "Hey, food is ready. Come for it." And they would go for it. They [girls] also can't go there.

They feared their ore to die, because if a woman sleeps with a man. . . . Sleeping, she could sleep but not commit adultery [*kusihana*]. They thought maybe a woman can steal herself and go and sleep elsewhere.

They [girls who were not in their good days/menstruating] were feared at the smelting. If they insisted on coming and you looked at the tuyere, you'd see total darkness. So the ore dies, then they say, "Someone has spoiled it."

For the ore to be ready, it's supposed to be very red, pure red after it has formed. But if it is spoiled, it is very black. It's extremely black. As black as your recorder here.

They didn't blame anybody [if the iron turned black] because they didn't know who caused it. They wouldn't know who had trouble. If they knew they wouldn't have allowed that person to come. It wasn't a [court] case. It was bad luck.

[An aside on other times when a "prison" is used.] If there is a ceremony being performed by the *nyakatagara,* she would prevent people from coming. They put there a prison. If there is something important involving a *nyakatagara,* they put a prison. Family things, maybe. If the *nyakatagara* decided to be possessed, or if they were going to instruct children in that home, or if they were to look for a god to strengthen them, that's when they put their things to prevent people.

Sacrifice

The slaughter is for the furnace hearth.

At the discovery of the mine, they would slaughter to bewitch any evil that would spoil the mine. Therefore, even at the smelting, they slaughtered so that the ore didn't get spoiled. That is why they even sprinkled people with blood. They didn't cook it [the sheep], they simply roasted it. They would eat and finish it there; it did not stay overnight. It was done at every smelting. For every smelting of ore that was the first ceremony they performed.

When they were going to smelt, that's when he brought his *nyakatagara*. Then they would sacrifice and then they got their ore.

The smith of ore pleads to the *nyakatagara* earlier. The god would come to the home if they were going to smelt. So when he gets up to smelt that ore, the owner of the ore kneels down in front of the *nyakatagara* who says, "Bring your hands. Poo, poo, poo. Bring your head. Go and work well and get income." Assuming I am *nyakatagara* now, I tell you, "Go to your home. That is all your wealth. You'll get a wife. You'll get a cow. Go and work. Poo." [Adyeri pretends to spit.]

If you were going to smelt tomorrow, you'd go and collect her today. So the *nyakatagara* would come and bring millet and mushroom and dried meat of a cow, plus all her other things. Then she would sleep there. Then the following day you'd start smelting your ore. When you finished, she went back to her home.

They slaughtered it when they were bellowing. Then they would sprinkle with the sprinkler [*ekimaso*] so that the ore doesn't die. They put the sprinkler in the sheep's blood and sprinkled it in the furnace and on the men who were bellowing. The blood gets into the pit. They sprinkle the blood onto the charcoal. [I could not find a definition of *ekimaso* in the literature.]

Why they slaughter a sheep is because it is supposed to bring good luck. "Let all the money come here." It is called a gentle thing [*kibonde*]. Yes, it is luck.

It's the discoverer who brought it and said, "Here is the sheep." Or if someone else brought the sheep, he would negotiate. The smith asked, "What do you want?" Then the other said, "I want a hand knife" or "I want a sickle." Then they slaughtered and started roasting.

Smelting

The smelters went out at about 3 A.M. to go and smelt the ore. By 12:00, they start peeking at the ore to see if it is ready. They might be able to get the iron at about 3:00 P.M. on that day. They feared the sun, that it doesn't shine on them too much, and they feared the wind.

Those smelters who knew how to smelt —it was their job. They worked together to make the ore ready. If they wanted to bring in others, it was up to them but their job was to smelt. They feared sharing the profits. That's why they used two smelters. If one took a hoe and the other took a hoe, then how much iron would be left? That is why two worked together. If the iron was ready, they would split the one piece for the workers. He would be very careful about the [number of] workers because if he had many, then he wouldn't be able to pay them. So he would put two to work—it was their job.

When he takes part in the smelting, he would eat a salary. He doesn't work for free. When someone is the bellower [*omujuguzi*]—all his muscles come out—he would have to be paid. Everybody had enough job for himself.

You do not select clan at a smelt. You only choose one who knows how to smelt.

A smelter did not wear clothes. He tied a sheep hide [around him]. A cloth would burn.

You put the *entăbo* and the ore in, then you bring the charcoal and you put the charcoal in the pit. Then the bellows are set up. Then you smelt and smelt and smelt. Then the ore and the charcoal and the *entăbo* talk loudly so that if you are seated there, you run away.

You cannot add on charcoal if the ore is lit but if you have your basket of ore, you can add on. No adding on charcoal, but you can add on ore.

When you are bellowing, you squat. However, there's a difference. At the smelt, you bellow while seated on a chair/throne [*ekitebe*]. If he is to squat, for how long will he squat? So he'd put up a structure like that chair you are seated on and he would sit in your sitting position [with legs open] while the hands are working without getting tired.

He is [*omutemi*] capable of making the bellows make loud sounds and beat the *obulindi*. [Davis (1938, 116) defines *omutemi* as "feller of trees," although it seems to mean the bellower in this context.] Even the passersby are able to hear. When he held the stick for bellowing in his hands, this finger to the third finger worked saying, "Ti, ti, ti." When he is bellowing holding the stick, he is making the *obulindi*. While you bellow, you are beating the *obulindi*. The noises come from the sticks. These *obulindi* are the ones that amuse people. [I could not find a definition for *obulindi* in the literature.]

It depended on someone's strength [when bellowing] and when he got tired. If he got tired, he would then say, "I am tired. Who is helping me?" The other would then come in and sit quickly. Smelting is like driving a car. If a driver sets off, when he's tired, another one drives.

Red earth [*etaka eri kutukura*] is kept ready during the smelting. You'd put it when the ore is about to form so that it's able to stick with the ore as it formed together with the *entăbo*. When the iron starts sparking, he then sprinkles in the earth. They add it to make the *entăbo* and the ore become hard [*kuguma*], to be able to stick together. They bellowed harder and harder while they added the red earth. The red earth that doesn't stick goes down to join the slag. So the red earth will have helped it to stick like gum.

This one is *ghee* [meaning the red earth is like lard], it sticks together. The *entăbo* is also like *ghee,* but it is very important. It is the one that embraces [*kufumbata*] the iron. You will know [the difference] because the stones of the *entăbo* will not be difficult to see.

When the *emisasa* and the *emihakwa* [types of charcoal] were cooking well, the iron was hissing; it made the iron hiss [*kusara*] and form. So the hissing of the iron was the *emisasa*.

When the iron is ready, then comes the sparks. There are sparks that look like stars. They rise and rise. People can even run away. Then it hisses and hisses and hisses. Then he says, "Yaa." Don't you see, you are sitting there. You'd run away as the sparks are flying. The one who is guarding the ore would be there waiting with the sprinkler. He sprinkles water from the water pot, so that he reduces the heat. He sprinkles water. When it hisses and it is ready, it then coagulates [*kukwāta*].

Someone is bellowing while the other is watching. While the one is bellowing, the other is able to see that the iron is almost ready. When it is ready, it then starts precipitating. He can see the water [iron] dropping [*kutōnya*], like they are squeezing oil. It would drop on the dried reeds. They used to put it there so that the ore does not get spoiled; so it could not pass through the dried reeds. When it reached the dried reeds, it would stick there and the slag went down. Then the iron stays properly without the slag. If the slag goes down and the iron starts hissing, then they say the iron is good/beautiful [*kusemera*].

When it finished bulging, they put more strength. "Put in more strength and bellow. Ohh, it's ready." That's how they would see it, dropping, dropping. That water would drop after it has bulged. They would see through the tuyere, in its small hole.

Before it started hissing, he peeks in the tuyere again. For the ore to be ready, it is the smelter who sees it. He sees and says, "The ore is going to be good! Ohh!" When it is nice, it is so red. He says, "Bring the *nyakatagara* to see." She also comes and peeks. Meanwhile the one who is bellowing has fixed his eyes on the tuyere. So *nyakatagara* fills her mouth with water and spits, "Let it be white," and spits again, "Let it be pure white." Then it will be very good.

If he sees that the ore had become black, that means the ore has died. You cannot see it dripping. That dripping is what is iron. It bulges and bulges. Instead there will be no bulging at all and it will be very, very black. It is dead.

When the sparks start rising and the smelter sees them, he bellows harder without breathing until the iron is served.

The smelter will see that if the slag expands a lot and not the iron, then he will say, "Oh, the tuyere is going to get a problem. So whoever has the tongs [*ruhana*], clear it, clear it." Then he continues to smelt.

When it's ready, they call it iron [*ebyoma*]. The stones have come out and the slag has remained up and there is iron. At the smelting of the ore, there are the twins. It is a good thing. It is good because you can get wealthy. If someone produces for you two children every day, then she has done a great job. Even then when they smelt in this place and get a big piece of iron, it is good. Maybe you can break it up into six or eight pieces and those are the twins. Many twins. That is why mother of twins and father of twins is very important. We say the father of the twins has had children with the mother of twins and among those children is the iron.

When it is ready, you put on your song. "It had hissed but lacked the tuyere." Then they start dancing. They are happy because their thing has become nice.

That Adyeri [the pet name of the *omuchwezi* Ntogota], he escorts you. He is Ntogota. He will escort you so that the iron hisses. Then when it hisses, it lacks a tuyere, then it is ready to make. [I am unsure of the meaning here—maybe strength of bellowing is lacking or the tuyere is clogged.]

This is how it was sung:

> Ntogota come and accompany me, it almost was hissing but there is no tuyere.
>
> Woman and child come and accompany me, it is almost hissing but there is no tuyere.
>
> Cow and sheep accompany me, it is almost hissing but there is no tuyere. . . .

Meanwhile others sang the chorus and they were very happy. It means the ore was almost hissing but there was no fire from the tuyere. The ore was almost ready.

They also sang:

> Say, say, say the hammer widens.
> The wife doesn't know what brought her, if
> the woman doesn't know the tuyere,
> she doesn't know what brought her.
> Say, say, say the hammer widens.

If a woman produces a baby girl on that day they are smelting ore, they call her "[*Kabahēsi*]." Again she gets married to smiths. That is a smith's person. Even when she produces children, they are smith's children.

[After the iron is ready] then they start serving [*kwihura*] the iron.

SERVING

For the two baskets of ore you put in, you get a big piece of iron. It would be heavy. You see that the iron is ready, so the servers bring tongs [*emihana*] to serve. They [the tongs] were 6 feet long. You know, they are four servers, two this way and two that way. They would bring the tongs, push them in, remove the slag, and the iron remained in the middle. Then they push in their tongs, pierce [*kucumita*] the iron, pull it out, and throw it there.

They get sticks with a knob and beat the iron and beat the iron. So they hit the iron with strength. They don't use stones to hit the iron because they will spoil it. They use sticks. You see, when they get it from the furnace, it is very soft. It's like clay. When it is cold and they've beaten it and it's lost its softness, they push it into the fire again and bellow. They bellow and bellow and the sparks come out. They then remove it and beat the second time. They beat and beat and beat and get an iron. Then they mold it.

[An aside about the servers.] They would do their other jobs. If they had not been called upon to smelt or to serve or any other assistance, they would go about their own jobs like feeding their cattle or digging. That is all they did.

Then the one who is supposed to cut it comes. He breaks it into parts. He was not a smith. His job was to accurately split the iron. He splits it with an axe [*endemu*] after which he beats it to make them equal in size [*kwinganaingana*]. Then the owner would say, "It is cooling. Put it back to get cooked. Break it into two again. Split it again." These pieces would remain his own iron [the owner of the ore]. It is the splitter who knew how many tools could be made [out of a lump of iron]. If someone is to take a small piece of iron, it would be broken off.

[The splitter also used] an axe that cuts iron. That axe was put in steel, to become hard so that when you used it to cut, it did not break. So that it did not break the cutting edge. Even now you can see iron that is from springs that they have put in steel. If you were not careful, it would simply break up *[kukatŭka*]. It was not made to cut wood or anything but iron. The axe was simply iron, but they put it in steel wisely in another furnace [I believe that Adyeri is talking about quenching.] Then it would bulge and they put it out to cool. But iron and steel is your language of English. What they did is they put the iron in steel wisely then they cooled it with water slowly, slowly so the sharp blade would never get spoiled.

[The splitter also used] the stone hammer, a stone like this. He would lift it and he would BAAAAAH. And then he would beat the iron. Then he lifts the stone hammer and he beats. BAAAAH. BAAAAH. And the sparks go. We don't know how they discovered the stone hammer. It is baffling [*kusobera*]. They got them from Rwiimi. They were round boulders that are brought by water.

Payments at the Serving

The discoverer knows his workers. The day he smelts he would pay them [at the serving]. He would give them their due salary. Someone would be paid according to what he did.

You know they are like a king, a [*katakiro*], and a layman [the discoverer, his primary assistant, and a worker]. The discoverer would then say, "Give that one this. Give the other one this."

The miners get more because by the time they went to the mine they would have negotiated. Because digging the mine and getting the ore was a very cumbersome thing. When they mined and the ore was smelted and the iron was made, they would then split the iron in four pieces, "That one is a piece for the miners." Then the owner of the mine would take his piece and miners would also take theirs.

They [the servers] were also paid a very small piece of iron. They are not paid a lot. They would decide to put their pieces together and get at least a needle [*empindo*] and a hand knife, which they wouldn't get if they used their pieces individually.

After they served and the server finished his job, he was paid a piece of iron from which he could get a knife. It's used for cutting. So when they retired, the discoverer would say, "Here you are. Take this and use it the way you want."

Other Information about the Serving

If you finished smelting, the iron was ready, and you served the iron—you put the irons there and they were split—then the bellows were removed and the slag remained. One bellows is put upside down and the other is put upside down [*kujumika*] so that even if it rains, it does not rain in them. Even the sticks would be out.

When there was any bathing to be done by the smelters, they would prepare the female bellow or even the male bellow, then they bring the slag and put it there. They would put the water in the bellows and it would heat very fast and the smelters would bathe. They [the bellows] were their basins. Did they have any at the smelt? Would they have to bring their basins every time they smelted? It was because they came from afar. And even if they came from near, they did not want to disturb their people from home. They never used to put their bellows on the cooking pit [of their wife].

The old men and good young men would come [to the serving]. Old women and other women would come. Then they would drink beer. You know when there was beer you would all come with your cup. They would put them there and you would fill it. Then you'd dance. But the children were not allowed because they would drink beer.

No, they [girls] were not allowed to come. It was a ritual because girls were not able to keep themselves. Or, a child will pass gas from there. There were days when the women went in their days of not being good [menstruating], so they were not allowed to come.

After they have finished smelting and they have served their iron, then they sing happily. They are songs of the pagans. *Ntogota, Ntogota* was their way of doing things. For example, when the king is having a ceremony in his palace, he had a way he did it. That is how these people also did it. There are about four or five songs and dancing. They would wrap themselves in sheep's hide [around the waist], then others would lift the hammer stone, then they sing and dance to amuse people. They would drink beer and get drunk. They are happy because ore has come and they are going to be rich.

Protecting the Furnace or the Serving

Other ceremonies might be performed [to protect the furnace]. For example, when the village chiefs came to arrest the smiths, the ones who were bellowing are told to continue bellowing. Meanwhile the smith is kneeling down because, by then, his knees are numb. Down there is slag, so he tells them to keep bellowing. So he tells the bellowers, "Play your part." As they advance, he then gets the slag and hurls it at the party who want to arrest him.

Slag is the one that is made of the refuse, so he tells those who are smelting to do their "knowledge." They fix their serving tongs, pull out the slag, and hurl it at the chief, so when he falls, the slag burns him excessively. It was a rule, they never allowed people to invade smiths. If he allowed them [the chief and his assistants] to come near, they would arrest him because he could not stand; he's numb, he's there kneeling. He had no back, so the slag was his defense, it was his stick. It was his weapon.

No, slag has never done anything and it is still there where they smelted. Its use was there during days of rebellion. If they came prepared to cheat the iron of the smith, he would tell the bellower, "Bellow with strength, bellow with strength." The slag would be red hot. After seeing people come closer to catch them, he stuck the tong in the slag and hurled it at the person. He fell down and died. They all ran away.

FORGING

The Smith

The smiths did not do other jobs, except their daily jobs like digging. A smith would get his cows. He would feed them and he comes back and sits there. If he is forging, he would employ a herdsman to do the work while they forged. Or if he had goats, he would tie them to graze. He would dig his food.

In Milongo, the subcounty of Butiiti, there can be one smith. And then in another subcounty, like Mukunyu, there would be another smith. The one in Mukunyu might make very big tools and many other wonderful things, whereas the one in the village like Mbale would make household tools like sickles and spears. So everyone would forge what he thought was good for him. There were not very many smiths. Smiths were not widespread. Forging is a very big job and it is held carefully.

The smith, the owner of the forge, is the one who made the final decisions. If someone came and he agreed to pound the iron, then they agreed, "If I make your iron, you'll give me this." If he [not sure whether "he" is the smith or the customer] sees the iron is so nice for him and he cheats, it is the chief who will make the final decision. He will say, "Give that piece of iron to this one." Yes, the chief will decide who gets the piece. Those [cases] were settled by the chiefs.

For him [the smith], he settled those [problems] of the forge. Anything that concerns the forge, like those who cheat each other of iron. They can be forging, then one steals iron and brings it to another forge. Then the other one reports him and says, "My iron got lost. It looks like this one. That is my iron." So they bring it to the chief smith to judge [*kuramura*]. "How did you get that piece of iron?" Then he says, "This iron, I got it like this and this." "Is there a witness? Bring him." Those are the cases he settles.

[The smith is very important when] there is a function that is led by *omuchwezi* Ntogota. If the chief smith goes there—the one who dances for that hammer—that function is nice. If he sings for the hammer, people will be climbed by the spirit. It comes from those songs of the hammer you heard that day. There would be about four people who fell. Then they take them to the shrine. At a function, if that clan it is not led by Ntogota, it won't matter. Even if he [the smith] sang, people wouldn't fall.

A smith was never mean or unhelpful. Their rule is to be kind. If someone brought a broken knife—if it broke where it entered the handle—and he came and the smith asked him, "What is it?" He says, "My knife is broken." [The smith] would say, "Bring it here," and he repairs it. But he won't ask for money. Pum, pum, pum [light taps of the hammer] and he gives it. This means that a smith had to be kind; he was supposed to treat everyone equally. And he was not supposed to be greedy. For everything he did—"bring money," no.

A smith never hid his money. When he got money he would buy goats. He would get cows. Therefore, from the cows, he got a wife.

He's a smith. How could he lead them [as a chief]? He stayed at this forge. He never went with chiefs. If they say, "Bring hunters," he won't go there. When they asked for food taxes [*omusenga*] for the king, he doesn't give it.

They would arrest him if he refused to pay taxes or do communal work, but the smith wouldn't allow his people to be arrested. Whoever bragged to go and arrest him is the one who died. They [chiefs, soldiers] learned that it is not easy to arrest a smith. Then they stopped.

They [smiths] were friends. They would be blood brothers [*omukago*].

[The smith wore copper instead of wearing his iron because] it was copied from other countries. The traders who came this way to buy things brought copper [*omulinga*] to sell. The bracelet [*ekikomo*]. Even now, if there is a function, if the king calls you, the smith or the chief smith has to wear this on his hand. Even now it's there. The smith wears copper. If they ask, "Where is the chief smith?," you come.

They liked it [copper]. It was fashion. For example some time ago, you had to remove your bottom row front two teeth to marry a girl. The girls who removed their bottom row teeth and the boys who removed them are the ones who got married. If you did not remove your teeth, no. It's like scarification [*engondo*]. Anybody who was not scarified did not marry. Even if she was very beautiful she wouldn't marry. She was nothing. That was also a fashion.

Now, if they are scarifying him/her, he'll lay down face upward. The one who cuts [*omusazi engondo*] gets his needle [*empindo*] and small knife [*akahyo*]—those two. He pushes here and cuts, pushes here and cuts. He holds the skin and makes the pattern of W, like W in school. Takes one line and brings back another. That is not the job of a smith. But the smith was scarified.

The Forge

He had his home and his wife, his favorite wife. Then he would build another house for another wife there. Then he would build for another wife on the other side. All those women would stay there in their homes. So he would go to one home, spend there two days, then go to another home, spend there another two days. So if there were four or five wives, then each would get two days. Then he would come back to his favorite wife. Then he would also stay with her for two days, then he would go back to his other wives so they don't feel lonely. If he wanted to forge, he would go back to his first wife. He only had one forge [*isăsa*].

The forge he builds in his front yard very permanently. The purpose of a forge being in the front yard is to attract passersby, for example, those from Kabarole, Fort Portal, and Kyenjojo. They would pass, see the smith, and say, "Are you there?" "Yes, I am here." Then another one will say, "I am going to buy my thing from the smith in Nkinga."

For those who forged every day, [his forge] looked like a traditional market [*empinga*]. People come and buy things and go.

[*Ihēsero*] is the same as [*isăsa*]. That is where they forge from. It is nearly called a school.

It is not a house. It is like a house but where air can pass. It is an open structure. If he wants he can even roof it, but he'd leave doors to allow in light. That's where he works daily. He knows that he needs an anvil [*oruhīja*] where he will pound. When he digs the pit, he doesn't make it so deep. At the bottom, you make it nice so that the iron goes in straight.

Charcoal for forging came from the *emihakwa* and *emisasa* [types of trees for charcoal]. There are other trees in the forest called *ensoko*. The dried reeds are there to light the pit. If the charcoal is lit, then you put in the iron.

Hammers

The stone hammer used to be a stone like this. He would lift it and he would BAAAAAH. And then he would beat the iron. Then he lifts the stone hammer and he beats. BAAAAH. BAAAAH. And the sparks go. Then those who are seated there run away until the iron joins together.

When a child was going to forge, they first gave him the hammer of *omwangatta*. Because of its overuse, it had reduced in size. It was called "*omwangatta*"—"that one I have given you, a thing of wealth, keep it safely; it is the one that rules the hammers." [I could not find a translation of this word in the literature.] That hammer was "*kamaramasu*"—"one that saves you from boredom or loneliness"—meaning that one that takes away all your sorrow from his home. That is the old hammer. It was used to help to forge a hoe, forge a sickle; it would forge this and that. It is also for putting final touches to small tools, like the needle. The *omwangatta* is up there [the flat crest at the top of the hammer]. That is where you put the needle [on the flattened crest] and you beat it. The hammer is down.

There are many hammers. There is one that is very big that hits the big piece of iron which makes the hoe and the axe. Then there is a small one that is capable of making knives, a sickle, and a mat needle. They look alike. Then there is one that is slightly bigger that makes spears. That hammer requires a lot of skill to use; to make the spear ridge in the middle. A smith has to be very careful and must have very good eyes that are accurate. He should not have bad sight. He has to target and make something correctly. There are several hammers. Like a craftsman, he has several tools—big ones, small ones.

Also in the family of hammers . . . he was given the hammer that puts the final touches after he has finished forging, for example, a knife, a spear, or a basket needle [*orukăto*]. It will help him to pound and lengthen it out properly. That is the small one. Then he gives him another hammer, a big hammer. It stays there, it stays there with its appetite—it was called one with big appetite [*karamairu*]. *Karamairu*, that's the one that forged a hoe after the hoe has been pounded with the hammer stone. That is the hammer. It is the one that makes the hoe; it was a hoe of strength.

They did not have other names, unless someone named it. They would say, "this is my big hammer." If a tool was to be forged, the big hammer would come. A small tool—a small hammer would be caught. For example, that hammer that she [myself, Akiiki] saw and left here, it was called "*Rujonjoza*" [Davis (1938, 54) defines *kujonjoza* as "to abuse."] *Rujonjoza*, it's just a thing

Plate 4.3 Adyeri's family hammers and clay tuyere

that is there. That is a name he [another member of Adyeri's family] named it. How would you call it?

Rujunjonza, it's there in the house. You know, it gives birth [*kuzāra*] and its children are there. It is female. It produced. It has its child. Send me "trap" [*batega*] and "abuse" [*rujonjoza*]. The stone hammer is the husband of *rujonjoza*. However big an iron will be, you use the stone hammer and it will be finished. "Abuse" and "trap" simply irons/straightens out [*kugorra*] the iron.

This one ["abuse"] is the one that is old. This one is the mother. It will do anything that has gone wrong. That one ["trap"] is its child. The child will also sit and work with its mother. You hold them and see. Have you felt its strength?

It is the bellows that conform to the way things were created—husband and wife. They should always stay together. So the people said, "Let there be a male and a female hammer."

[*Adyeri's nephew speaks in the following extended paragraph with three sections. No other smiths we interviewed corroborated his claims about being climbed or caught by the spirit of the hammer.*]

I am helping [*kukonyera*] it [by spitting on it]. "Rest, rest" [he says to the hammers]. The one who made these was very old and died. He was an important old man [*mzee mukuru*]. He used to live in Mbale there. They [the hammers] were for our great grandfather. Yes, our great grandparents forged with these hammers. And when they had used them, they also left them to their sons so that they could do the job. . . . The hammer is like a spirit. It chooses you and it can even make you run mad [*kugwa iraro*] after it has chosen you for itself. When it says, "You should forge," then you forge. Even if you don't forge something very big, at least forge a mat needle or a basket needle. When you hear the song, "I slept when I had been climbed by white," that is the one. That means I've been climbed by the hammer [white is the iron hammer]. If it climbs you, can you also sleep? You run mad and if they do not tie you with ropes; it is not good. [The nephew holds the both hammers between his legs and caresses them.] I was 11 years. That's when they gave me the hammers. When my father died. That is when he initiated/educated [*kutendeka*] the hammer. Do you know what *kutendeka* means? That's when he initiated me. . . . That work [smithing] is the work of the clan. Even if this job is for the clan, these hammers choose their person who hold them and use them. Don't think all the members of the clan hold those hammers and use them. They will choose only one person who will start working. The clansmen can come and work. If a clansman brings his iron, you forge it.

People of long ago, when they were singing, they would say, "Now that we have sung those songs, let's sing for the hammer." The hammer is the leader of all. So they start singing for the hammer. Those who want to copy will copy and sing.

"Say the hammer widens [*Gambe enyondo mugalihya*]" [this is the first verse of a song] means the hammer is the one that widened everything. The woman is of the hammer. If she enters a home, she produces for the clan. The one who buys the cow is for the hammer because it can produce many other cows. The motorcar is for the hammer. A car cannot move. It is smiths who forged it. Everything is for the hammer "Widen [*Mugalihya*]."

"*Mugalihya*" is a name of a hammer because you know it widens. It widens all things. It widens a house like this and puts a cow there. It widens money; he gets a hammer and forges. He gets a hoe, he uses a hoe to marry a wife, he buys a cow and goats, and then the home widens. Then the woman he marries produces a child. That child produces another and that one also produces a child.

Forging

When he starts, he asks, "Is the place where I put the forge proper? Are the places for the bellows and the water sprinkling pot to sprinkle the iron there?" He needs to know there is a forest where charcoal will be got from; where he will cut it; where there is *emihakwa* [type of wood for charcoal]. Then he got the hammer stone. These days people use axes, but for him, he uses a big stone. When he is finished preparing—he has dug the pit, the anvil is there, the person who will pound [*omurubiki*] is there—then he starts his job.

Someone then brings his iron, "What do you want from your iron?" "I want hoes." So he asks again, "How many hoes?" The other replies, "Two hoes." So the reply is, "If you are getting two hoes, then I will take one." They come to a compromise and he takes one. There are those who bring beer. Those who have come to an agreement to pay him will pay him. He then puts the iron and he straightens it; a small piece can stretch up to there. He then heats it. Then he does his job of smithing.

The smith sits here and he guards against the person pounding because he is the one who sends the piece to the pounder to pound. The pounder takes care that the stone does not fall from his hands and hits the smith. If it hits his head, he will die. Then the smith starts forging tools.

A good smith prepares his forge early. Smithing is not as cumbersome as to bellow ore [*kujuguta obutale*]. There will be someone bellowing. He [the smith] removes the iron, then he gives it to the pounder—they don't wear clothes, they wear a loincloth. The smiths never wear clothes; they would fear it to burn. When he finishes forging the iron someone brought for him and it is time for retiring, he would say, "Unstretch the bellows and we go home." So he would ask, "Is there water?" They would answer, "Yes." Then they would put water in the bellow and he sits there and bathes. That is a smith. He is the one who forges. He forges iron from the ore; he forges all kinds of iron tools.

Sheep, the hide of a sheep. They wore the hide of a sheep because, if the ore hissed a lot, they feared the cloth would burn and get finished. That hide he wore like this. When he was forging, wouldn't he have something he wore under there [points to under his leg]?

At forging, you wouldn't be nepotistic because there are people who know how to pound. That is a department of very strong men with a chest who can pound the iron with strength. And there are others with no strength. They cannot lift that stone off the ground to hit that iron. Would you choose such a person and give him a job!?

There are two workers and the other one you had is the wife who brings water and food. She places some water beside the small pit so that if the water in the small pit is finished, then the smith can pour in what she brought. So she's the third. The two—one is a bellower and one is a smith. If it's an ordinary forge, the pounder is not there. But if there is iron that needs to be pounded, then he comes and is the third; the wife is the fourth.

You squat. You bellow while squatting.

Spring iron. If this does not have steel, it cannot fall [*kugwa*] and rise [*kwimuka*]. But if it is soft and it falls, it could come back. That is the one that can take hold of one another [*kukwātana*]. These are the ones. Those are all irons but they are not equal to this one. This one [iron made from ore], if you beat it with a hammer, it won't break. But this one [iron from leaf springs of cars or trucks] if you beat it with a hammer, it will break. When you take it out and you beat it, it breaks because it will have gotten excessively ready [*kuhingurana*].

To be able to know it [iron made from ore] is ready, when you put it in the fire, it released electricity. We removed it from the fire and beat it. We could put it in the fire two or three times as we made it long [*kuraiha*] and made it wide [*kusorora*]. Then we can then cut it and make a hoe.

If the springs release electricity, then they are broken. They shouldn't release electricity. I do not bellow to make it excessively ready . . . like stars [*obunyunyuzi*].

If the smith was there forging and he put the iron there, if he removed it from the fire and beat it, and if the sparks went all over the place and fell on him, they would burn him. If it fell on you, it would burn out very quickly but it would burn you because it hisses a lot. This spring iron won't burn you quickly, because it does not hiss. They do not want it to hiss. If it hisses a lot, you will have lost.

[When you made a knife and a very small piece remained], you would make a mat needle [*orukăto*]. Or you would wind [*kumyora*] it to make a

Plate 4.4 Toro smith working at his forge

needle for making baskets. They never threw away a piece to get wasted/die for nothing [*kufa era bussa*].

Long ago we had sticks. You would fix the knife in two sticks and join it. A sickle enters a stick. The meat cutting knife [*entahirizo*] enters the stick. The hand knife enters a stick. The dagger [*empirima*] enters the stick.

They cut a handle [*omuhini*] and tie the hoe. There are things to tie it there, not those fibers. The ones they use to tie the hoe are for thatching the house. They would tie it so tightly so that it does not wiggle out. The second way is to tie with strips [*enjuza*] of papyrus [*orufunjo*] from the swamp. Also, they used to tie *omubugo*. [I could not find a translation of this word in the literature.] It's there in the forest. They would get pieces like this and use.

Then you'd make it [the handle] black [*kuziga*]. That's what you held. So you'd hold it like this with the blade here and you cut. The smith [did that]. He would forge his wood. He would not give you a knife without putting it in sticks. Making it black was its beauty. You scorch it. You used a piece of iron that was ready [to scorch it]. When he wants that stick to be black, he passes it on the fire, like this.

They got the whetstone/polishing stone [*ihyoro* or *emunyu*] for beautifying [*kusemeza*] the king's spear "*Erihango*." It's what whitened [*kwēza*] the king's spears. It is a stone that is softish [*orobera*] and it is white. When you use it, it is sandy. If they put it on the spear, it will shine [*kumulīkana*]. They also smear it with *ghee*/lard to make it glitter [*kumeresera*]. Give me my spear. Bring. Now, this spear is dirty/black [*kwiragura*]. If you use the whetstone, it will shine. That is our gun, we stay with it. If you also want to rub your spear, to make it shine, you can. These days the whetstones are still there at Kyehara village.

Welding

It's called to unite [*kuteraniza*] the iron.

You go to the forge and light it. We could get about 12 old, useless hoes [*enfūni*]. Those are old hoes that stopped digging. They are hoes from our iron ore. You see, they want to make one iron become another. Not the European kind. So he brings the iron, he puts it there. Then we mold [*kubumba*] them like this.

You get the piece and the other piece. Then you smear [*kusīga*] the piece to make it red [*kutukura*]. That red earth is mud mortar [*obudongo*]. It looks like clay. It looks like the *entăbo* [the red clay-like ore] for putting in the ore. It is soft that you have made into dough. Then you smear it on the other piece. You level [*kwinganiza*] them together. Then you put it [the red earth] in the middle. Even if he wants to add a third piece, he would still smear it.

Then he takes it slowly and puts it on the fire. Then the others bellow and the iron heats up [*kusensĕra*] [In the context of this discussion, he meant that the iron heated up. Davis (1938, 158) translates the word as "to creep in or out."] When it heats up, the red earth seizes [*kukwata*] onto the iron that is on top. The indication that it has stuck is the sparks. There are so many! Then it sticks. Then you remove it. It hisses and he bellows; it hisses and he bellows.

When it sticks and the bellows are pumping, he gets a tong and he uses it to lift the iron out. He puts it on the anvil. Then the pounder pounds while the smith is holding for him. Like this and like this. He hits it hard to make them take hold of one another [*kukwataniza*]. Then he places it in the fire again. When he has finished making it together, he then changes it to the other side and puts it in the fire again with bellowing. There are so many sparks. He then changes it and beats it like this with the stone hammer. Slowly, slowly, slowly. Then he puts it back in the fire. He changes it this way again and he beats slowly, slowly, until he has molded it into a big piece of iron. Then they know that this hoe has been made out of iron that had been stuck together. Then he prepares to get the bigger iron.

If it hasn't stuck properly, he dips it in the water pit. It cools. Then they put on more red earth.

Forging Objects, Including a Hoe

They forged those that people wanted. They forged a knife, grass cutting knife, hoe, digging tool [*ekihoso*], spear [*icumu*], spike at the end of a spear [*omuhunda*]. . . . A spear is something that is very, very expensive. It is like a gun [*embundu*]. It's the one you married with. There are other important things, like the basket needle, mat needle, knife for pruning banana leaves [*ekisalizo*], and many, many others.

A hoe was very profitable. It is the one that married a wife. It would marry the wife—only one hoe. And in a hoe, someone would get a calf. If someone had many cows, he would get one calf and use it to buy a hoe. All those are valuable.

[Adyeri's father was a "king's smith." Here he describes the objects that his father made for the king and for his household.] He would make basket needles for the queens [*omugo*]. He made small knives for making the king's nails nice. He forged razors [*orumaiso*] for shaving the king. That was his job that he did.

The tools are the same [for the smith or the king's smith]. It is the smith who made the difference. All the tools looked alike.

The thing that disturbs you to get out of iron is a hoe. A hoe is made from a big piece of iron with strength. A hoe cannot be made from small things. From such, you get a basket needle, a knife—small, small things.

You can take two or three days to forge a hoe. You might make this part today, then if you are satisfied, the following day you pound the other part. On the final day, you make a complete hoe. That first day you come with the pounding stone. You pound here and you pound there, then you level it properly. It might take three days. . . . They first forge that round thing. They beat it like this and it becomes tall/stretches out. It is from there that they estimate and break off [*kuchwaho*] a piece that will make *ensokoro* [I cannot find a translation of this word in the literature. I believe that it means a large piece of worked iron.] It is that piece that he is going to pound on the anvil. He pounds while he is pulling [*kusĭka*] and pounds it while he is widening it. If he is pounding it like this and this, he is spreading it. If he pounds it like this, he is flattening/widening it. Meanwhile the smith is holding it for him; he used reed tongs to hold the iron. He changes it slowly and the other one beats. When he has seen that the *ensokoro* was finished, he then. . . . Yes, *ensokoro,* you can make a hoe out of it. *Ensokoro* was the last thing—it was wealth. From it came something of wealth.

[Adyeri brings in worn hoes.] Those hoes were eaten by the earth. Those were the first hoes. That is the one that was brought by the Europeans when they came. They called it *ekidimu*. They also called them *hulisi*. [I could not find a translation of this word in the literature.] They [Europeans] used to send them.

You know the king's spear, "*Erihango,*" was different in the way it was made unique [*kutekerwa*]. [I could not find a translation of this word in the literature.] And even the way it looked. It was glittering. For ordinary spears, they only put the blade edge [*obwogi*] for spearing the animal. They cannot make it as nice as the king's. There is a polishing stone called *emunyu*. It is the one they use to stop the spear from rusting [*kumŏma*]. The one who makes the king's spears unique has to make sure that there is not even a dot [of rust]. He has to make it very, very nice.

Wire Making

[This discussion was by a friend and colleague of Adyeri.]

There were other things we tried to make, like making *omugāga* where we pulled [*kusĭka*] wires [*orunyerre*]. Where we made the *omugāga* to get the wires, it wasn't fit for people to come there. [If people came there], it would break. That is where there were those rituals. [*I could not find a translation of* omugāga *in the literature that made sense in this context. Davis (1938, 100) defines it as a "roll of cloth on which bead ornaments are kept." The verb* kugāga *means "to grow rich; do certain kind of bead-work (covering gourds, etc.)" (Davis 1938, 34). After considerable thought, I believe that it was probably the iron drawplate through which wire was repeatedly pulled to give it a particular thickness.*]

Omugāga is where the wires came from that women wore. A wire of copper. You then pulled it and pulled it and you got a very small thing. And that very small thing that you got is what they rolled up [*kuzinga*] and got the wires that they wore.

That thing [where you pulled the wire through] was also a hammer we had forged. It was an iron of a bar [*omutēhimbwa*]. It was sharp on this side and this side, then we made it bigger here. Then in the middle there was a hole. The one who taught me how to forge is the one who had those things. After we forged it, in the middle, we put a hole [*ekihŭru*] in it. We used to call it *kalitundu*. It was those small hammers we used to call *kalitundu*. [I could not find a translation of this word in the literature.]

Then we would get a wire and put it inside like this. Then we held it like this. We used to pull that iron that we had put the wire through. We pulled and pulled and pulled. We even had cow *ghee*/lard. We used to smear it [on the wire] and it would slide easily. When you finished putting it through, you could then beat it there and again put it through. And we pulled again and pulled it through and pushed it through again until it became very thin. Then we removed it. Out of that small iron tool you get something very long from here out to the road there.

Avoidances at the Forge

I prepare myself when I'm going to start work tomorrow. Before I forge I cure/ward off [*kutamba*]. I first drive away bad/evil [*ekibi*]. I wake up early in the morning. I stop evil, I stop what will come like permanent evil. I send away eating. I have my water in my water bowl and the sprinkler. I clean and clean before I start to work because I will have healed evil in the morning. If you come with whatever you come with, you will give it to me. If you come with food, you'll give it to me. If you've brought money, you put it there. There is no problem. [*His mention of sending away eating is not clear. Reference to "eating" is made in a number of instances when something is at a new beginning, such as a new kingship or a marriage. In this context, perhaps it means to prevent new things, like evil, at the forge.*]

Those avoidances, the main avoidances, are the ones that killed [*kwita*] the iron. If someone slept badly with another. If such a person came and stepped around your forge in the morning while you were preparing yourself, then that day you wouldn't work. The iron would die. But what has happened now and replaced this is that, if you wake up and you are going to forge, you say your prayers and you do like this [makes the sign of the cross]. Then you work. All the evil [*obubi*] will have gone. But long ago Satan had power [*obusobozi*] on all his things and on all his people. Before people knew God, Satan had spoiled [*kunyaga*] everything. They used to put horns of goats there; there you would tie medicine [*omubazi*]. They would plant a charm [*engisa*] here [in the doorway; Davis (1938, 125) defines it as "wooden charms to prevent disease"]. They would plant horns to guard [*kulinda*] the house. That was Satan, but now God. Now we pray for everything.

It's only the god who was able to stop any problems. If he [the smith] was making tools and they were getting spoiled and he was making things that were not coming out, then he would call the *nyakatagara* who would come very quickly and blow [*kuhuha*] the forge. Then she would spit at the anvil and say, "If there is a witch [*omurogo*], if there is any bad person." Ntogota had authority to call Kagoro [another god for different clans]. If, for example, someone had sent you a horn in the middle of your doorway, Ntogota would call Kagoro to pull it out. So the lightening strikes, upsets the place, and removes the horn. A smith [of the Abachwamba clan] does not wear a charm on the neck or around the waist. He trusts only Ntogota. If there is anything wrong, Ntogota will come and remove it.

If there is anything that went wrong or the iron spoiled or they make tools that got spoiled, they call the *nyakatagara* who divines for the god. A woman. She comes and brings the layings [*emyarro*]. [Davis (1938, 121) defines *emyarro* as "grass, etc. used for spreading in houses of bachwezi." Bachwezi is the plural of "god."] Then they prepare millet. He [the smith] sits there and places his case/problem [*kutongana*]. He kneels in front of the *nyakatagara* and says, "My things are spoiled. When my bull is in heat, it runs away. When the woman gets pregnant, she miscarries. They forged tools and they are getting spoiled. What went wrong? Was it the offering or is it the way we slaughtered it? All the things are against me." So the *nyakatagara* fills her cheeks with water and spits at the house. [She says,] "If it is me, then your things will produce." By then she is speaking in the name of Ntogota. "If it is me, then your cows will go in heat. Your goats and women will produce properly. Come here near me." So he comes near. Then she spits saliva on him. If it is not him [*omuchwezi* Ntogota], then so what?

Someone can come and do bad things there. For example, if you brought a piece of iron and you want something made out of it, then someone comes and sneezes [*kwesemura*], then that iron won't come out.

You pray to god, but the day you are going to forge, you don't join with a woman. You sleep on one side.

You did not speak aloud what you were making. For example, someone can come and ask, "What are you forging out of that?" When you who are forging hasn't finished your work, you will not say that, "I am making thing X." If you tell him, "I am making thing X," it can break right away. He will bewitch it.

[A girl who was a daughter of a smith could not be a smith], but if she came to her father's forge when he is forging and there is no one bellowing, she could bellow. She could not squat for the bellows. Even when she is bellowing, she kneels and bellows. That way—they fear squatting [*kusitama*]. [Squatting is considered improper for women.]

[They weren't careful about girls who were menstruating because] there was no bad luck, since there was no ore. It is the ore that was protected from that kind of thing. With forging, it wasn't special.

If the smith in Kiganda forged things or if the king came to the palace—there was a palace up here in Nkinga—and smiths brought things to present to the king, then the king said, "Oh, this smith has done very good things and he's better than all his fellow smiths." Then they would bewitch [*kuroga*] him. "At least he should die so that he is not better than us." They had their medicine they used to bewitch people. They would look for medicine at a witch doctor's [*omufumu*] place, one who bewitched people. He would give him the medicine and tell him, "Go and lay a trap [*kutega*] of this medicine for him." Tomorrow they would find him dead. They did not bewitch him as a smith but as any other person. But the smiths had clans. In our clan no child was allowed, if he had a home, to bring a witch doctor to plant horns in that house or in the doorways like there and there. Lightening would strike that house and remove it.

In my clan, no child can wear a charm inside to prevent him from being bewitched and die, no. Or to plant a horn in the compound to prevent people from killing him. No. And in most cases, if someone came and put things to bewitch us, while you are seated here, you'll hear BAH! and lightning will strike. You see when it has thrown them out. That is what our god Ntogota said, "No wearing anything. No doing that, no doing anything." He told the whole clan, our clan. We the Abachwamba should never wear a talisman or plant horns. No.

But you must wash [*kuogya*] it [the hammer]. Do you know what washing is? Washing this hammer—you slaughter a sheep for it, you get it its beer, you cook millet and people eat. People sleep there until daybreak.

You buy a sheep or if you have one at home, you wake up early in the morning and you slaughter it. [You slaughtered the sheep] once a year. That sheep is the function/sacrifice/ceremony of the forge. It is the one we eat. It's the smith who slaughters it. When the *nyakatagara* comes, you slaughter the sheep. The hammer, that is most important. That hammer, the head of the house, the *nyakatagara* smears it with blood. Then it can start working.

The *nykatagara* came [to the forge] with her layings, tree scrapings. Then she says, "Heh. All the children should be nice. All the things we make should be nice." The job she'd do, she'd come to the forge and prepare her layings—put them there on the side of the wall. She even went to the house and did things there. Then, before she left, she prepared her pot/pipe [*enyungu*] of food, of millet. If it is ready, she would serve it after she put the layings there. All the clansmen would eat that millet. We would have our beer, so we drank. She drank a little and blew some on the walls and also on the hammer. And when she finished, she'd come and sit there. And before she went, you rewarded [*kusumika*] her with intestines. Then our job started.

Payments for Forging and the Market

If he [the smith] got iron enough to make five hoes, then he'd get something. Each one would be brought. If someone's daughter wants to get married, they'd come and buy a hoe. If someone had a heifer and wants a hoe, they would exchange. If you wanted money instead of a heifer, he knew what to do. That's how wealth came. If he forged and he got good tools, he kept them there. If someone wanted to buy, he would buy. That's how things bought each other. It's like barter trade. He lifts a cow and gives him. The other lifts a hoe and gives it to him. If he lifted a hoe and gave it to him, the other lifted a daughter and gave it.

You see when we smiths are buying/selling, we do not bargain. If you come to buy something, I do not bargain. Whatever money I have told you, that is it.

When someone brought his sickle and said, "I want you to forge my sickle." The smith would tell him, "Go and bring charcoal so that I can repair your sickle." So he would go and cut the tree, put the charcoal in the raft, bring it, and his sickle would be repaired. Or if his hoe was broken, "Hey, my hoe is broken. I want you to repair it for me." The smith would say, "If you want your hoe repaired, go and bring a raft full of charcoal." Of course, he used it for other things. Doesn't he make a profit? He knew how to do it.

He [a customer] would say, "I have this payment." Then you say, "Aah or no. Bring this payment. If you are bringing 100 shillings, it's not enough. Bring 200." "200, here it is." Then he [the smith] puts it in the forge.

He [a customer] would bring nearly a full basket [of cowries] just to buy that iron. He would carry it on his head. It wasn't money that was so useful. A whole big basket would be equivalent to maybe 50 shillings in old money. On the other hand, he would bring a big bull if he wanted a piece big enough to make a hoe. He would call you [the smith] to go and see the bull and if you agreed, he'd come and take the hoe.

He gets a big piece of iron, like these days when there are so many springs, then he breaks off knives and piles them there. Meanwhile, if the season for harvesting millet has come, he would know that many would want the hand knives. Someone comes, puts their money, and takes. If he wanted to sell them faster, he would put them in a bag like hers and take them. Then people would say, "The smith has passed. The smith has passed." Then they say, "Hello smith, what do you have there? Are there needles in your bag? Are there basket needles?" And you think you got a lot of money? You only got 10 shillings.

It depended on what certain areas wanted. He would then choose a day on which he would travel. Like now, there has been a group that has been making sickles. He would be told to bring another 100 sickles. From there he would have to make a sickle every day. If they got finished, then he would decide on when to make more.

He [the smith] would send those [to the market] that he thought were faithful. If he sent the unfaithful ones, they would sell and drink the money. If he had his bag, he would take them [the objects]. But if he was busy, maybe making banana knives, he would ask his son to take and sell what he had made. Or if it was a market day, he would give them to his child. He put them in his bag and went.

[Different smiths at a market] could come from a place like Nyakungu. He would also bring his objects, put them in his own stall, while yours are in another stall. So it depended on the customers. They [customers] bought from the stall which they thought had better irons.

Learning to Forge

It all started off if your father was a smith. You see what he does. He would give us jobs to learn how to bellow. You'd eventually learn how to bellow. If you were lucky and you learned how to forge, you see something being forged at home and you learn. He would tell you, "Forge that iron." You would see. Then he tells you, "Handle it this way. Straighten it this way." So the iron goes. "When you do it this way, it widens. Now you hold it this way. Now it's not nice. Hold it again." If it wasn't nice, he would slap him. "Now level it like this." If you forged well or you pounded well, you got a reward. So you get an income. I was 14 [when I started learning to forge].

You make like a picture; like in the past, we made things out of clay. You mold a cow. You put horns with clay. Even when you are forging and there is clay, a child will start with the clay. He will beat the clay and it becomes long or in a different way. So you find that he also learns on that clay. Or even mud, he starts beating it with sticks. All those teach him. When he reaches an iron, then he'll work on it.

If you were not in school, you would do a few things. As you play with sticks, you learn, even in a forge. That is what you do. You can start with just cutting simple iron sheets roughly. Then you cut and you join, you throw away, you cut, and join and throw away, meanwhile you are learning. Today you just get iron and roll it and make a spear base point. Then tomorrow you will make an iron. When your father came and saw, he would now say, "Mold it this way." And then he would tell you when you beat like this, "The iron will widen. If you beat like this, it will straighten."

He [the smith] would see what he [the student] has made. You know, there is no school where to teach it on the blackboard. He learns by sight. It's like a school. He simply looks on what others are making and he learns. He sees how they are pounding and he's also given a small stone hammer to pound.

Then he learns how to pound the iron without being burned. They would warn him, "You are holding the stone badly." If he worked properly, his parent would say, "You've worked well." They would give him a small piece of iron and tell him, "Make a hand knife [*omuhyo gwe engaro*]." Then he starts forging and gets a hand knife. If he makes a mistake, they tell him, "You made a mistake." But if he makes it well, then he has learned. So if the smith is about to die, he says, "My son is a smith." He's the one to whom he leaves his hammer and all the things related to smithing.

When I am teaching them, I do not touch their hands and tell them, "Do like this." He has his eyes so he will see what I am doing. Then he also catches. He sees how I forge. He sees how I cut the iron. Then he also does the same; he copies [*kusubiriza*]. He works while watching me and he goes forward. [You will know his success] because what he will have made will start looking like mine.

And to add to that, say you are making your things and you take them to the market when they are not very straight and level. When someone is buying, he will say, "Hey, my friend, why haven't you made it very straight and level here?" So you go back home and make it straight and say, "Eh, they didn't buy so let me make them better." Then returning home, you make it level. It's like being in P1, then you go to P2, then they say, "Go back, repeat please. Repeat this." Then you learn and straighten up. [P1 and P2 are primary school grade levels in Uganda.]

To be able to make something—to see that it is straight and it is hard. I could see money in it. It took about, let me say, half a year.

[A smith would also allow boys from outside the family to come and learn.] He would also be there and also learn. It's like children going to school. They all see with their eyes what they've been taught. The one who is able to learn/catch, will learn. The one who can't, will leave. What will he do?

Opening a New Forge: General

If your father is there forging, why would you build a forge? You help him with pounding the iron. I've told you, this is a forge here. The master/elder smith [*omuhēsi omukuru*] is there. Now the iron is ready. Meanwhile the stone hammer would be on this side. He will be on his anvil. When it's ready, you pass it on to him. Then he pounds it. He passes it on to you, then you straighten it up. Or, if your father grows older and older, he retires and tells you to forge. So you forge all the things you saw your father forging.

If a forge collapses or the one who built it died, the young ones will have to build a new one. Or he calls the master/elder smith and asks [to build his own forge]. The smiths would help him. They would say, "This child has reached forging. Let him go and forge from Butiiti. He has learned. This one will forge. You've given him an iron to pound, he knows. Let him go and make his own forge."

If you [the master smith] are still alive, you go and plant a tree [*kusīmba omuti*] for him. "This is your area" and then you plant the tree. If you go to a new place, you look for a bark cloth tree [*omutoma*] [Davis (1938, 184) defines this as a "tall tree from which a white bark cloth is obtainable. Antiaris africana."] You chop an *omuyamoya.* You chop another tree; it's there. You put four posts. Then you chop an *emilaba* and you put them there. [I could not find translations for either of these types of wood in the literature.] When you finish, you go into your house and sleep. The following morning you wake up very early, the charcoal will be there, the iron will also have slept there. Then in the morning you start forging. You will have entered a forge. That day you enter it, you eat and drink and forge as you go on. You buy the sheep you slaughter for the ceremony for when you enter a new forge. You buy a sheep.

Opening a New Forge: The Anvil

It's a big stone. They deliberately got it and made sure it didn't split/break and was very hard. So when he plans to go to look for the anvil on which the iron is made, he also wonders if will he get good people to hammer.

If you, the father, know where to get the anvils, the good ones, you would say, "The anvil is on the other hill. Go and get it." He [the new smith] chooses people, about 20 or 30. They go and dig it up. It's like, if it is as big as this, it would be enough for ore, but if it is smallish. . . . They always went for those where iron from ore could be hammered. They would get a rope that was used to trap animals and they would tie it. Then they would have six people on one side and six on the other side to be able to bring it. They carry it like this—like a person who is sick. Then they bring it and plant it there. Then they sing very big songs like those they sang yesterday. Then the *nyakatagara* comes. The *nyakatagara* that mediates that god, she fills her mouth with water, spits on the anvil and says the following: "Forge tools. Get a lot of wealth. Who will forge from here and . . ." To get the anvil from the forest, it was also followed by a feast [*obugenyi*]. They would then sing songs of smiths. Then people would fall as we have already talked about.

There are experts who also went and discovered them. Like they find ore. He would go with his tool that would tell him. He would knock/pound [*kuhonda*] on each stone. He would knock one and knock and knock. He would see that pieces don't break off. Even if it is deep down they say, "We will get it." [He used] the hammer, the *omwangata.* He would use it to knock the stone to know that if it is just a stone, it will break when they put the iron there. It [the new anvil stone] is very hard and it has strength. It does not crack/shatter [*kuhomōka*]. You beat like this and no stone will break off. That is the anvil.

After the anvil had come and they put it there, they bring other hammers. They knock it to remove the small stones so that they do not bring in bumps as iron is leveled. Then that's when it is ready for forging a hoe.

It was finished, but in digging to plant it, they used to slaughter a white chicken. They would cut it and let the blood go where it [anvil] was going to sleep. Whenever they were going to plant an anvil, they brought the *nyakatagara* of that house. She's the one who cuts and afterwards, she puts the sprinkler on those who have come to plant it.

They plant the anvil and the *nyakatagara* opens [*kwigura*] it. Under that anvil—you lift it up. Long ago there used to be coin money. So you put one shilling and you plant the anvil. The cowrie shells stay in the anvil. [The cowrie shells are an alternative to coins.] The problem is putting the anvil there without rewarding it. Then they forge from there. First, they forge a basket needle that is the gift/payment to the *nyakatagara*. That is the first thing they forge.

On the anvil? It would also be healed. It's only the anvil and the hammers [where blood was put on]. All the smiths who have come will eat that meat [mutton]. And the biggest problem would be—you cannot enter my forge without eating or drinking. You eat and drink since you have intruded on me. If you go without eating, you go on spreading bad words about me—that you came to my forge and I refused to give you food and drinks. So you must eat and drink however little. Or, what I can do is forge you a knife and give it to you. But you don't pay for it. It's a rule. You don't go out before you've eaten. You do not go without anything when you've entered a forge. At least I give you a needle and you go and make a mat.

Bringing in the anvil is not something special, but when they collected to bring it here, the *nyakatagara* is the one who led [*kwebembera*] them. She came ahead of it. They sang and danced, "When we were dead . . .", they would sing that song that was there.

"When we were finished . . ." Then the others replied:
"Say the hammer widens."
"We were saved by white." That is all.
"In the days of eating mud."
"Say the hammer widens."
"We were saved by white."
"In the days of eating clay."
"Say the hammer widens."
"We were saved by white."

When hunger had struck, they are clay, they ate mud, they were saved by white—the hammer. That is the song they sang. Up to when they reached there.

They would sing those songs of smiths [when they brought a new anvil]:
"I slept while the bellows were nice; I slept while the bellows were nice."
"Short, stout, [tuyere], where did you sleep?"
"I slept while the bellows were nice. I slept while the bellows were nice."
"Abwooli, who is sweeping, where did you sleep?"
"I slept while the bellows were nice."

Meanwhile people are dancing in a circle tied with those things [unspecified objects around the waist]. Someone is hitting the hammer and another is singing, "It's nice, it's nice." Then the chorus sing. They have brought their anvil and the bellows are nice. They are happy.

Opening a New Forge: The Hammer

The hammer came on the day they planted the anvil. The father handed it to him [new smith]. They then put up the bellows and forged the needle. Of that home, the children and the women came. All came of the clan. The *nyakatagara* would sprinkle with water.

When they've built the forge and he wants to give his son a hammer to go there, the father would tie his hammers in a hide. If he's taking a certain hammer, while the son is building, he ties it in a sheep's hide. He would put it under his arm/hide it. He goes there, he finds the son is building the forge. Meanwhile, he's with the *nyakatagara*.

There are people who forge the hammer. If his father is still alive, he gets a good piece of iron and he takes it to him and his father makes one. He pounds it this way and that way and makes him a hammer—a good one. Then he puts it in steel because the other fire has burned it so hard. It is very delicate so it goes in steel, then it goes/changes into iron. They put it in early so that it can be long-lasting, so it does not fold. The hammer is very big and heavy. He holds it in one hand while holding the iron in the other. Then he hits like this. The hand of the smith is very strong because he uses it a lot. If a smith beats you, ahh . . .

Since the people of that clan brought a hammer, the *nyakatagara* puts a blessing [*ekitambo*] on them. If she hasn't used a sprinkler, then she fills her mouth with water and spits on them. [*Kutamba* means to cure, but when used in the context of a *nykatagara* for the god, it suggests that the hammer and the clan members are getting the spirit or god and its blessing.]

Ntogota has come when they are handing him the hammer. And they sing: "Ntogota come and accompany me, it almost was hissing but there is no tuyere."

Yes, he escorted you. "Ntogota come and accompany me, it almost was hissing but there is no tuyere. Woman and child come and accompany me, it almost was hissing but there is no tuyere. Cow and sheep come and accompany me, it almost was hissing but there is no tuyere." . . . That's it. If the ore hisses and the tuyere is not there, they say, "The ore has no tuyere." When you hit that [iron], all the people start dancing. It's a function for bringing in [*kutahya*] the hammer. [When a man marries, he "brings in" his wife.]

Nyakatagara, isn't she the *nyakatagara* for that clan? She would go with him. When he reaches there, he [the new smith] unties the hide, she looks in his eyes like this, "I give you this hammer. I give you to eat. I've given you wealth and the ability to get it. You should always work with kindness [*embabazzi*]. Now, never cheat, never be unscrupulous. Here is your hammer." He [the new smith] holds it. Then he takes it. He goes where he has planted the anvil, then he beats there four times. The father tells the son, "Beat there four times, one, two, three, four. Stop there. Now, people who come from there, help them. Those who come from this way, help them. Those who come from the other side, help them. Never discriminate/segregate [*kusorora*] and say, 'What have they come to do?' All of them have come to the forge. They all want to be healed. You heal them now. Never have anger and never quarrel. Here is your hammer." Then he says, "Sit now and forge." Now he starts forging on the anvil. While the bellower is bellowing the bellows, he forges a needle, a nice one. Then he forges a second one. One of the needles will be taken by the *nyakatagara*. The second one will be taken by his mother.

The *nyakatagara* would have handed him [the new smith] the hammer. The *nyakatagara* would give that child a hammer. Then she says, "My child, I've handed you this hammer. If someone is hungry and wants a hoe, or his hoe is broken, never refuse to help him. I've handed you this hammer, forge the king's spears and the needle. I hand you this hammer. Forge for the deformed/lowest class and the respected. Whatever they bring for you to forge, you forge. Never be angry. A smith never has anger. Don't shout at someone when he brings something and bark at him and tell him, 'Take your stuff.' " They advise him so much so that he is a good person; so that people are all happy with him. They also sing a song at handing him the hammer. There is a god Ntogota.

He gives her [his mother] a knife. Why he gives his mother a knife is that it will enable her to peel food. That knife, if she is going to make a basket, it will help her to do the splitting of the papyrus reed. That is why he gives her a knife, it is very important. It will help that child; he will never see problems. And that knife, that peeler does so many things—not only her work, but her son's too.

Give him [his father] anything? He was his child. He was learning those things he did, there was nothing to give his father. He only gave to those who were concerned. It was his father who wanted the best for his son, he did not need anything from him. He gave to the *nyakatagara* because it was the *nyakatagara* who mediated the god in that home. She was the one who spat saliva on them for doing everything. It was that *nyakatagara* who they feared most of all. Even his father feared the *nyakatagara*.

For the job the *nyakatagara* did of opening the forge, she got a basket needle or a hand knife. Only that. She didn't ask for anything else, except if she was digging and the hoe broke or the needle got lost, the *nyakatagara* of that place would come and ask, and the smith would give her. She would never buy [from a smith].

You called the *nyakatagara* and if she came, she would fill her mouth with water. She blows on the poles, "Let this forge live long." Then she finished so that the forge can live long and be long lasting. They were rituals of people of long ago. They used to uphold them and they would work. If you knelt down for a god, "I am going to work, here is my 1200 shillings. Let me work and get wealth. They should not sack me from my job. Let me be strong until I come back." Then he put money there. He [the clansman who asked for help] would go and get that money [wealth]. But these days, things have changed. What can we do? Things have changed. Religion spoiled them.

After Forging

After the smith forged tools, he and the pounder prepared themselves to relax. And if there were people around, then the smith would say, "Bring our brew," and we started drinking. So each would fill his cup and drink. Then he would say, "Now let's start dancing." When they danced that dance and hit the iron, the god/spirit would break [*kwatika*] and someone would fall. They called the *nyakatagara* of that home to lift her and take her to the shrine.

When smiths have finished forging and they've gathered together or they've made the anvil enter or if a woman is married, they dance.

You'd hit the tools, the hoes together. So as you hit, you danced and danced. It's only when you hit iron. That's when he [the god/spirit] comes. While you are still hitting and dancing, then you see someone fall.

You start and they answer:

"The king's smith, if he is selling, he does not bargain." [repeated four times]

"Say the hammer widens." [repeated three times]

Chorus: "If he is selling, he does not bargain."

"The child of the hammer." [repeated three times]

"The wife of the hammer." [repeated three times]

Chorus: "If he is selling, he does not bargain."

"The king's smith cannot bargain when selling," implying that when a king's smith was buying, he did not force a sale/bargain. Others join in and dance. Then others beat the iron to the rhythm. People used to fall there.

"The king's smith is not supposed to negotiate." Long ago there were peo-

Plate 4.5 Mining dance by members of the Abachwamba clan. Dancer in foreground is dancing with a hammer.

ple who would fall there so they initiate them from there. They initiate them into spirit possession.

[During the day when Adyeri and his clansmen sang and danced the smithing songs, one participant wore a hat and "skirt" that are described here.] This one is elephant grass. Dried grass. Sprinkler, I was wearing a sprinkler [the grass on his head]. It's for a ceremony/ritual. I did not carry cowrie shells in my hands.

"Clansmen thank you." [repeated three times]

Chorus: "I slept when the bellows were nice/happiness/joy/wealth."

"Nice, nice, nice, nice . . ."

Chorus: "I slept when the bellows were nice/happiness/joy/wealth."

"Nice, nice, nice, nice . . ."

Short legged, where did you sleep? [repeated three times]

Chorus: "I slept when the bellows were nice/happiness/joy/wealth."

"Nice, nice, nice, nice . . ."

"Appreciate, appreciate." [repeated four times]

Chorus: "I slept when the bellows were nice/happiness/joy/wealth."

"Nice, nice, nice, nice . . ."

"Clansmen thank you." [repeated three times]

Chorus: "I slept when the bellows were nice/happiness/joy/wealth."

"Nice, nice, nice, nice . . ."

This means he spent the night where they were dancing/singing. They are good things; the bellows were nice. It has enabled people to go there; the bellows were nice. If the bellows are there, that home is very rich. That bellows.

"Wife of the hammer."

Chorus: "Say the hammer widens."

"Child of the hammer."

Chorus: "Say the hammer widens."

"Hammer of father."

Chorus: "Say the hammer widens."

"This is my hammer."

Chorus: "Say the hammer widens."

"Knowledge of the hammer."

Chorus: "Say the hammer widens."

"White person of the hammer."

Chorus: "Say the hammer widens."

"Toro of the hammer."

Chorus: "Say the hammer widens."

"Person of Kenya of the hammer."

Chorus: "Say the hammer widens."

"People of the hammer."

Chorus: "Say the hammer widens."

"Car of the hammer."

Chorus: "Say the hammer widens."

"Smiths of the hammer."

Chorus: "Say the hammer widens."

There are other dances. They do not concern the hammer. Those songs are just to make people happy at that time. Those are sung when they are marrying in our traditional way.

References

Adams, R. M. 1996. *Paths of Fire: An Anthropologist's Inquiry into Western Technology*. Princeton, N.J.: Princeton University Press.

Allan, W. 1965. *The African Husbandman*. New York: Barnes and Noble.

al-Tunisi, M. O. 1845. *Voyage au Darfour*. Paris.

———. 1851. *Voyage au Ouadday*. Paris.

Anciaux de Faveaux, E., and P. de Maret. 1980. "Vestiges de l'Age du Fer dans les environs de Lubumbashi" *Africa-Tervuren* 26: 1–7.

———. 1984. "Premieres datations pour le fonte du cuivre au Shaba (Zaire)." *Bulletin de la Société Royale Belge d'Anthropologie et de Préhistoire* 95: 5–20.

Anonymous. 1961. "An Ancient Smelting Craft Revived." *Horizon* 3(8): 30–32.

Anquandah, J. 1982. *Rediscovering Ghana's Past*. Accra: Sedco; London: Longman.

———. 1993. "Urbanization and State Formation in Ghana during the Iron Age." In T. Shaw, P. Sinclair, B. Andah, and A. Okpoko, eds., *The Archaeology of Africa: Food, Metals and Towns* (643–651). London: Routledge.

Aremu, D. A. 1993 "Demonstration of Brass Casting at Obo Aiyegunle, Kwara State." In B. W. Andah, ed., *Cultural Resource Management: An African Dimension* (209–217). Ibadan: Wisdom Publishers.

Arkell, A. J., B. Fagan, and R. Summers. 1966. "The Iron Age in Sub-Saharan Africa." *Current Anthropology* 7: 451–484.

Arnot, F. S. 1875. *Garenganze*. London: Frank Cass.

Asombang, R., J. M. Essomba, and J. P. Ossah-Mvondo. 1991. "Reconaissance archéologique dans l'arrondissement de Zoétélé, province du sud, Cameroun méridional." *Nyame Akuma* 35: 17–21.

Atangana, C. 1989. "Archéologie du Cameroun méridional: Étude du site d'Okolo." Ph.D. diss., University of Paris I: Pantheon-Sorbonne.

———. 1992. "Les fosses d'Okolo (sud du Cameroun): Fouilles et axes de recherches." *Nyame Akuma* 38: 7–13.

Atherton, J. 1984. "La Préhistoire de la Sierra Leone." *L'Anthropologie* 88(2): 245–261.

Avery, D. H., N. J. van der Merwe, and S. Saitowitz. 1988. "The Metallurgy of the Iron Bloomery in Africa." In R. Maddin, ed., *The Beginning of the Use of Metals and Alloys*. Cambridge, Massachusetts.

Bancroft, J. A. 1961. *Mining in Northern Rhodesia*. London: British South Africa Company.

Barndon, R. 1996. "Fipa Ironworking and Its Technological Style." In P. R. Schmidt, ed., *The Culture and Technology of African Iron Production* (58–73). Gainesville: University Press of Florida.

Barnes, H. B. 1929. "Iron Smelting among the Ba-Ushi." *Journal of the Royal Anthropological Institute* 76: 189–194.

Bathily, M. S., M. O. Khattar, and R. Vernet. 1992. *Les Sites neolithiques de Khatt Lemaiteg (Amatlich) en Mauritanie occidentale*. Nouakchott: Centre Culturelle Francais.

Battell, A. 1859. *The Strange Adventures of Andrew Battel of Leigh in Angola and Adjoining Regions*. Edited by E. Ravenstein. London: Hakluyt Society.

Beckombo-Priso, M. 1981. "Essai sur le peuplement de la region cotiere du cameroun: Les populations dites Dwala." In C. Tardits, ed., *Contribution de l'ethnologie à l'histoire des civilizations du Cameroun* (503–520). Paris: Editions du CNRS.

Bernus, E. 1981. *Touaregs nigériens: Unité culturelle et diversité régionale d'un peuple pasteur*. Paris: Editions de l'ORSTOM.

———. 1983. "Place et rôle du foreron dans la société touarègue." In N. Echard, ed., *Métallurgies africaines: Nouvelles contributions* (237–251). Paris: Mémoires de la Société des Africanistes.

Bernus, E., S. Bernus, P. Cressier, P. L. Gouletquer, and Y. Poncet. 1984. *La Région d'In Gall–Tegidda-n-Tesemt (Niger) I: Introduction, Méthodologie—Environnement* Niamey: Etudes Nigériennes No. 48.

Bernus, S., and P. Cressier, eds. 1991. *La Région d'In Gall–Tegidda-n-Tesemt (Niger) IV:* Azelik—Takadda *et l'implantation sédentaire médiévale*. Niamey: Etudes Nigériennes No. 51.

Bernus, S., and N. Echard. 1985. "Metalworking in the Agadez region (Niger): An Ethno-Archaeological Approach." In P. T. Craddock and M. J. Hughes, eds., *Furnaces and Smelting Technology in Antiquity*. British Museum Occasional Papers No. 48 (71–80). London: British Museum.

———. 1992. *La Région d'In Gall–Tegidda-n-Tesemt (Niger) V: Les Populations actuelles*. Niamey: Etudes Nigériennes No. 52.

Bernus, S., and P. L. Gouletquer. 1976. "Du cuivre au sel: Recherches ethno-archéologiques sur la région d'Azélik (campagnes 1973–1975)." *Journal des Africanistes* 46(1–2): 7–68.

Birmingham, D. 1966. *Trade and Conflict in Angola*. London: Oxford University Press.

Birmingham, D., and S. Marks. 1977. "Southern Africa." In R. Oliver, ed., *Cambridge History of Africa,* vol. 3 (567–620). Cambridge: Cambridge University Press.

Bisson, M. S. 1975. "Copper Currency in Central Africa: The Archaeological Evidence." *World Archaeology* 6: 276–292.

———. 1976. *The Prehistoric Copper-Mines of Zambia*. Ann Arbor, Mich.: University Microfilms International.

———. 1983. "Trade and Tribute Archaeological Evidence for the Origin of States in South-Central Africa. "*Cahiers d'Etudes Africaines* 22: 343–361.

———. 1989. "Continuity and Discontinuity in Copperbelt and North-Western Province Ceramic Sequences." *Nyame Akuma* 31: 43–46.

———. 1992. "A Survey of Late Stone Age and Iron Age Sites at Luano, Zambia." *World Archaeology* 24: 234–248.

———. In prep. *Luano and the Later Prehistory of the Zambian Copperbelt.*

Bisson, M. S., and J. H. Robertson. 1979. "Archaeology at Kansanshi Mine: Preliminary Notes on the 1978 Rescue Excavations." *Nyame Akuma* 14: 66–68.

Bocoum, H. 1986. "La métallurgie du fer au Sénégal: Approche archéologique technologique et historique." Ph.D. diss., University of Paris I: Pantheon-Sorbonne.

———. 1987. "Métallurgie et Couvert Végétal dans la Moyenne Vallée du Sénégal et dans les Régions Voisines." *Notes de Biogéographie* 3: 67–78.

———. 1990. "Contribution à la connaissance des origines du Takrur." *Annales de la faculté des Lettres et Sciences Humaines* 20: 159–178.

Bohannon, P. 1959. "The Impact of Money on an African Subsistence Economy." *Journal of Economic History* 19(4): 491–503.

Bonte, J. G., and P. Bonte. 1991. "Introduction." In J. G. Galaty and P. Bonte, eds., *Herders, Warriors, and Traders: Pastoralism in Africa* (3–30). Oxford: Westview Press.

Bourdieu, P. 1979. *La Distinction: Critique sociale du jugement*. Paris: Editions de Minuit.

Bower, J. G. 1927. "Native Smelting in Equatorial Africa." *The Mining Magazine* 37(3): 137–147.

Bradley, K. 1952. *Copper Venture*. Kitwe: Mufulira Copper Mines Limited.

Brock, B. B. 1963. "On the Structure and Sedimentation of the Katanga Basin." In J. Lombard and P. Nicolini, eds., *Symposium on Copper in Africa, Part II* (116–124). Association of African Geological Surveys.

Brooks, R. n.d. "Smelting at Musonoi." National Archives of Zambia No. Br/1/1. Unpublished photo album, 10 photos.

Browne, W. G. 1799. *Travels in Egypt, Syria and Africa*. London: Longman and Rees.

Buleli, N. 1993. "Iron-Making Techniques in the Kivu Region of Zaire: Some of the Differences between the South Maniema Region and North Kivu." In T. Shaw, P. Sinclair, B. Andah, and A. Okpoko, eds., *The Archaeology of Africa: Food, Metals and Towns* (468–477). London: Routledge.

Burton, R. F. 1873. *The Lands of Cazembie: The Diary of Dr Francisco Jose Maria de Lacerda e Almeida*. London: Frank Cass.

Cahen, L., and N. J. Snelling. 1966. *The Geology of Equatorial Africa*. Amsterdam: North Holland Publishing.

Calvert, A. 1912. *Nigeria and Its Tin Fields*. London: Edward Stanford.

Calvocoressi, D., and N. David, 1979. "A New Survey of Radiocarbon and Thermoluminescence Dates for West Africa." *Journal of African History* 20: 1–29.

Caton-Thompson, G. 1931. *The Zimbabwe Culture*. London: Oxford University Press.

Célis, G. 1989. "La métallurgie traditionnelle au Burundi, au Rwanda et au Buha: Essai de synthèse." *Anthropos* 84: 25–46.

Célis, G., and E. Nzikobanyanka. 1976. *La Métallurgie Traditionnelle au Burundi: Techniques et Croyances*. Tervuren: Royal Museum for Central Africa.

Chaplin, J. H. 1961. "Notes on Traditional Smelting in Northern Rhodesia." *South African Archaeological Bulletin* 16(62): 53–60.

———. 1962. "A Preliminary Account of Iron Age Burials with Gold in the Gwembe Valley, Northern Rhodesia." *Proceedings of the First Federal Science Congress*, Salisbury, 1960, 397–406.

Chibanza, S. J. 1961. *Kaonde History.* Central Bantu Historical Texts I, Part II. Livingstone: Rhodes Livingstone Institute.

Chikwendu, V. E., P. T. Craddock, R. M. Farquhar, T. Shaw, and A. C. Umeji. 1989. "Nigerian Sources of Copper, Lead, and Tin for the Igbo-Ukwu Bronzes." *Archaeometry* 31(1): 27–36.

Chikwendu, V. E., and A. C. Umeji. 1979. "Local Sources of Material for the Bronze, Brass Industry." *West African Journal of Archaeology* 9: 151–165.

Childs, S. T. 1998a. "'Find the *ekijunjumira*': Iron Mine Discovery, Ownership and Power among the Toro of Uganda." In A. B. Knapp, V. C. Pigott, and E. W. Herbert, eds., *Social Approaches to an Industrial Past: The Archaeology and Anthropology of Mining* (123–137). London: Routledge.

———. 1998b. "Social Identity and Craft Specialization among Toro Iron Workers in Western Uganda." In C. L. Costin and R. P. Wright, eds., *Craft and Social Identity* (109–121). Archeological Papers of the American Anthropological Association No. 8. Washington, D.C.: American Anthropological Association.

———. 1991a. "Style, Technology, and Iron Smelting Furnaces in Bantu-Speaking Africa." *Journal of Anthropological Archaeology* 10: 332–359.

———. 1991b. "Iron as Utility or Expression: Reforging Function in Africa." In R. Ehrenreich, ed., *Metals and Society: Theory beyond Analysis*. Philadelphia: MASCA Research Papers in Science and Archaeology, Vol. 8, No. 2, 57–67.

———. 1991c. "Transformations: Iron and Copper Production in Central Africa." In P. Glumac, ed., *Recent Trends in Archaeometallurgical Research*. Philadelphia: MASCA.

———. 1996. "Technological History and Culture in Western Tanzania." In P. R. Schmidt, ed., *The Culture and Technology of African Iron Production* (277–320). Gainesville: University Press of Florida.

———. 1999. " 'After All, a Hoe Bought a Wife': The Social Dimensions of Ironworking among the Toro of East Africa." In M. A. Dobres and C. R. Hoffman, eds., *The Social Dynamics of Technology: Practice, Politics and World Views* (23–45). Washington, D.C.: Smithsonian Institution Press.

Childs, S. T., and W. J. Dewey. 1996. "Forging Symbolic Meaning in Zaire and Zimbabwe." In P. R. Schmidt, ed., *The Culture and Technology of African Iron Production* (145–171). Gainesville: University Press of Florida.

Childs, S. T., and D. Killick. 1993. "Indigenous African Metallurgy: Nature and Culture." *Annual Review of Anthropology* 22: 317–337.

Cissé, Y. 1964. "Notes sur les Sociétés de Chasseurs Malinké." *Journal de la Société des Africanistes* 34(2): 175–226.

Clark, J. D. 1957. "Pre-European Copper Working in South-Central Africa." *Roan Antelope* 6(5): 12–15.

Cline, W. 1937. *Mining and Metallurgy in Negro Africa*. Menasha, Wis.: George Banta.

Clist, B. 1989. "Archaeology in Gabon 1886–1988." *African Archaeological Review* 7: 59–95.

Coghlan, H. H. 1975. *Notes on the Prehistoric Metallurgy of Copper and Bronze in the Old World*. Oxford: Oxford University Press.

Cohen, R. 1987. *The Kanuri of Borno*. Prospect Heights, Ill.: Waveland Press.

Collett, D. P. 1993. "Metaphors and Representations Associated with Precolonial Iron-Smelting in Eastern and Southern Africa." In T. Shaw, P. Sinclair, B. Andah, and A. Okpopo, eds., *The Archaeology of Africa: Food, Metals and Towns* (499–511). London: Routledge.

Connah, G. 1975. *The Archaeology of Benin and Other Researches in and around Benin City, Nigeria*. London: Oxford University Press.

———. 1981. *Three Thousand Years in Africa*. Cambridge: Cambridge University Press.

———. 1987. *African Civilizations*. Cambridge: Cambridge University Press.

Conte, E. 1991. "Herders, Hunters and Smiths: Mobile Populations in the History of Kanem." In J. G. Galaty and P. Bonte, eds., *Herders, Warriors, and Traders: Pastoralism in Africa* (223–247). Oxford: Westview Press.

Cornevin, R. 1962. *Les Bassari du Nord-Togo*. Paris: Berger-Levrault.

Coy, M. W. 1982. *The Social and Economic Relations of Blacksmiths among Kalenjin-Speaking Peoples of the Rift Valley, Kenya*. Ann Arbor, Mich.: University Microfilms International.

———. 1989. "Being What We Pretend to Be: The Usefulness of Apprenticeship as a Field Method." In M. Coy, ed., *Apprenticeship: From Theory to Method and Back* (115–135). Albany: State University of New York Press.

———. n.d. "A contribution to the study of East African Blacksmiths." Unpublished manuscript.

Craddock, P. T. 1995. *Early Mining and Metal Production*. Washington, D.C.: Smithsonian Institution Press.

Craddock, P. T., J. Ambers, D. Hook, R. M. Farquhar, V. E. Chikwendu, A. C. Umeji, and T. Shaw. 1997. "Metal Sources and the Bronzes from Igbo-Ukwu, Nigeria." *Journal of Field Archaeology* 24: 405–429.

Craddock, P. T., V. E. Chikwendu, A. C. Umeji, R. M. Farquhar, and T. Shaw. 1993. "The Technical Origin of the Igbo Bronzes." In B. W. Andah, C. A. Folorunso, and I. Okpoko, eds., *Imprints of West Africa's Past* (101–201). Ibadan: Wisdom Publishers.

Cunnison, I. 1959. *The Luapula Peoples of Northern Rhodesia*. London: Manchester University Press.

da Gama, V. 1962. *Documents on the Portuguese in Mozambique and Central Africa, 1497–1840, Vol. 1*. Lisbon: Centro de Estudos Historicos Ultramarinos.

Daniels, S. G. H. 1967. "A Note on Iron Age Material from Kamusongolwa Kopje, Kasempa." *South African Archaeological Bulletin* 22: 142–150.

Dark, P. 1973. *An Introduction to Benin Art and Technology*. London: Oxford University Press.

Darling, P. J. 1983. "Iron-Smelting in and around Hausaland, Northern Nigeria." Paper presented at the ninth congress of the Pan African Association for Prehistory and Related Studies, Jos, Nigeria.

Dart, R. A. 1924. "Nickel in Ancient Bronzes." *Nature* 113: 888.

David, N., R. Heimann, D. Killick, and M. Wayman. 1989. "Between Bloomery and

Blast Furnace: Mafa Iron-Smelting Technology in North Cameroon." *African Archaeological Review* 7: 183–207.

David, N., and I. Robertson. 1996. "Competition and Change in Two Traditional African Iron Industries." In P. R. Schmidt, ed., *The Culture and Technology of African Iron Production* (128–144). Gainesville: University Press of Florida.

Davidson, B. 1969. *A History of East and Central Africa: To the Late Nineteenth Century*. Garden City, N.Y.: Anchor Books.

Davis, M. B. 1938. *A Lunyoro-Lunyankole-English and English-Lunyoro-Luankole Dictionary*. Kampala: The Uganda Book Shop.

de Barros, P. 1985. *The Bassar: Large-Scale Iron Producers of the West African Savanna.* Ann Arbor, Mich.: University Microfilms International.

———. 1986. "Bassar: A Quantified, Chronologically Controlled, Regional Approach to a Traditional Iron Production Centre in West Africa." *Africa* 56: 148–174.

———. 1988. "Societal Repercussions of the Rise of Large-Scale Traditional Iron Production: A West African Example." *African Archaeological Review* 6: 91–113.

———. 1990. "Changing Paradigms, Goals and Methods in the Archaeology of Francophone Africa." In P. Robertshaw, ed., *A History of African Archaeology* (155–172). London: Heinemann.

de Beaucorps, R. 1951. *L'Evolution Economique chez les Basongo de la Luniungu et de la Gobari.* Brussels: Mémoires de l'Institut Royal Colonial Belge.

de Columbel, V. 1986. *Phonologie Quantitative et Synthétique avec Application à l'Ouldémé, Langue Tchadique du Nord-Cameroun*. Langues et Cultures Africaines No. 7. Paris: Société d'Etudes Linguistiques et Anthropologiques de France.

de Hemptinne, M. 1926. "Les Mangeurs de cuivre du Katanga." *Congo* 1(3): 371–403.

de Heusch, L. 1972. *Le roi ivre ou l'origine de l'etat.* Paris: Gallimard.

———. 1975. "Le Roi, les Forgerons et les Premiers Hommes dans l'ancienne Société Kongo." *Systèmes de Pensée en Afrique Noire*. Paris.

———. 1982. *Rois Nés d'un Coeur de Vache: Mythes et Rites Bantous II*. Paris: Gallimard.

de Maret, P. 1977. "Sanga, New Excavations, More Data, and Some Related Problems." *Journal of African History* 18: 321–337.

———. 1979. "Luba Roots the First Complete Iron Age Sequence in Zaire." *Current Anthropology* 20(1): 233–235.

———. 1980. "Ceux qui jouent avec le feu: La place du forgeron en Afrique Centrale." *Africa* 50: 263–279.

———. 1981. L'evolution monetaire du Shaba central entre le 7[e] et le 18[e] siecle." *African Economic History* 10: 117–149.

———. 1982. "New Survey of Archaeological Research and Dates for West-Central and North-Central Africa." *Journal of African History* 23: 1–15.

———. 1985a. "Recent Archaeological Research and Dates from Central Africa." *Journal of African History* 26: 129–148.

———. 1985b. "The Smith's Myth and the Origin of Leadership in Central Africa." In R. Haaland and P. Shinnie, eds., *African Iron Working: Ancient and Traditional.* (73–87). Bergen: Norwegian University Press.

———. 1991. *Fouilles Archéologiques dans la Vallée du Haut-Lualaba, Zaire. III. Kamilamba, Kikulu, et Malemba-Nkulu, 1975*. Tervuren: Royal Museum for Central Africa.

de Maret, P., and G. Thiry. 1996. "How Old Is the Iron Age in Central Africa?" In P. R. Schmidt, ed., *The Culture and Technology of African Iron Production* (29–39). Gainesville: University Press of Florida.

Derricourt, R. M. 1977. *Prehistoric Man in the Ciskei and Transkei*. Cape Town: Struik.

Devisse, J., and R. Vernet. 1993. "Le bassin des vallées du Niger: Chronologie et espace." In *Vallées du Niger* (11–37). Paris: Editions de la Reunion des Musées Nationaux.

Dewey, W. J. 1985. "Shona Ritual Axes." *Insight,* June 1–5.

———. 1986. "Shona Male and Female Artistry." *African Arts* 19(3): 64–67.

Dewey, W. J., and A. F. Roberts. 1993. *Iron, Master of Them All*. Iowa City: University of Iowa Museum of Art and the Project for Advanced Study of Art and Life in Africa. 5 to July 15, 1993

d'Hertefelt, M., and A. Coupez. 1964. *La Royauté Sacré de l'Ancien Rwanda*. Tervuren: Annales of the Royal Museum for Central Africa.

Dieterlen, G. 1957. "The Mande Creation Myth." *Africa* 27(2): 124–139.

Dillon, R. G. 1981. "Notes on the Pre-Colonial History and Ethnography of the Meta." In C. Tardits, ed., *Contribution de la recherche ethnologique à l'histoire des civilisations du Cameroun* (361–370). Paris: Editions du CNRS.

Diop, L. M. 1968. "Métallurgie traditionnelle et âge du fer en Afrique." *Bulletin de l'IFAN* 30, Series B (1): 10–33.

dos Santos, J. N. 1891. *Ethiopia Oriental*. Lisbon: Bibliotheca de Classicos Portugueses.

Doumbia, P. E. N. 1936. "Etude du Clan des Forgerons." *Bulletin du Comité d'Etudes Historiques et Scientifiques de l'Afrique Occidentale Française* 19(2–3): 334–360.

Dugast, S. 1986. "La pince et le soufflet: Deux techniques de forge traditionnelles au Nord-Togo." *Journal des Africanistes* 56(2): 29–53.

———. 1988. "Déterminations economiques versus fondements symboliques: La chefferie de Bassar." *Cahiers d'Etudes Africaines* 110, 28(2): 265–280.

Dupré, M.-C. 1981–82. "Pour une Histoire des Productions: La Métallurgie du Fer chez les Téké: Ngungulu, Tio, Tsaayi (République du Congo)." *Cahiers del'ORSTOM, Série Sciences Humaines* 18(2): 195–223.

Echard, N. 1992. "A propos de la métallurgie: Système technique, organisation sociale et histoire." In E. Bernus and N. Echard, eds., *La Région d'In Gall-Tegidda-n-Tesemt: V. Les Populations Actuelles,* Series 52 (7–60). Niamey: Etudes Nigeriennes.

———, ed. 1983. *Métallurgies Africaines: Nouvelles contributions*. Paris: Mémoires de la Société des Africanistes.

Eckert, H. E. 1974. "Les Fonduers de Koni." *Géographie: Annales de l'Université d'Abidjan* 6: 169–189.

Essomba, J. M. 1985. "Archéologie et histoire au sud du Cameroun: découverte de hauts fourneaux en pays Bassa." *Nyame Akuma* 26: 2–4.

———. 1986. *Bibliographie critique de l'archéologie camerounaise*. Yaoundé: Librairie Universitaire.

———. 1987. "Le fer dans le dévelopement des sociétés traditionnelles du sud Cameroun." *Annales de la faculté des lettres et sciences humaines* 3(2): 33–65.

———. 1992a. "Archéologie du sud du Cameroun: Notes préliminaires de recherches au site de Nkometou (Mfomakap)." In J. M. Essomba, ed., *Archéologie au Cameroun* (229–246). Paris: Karthal.

———. 1992b. *Civilisation du fer et sociétés en Afrique Centrale: Le cas du Cameroun méridional Collections "Racines du Présent."* Paris: L'Harmattan.

———. 1993. *Le fer dans le passé des sociétés du sud Cameroun*. Paris: L'Harmattan.

Estermann, C. 1976. "The Non Bantu People." In G. D. Gibson, ed., *Ethnography of Southwestern Angola* (1–49). New York: Africana Publishing.

Evers, T. M. 1974. "Ancient Mining in Southern Africa." *Journal of the South African Institute of Mining and Metallurgy* 74: 217–226.

Fagan, B. M 1969. "Early Trade and Raw Materials in South-Central Africa." *Journal of African History* 10(1): 1–13.

Fagan, B. M., D. W. Phillipson, and S. G. H. Daniels. 1969. *Iron Age Cultures in Zambia, Vol.* 2. London: Chatto and Windus.

Fallers, L. A. 1965. *Bantu Bureaucracy*. Chicago: University of Chicago Press.

Farquhar, R. M. 1998. "Provenance of Copper-Rich Metallic Artifacts from the Congo, Based on Chemical and Lead-Isotope Concentrations." In Z. Volavka, ed., *Crown and Ritual the Royal Insignia of Ngpyo* (272–283). Toronto: University of Toronto Press.

Filipowiak, W. 1985. "Iron Working in the Old Kingdom of Mali." In R. Haaland and P. Shinnie, eds., *African Iron Working: Ancient and Traditional* (36–49). Bergen: Norwegian University Press.

Fisher, R. 1970. *Twilight Tales of the Black Baganda*. London: Frank Cass.

Flight, C. 1973. "A Survey of Recent Results in the Radiocarbon Chronology of Northern and Western Africa." *Journal of African History* 14: 531–554.

Fowler, I. 1990. "Babungo: A Study of Iron Production, Trade and Power in a Nineteenth Century Ndop Plain Chiefdom (Cameroons)." Ph.D. diss., University College, London University.

Fox, C. 1986. "Asante Brass Casting." *African Arts* 19(4): 66–71.

Franklin, U., and Z. Volavka. 1998. "Technical Studies." In Z. Volavka, ed., *Crown and Ritual the Royal Insignia of Ngpyo* (257–272). Toronto: University of Toronto Press.

Freeman-Grenville, G. S. P. 1962. *The East African Coast*. Oxford: Clarendon Press.

Friede, H. M. 1980. "Iron Age Mining in the Transvaal." *Journal of the South African Institute of Mining and Metallurgy* 80: 156–165.

Friede, H. M., and R. H. Steel. 1975. "Ingot Casting and Wire Drawing in Iron Age Southern Africa." *Journal of the South African Institute of Mining and Metallurgy* 76(4): 232–237.

———. 1976. "Tin Mining and Smelting in the Transvaal during the Iron Age." *Journal of the South African Institute of Mining and Metallurgy* 76: 461–470.

———. 1977. "An Experimental Study of Iron-Smelting Techniques in the Southern African Iron Age." *Journal of the South African Institute of Mining and Metallurgy* 77: 233–242.

———. 1986. "Traditional Wooden Drum Bellows of South-Western Africa." *South African Archaeological Bulletin* 41(143): 12–16.

Frobenius, L., A. Martius, and L. von Wilm. 1921. *Atlas Africanus*. Frankfurt: Forschungs Institut für Kultur-Morphologie.

Galaty, J. G. 1982. " 'Being 'Maasai'; Being 'People-of-Cattle': Ethnic Shifters in East Africa." *American Ethnologist* 9(1): 1–20.

Gardi, R. 1969. *Unter afrikanischen Handwerkern*. Bern.

Gardin, J. C. 1979. *Une Archéologie Théorique*. Paris: Hachette.

Garlake, P. 1970a. "Portuguese References and Copper Ingots." *South African Archaeological Bulletin* 25(1): 41–43.

———. 1970b. "Iron Age Sites in the Urungwe District of Rhodesia." *South African Archaeological Bulletin* 25(3): 25–44.

———. 1973. *Great Zimbabwe*. New York: Stein and Day.

———. 1982. *Life at Great Zimbabwe*. Gweru: Mambo Press.

Garlick, W. G. 1961. "Structural Evolution of the Copperbelt." In F. Mendelsohn, ed., *Geology of the Northern Rhodesian Copperbelt* (89–93). London: Macdonald.

Garrard, T. 1973. "Studies in Akan Gold Weights (4) Their Date." *Transactions of the Historical Society of Ghana* 14: 149–168.

Garrard, T. F. 1980. *Akan Weights and the Gold Trade* London

———. 1982. "Myth and Metrology: The Early Trans-Saharan Gold Trade." *Journal of African History* 23: 443–461.

Gell, A. 1988. "Technology and Magic." *Anthropology Today* 4: 6–9.

Gibbs, J. L., Jr. 1988. "The Kpelle of Liberia." In *Peoples of Africa: Cultures of Africa South of the Sahara* (197–240). Prospect Heights, Ill.: Waveland Press.

Godelier, M. 1982. *La Production des grands hommes*. Paris: Fayard.

Goucher, C. L. 1981. "Iron Is Iron 'til It Is Rust: Trade and Ecology in the Decline of West African Iron-Smelting." *Journal of African History* 22: 179–189.

———. 1984. "The Iron Industry of Bassar, Togo: An Interdisciplinary Investigation of African Technological History." Ph.D. diss., University of California, Los Angeles.

Goucher, C. L., and E. W. Herbert. 1996. "The Blooms of Banjeli: Technology and Gender in West African Iron Making." In P. R. Schmidt, ed., *The Culture and Technology of African Iron Production* (40–57). Gainesville: University Press of Florida.

Grébénart, D. 1987. "Characteristics of the Final Neolithic and Metal Ages in the Region of Agadez (Niger)." In A. Close, ed., *A Prehistory of Arid North Africa: Essays in Honor of Fred Wendorf* (287–316). Dallas: Southern Methodist University Press.

———. 1979a. "La préhistoire de la République du Niger: État actuel de la question." *Recherches Sahariennes.*"1: 37–70.

———. 1979b. "Recherches sur la préhistoire au Niger." *Recherches Sahariennes* 1: 207–224.

———. 1983. "Les métallurgies du cuivre et du fer autour d'Agadez (Niger) des origines au début de la période médiévale: Vues générales." In N. Echard, ed., *Métallurgies africaines: Nouvelles contributions* (109–125). Paris: Mémoires de la Société des Africanistes.

———. 1985. *La Région d'In Gall–Tegidda n Tesemt (Niger) II: Le Néolithique Final et les Débuts de la Métallurgie*. Niamey: Etudes Nigériennes.

———. 1988. *Les premiers métallurgistes en Afrique Occidentale*. Paris: Errance.

Gray, R., and D. Birmingham. 1970. *Pre-Colonial African Trade*. London: Oxford University Press.

Haaland, R. 1980. "Man's Role in the Changing Habitat of Mema during the Old Kingdom of Ghana." *Norwegian Archaeological Review* 13: 31–46.

———. 1985. "Iron Production, Its Socio-Cultural Context and Ecological Implications." In R. Haaland and P. Shinnie, eds., *African Iron Working: Ancient and Traditional* (50–72). Bergen: Norwegian University Press.

Haaland, R., and P. Shinnie, eds. 1985. *African Iron Working: Ancient and Traditional*. Bergen: Norwegian University Press.

Haddon, A. C. 1908. "Copper Rod Currency from the Transvaal." *Man* 65: 21–22.

Hahn, H. P. 1997. *Techniques de Métallurgie au Nord-Togo Collections*. Patrimoines No. 6. Lomé: Presses de l'Université du Bénin.

Herbert, E. W. 1984. *Red Gold of Africa*. Madison: University of Wisconsin Press.

———. 1993. *Iron, Gender, and Power: Rituals of Transformation In African Societies*. Bloomington: Indiana University Press.

Hiernaux, J., E. Longrée, and J. De Buyst. 1971. *Fouilles archaéologiques dans la vallée du Haut-Lualaba, I. Sanga, 1958*. Tervuren: Musée Royale de l'Afrique Centrale.

Hodder, I. 1982. *Symbols in Action*. Cambridge: Cambridge University Press.

———. 1986. *Reading the Past*. Cambridge: Cambridge University Press.

Hodge, M. A. 1996. "Political Organization of the Central Provinces." In F. F. Berdan, R. E. Blanton, E. H. Boone, M. G. Hodge, M. E. Smith, and E. Umberger, eds., *Aztecs Imperial Strategies* (17–45). Washington, D.C.: Dumbarton Oaks.

Holl, A. 1985. "Background to the Ghana Empire: Archaeological Investigation on the Transition to Statehood in the Dhar Tichitt Region (Mauretania)." *Journal of Anthropological Archaeology* 4: 73–115.

———. 1988a. *Houlouf I: Archéologie des Sociétés Protohistoriques du Nord-Cameroun*. Oxford: British Archaeological Reports.

———. 1988b. "Transition du néolithique à l'age du fer dans la plaine péritchadienne: Le cas de Mdaga." In D. Barreteau and H. Tourneux, eds., *Le milieu et les hommes: Recherches comparatives et historiques dans le bassin du lac Tchad* (81–109). Paris: Editions de l'ORSTOM.

———. 1990. "West African Archaeology: Colonialism and Nationalism." In P. T. Robertshaw, ed., *A History of African Archaeology* (296–308). London and New York: J. Currey.

———. 1991. "L'Age du fer ancien: Cameroun." In R. Lanfranchi and B. Clist, eds., *Les Origines de l'Afrique Centrale* (192–196). Libreville: Editions Sépia.

———. 1993. "Transition from Late Stone Age to Iron Age in the Sudano-Sahelian Zone: A Case Study from the Perichadian Plain." In T. Shaw, P. Sinclair, B. Andah, and A. Okpoko, eds., *The Archaeology of Africa: Food, Metals and Towns* (330–343). London: Routledge.

———. 1997. "Metallurgy, Iron Technology and African Late Holocene Societies." In R. Klein-Arendt, ed., *Traditionelles Eisenhandwerk in Afrika* (13–54). Koln: Heinrich Barth Institut.

Huard, P. 1960. "Contribution à l'étude du cheval, du fer et du chameau au Sahara oriental I: le fer." *Bulletin de l'IFAN* 22, Series B (1–2): 136.

———. 1964. "Nouvelle contribution à l'étude du fer au Sahara et au Tchad." *Bulletin de l'IFAN* 24, Series B (3–4): 297–397.

Huffman, T. N. 1986. "Iron Age Settlement Patterns and the Origins of Class Distinction in Southern Africa." In F. Wendorf and A. Close, eds., *Advances in World Archaeology 5* (291–338). New York: Academic Press.

———. 1989. *Iron Age Migrations*. Johannesburg: Witwatersrand University Press.

Huffman, T. N., H. D. van der Merwe, M. R. Grant, and G. S. Kruger. 1995. "Early Copper Mining at Thakadu, Botswana." *Journal of the South African Institute of Mining and Metallurgy* 95: 53–61.

Hupfeld, V. F. 1899. "Die Eisenindustrie in Togo." *Mitteilungen aus den deutsche Schutzegebieten* 11 175–194.

Ibn Batutta. 1929. *Travels in Asia and Africa, 1325–54*. Translated by H. A. R. Gibb. London: Routledge and Kegan Paul.

Inskeep, R.R. 1962. "Some Iron Age Sites in Northern Rhodesia." *South African Archaeological Bulletin* 17: 136–180.

Izard, M. 1983. "Le royaume Yatenga et ses forgerons: Une recherche d'histoire du peuplement (Haute-Volta)." In N. Echard, ed., *Métallurgies Africaines: Nouvelles Contributions* (253–279). Paris: Mémoires de la Société des Africanistes.

———. 1985. *Gens du Pouvoir, Gens de la Terre*. Cambridge and Paris: Cambridge University Press and Editions de la Maison des Sciences de l'Homme.

Jaggar, P. J. 1973. "Kano City Blacksmiths: Precolonial Distribution, Structure and Organization." *Savanna* 2(1): 11–25.

Jézégou, M. P., and B. Clist. 1991. "L'Age du fer ancien: Gabon." In R. Lanfranchi and B. Clist, eds., *Aux Origines de l'Afrique Centrale* (202–207). Libreville: Editions Sépia.

Johansson. 1967. *Nigerian Currencies*. Translated by J. Learmont. Norkopping, Sweden.

Johnston, H. H. 1908. *George Grenfell and the Congo*. 2 vols. London: Hutchinson.

Kense, F. J. 1983. *Traditional African Iron Working*. Calgary: University of Calgary Press.

———. 1985a. "Western Gonja Archaeology Project: Preliminary Report." *Nyame Akuma* 26: 18–20.

———. 1985b. "The Initial Diffusion of Iron to Africa." In R. Haaland and P. Shinnie, eds., *African Iron Working: Ancient and Traditional* (11–27). Bergen: Norwegian University Press.

Kiethega, J. B. 1983. *L'Or de la Volta Noire: Exploitation traditionnelle, Histoire et Archaeologie*. Paris: Karthala.

———. 1996. "La Metallurgie lourde du fer au Burkina Faso." Ph.D. diss., University of Paris I: Pantheon-Sorbonne.

Killick, D. J. 1990. "Technology and Its Social Setting: Bloomery Iron Smelting at Kasungu, Malawi, 1860–1940." Ph.D. diss., Yale University.

Killick, D., N. J. van der Merwe, R. B. Gordon, and D. Grébénart. 1988. "Reassessment of the Evidence for Early Metallurgy in Niger, West Africa." *Journal of Archaeological Science* 15: 367–394.

Kinahan, J., and J. C. Vogel. 1982. "Recent Copper-Working Sites in the Khuiseb Drainage, Namibia." *South African Archaeological Bulletin* 37(135): 44–45.

Kiriama, H. O. 1993. "The Iron-Using Communities in Kenya." In T. Shaw, P. Sinclair, B. Andah, and A. Okpoko, eds., *The Archaeology of Africa: Food, Metals and Towns* (484-498). London: Routledge.

Kirsch, H. 1968. *Applied Mineralogy for Engineers, Technologists and Students*. London: Chapman and Hall.

Kiyaga-Mulindwa, D. 1993. "The Iron Age Peoples of East-Central Botswana." In T. Shaw, P. Sinclair, B. Andah, and A. Okpoko, eds., *The Archaeology of Africa: Food, Metals and Towns* (387–389). London: Routledge.

Klose, H. 1964. *Klose's Journey to Northern Ghana 1894* (trans. I. Killick from Klose 1899, *Togo unter deutscher Flagge: Reisebilder und Betrachtungen*) Berlin: Reimer, 285–544.

Koert, W. 1906. "Das Eisenlager van Bangeli in Togo." *Mitteilungen aus den deutsche Schutzgebieten* 19: 113–131.

Kuevi, D. 1975. "Le travail et le commerce du fer au Togo avant l'arrivée des Européens." *Etudes Togolaises* 11–12: 22–43.

Kun, Nicholas de. 1965. *The Mineral Resources of Africa*. Amsterdam: Elsevier Publishing.

Kuper, H. 1988. "The Swazi of Swaziland." In J. L. Gibbs Jr., ed., *Peoples of Africa: Cultures of Africa South of the Sahara* (479–512), Prospect Heights, Ill.: Waveland Press.

Laburthe-Tolra, P. 1981a. "Essai de synthèse sur les populations dites 'béti' de la région de Minlaba (sud du Nyong)." In C. Tardits, ed., *Contribution de l'ethnologie à l'histoire des civilisations du Cameroun* (533–546). Paris: Editions du CNRS.

———. 1981b. *Minlaba I: Les seigneurs de la forêt*. Paris: Publications de la Sorbonne.

Ladame, F. 1921. "Le droit des indigenes sur les mines de cuivre du Katanga." *Congo* 2: 685–691.

Laing, A.G. 1825. *Travels in the Timanee, Kooranko and Soolima Countries of Western Africa*. London: John Murray.

Laman, K. 1953–57. *The Kongo*. 2 vols. Uppsala: Studia Ethnographica Upsaliensia.

Lambert, N. 1971. "Les industries sur cuivre dans l'Ouest Saharien." *West African Journal of Archaeology* 1: 9–21.

———. 1975. "Mines et métallurgies antiques dans la région d'Akjoujt." *Annales de l'Institut Mauritanien de la Recherche Scientifique* 1: 6–25.

———. 1983. "Nouvelle contribution à l'étude du chalcolithique mauritanien." In N. Echard, ed., *Métallurgies Africaines: Nouvelles Contributions* (63–87). Paris: Mémoires de la Société des Africanistes.

Lanfranchi, R., and B. Clist, eds. 1991. *Les Origines de l'Afrique Centrale*. Libreville: Editions Sépia.

Larick, R. 1986. "Smelting and Inter-Ethnic Conflict among Pre-Colonial Maa-Speaking Pastoralists of North-Central Kenya." *The African Archaeological Review* 4: 165–174.

———. 1991. "Warriors and Blacksmiths: Mediating Ethnicity in East African Spears." *Journal of Anthropological Archaeology* 10: 299–331.

Latour, B. 1993. "Ethnography of a "High-Tech Case: About Aramis." In P. Lemonnier, ed., *Technological Choices* (372–398). London: Routledge.

Lawson, T. D. 1972. "Géologie et perspectives economiques e la formation ferrifère de la cuvette du Buem au Togo." Projet du Fonds Spécial ONU: Mines et Eaux. Bureau National de Recherches Minières, Lome (Togo). Mimeographed.

Leach, E. 1976. *Culture and Communication*. Cambridge: Cambridge University Press.

Lebeuf, J. P. 1969. *Carte archéologique des abords du lac Tchad*. Paris: Editions du CNRS.

———. 1981. *Supplément à la carte archéologique des abords du lac Tchad*. Paris: Editions du CNRS.

Lebeuf, J. P., A. M. D. Lebeuf, F. Treinen-Claustre, and J. Courtin. 1980. *Le Gisement Sao de Mdaga (Tchad)*. Paris: Société d'Ethnographie.

Lechtman, H. 1977. "Style in Technology—Some early thoughts." In H. Lechtman and R. Merrill, eds., *Material Culture: Styles, Organization and Dynamics of Technology* (3–20). St. Paul: West Publishing.

Lekime, F. 1966. *Katanga, Pays Du Cuivre*. Verniers: Editions Gèrard.

Lemonnier, P. 1992. *Elements for an Anthropology of Technology*. Ann Arbor: University of Michigan Press.

———. 1993. "Introduction." In P. Lemonnier, ed., *Technical Choices* (1–35). London: Routledge.

Levi-Strauss, C. 1966. *The Savage Mind*. Chicago: University of Chicago Press.

Levtzion, N. 1973. *Ancient Ghana and Mali*. London: Methuen.

Levtzion, N., and J. F. P. Hopkins, eds. 1981. *Corpus of Early Arabic Sources for West African History*. Cambridge: Cambridge University Press.

Levy, T. E., and A. Holl. 1988. "Les societes chalcolithiques de la Palestine et l'emergence des chefferies." *Archives Europeennes de Sociologie* 29: 283–316.

Lhote, H. 1952. "La connaissance du fer en Afrique Occidentale." *Encyclopédie mensuelle d'Outre-mer*, 269–272.

Lihoreau, M. 1993. *Djorf Torba: Necropole Saharienne Anteislamique*. Paris: Karthala.

Lindblom, G. 1926. "Copper Rod 'Currency' from Palabora, N Transvaal." *Man* 26: 144–147.

Livingstone, D. 1857. *Missionary Travels and Researches in South Africa*. London: John Murray.

———. 1874. *Last Journals, Vol. 2*. London: John Murray.

Lloyd, P. C. 1988. "The Yoruba of Nigeria." In J. L. Gibbs Jr., ed., *Peoples of Africa: Cultures of Africa South of the Sahara* (547–582). Prospect Heights, Ill.: Waveland Press.

Lombard, J. 1957. "Aperçu sur la technologie et l'artisanat Bariba." *Etudes Dahoméenes* 18: 7–60.

MacDonald, K. C., and W. van Neer. 1994. "Specialized Fishing in the Later Holocene of the Mema Region (Mali)." In W. van Neer, ed., *Fish Exploitation in the Past*, Series 274 (243–251). Tervuren: Annales du Musee Royal de l'Afrique Centrale, Sciences Zoologiques.

Manima-Moubouha, A. 1987. "A propos des recherches archéologiques sur la métallurgie du fer et du cuivre en R.P. du Congo." *NSI* 1: 3–5.

Martinelli, B. 1982. *Métallurgistes Bassar: Techniques et Formation Sociale*. Etudes et Documents de Sciences Humaines, Series A, No. 5. Lomé: University of Benin.

Martins, J. V. 1966. *A Idade dos Métais na Lunda*. Lisbon.
Mauny, R. 1951. "Un age du cuivre au Sahara Occidental." *Bulletin de l'Institut français d'Afrique noire* 13: 168–180.
———. 1952. "Essai sur l'histoire des métaux en Afrique Occidentale." *Bulletin de l'IFAN* 14(2): 545–595.
———. 1953. "Autour de l'introduction du fer en Afrique Occidentale." *Encyclopédie mensuelle d'Outre-mer*, 109–110.
———. 1967. "Datation au C14 des sites ouest africains de l'âge du fer." In H.-J. Hugot, ed., *Actes du VI* e *Congrès Panafricain de Préhistoire et d'Etudes du Quaternaire*. (533–539). Chambery: n.p.
Mbida, C. 1992a. "Fouilles archéologiques au sud Cameroun: Résultats préliminaires de la mission de l'été 1990." *NSI* 10/11: 6–8.
———. 1992b. "Archaeological Research in South Cameroon: Preliminary Results on the 1990 Field Season." *Nyame Akuma* 37: 2–4.
McIntosh, R. J. 1998. *The Peoples of the Middle Niger: Island of Gold*. Oxford: Blackwell Publishers.
McIntosh, R. J., and S. K. McIntosh. 1980. *Prehistoric Investigations in the Region of Jenne, Mali*. Oxford: British Archaeological Reports.
———. 1988. "From Siècles Obscurs to Revolutionary Centuries on the Middle Niger." *World Archaeology* 20(1): 141–165.
McIntosh, S. K.1993. "A Tale of Two Floodplains: Comparative Perspectives on the Emergence of Complex Societies and Urbanism in the Middle Niger and Senegal Valleys. In P. Sinclair, ed., *East African Urban Origins in World Perspective*. New York: Routledge and Kegan Paul.
———. 1994. "Changing Perceptions of West Africa's Past: Archaeological Research since 1988." *Journal of Archaeological Research* 2(2): 165–198.
McNaughton, P. R. 1988. *The Mande Blacksmiths*. Bloomington: Indiana University Press.
Meillassoux, C. 1978. "The Economy in Agricultural Self-Sustaining Societies: A Preliminary Analysis." In D. Seldon, ed., *Relations of Production: Marxist Approaches to Economic Anthropology* (127–156). London: Frank Cass.
Melland, F. 1923. *In Witch-Bound Africa: An Account of the Primitive Kaonde Tribe and Their Beliefs*. London: Frank Cass.
Mellart, J. 1967. *Catal Hûyûk*. London: Thames and Hudson.
Mendelsohn, F., ed. 1961. *Geology of the Northern Rhodesian Copperbelt*. London: Macdonald.
Middleton, J. 1992. *The Lugbara of Uganda*. 2nd ed. San Diego: Harcourt Brace Jovanovich.
Miller, D. E. 1994. "Kaonde Copper Smelting Technical Versatility and the Ethnographic Record." In S. T. Childs, ed., *Society, Culture and Technology in Africa* (79–85). MASCA Research Papers in Science and Archaeology, Vol. 11 (supplement). Philadelphia: University of Pennsylvania Museum of Archaeology and Anthropology.
Miller, D. E., and N. J. van der Merwe. 1994. "Early Metal Working in Sub-Saharan Africa: A Review of Recent Research." *Journal of African History* 35: 1–36.
Miracle, M. P. 1962. "The Copperbelt—Trading and Marketing." In P. Bohannon and G Dalton, eds., *Markets in Africa* (197–243). New York: Doubleday.

Monimo, Y. 1983. "Accoucher du fer: La métallurgie Gbaya (Centrafrique)." In N. Echard, ed., *Métallurgies Africaines: Nouvelles Contributions* (281–309). Paris: Mémoires de la Société des Africanistes.

Monteiro, J. J. 1875. *Angola and the River Congo.* 2 vols. London: Frank Cass.

Muhammed, I. M. 1993. "Iron Technology in the Middle Sahel/Savanna: With Emphasis on Central Darfur." In T. Shaw, P. Sinclair, B. Andah, and A. Okpoko, eds., *The Archaeology of Africa: Food, Metals and Towns* (459–467). London: Routledge.

Nachtigal, G. 1871. *Sahara and Sudan.* London: H. Hurst.

Nadel, S. F. 1942. *A Black Byzantium: The Kingdom of Nupe in Nigeria.* London: Oxford University Press.

Neaher, N. 1979. "Akwa Who Travel." *Africa* 49: 352–366.

Neher, G. 1964. "Brass Casting in Northeast Nigeria." *Journal of the Nigerian Field Society* 29(1): 16–27.

Nenquin, J. 1963. *Excavations at Sanga, 1957.* Tervuren: Musée Royale de l'Afrique Centrale.

Ngijol Ngijol, P. 1980. *Les Fils de Hitong.* Yaoundé: Centre d'édition et de production pour l'enseignement et la recherche.

Ngoa, H. 1981. "Tentative de reconstruction de l'histoire recente des Ewondo." In C. Tardits, ed., *Contribution de lethnologie à l'histoire des civilisations du Cameroun* (547–562). Paris: Editions du CNRS.

Nkolo Foe. 1985. *La Naissance du Monde Selon le Mvet: Contribution à l'Etude des Cosmogonies Africaines.* Ph.D. diss., University of Yaoundé.

Okafor, E. E. 1992. "Early Iron Smelting in Nsukka-Nigeria: Information from Slags and Residues." Ph.D. diss., University of Sheffield.

———. 1993. "New Evidence on Early Iron-Smelting from Southeastern Nigeria." In T. Shaw, P. Sinclair, B. Andah, and A. Okpoko, eds., *The Archaeology of Africa: Food, Metals and Towns* (432–448). London: Routledge.

Oliver, R., and G. Mathew. 1963. *History of East Africa, Vol. 1.* Oxford: Clarendon Press.

O'Neill, P., F. Muhly Jr., and W. Lambrecht. 1988. *The Tree of Iron.* Foundation for African Prehistory and Archaeology. 16-mm film, video.

Ossah-Mvondo, J. P. 1990. "Recherches archéologiques dans le nord-ouest: Le site métallurgique de Ba/." *Nyame Akuma* 33: 2.

———. 1991. "Problèmes et méthodes de la recherche archéologique en pays forestiers: La province du sud et ses environs." *Nyame Akuma* 36: 47–52.

———. 1992a. "Identification du site métallurgique de Mandoumba, Centre Cameroun: Les premières données archéologiques." *Nyame Akuma* 38: 17–19.

———. 1992b. "Prospection archéologique dans le département du Ntem, Province du sud Cameroun." *NSI* 10/11: 9–12.

———. 1993. "Prospection des sites d'habitat dans les arrondissements de Djoum et Mintom (sud Cameroun)." *Nyame Akuma* 39: 15–19.

Paques, V. 1967. "Origines et caractères du pouvoir royal au Baguirmi." *Journal de la Société des Africanistes* 37: 183–214.

Paris, F. 1984. *La Région d'In Gall–Tegidda-n-Tesemt (Niger) III: Les Sépultures du Néolithique Final à l'Islam.* Niamey: Etudes Nigeriennes No. 50.

———. 1996. *Les Sepultures du Sahara Nigerien du Neolithique a l'Islamisation*. Paris: Editions de l'ORSTOM.

Paris, F., A. Person, G. Quechon, and J. F. Saliege 1992. "Les debuts de la metallurgie au Niger Spetentrional (Air, Azawagh, Ighazer, Termit)." *Journal des Africanistes* 62(2): 55–68.

Pereira, D. P. 1937. *Esmeraldo de Situ Orbis*. Edited and translated by G. H. T. Kimble. London: Hakluyt Society.

Phillipson, D. W. 1968a. "The Prehistory of the Copper Industry in Zambia." *Horizon* 10(4): 4–8.

———. 1968b. "The Early Iron Age in Zambia: Regional Variants and Some Tentative Conclusions." *Journal of African History* 9: 191–211.

———. 1970. "Notes on the Later Prehistoric Radiocarbon Chronology of Eastern and Southern Africa." *Journal of African History* 11(1): 1–15.

———. 1974. " Iron Age History and Archaeology in Zambia." *Journal of African History* 15: 1–25.

———. 1985. *African Archaeology*. Cambridge: Cambridge University Press.

———. 1993. *African Archaeology*. 2nd ed. Cambridge: Cambridge University Press.

Phillipson, D. W., and B. M. Fagan. 1969. "The Date of the Ingombe Ilede Burials *Journal of African History* 10: 199–204.

Pole, L. M. 1974. "Iron Smelting in Northern Ghana." *National Museum of Ghana Occasional Papers* 6: 5–40.

———. 1975. "Iron-Working Apparatuses and Techniques: Upper Region of Ghana." *West African Journal of Archaeology* 5: 11–39.

———. 1976. "Iron-Working Apparatus and Techniques: Upper Region of Ghana." *West African Journal of Archaeology* 5: 11–39.

Pomel, S., E. Shulz, and R. Baumhauer. 1991. "Changement dans le région de bordure des savanes à l'Holocène: Seguedine (Kaouar, Nord-Est Niger): Interactions de l'homme et du climat." Paper presented at Cinquième Colloque Mega-Tchad: L'Homme et le Milieu végétal, September 18–20, Paris-Sévres.

Poncet, Y. 1983. *La Région d'In Gall–Tegidda-n-Tesemt (Niger): Atlas*. Niamey: Etudes Nigeriennes No. 47.

Posnansky, M. 1973. "Aspects of Early West Africa Trade." *World Archaeology* 5: 149–162.

———. 1975. "Archaeology, Technology, and Akan Civilization." *Journal of African Studies* 2: 24-38.

———. 1977. "Brass Casting and Its Antecedents in West Africa." *Journal of African History* 18: 287–300.

Reefe, T. 1981. *The Rainbow and the Kings*. Berkeley and Los Angeles: University of California Press.

Rehder, J. E. n.d. "The Smelting of Copper." Unpublished manuscript (cited with permission).

Rein-Wührmann, A. 1925. *Mein Bamumvolk im Grasland vo Kamerun*. Stuttgart.

Renfrew, C. A. 1984. *Approaches to Social Archaeology*. Edinburgh: Edinburgh University Press.

Richter, D. 1980. "Further Considerations of Caste in West Africa. *Africa* 50(1): 37–54.

Rickard, T. A. 1927a. "Curious Methods Used by the Katanga Natives in Mining and Smelting Copper." *Engineering and Mining Journal Press* 123: 51–58.

———. 1927b. "Reply to Walker." *Engineering and Mining Journal Press* 123: 732.

Robertshaw, P. T. 1990. *A History of African Archeology*. London: J. Currey.

Roscoe, J. 1923a. *The Bakitara or Banyoro: The First Part of the Report of the Mackie Ethnological Expedition to Central Africa*. Cambridge: Cambridge University Press.

———. 1923b. *The Banyankole: The Second Part of the Report of the Mackie Ethnological Expedition to Central Africa*. Cambridge: Cambridge University Press.

———. 1924. *The Bagesu and Other Tribes of the Uganda Protectorate: The Third Part of the Report of the Mackie Ethnological Expedition to Central Africa*. Cambridge: Cambridge University Press.

Rowlands, M., and J. P. Warnier. 1993. "The Magical Production of Iron in the Cameroon Grassfields." In T. Shaw, P. Sinclair, B. Andah, and A Okpoko, eds., *The Archaeology of Africa: Food, Metals and Towns* (512–550). London: Routledge.

Rustad, J. 1980. "The Emergence of Iron Technology in West Africa, with Special Emphasis on the Nok Culture of Nigeria." In B. K. Swartz and R. A. Dumett, eds., *West African Culture Dynamics* (227–245). The Hague: Mouton Publishers.

Sabi-Monra, S. 1991. *Tradition Orale and Archéologie: Enquête sur la Métallurgie Ancienne du Fer dans le Borgou Oriental*. Mémoire de Maîtrise d'Histoire, Faculté des Lettres, Arts et Sciences Humaines, Université Nationale du Bénin.

Samtouna, I. 1990. *La Métallurgie Ancienne du Fer dans la Région de Koumbri (Yatenga, Burkina Faso)*. Etudes sur l'Histoire et l'Archéologie du Burkina Faso 4. Stuttgart: Franz Steiner Verlag.

Schaffer, M., and C. Cooper. 1987. *Mandinko: An Ethnography of a West African Holy Land*. Prospect Heights, Ill.: Waveland Press.

Schimmin, I. 1893. "Journey to Gambisa's" In F. W. McDonald, ed., *The Story of Mashonaland*. London: Mission House.

Schmidt, P., and R. Asombang. 1990a. "Rock-Shelters and a Greater History of the Bamenda Grassfields, Cameroon." *Nyame Akuma* 34: 5–10.

———. 1990b. "Archaeological Survey in Northwestern Cameroon." *Nyame Akuma* 34: 10–16.

Schmidt, P. R. 1978. *Historical Archaeology: A Structural Approach in an African Culture*. Westport, Conn.: Greenwood Press.

———. 1983a. "Cultural Meaning and History in African Myth." *International Journal of Oral History* 4: 183.

———. 1983b. "An Alternative to a Strictly Materialist Perspective: A Review of Historical Archaeology, Ethnoarchaeology, and Symbolic Approaches in African Archaeology." *American Antiquity* 48: 62–79.

———. 1988. "Reproductive Symbolism in Iron Smelting among the Barongo." Chicago: Paper presented at the 38th annual meeting of the African Studies Association, Chicago.

———. 1990. "Oral Traditions, Archaeology, and History: A Short Reflective History." In P. Robertshaw, ed., *A History of African Archaeology* (252–270). Portsmouth, N.H.: Heinemann.

———. 1996a. "Cultural Representations of African Iron Production." In *The Cul-*

ture and Technology of African Iron Production (1–28). Gainesville: University Press of Florida.

———. 1996b. "Reconfiguring the Barongo: Reproductive Symbolism and Reproduction among a Work Association of Iron Smelters." In *The Culture and Technology of African Iron Production* (74–127). Gainesville: University Press of Florida.

———, ed. 1996c. *The Culture and Technology of African Iron Production*. Gainesville: University Press of Florida.

———. 1997. *Iron Technology in East Africa: Symbolism, Science, and Archaeology*. Bloomington: Indiana University Press.

Schmidt, P. R., and D. H. Avery. 1983. "More Evidence for an Advanced Prehistoric Iron Technology in Africa." *Journal of Field Archaeology* 10(3): 421–434.

Schmidt, P. R., and S. T. Childs. 1985. "Innovation and Industry during the Early Iron Age in East Africa: The KM2 and KM3 Sites of Northern Tanzania." *African Archaeological Review* 3: 53–94.

Schmidt, P. R., and B. B. Mapunda. 1997. "Ideology and the Archaeological Record in Africa: Interpreting Symbolism in Iron Smelting Technology." *Journal of Anthropological Archaeology* 16: 73–102.

Schulz, E. 1991. "A Neolithic Revolution in the Sahara? Background to the Resources of Human Alimentation during the Holocene of the Central and Southern Sahara." Paper presented at the Cinquième Colloque Mega-Tchad: L'Homme et le Milieu végétal, September 18–20, Paris-Sèvres.

Seignobos, C. 1986. "Les Zumaya ou l'Ethnie Prohibée." Expanded version of a paper presented at the Third Colloque Internationale Méga-Tchad, September, Paris.

Shaw, T. 1970. *Igbo-Ukwu*. 2 vols. London: Faber and Faber.

Shaw, T., P. Sinclair, B. W., Andah, and A. Okpoko, eds., 1993. *The Archaeology of Africa: Food, Metals and Towns*. London: Routledge.

Shinnie, P. L. 1985. "Iron Working at Méroe." In R. Haaland and P. Shinnie, eds., *African Iron Working: Ancient and Traditional* (28–35). Bergen: Norwegian University Press.

———, ed. 1971. *The African Iron Age*. Oxford: Clarendon Press.

Shinnie, P. L., and F. J. Kense. 1989. *Archaeology of Gonja, Ghana: Excavations at Daboya*. Calgary: University of Calgary Press.

Spencer, P. 1973. *Nomads in Alliance: Symbiosis and Growth among the Rendille and Samburu in Kenya*. London: Oxford University Press.

Stanley, G. 1929. "Primitive Metallurgy in South Africa." *South African Journal of Science* 36: 739.

Stayt, H. A. 1931. *The Bavenda*. London: Oxford University Press.

Steel, R. H. 1974. "Iron Age Copper Mine 47/73." *Journal of the South African Institute of Mining and Metallurgy* 74: 244.

———. 1975. "Ingot Casting and Wire Drawing in Iron Age Southern Africa." *Journal of the South African Institute of Mining and Metallurgy* 76(4): 232–237.

Sterner, J., and N. David. 1991. "Gender and Caste in the Mandara Highlands: Northeastern Nigeria and Northern Cameroon." *Ethnology* 30(4): 355–369.

Strathern, A. 1971. *The Rope of Moka: Big Men and Ceremonial Exchange in Mount Hagen, New Guinea*. Cambridge: Cambridge University Press.

Summers, R. 1969. *Ancient Mining in Rhodesia and Adjacent Areas*. Salisbury: National Museums of Rhodesia.

Swan, L. 1995. *Early Gold Mining on the Zimbabwe Plateau: Changing Patterns of Gold Production in the First and Second Millennium AD*. Uppsala: Studies in African Archaeology.

Tainter, J. A. 1988. *The Collapse of Complex Societies*. Cambridge: Cambridge University Press.

Talmari, T. 1991. "The Development of Caste Systems in West Africa." *Journal of African History* 32: 221–250.

Tardits, C., ed. 1981a. *Contribution de la recherche ethnologique à l'histoire des civilizations du Cameroun*. Paris: Editions du CNRA.

———. 1981b. "Le Royaume Bamoun: Chronologie—implantation des populations—commerce et economie—diffusion du mais et du manioc." In *Contribution de la recherche ethnologique à l'histoire des civilizations du Cameroun* (401–420). Paris: Editions du CNRA.

Todd, J. A. 1977. "Caste in Africa?" *Africa* 47(4): 398–412.

———. 1985. "Iron Production by the Dimi of Ethiopia." In R. Haaland and P. Shinnie, eds., *African Iron Working: Ancient and Traditional*. (88–101). Bergen: Norwegian University Press.

Togola, T. 1993. *Archaeological Investigations of Iron Age Sites in the Mema Region Mali (West Africa)*. Ann Arbor, Mich.: University Microfilms International.

———. 1996. "Iron Age Occupation in the Mema Region, Mali." *African Archaeological Review* 13: 91–110.

Treinen-Claustre, F. 1982. *Sahara et Sahel à l'Age du Fer: Borkou, Tchad*. Paris: Mémoires de la Société des Africanistes.

Trevor, T. G. 1912a. "Some Observations on Ancient Workings in the Transvaal." *Journal of the Chemical, Metallurgical, and Mining Society of South Africa* 12: 267–275.

———. 1912b. "Some Observations on Ancient Workings in the Transvaal." *Journal of the Chemical, Metallurgical, and Mining Society of South Africa* 13: 148–149.

———. 1930. "Some Observations on the Relics of Pre-European Culture in Rhodesia and South Africa." *Journal of the Royal Anthropological Institute* 33: 389–399.

Trigger, B. G. 1969. "The Myth of Méroe and the African Iron Age." *African Historical Studies* 2: 23–50.

———. 1993. *Early Civilization: Ancient Egypt in Context*. Cairo: American University in Cairo Press.

Tuden, A., and L. Plotnicov, 1970, "Introduction." In A. Tuden and L. Plotnicov, eds., *Social Stratification in Africa* (1–29). New York: The Free Press.

Turner, V. 1967. *The Forest of Symbols*. Ithaca, N.Y.: Cornell University Press.

Tylecote, R. F. 1962. *Metallurgy in Archaeology*. London: Edward Arnold.

———. 1975. "The Origin of Iron Smelting in Africa." *West African Journal of Archaeology* 5: 1–9.

———. 1983. "Archaeometallurgical Finds and Their Significance." In N. Echard, ed., *Métallurgies Africaines: Nouvelles Contributions*. (1–11). Paris: Mémoires de la Société des Africanistes.

———. 1992. *A History of Metallurgy*. 2nd ed. London: Institute of Materials.

van Beek, W. E . A. 1987. *The Kapsiki of the Mandara Hills*. Prospect Heights, Ill.: Waveland Press.

van der Merwe, N. J. 1980. "The Advent of Iron in Africa." In T. A. Wertime and J. D. Muhly, eds., *The Coming of the Age of Iron* (463–506). New Haven, Conn.: Yale University Press.

van der Merwe, N. J., and D. H. Avery. 1982. "Pathways to Steel." *American Scientist* 70: 146–155.

———. 1987. "Science and Magic in African Technology: Traditional Iron Smelting in Malawi." *Africa* 57(2): 143–172.

van der Merwe, N. J., and R. Scully. 1971. "The Phalaborwa Story: Archaeological and Ethnographic Investigation of a South African Iron Age Group." *World Archaeology* 3(2): 178–196.

van Grunderbeek, M. C. 1992. "Essai de délimitation chronologique de l'Age du Fer Ancien au Burundi, au Rwanda et dans la région des grands lacs." *Azania* 27: 53–80.

van Grunderbeek, M. C., E. Roche, and H. Doutrelepont. 1982. "L'âge du fer ancien au Rwanda et au Burundi: Archéologie et environnement." *Journal des Africanistes* 52(1–2): 5–58.

Van Noten, F. 1983. *Histoire Archéologique de Rwanda*. Tervuren: Royal Museum for Central Africa.

van Warmelo, N. J. 1940. "The Copper Mines of Musina." In *South African Ethnological Publications No. 8* (81–86). Pretoria: Department of Native Affairs.

Vanacker, C. 1979. *Tegdaoust II, Recherches sur Aoudaghost: Fouilles d'un Quartier Artisanal*. Paris: Mémoire de l'Institut Mauritanien de la Recherche Scientifique 2.

Vansina, J. 1955. "Initiation Rituals of the Bushong." *Africa* 25: 138–153.

———. 1966. *Kingdoms of the Savanna*. Madison: University of Wisconsin Press.

———. 1973. *The Tio Kingdom of the Middle Congo 1880–1892*. London: Oxford University Press.

———. 1978. *The Children of Woot: A History of the Kuba People*. Madison: University of Wisconsin Press.

———. 1990. *Paths in the Rainforests: Toward a History of Political Tradition in Equatorial Africa*. Madison: University of Wisconsin Press.

———. 1995. "New Linguistic Evidence and the 'Bantu Expansion.' " *Journal of African History* 36: 173–195.

Vaughan, J. H., Jr. 1970. "Caste Systems in Western Sudan." In A. Tuden and I. Plotnicov, eds., *Social Stratification in Africa* (59–92). New York: The Free Press.

Vernet, R. 1986. *La Mauritanie des Origines au Début de l'Histoire*. Nouakchott: Centre Culturel Français A. de St Exupéry.

———. 1993a. "Préhistoire des bassins affluents de la rive gauche du fleuve Niger." In *Vallées du Niger* (63–74). Paris: Editions de la Reunion des Musées Nationaux.

———. 1993b. *Préhistoire de la Mauritanie*. Nouakchott: Editions Sépia.

Vogel, J. O. 1971. *Kumadzulo*. Lusaka: Oxford University Press.

———. 1972. "On Early Iron Age Funerary Practise in Southern Zambia." *Current Anthropology* 13: 583–586.

———. 1975. "Kabondo Kumbo and the Early Iron Age in the Victoria Falls Region." *Azania* 10: 49–76.

Volavka, Z. 1998. *Crown and Ritual: The Royal Insignia of Ngoyo*. Toronto: University of Toronto Press.

von Morgen, C. 1982. *A travers le Cameroun du sud au nord*. Paris: Publications de la Sorbonne.

Walker, G. L. 1925. "Ancient Copper Mining and Smelting in Central Africa." *Engineering and Mining Journal Press* 120: 811–816.

———. 1927. "Ancient Copper Smelting." *Engineering and Mining Journal Press* 123: 573–574.

Walton, J. 1957. "Some Features of the Monomatapa Culture." In J. D. Clark, ed., *Third Pan-African Congress on Prehistory* (336–356). London: Chatto and Windus.

Warnier, J.-P. 1975. *Pre-Colonial Mankon: The Development of a Cameroon Chiefdom in Its Regional Setting*. Ann Arbor, Mich.: University Microfilms International.

———. 1981. "L'histoire pré-coloniale de la chefferie de Mankom (département de la Mezam)." In C. Tardits, ed., *Contribution de la recherche ethnologique à l'histoire des civilisations du Cameroun* (421–436). Paris: Editions du CNRS.

———. 1984. "Histoire du peuplement et génèse des paysages dans l'ouest camerounais." *Journal of African History* 25: 395–410.

———. 1985. *Echanges, développement et hiérarchies dans le Bamenda pré-colonial*. Wiesbaden: Franz Steiner Verlag.

———. 1992. "Rapport préliminaire sur la métallurgie du groupe Chap." In J. M. Essomba, ed., *L'Archéologie au Cameroun* (197–210). Paris: Karthala.

Warnier, J. P., and I. Fowler. 1979. "A Nineteenth Century Ruhr in Central Africa." *Africa* 49(4): 329–351.

Welsby, D. A. 1998. *The Kingdom of Kush: The Napatan and Meroitic Empires*. Princeton, N.J.: M. Wiener Publishers.

Were, P. O. 1972. "The Origin and Growth of the Iron Industry and Trade in Samia (Kenya)." Baccalaureate dissertation, University of Nairobi.

Wertime, T. E., and J. D. Muhly, eds. 1980. *The Coming of the Age of Iron*. New Haven, Conn.: Yale University Press.

Wiesmuller, B. 1996. "Untersuchungen zur Chronologie der fruhen Eisenzeit in Afrika anhand linguistischer, archaologischer und naturwissenschaftlicher Quellen." *Beitrage zur Allgemeinen und Vergleichenden Archaologie* 16: 139–214.

———. 1997. "Moglichkeiten der interdisziplinaren Zusammenarbeit von Archaologie und Linguistik am Beispiel des fruhen Eisenzeit in Afrika." In R. Klein-Arendt, ed., *Traditionelles Eisenhandwerk in Afrika* (55–90). Koln: Heinrich Barth Institut.

Wilhelm, H. 1981. "Le commerce pré-colonial de l'ouest (plateau Bamiléké-Grassfields, régions Bamoun et Bafia)." In C. Tardits, ed., *Contribution de la recherche ethnologique à l'histoire des civilisations du Cameroun* (485–502). Paris: Editions du CNRS.

Willett, F. 1967. *Ife in the History of West African Sculpture*. New York: McGraw-Hill.

———. 1971. "A Survey of Recent Results in the Radiocarbon Chronology of Western and Northern Africa." *Journal of African History* 12: 339–370.

Williams, D. 1974. *Icon and Image: A Study of Sacred and Secular Forms of African Classical Art*. New York: New York University Press.

Williams, M. A. J., and H. Faure, eds. 1980. *The Sahara and the Nile*. Rotterdam: A. A. Balkema.

Willis, R. G. 1981. *A State in the Making: Myth, History and Social Transformation in Precolonial Ufipa*. Bloomington: Indiana University Press.

Wilson, M. 1957. *Rituals of Kinship Among the Nyakyusa*. London: Oxford University Press.

Wise, R. 1958. "Some Rituals of Iron-Making in Ufipa." *Tanganyika Notes and Records* 50: 106–111; 51: 232–238.

Woodhouse, J. 1998. "Iron in Africa: Metal from Nowhere." In G. Connah, ed., *Transformations in Africa* (160–185). London: Leicester University Press.

Wright, B. L. 1989. "The Power of Articulation." In W. Arens and I. Karp, eds., *The Creativity of Power*. Washington, D.C.: Smithsonian Institution.

Zangato, E. 1991. "Etude du Megalithisme dans le Nord-Ouest de la Republique Centrafricaine." Ph.D. thesis, University of Paris X: Nanterre

———. 1993. "La question des datations des megalithes du centrafrique: Nouvelles perspectives." In D. Barreteau and C. von Graffenried, eds., *Datations et chronologie dans le Bassin du lact Tchad*. (51–75). Paris: Editions de l'ORSTOM.

———. 1999. *Societes prehistoriques et megalithes dans le nord-ouest de la Republique Centrafricaine*. Oxford: British Archaeological Reports.

Author Index

Adams, R. McC., 2, 3, 19, 58
Allan, W., 141
al-Tunisi, M. O., 177
Anciaux de Faveaux, E., 103, 115, 118, 121
Andah, B. W., 9
Anonymous, 101
Anquandah, J., 187, 188
Aremu, D. A., 100
Arkell, A. J., 6
Arnot, F. S., 83, 112, 122
Asombang, R., 50, 64
Atangana, C., 59
Atherton, J., 156
Avery, D. H., 6, 7, 150, 151, 153, 164, 165, 167

Bancroft, J. A., 84, 87
Barndon, R., 153, 154, 155, 158, 166, 168, 169, 171
Barnes, H. B., 190
Bathily, M. S., 11
Battell, A., 88
Bekombo-Priso, M., 79
Bernus, E., 24, 26, 84, 88, 182
Bernus, S., 13, 23, 24, 26, 37, 39, 83, 126, 145
Birmingham, D., 83, 116, 128, 145
Bisson, M. S., 84, 91, 92, 99, 100. 101,.103, 105, 113, 114, 115, 118, 10, 121, 122, 124, 134, 137, 141, 143, 144, 145, 170, 172, 186
Bocoum, H., 15, 18, 190
Bohannon, P., 113
Bonte, P., 179, 181, 182
Bourdieu, P., 43
Bower, J. G., 88
Bradley, K., 83
Browne, W. G., 177
Buleli, N., 151, 153
Burton, R. F., 83, 111

Cahen, D., 86
Calvert, A., 109
Calvocoressi, D., 89
Caton-Thompson, G., 121
Célis, G., 161, 167, 181
Chaplin, J. H., 100, 101
Chibanza, S. J., 141
Chikwendu, V. E., 85, 114, 126, 133
Childs, S. T., 7, 148, 153, 155, 158, 162, 166, 167, 169, 171, 172, 173, 178, 190, 191, 201
Cissé, Y., 169
Clark, J. D., 134
Cline, W., 98, 99, 103, 104, 105, 107, 171, 179, 180, 181, 183
Clist, B., 14, 15
Coghlan, H. H., 91
Cohen, R., 153
Collett, D. P., 164, 170, 179
Connah, G., 15
Conte, E., 158, 182, 183
Cooper, C., 160, 175

Cornevin, R., 159, 184
Coupez, A., 181
Coy, M. W., 154, 155, 159, 160, 161, 174, 179, 180, 183, 184
Craddock, P. T., 85, 89, 92, 109
Cressier, P., 13, 24, 89
Cunnison, I., 128

da Gama, V., 83
Daniels, S. G. H., 118
Dark, P., 153, 158
Darling, P. J., 159
Dart, R. A., 141
David, N., 23, 89, 151, 152, 154, 159, 169, 174, 176, 177, 178, 183, 184
Davidson, B., 161
Davis, M. B., 203, 210, 217, 220, 223, 238, 246,
de Barros, P., 6, 147, 149, 151, 152, 153, 154, 155, 157, 159, 174, 176, 184, 185, 186, 187, 189, 190, 191, 194, 197
de Beaucorps, R., 154
De Buyst, J., 115, 118
de Columbel, V., 177
De Crits, E., 64, 67
de Hemptinne, M., 83, 87, 92, 96, 97, 103, 112, 122, 141
de Heusch, L., 148, 149, 181, 187
de Maret, P., 6, 15, 59, 60, 91, 103, 112, 115, 118, 121, 140, 145, 148, 149, 150, 152, 153, 154, 158, 161, 162, 164, 167, 170, 172, 178, 180, 181, 182, 183, 184
Derricourt, R. M., 150
Devisse, J., 14
Dewey, W. J., 148, 150, 158, 162, 169, 171, 172, 173
d'Hertefelt, M., 181
Dieterlen, G.,148
Dillon, R. G., 74, 76
Diop, L. M., 7, 9
Dos Santos, J. N., 111
Doumbia, P. E. N., 160
Dugast, S., 151, 152, 186, 191
Dupré, M.-C., 147, 152, 156, 158, 159

Echard, N., 7, 23, 24, 26, 37, 84, 153, 190
Eckert, H. E., 170
Essomba, J. M., 15, 38, 60, 61, 62, 63, 75.76, 149, 151, 152, 153, 154, 155, 156, 167, 168, 190, 199
Estermann, C., 151
Evers, T. M., 92, 112

Fagan, B. M., 105, 112, 122, 125, 144
Fallers, L. A., 161
Farquhar, R. M., 131
Faure, H., 109
Filipowiak, W., 158, 174
Fisher, R., 149
Flight, C., 10
Fowler, I., 64, 67, 70, 151, 152, 153, 155, 157, 158, 159, 160, 166, 167, 169, 170, 173, 174, 176, 191
Fox, C., 109, 110
Franklin, U., 131
Freeman-Grenville, G. S. P., 145
Friede, H. M., 83, 92, 104, 105, 125
Frobenius, L., 103

Galaty, J. G., 174, 179, 181, 182
Gardi, R., 165
Gardin, J. C., 18
Garlake, P., 91, 103, 121, 122, 162
Garrard, T. F., 9, 109
Gell, A., 164
Godelier, M., 77
Gordon, R. B., 89
Goucher, C. L., 148, 151, 168, 170, 172, 173, 186
Gouletquer, P. L., 37, 39, 84
Gray, R., 83, 116, 128, 145
Grébénart, D., 9, 10, 13, 14, 24, 26, 27, 32, 34, 37, 89

Haaland, R., 6, 48, 58, 147, 148, 150, 151, 153, 154, 158, 177, 183, 186
Haddon, A. C., 112
Hahn, H. P., 152, 165, 168, 172, 186
Herbert, E. W., 84, 85, 88, 105, 109, 111, 113, 114, 122, 125, 148, 151, 155, 158, 160, 161, 162, 163, 164, 167, 168, 169, 170, 171, 173, 174, 178, 179, 181, 182
Hiernaux, J., 115, 118
Hodder, I., 166

Hodge, M. A., 58
Holl, A., 6, 7, 8, 10, 13, 15, 20, 58, 89, 156, 186
Hopkins, J. F. P., 48
Huard, P., 6
Huffman, T. N., 91, 92, 102, 124, 162
Hupfeld, V. F., 192

Ibn Batutta, 48, 113
Inskeep, R. R., 121
Izard, M., 23

Jaggar, P. J., 153, 154, 159, 184
Jézégou, M. P., 14
Johansson, 113
Johnston, H. H. 113, 114

Kense, F. J., 5, 7, 8, 14, 15, 16, 18
Kiethega, J. B., 1
Killick, D., 7, 13, 26, 89, 151, 153, 154, 158, 159, 160, 166, 167, 168, 169, 170, 172, 190, 191
Kinahan, J., 88
Kiriama, H. O., 169
Kirsch, H., 95
Kiyaga-Mulindwa, D., 188
Klose, H., 153, 155, 176
Koert, W., 192
Kuevi, D., 152, 186
Kun, N., 85
Kuper, H., 169

Laburthe-Tolra, P., 61, 75
Ladame, F., 96
Laing, A. G., 156
Laman, K., 131
Lambert, N., 88, 90, 113
Lanfranchi, R., 15
Langrée, E., 115, 118
Larick, R., 149, 153, 174, 179, 180, 186
Latour, B., 4
Lawson, T. D., 192
Leach, E., 170
Lebeuf, A. M. D., 15
Lebeuf, J. P., 15
Lechtman, H., 166
Lekime, F., 97
Lemonnier, P., 19, 20, 21, 23
Levi-Strauss, C., 165
Levtzion, N., 48, 58
Levy, T. E., 20
Lhote, H., 7, 9
Lihoreau, M., 9
Livingstone, D., 83, 105, 112
Lloyd, P. C., 153
Lombard, J., 160, 176

MacDonald, K. C., 51
Mapunda, B. B. M., 38, 96
Marks, S., 83
Martinelli, B., 148, 152, 153, 154, 155, 176, 184, 191
Martins, J. V., 171
Martius, A., 103
Mathew, G., 136
Mauny, R., 6, 7, 89
Mbida, C., 58, 69, 67
McIntosh, R. J., 15, 48, 126, 153, 160, 173, 186, 188, 190
McIntosh, S. K., 15, 126, 160
McNaughton, P. R., 151, 158, 160, 167, 169, 170, 173, 174, 175, 178, 184, 188, 190
Meillassoux, C., 147, 155, 184
Melland, F., 100, 144
Mellart, J., 6
Middleton, J., 183
Miller, D. E., 6, 95, 99, 100, 141, 147
Miracle, M. P., 137
Monimo, Y., 23
Monteiro, J. J., 112, 113
Muhammed, I. M., 177, 188
Muhly, J. D., 7

Nadel, S. F., 153, 158
Neaher, G., 109
Nenguin, J., 115, 118
Ngijol Ngijol, P., 79
Ngoa, H., 61
Nkolo Foe, 149, 156
Nzikobanyanka, E., 161, 167, 181

O'Neill, P., 162
Okafor, E. E., 14, 18, 23, 173

Oliver, R., 126
Ossah-Mvondo, J. P., 59, 62, 64, 67

Paques, V., 160
Paris, F., 14, 24, 32, 43, 45, 76
Pereira, D. P., 88
Phillipson, D. W., 7, 8, 15, 124, 134
Plotnicov, L., 174
Pole, L. M., 151, 168, 169, 170
Pomel, S., 109
Poncet, Y., 24, 25, 45
Posnansky, M., 107, 109, 187

Reefe, T., 158
Rehder, J. E., 95
Rein-Wührmann, A., 159
Renfrew, C., 23
Richter, D., 174, 175, 176, 184
Rickard, T. A., 86
Robert-Chaleix, D., 194
Roberts, A. F., 148, 150
Robertshaw, P. T., 6
Robertson, I., 152, 154, 159, 177
Robertson, J. H., 134
Roscoe, J., 151, 152, 167, 168, 172, 181, 183
Rowlands, M., 67, 71, 72, 153, 164, 167, 170, 176, 190
Rustad, J., 7, 10

Sabi-Monra, S., 151, 153, 154, 155, 158, 160, 166, 168, 169, 176, 178, 186, 187, 190
Samtouna, I., 152, 158, 161, 184
Schaffer, M., 160, 175
Schimmin, I., 170
Schmidt, P. R., 6, 7, 14, 23, 38, 64, 67, 96, 148, 159, 151, 156, 161, 162, 163, 164, 165, 166, 167, 168, 169, 170, 171, 172 174, 181, 182, 185, 186, 190, 191
Schulz, E., 26, 29
Scully, R., 91, 101, 102, 125
Seignobos, C., 159
Shaw, T., 7, 8, 107, 109, 114
Shinnie, P. L., 6, 8, 15, 16
Snelling, N. J., 85
Sognane, M., 194
Spencer, P., 179
Stanley, G., 102
Stayt, H. A., 94, 101, 124
Steel, R. H., 88, 102, 103, 104, 105, 125
Sterner, J., 169, 174, 176, 177, 178, 183, 184
Strathern, A., 155
Summers, R., 83, 88, 91
Swan, L., 1

Tainter, J. A., 23
Talmari, T., 160, 161, 174, 183
Tardits, C., 75, 76
Thiry, G., 167
Todd, J. A., 174, 177, 178
Togola, T., 48, 49, 51, 57, 58, 59, 76, 147, 158
Treinen-Claustre, F., 15
Trevor, T. G., 141
Trigger, B. G., 4, 8, 20, 21, 58, 90, 102
Tuden, A., 174
Turner, V., 111
Tylecote, R. F., 6, 18, 88, 95

Umeji, A. C., 85, 114, 133

van Beek, W. E. A., 154
van der Merwe, N. J., 3, 6, 7, 9, 91, 96, 101, 102, 125, 147, 150, 151, 153, 164, 167
van Grunderbeek, M. C., 7, 15
van Neer, W., 51
van Noten, F., 167
Vanacker, C., 186
Vansina, J., 15, 23, 77, 70, 89, 128, 145, 158, 160
Vaughan, J. H., 160, 161, 174, 177, 183
Vernet, R., 10, 12, 14, 89, 90
Vogel, J. C., 88
Vogel, J. O., 118, 149
Volavka, Z., 84, 87, 105, 128, 130, 131, 132, 133
von Morgen, C., 75, 80
von Wilm, L., 103

Walker, G. L., 83, 86, 87, 131
Walton, J., 121

Warmelo, N. J., 94
Warnier, J. P., 64, 67, 70, 71, 72, 76, 153, 157, 158, 164, 167, 170, 176, 190
Welsby, D. A., 1, 4, 20
Were, P. O., 154, 183
Wertime, T. E., 7
Wiesmuller, B., 7, 13
Wilhelm, H., 74
Willett, F., 10, 108, 109, 110, 163
Williams, D., 109
Williams, M. A. J., 108
Willis, R.G., 162
Wilson, M., 171
Wise, R., 162
Woodhouse, J., 10, 11, 16, 90
Wright, B. L., 174, 184

Zangato, E., 14

Subject Index

Abstinence (male sexual): for smelting, 169; for smithing, 172
Adams, R., xv
Adwinfuo (ironworkers district), 187
Africa Association, xv
Afunfun, 28, 87, 89,161
Agadez, 86–7
Akan gold weights, 109
Akjoujt, 10, 12–3, 86, 89
Akumbi mound group, 51
Alaska mine, 88
Ancestor cults, 26
Ancestors, influence over smithing by (Shona), 167, 173, 187
Ancient workings (Zimbabwe), xvii
Animal interments, 32. *See also* Mortuary patterns
Anvil, 234, 238, 239, 241, 245, 246–7, 248; and hammers as head rests, 139
Anyokan, 31
Archaeology: cultural phases, determination of, 5, 7; nomenclature, 19; proposed research design, 18–20; research (non-metallurgical), 17–8; systematics discussed, 3
Artisan villages, western and eastern Sudan, 187
Atlantic trade, 62, 74, 77
Axe, xx, 226. *See also* Ceremonial axes
Azelik, 86–7, 89

Babungo (Cameroon), 157, 173–4
Bacwezi, sacred ironworking cult, 169, 181
Bahaya, dynasties of, 181
Baines, T., xvi
Baisengobi, 161
Bambudye secret society, 162
Bamenda Plateau. *See* Ironworking
Bamum, 158, 159
Bantu-speaking farmers, xix
Baquirmi kingdom (Chad). *See* Smith kings
Barongo (Tanzania), 185; female participation in ironworking, 151
Bassa, involvement in exchanges, 78
Bassar region, 157; access to production, 159; Bandjeli Zone, 192–4; extended family production, 198; growth of smelting industry, 191–2; intensification of production and clan affiliation, 198; iron production, 191–8; Kabu-Bassar axis, 194–8; large scale production, 171–2; organization of production and labor, 149; regional specialization in western Bassar, 187; smelting ritual, 168; smelting and smithing in separate villages, 187
Bellows, 103–5, 205, 206, 212–4, 216–7, 218, 227, 233, 234, 248, 250, 252
Bellows clays, 183
Bembe mine, 86, 88, 131
Benin (Nigeria), 87, 108, 184; smith's hammer and anvil, 162
Benue rift, 85–6, 109
Beti, 80; migration epic, 61

Big men: as ironworkers, 154, 176; rise of, 77, 76, 154, 155–6
Bimbia, coastal entrepôt, 78
Blood, 205, 222, 247
Boko Songho, 87, 131, 133
Borgu (Benin), taboos, 187
Bornu, smiths of, 177
Brass, 109
Bricolage, 165–6
Bride price (bride wealth), 24, 77, 150
Bronze, 109
Buffalo horn, 203
Buhaya kingdoms. *See* investiture
Bukino Faso, 1
Bunyoro, 161, 181; origin myth, 149
Burials: Berber, 45; caches (*see* Iron bloom); excavated, 149; furnishings, xx, 24; high status, 162–3; human (*see* Animal interments; Mortuary patterns)
Burundi, royal regalia, 181. *See also* Smith kings
Bushong origin myth, 148
Bwana Mkubwa mine, 88

Calabar, coastal entrepôt, 78
Cameroon, 1, 2, 59–80
Cameroon Grassfields, characterized, 157
Carnelian beads, 76
Carthage, as source of African metallurgy, 8
Carthaginian hypothesis, diffusion of iron explained by, 8
Cassava plantations, 90
Caste: defined, 174; hereditary, endogamous, 177; Hindu model of, 174; ironworkers and, 182–4; reasons for, 183–4; view, despised, inaccuracy of, 175
Castes: Eastern Sudan, 177; Interlacustrine East Africa and Sahel, 181–2; Mandara highlands, 176; Pastoralist societies of East Africa, 178–81; Southern Ethiopia, 177; West African Sudan, 174–6
Casting: copper, 102–3; lost-wax, 107–10
Cemeteries: with megaliths, 29–31, 43; significance of, 38, 45; as territorial markers, 28
Central African Republic, 1
Centralized polities: place of smiths in, 184; control of production and distribution in, 154, 157
Ceremonial axes or spears, 149, 162
Changa ironworkers, 180–1
Charcoal, 217–8, 219, 223, 230, 243, 246; burning, 151–2; making, 187
Chemistry of copper ores, 91
Chiefdoms, 67, 71; defined, 72; detecting in archaeology, 73; first appearance of, 72–4; settlement pattern of, 74
Chiefs, who once were ironworkers, 161
Chifumpa mine, 116
Chin Tadifet, 28, 31, 32; burials at, 32; tool types associated with, 74
Chokwe (Angola), 171
Clan, 202; affiliation and intensification of production, Bassar, 198
Classification in archaeology, 19
Clays, 184
Clump furnace, 67–8, 70
Congo, Republic of, early metal producing sites in, 15
Consumers: dead as, 45; and producers of metals, distinguishing between, 5
Copper, 83–145; analogous to gold, 84; earliest production of, 10–2; early history of, in Africa, 10, 12–4, 37, 39, 88–91; mining techniques, 91–4, 130–1; production, early experimentation at, 39; production estimates, 141–4; as social display, xv, 24; social significance of, 83–5, 110–2, 132–3, 145; trade, 125–8
Copper Age, cultures, 5
Copperbelt, Zambia, 1
Copper ingots. *See* ingots.
Copper metallurgy, early production, 13–4
Copper ores: chemistry of, 91; distribution of, 85

Copperworking: casting techniques, 102–3; earliest evidence, 12–4; smelter types, 37–8; smelting techniques, 94–102, 131–2; smithing techniques, 103–5
Corporate and trading monopolies: maintenance of, 184; West African Sudan smiths, 175
Cottage industry, metal production as, 23, 39
Cowrie shells, 203, 210, 243, 247, 252
Craft specialization, 151–2; full-time, 19, 23, 74; part-time, 12
Critical resources, 30–1
Cruciform ingots, 118–24
Culture: meaning, 20; process (change), 4–5, 19; selection, 20
Currency, 113–25, 133, 159; *manilla*, 113–4, 133; Neptune, 115; *Rotl*, 115

Daboya, 16
Dafur, smiths of, 177
Deaths (in mining), 208
Deforestation, 148, 154, 186
Deities, associated with ironworking, 169
Dekpassanware, early focus on, 191
Descent groups: multi-ethnic, ironworking, 185; prestige display, 45
Diffusion hypothesis and counter argument, 16–7
Dikuluwe mine, 87, 92, 116
Dimi smiths, 178
Diop, L. M., 8
Diviners, 168–9
Division of labor, 151–2
Do Dimmi, 14
Dogon origin myth, 148
Domestic corporations, 46
Dreams, 173
Drums, as life force, 171
Duala, coastal entrepôt, 78
Dwinfuor. *See* Adwinfuo

Ecological crisis, 75
Economic power, smiths', 175
Edea, 63, 78
Effects of ironworking, 149
Effects of metallurgy, 147, 150
Eghazer basin, 3, 24–48; average yield, 26; burial furniture, 40; categories of early metal artifacts, 39–40; chronology, 26; climatic history, 25; geology, 24–5; growing seasons of, 25–6; iron smelter varieties available in, 25; pastoralism in, 26; pasturage in, 25
Egyptian metallurgy, early, 5
Ekonda smelting rituals (Dem. Rep. Of Congo), 168
Endo ironworkers, 179
Entăbo (ore), 210, 211, 224
Enyigba mine, 87
Equatorial forest area, 64
Ethnicity and ironworking, 184–6
Etoile mine, 87, 115–6, 121
Exchange: networks, 12; patterns of, 76–80; social, 24

Failed smelts, reasons for, 166
Farmer/smith relationships, 176
Favoritism/nepotism, 209, 235
Female participation in ironworking, 151
Female rites of passage, associated with ceremonial axe decorations, 173
Fipa (Tanzania), 159
Foragers, 75
Forge, 207, 230; installation rituals, 172
Forging, xvii, 228, 234; tasks involved in, 151
Fuga smiths, 177
Funerals/burials, smiths' role in, 161
Furnaces: clays, 184, 187; clump, 67–8, 70; medicines in base of, 168; natural draft, 62

Gabon, early metal producing sites in, 14, 15
Gama, Vasco da, 83
Gender divisions, 151
Ghana Empire xvi, 2, 3, 58, 80; financing of, 58–9; integration of Mema region, 58
Gihang, Rwandan divine hero, 149

Glazed Sherd industry, 71–6; described, 72; chronology, 72; furnace types associated with, 72
Goats, 203
God/spirit, 202, 203
Gold, xv, xvi, 1, 2; analogous to copper, 84; production and trade, 1, 2; silent trade in, xvi; weights, Akan, 109
Gold-bearing quartz, reduction of, xvi
Goldfields, South Africa and Zimbabwe, 1
Goods, status-producing, 77
Grass (reeds) sprinkles (*efunga*), 219, 222, 224, 240, 247, 248, 250
Great Lakes region, early metallurgy, 14–5
Great Zimbabwe, xvii, 88, 121
Grey, G., xvii
Growing seasons, 25–6
Guelb Moghein, evidence of early copper working, 10
Guilds, 158, 184
Guilds, ironworker, 153–4
Gurage, smiths of, 177

Hammer: iron, 207, 229, 231–4, 235, 242, 246, 247, 248–50, 252; Nyanga, in royal investiture ritual, 181; stone, 226, 227, 231, 233, 234, 237
Handa (ingot), 119, 122–4
Harmony mine, 116
Hawsa state of Kano, 184
Hawsa trade network, 72
Hereditary kingship and smithing, 161
Hereditary, endogamous castes, 177
Hgoa, 61
Hierarchical society, rise of, 76–80
Hindu model of caste, 174
Hippo mine, 116
History characterized, 4
Hoe, xx, 202, 206, 209, 210, 213, 231, 234, 237, 238–9, 243, 247, 250
Hoe blades, iron, 150
Huange mines, 87
Hufrat-en-Nahas, 85
Human burials with animals. *See* Animal interments
Human reproduction metaphor, 168, 170

Ife, 87, 107–10
Igbo Ukwu, 87, 107–9, 126
Ikawaten, 34
In Gall-Teggida-n-Tsemt (Niger), 2, 3, 10, 13, 24–48, 168; chronology, 13, 37; copper smelter types, 37–8; early copper production, 13; metal production, 37; periodization, 13; variety suggests a pioneer phase, 38–9
Ingombe Ilede, 101, 105–7, 112, 121
Ingots, copper: cruciform, 118–24; *handa*, 119, 122–4; *lerale*, 125; *musuku*, 102, 124–5
Inland Niger delta, 3
Inland trade network, 78
Innovations, impact of, 3–5; acceptance of, 4; alternative responses, 4–5
Installation of new forge, ritual, 172
Intensification, resistance to, 156
Intermediaries in trading activities, 152
Investiture: Buhaya kingdoms, 152; characterized, 153; ironworkers' role in, 77, 161, 181; as a transformation process, 164
Iron: as cultural catalyst, 3–4; as dangerous, 156; hoe blades, 150; meteoritic, 5; tools, 150; as wealth, 150
Iron Age: culture complex, xix, 16; as true start of African history, 7
Iron bloom, 151; in burial caches, 149; specialists in, 152
Iron metallurgy: adoption, slow pace of, 156; chronology, 14–5; earliest evidence, 14–5
Iron production: centralized control of, 158; conquest to gain access to, 159; efficiency of, 153; intensification of, 61, 63–4, 174; political authority over, 158; scheduling, 178; seasonality of, 153, 178; wide range of things produced, 64
Iron products, 150; commodities exchanged for, 143; worth of, 154–5

Iron smelters: in Eghazer basin, 40; in Southern Forested region, 62, 65, 68
Iron technology, development of, 11
Ironworker guilds, 153–4; apprenticeship, 151
Ironworkers: attitude toward, farmers vs. pastoralists, 181; avoidance of habitation areas by, 190; district (Adwinfuo), 187; as divine heroes, 148–9; ethnicity of, 184–6; food and water for, 151; intermarriage and, 160; itinerant, 150; mobility due to deforestation, 186; mystique of, 190; professional, 153; relationship to dynasts, 159, 160; rewards to, 153; role in Bunyoro investiture, 181; spatial segregation of, 187; as threats to divine kings, 160; Tuareg aristocracy and, 182–4; who once were kings, 161
Ironworking, 148–9, 164; decline in due to deforestation, 186; effects of, 149; female participation in, 151; income from, 154; origin myths and, 148–9; spatial organization of, 187–90; technology (Bamenda Plateau), 67; universal aspects of, 164
Irungu (Bahaya deity associated with ironworking), 169
Islamic sultans, 159

Jenne-jeno (Mali), ironworking quarters at, 149
Joking relationships, 175

Kaiia, secret shrine association, 164
Kambove mine, 116
Kamusongolwa, 118, 140
Kanem (Chad), 182
Kano, 184
Kansanshi mine, 87, 90, 115–6, 133–45
Kaonde: mining techniques, 92–4; smelting techniques, 99–101
Kense, F. J., 5
Khatt Lemaiteg, 11
Kilembe mine, 85
Kingdoms, origins of, 76
Kingship, and smithing hereditary, 161
Kipushi mine, 86, 90, 116, 120–3
Knowledge, diffusion of, 153
Kobadi, 49
Kolima mound, 48
Kolwezi mine, 86, 92
Kongo (Angola), 128–30, 159; kingdom, 128–30; smith kings of, 161
Koni (Ivory Coast), 170
Kuba rivalry, with Luba, 158
Kumbi Saleh, 3, 58
Kushitic Period 1., use of iron, 4
Kwanyama (Angola), female participation in ironworking, 151

Labor-intensive tasks, women and children in, 151
Lacerda, Francisco de, 83
Land tenure, 26
Large scale producers, 152
Large scale production and reduction of ritual, 173–4
Late Stone Age, 38–50; settlements, 26
lerale (ingot), 125
Loango (Congo), smith kings of, 161
Lokop origin myth, 149
Lost-wax casting, 107–10
Luano: (Dem. Rep. Congo), 121; (Zambia), 118
Luba (Dem. Rep. Congo), 158; ceremonial axes, 149, 162; decorations, female rites of passage and, 173; smelting techniques, 97–9; smith kings of, 161
Luba-Lunda kingdoms, xvii
Lufilian Arc, 85
Luishia mine, 116
Lunda kingdom, 145
Lunga Valley (mines), 86
Lusunsi, 128–30

Maasi ironworkers, 179
Mafa of NW Cameroon: smiths, economic roles of, 177; wives generally potters, 177
Magic as superstition, 164
Magical powers, of smiths, 159–60, 175
Malachite, smelting of, xvii

Male associations, 154
Mali Empire, xv, xvi, 2
Mali state, 160
Malimba, coastal entrepôt, 78
Mande: origin myth, 148; smiths, varied economic roles of, 175
Mandoumba, 62
manilla (currency), 113–4, 133
Mansa Musa, xv
Marghi of NE Nigeria, 177; smiths relationship to farmers, 177; smith kings of Marghi, 160
Mauretania, 12, 13, 89–90
Mbanza Kongo, ironworkers district of capital, 187
Medicine hole (pots), 38, 62, 70, 167, 168
Medicines, 151, 167, 168, 171, 205, 206, 207; in furnace base, 168
Megalithic monuments 14, 43–6 (*see* Cemeteries); markers of status, 46; megalithic burial grounds, 29–31
Mema region (Mali), 2; 48–59; chronology, 49–52; Early Assemblage, 49–52; Late Assemblage, 75; Middle Assemblage, 51, 53–8, 75; periodization, 49; settlement patterns 57–8, 75
Men, principal smelters and smiths, 151
Menstruation, 242; taboo, 169, 170, 172
Meröe, xix; as diffusion point for metallurgy, 8
Messina mines, 87, 116
Metal artifacts, as elite display, 43
Metal edged weapons, 48
Metal production, socioeconomic model, 21–4
Metallurgy in Africa: chronology of, 10–5; cultural development, importance to, 5–6; effect on society, 80, 147, 150; search for cradles of, 8
Metallurgy, origins of: African continent, 7 (*see* Meröe; Carthage); as an archaeological problem, 17–8; autochthonous experimentation, 9; debate, 7–10; derived from Mediterranean, 7; diffusion routes search for, 8; Egyptian, early, 5; explanations, monophyletic, 7–9; explanations, polyphyletic, 9; summary of debate, 9–10
Metals, producers and consumers of, 5
Mindouli-Niari mines, 87, 130–1
Miners and mining, xvii, 26, 91–4, 130–1, 204–9; discovery of ore, 204; deaths, 208
Moorish nomads, 182
Mortuary patterns, 31–4
Mosani (Bariba deity associated with ironworking), 169
Muba (Dem. Rep. Congo), smith kings of, 161
Music and songs associated with smelt, 168
Musonoi, 92, 116
musuku (ingot), 102, 124–5
Mvet, oral literature of the, 149

Natural draft furnaces, 62
Naviundu site, 90, 115–6, 118
Ndop Plain industry, 67–71; settlement pattern, 70–1
Neolithic, 12–3
Neptune (currency), 115
Ngoyo kingdom, 128–33
Niari-Djoue mines, 87–8
Niger, earliest copper workings in, 13
Nile valley settlements, early appearance of iron in, 5
Nilotic pastoral people, 178
Nkomrtou, 61
Nok Culture, 1, 15
Noncapital economies, xix
Non-farming artisans, 176–7
Non-iron producing/working societies, 156–7
Nteni chiefships in Tanzania, 161
Ntogota, 203
Nubia, 1
Nupe, 184
Nyanga, hammer in royal investiture ritual, 181

O'Okiep mine, 88
Offering ritual, slaughter/sacrifice, 168, 171, 205, 221–2

Ogun (Yoruba deity associated with ironworking), 169
Ophir, xvi
Oral literature (Mvet), 149
Ore, 204, 205, 206, 207 (see also *Entăbo*); discovery of, 202, 204–5, 206, 209; drying the, 207, 211; settlement patterns related to, 70
Origin myths, 148–9
Otoumbi, early smelting furnaces at, 14

Pahouin (Beti, Bulu, Fang) origin myth, 148
Pan Mangueda, 63
Pastoral aristocracies of eastern Africa, 181
Pastoral Late Stone Age, 29–30
Pastoral societies: centralized, 161; of East Africa, 178–81; status of ironworkers in, 181
Pastoralists, 12, 26–9; mobility patterns, 29, 75 (*see* Transhumance patterns); view of smiths, 177
Phalaborwa mine, 87, 91, 116
Pharaonic Period, 1
Phillipson, D. W., 7
Phoenician settlements, 8
Political change, sanctioning, 78
Political power, ritual as means of accessing, 170
Political space, 45
Polities, centralized, rise and fall of, 186
Population movement, 75
Potter, 212–3
Potters: comparable to metalworkers, 178; as transformers, 178–9; wives of smiths, 177
Pre-German time, 62
Pre-Islamic burial grounds, 29
Prestige goods, 150, 154, 158
Problem-solving, African, 166
Procreation metaphor, 169, 170
Procreative analogy, 170
Procurement systems, 78
Products, iron. *See* Iron products

Rain, 207, 216, 227
Rank society, 74, 77; rise of, 76–80
Recycling, 22
Reduction of ritual and large scale production, 173–4
Regional specialization, western Bassar, 187
Regional trade, 152, 154
Rhanga, Buhaya divine hero, 149
Ritual: importance in broader social context, 171–2; importance to ironworking, 164; importance to successful smelt, 167; installing a new forge and, 172; large scale production and, 171–2; preserving sexual divisions and, 169–70; smelting, 167–74; smithing, 172–74
Rooiberg mine, 88
Rotl (currency), 115
Royal funerals/burials, 161
Royal Geographical Society, xvii
Royal regalia, 150, 161, 181
Royal tribute, 158
Ruashi mine, 86, 115–6
Rwanda: anvil/hammers as head rests, 149; smith kings of, 161

Saharan Late Stone Age, 37
Saharan Neolithic, 28
Sahelian Late Stone Age, 37
Sahelian Neolithic, 28
Sanaga-Lékié zone, 50–61
Sanga, 115, 118–20
Scientific discovery, 165
Seasonality of iron production, 153
Secrecy, to preserve monopoly, 173–4
Semi-permanent settlements, 34
Senufo of Ivory Coast, 175–6
Serving the melt, 225–8; related taboos, 220–1, 227
Sexual abstinence (male): for smelting, 169; for smithing, 172
Sexual division of labor, 141–52; smelting and smithing performed by men, 144–5; tasks for women and children, 151; female participation in ironworking, 151
Sexual divisions, means of preserving, 169–70

Sexual metaphor, 168, 170
Sexual symbolism and taboos, 164, 169–70; taboos explained, 169
Shaba Province (Congo), 1
Sheep (white), 205, 206, 214, 222, 234, 242, 246, 248. *See* Goats
Shin Wasaran, 32
Shinnie, P., pottery as marker of Iron Age, 16
Shona: ceremonial axe decorations and female rites of passage, 173; ceremonial axes, 149
Silent trade, xvi
Silver King mine, 116
Slavery, 78, 79; artisans as slaves, 181; slave raiding, 157, 189; slave raiding populations, avoidance of, 190
Smelt, reasons for failed, 166–7
Smelter, iron, 207, 218
Smelters: location of, 187–90; secrecy, 171
Smelting 222–4; copper, 94–102, 131–2; iron 164–7; monopoly of, 169; ritual, archaeological evidence, 167–8; tasks involved, 151
Smithing: copper, 103–5; smelting and, 187
Smith kings, 160–1
Smiths, 202, 228–9, 231, 234, 248; arcane practices of, 38; economic powers of, 150, 159–60; in investitures and funerals/burials, 77, 161; magical powers of, 150; relationship with farmers, 175–7; social status of, 76, 77; as transformers, 77. *See also* Medicine hole (pots)
Social and fertility relationship, 171
Social categories, 19
Social differentiation and metallurgy, 150
Social impetus, 21
Social model, interpreting archaeological data by, 2
Social prestige, 154
Social significance of copper, 83–5, 110–2, 132–3, 145
Social value, 21, 48
Socio-economic model of metal production, 21–4
Songhay, xvi
Songs and music associated with smelt, 168
Sorcerer, smiths as, 159, 175–6
Sorcery, smelt as victim of, 166–7
Southern Forested region (Cameroon), 59–80; chronology, 60–1
Spatial organization, 74, 75
Spear, 237
Special powers, belief in, 175
Specialization, 151–2, 187; in components of manufacture, 151; full-time, 19, 23, 74; part-time, 12; regional, 187; tasks in ironworking, 151; villages, 151; in working bloomery iron, 152
Spirit mediums, 202, 203, 204, 205, 209, 214, 221, 224, 241, 242, 246, 247, 248, 249–50
Stone hammer. *See* Hammer
Stone tumuli, 43. *See* Cemeteries
Sumptuary goods, 20
Sundiata Keita, founder of Mali state, 160
Symbolic links: smith's hammer and anvil, 162–3; king and ironworkers, 163
Symbolic sphere, 43
Systems theory, effects of innovations and, 20

Taboos: at the forge, 240–2; against menstruating women, 169; against smiths working near smelters, 187; regarding smelting, 169–71; regarding smithing, 172–4; and rituals, relaxation of, 174
Tasks: iron smelting, 151; forging, 151
Tchire Ouma, 14
Technical and ritual expertise, 164
Technology: innovations, effect of, 19–21; secret of, 153; style, 166; systems, 3
Tegadoust (Awdaghost) 58; separate ironworkers district, 187

Tenke-Fungurume mines, 87, 115–6, 120
Termit-Aïr, 15
Termit-Egaro area, early metallurgy, 14
Territorial cults. *See* Ancestor cults
Territorial expansion, ironworking in, 158
Territorial marking, 28. *See also* Ancestor cults; Mortuary patterns
Thakadu mines, 87, 90, 102, 116
Tio (Congo), smith kings of, 161
Tombouctou, xv
Trade: copper, 125–8; expeditions, 152; networks, 53, 67, 74, 76, 77, 152–3, 154; role in state formation, 78–9; specialists and middlemen, 152; trans-Saharan, xvi, 8, 58
Transformation: investiture, 162–4, 170; iron working as, 164
Transhumance pattern, 27–34
Trans-Saharan trade, xvi, 8, 58
Tribal units, 46
Tribute, 158
Trigger, B., 4
Tsumeb mines, 87–8
Tuareg (Niger), 182
Tuareg aristocracy, casted ironworkers and, 182–4
Tugen ironworkers, 179
Tuluk, stone axe workshop, 31
Tuyere, 212–3, 216, 218–9, 225, 248, 249; clays, 184
Twins, 214, 216, 224

Ukpo, 72
Umkondo mine, 87–8, 90
Urewe culture in eastern Africa, 15

Value, 154
Van der Merwe, N., 3
Venda: mining techniques, 94; smelting techniques, 101–2
Village society, 23
Volavka, Z., 128–33
Vute, territorial expanse of, 80

Wadai, smiths of, 177
Walata, 58
Warfare, 48
Wealth, 202, 205, 216, 222, 224, 239, 243, 246, 249, 250, 252; iron as, 150, 155
Weapons: iron (*see* Iron tools); manufacture as metaphor, 173; metal edged, 48
Welding, 237–8
West Africa: archaeological record, 2; demographic changes, 76; gold fields, 1; states, control of iron production in, 158
Western Grasslands 3, 64–74
Wilkinson, .W. F., xvii
Witchcraft, protecting smelt from, 168, 187
Wives: ironworkers', 204, 211, 229, 234, 238; smiths', 177
Woot, Yatenga divine hero, 148
Wum, 72

Yatenga origin myth, 148
Yeke: mining techniques, 92; smelting techniques, 95–7
Yoruba, 184

Zangato, E., 14

About the Authors

Michael S. Bisson is an associate professor of Anthropology at McGill University, Montreal. A specialist in the study of prehistoric technologies, his doctoral research included a two-year field study of ancient copper production on the Zambia–Congo border, including excavations at Kansanshi and Kipushi mines. His subsequent African research has focused on Late Stone Age and Iron Age settlement patterns and interactions in the Luano Stream drainage, Chingola, Zambia. He is currently investigating theoretical issues in European Paleolithic technology and typology.

Philip de Barros is an associate professor and director of the Archaeology Program at Palomar College. He has investigated traditional iron smelting among the Bassar in Togo, West Africa. His current research focuses on the Late Stone Age and iron-using cultures in western Africa, including excavations at the Agarade Rockshelter, as well as survey and excavations at Late Stone Age shell mounds and early agricultural sites in the Oti Valley in Togo. He has also spent considerable time in the field of cultural resource management in California.

S. Terry Childs is an archaeologist for the Archeology and Ethnography Program and leader of the Cultural Resources Web Team for the National Park Service. Her research over the last twenty-five years has focused primarily on African archaeology with a specialty in the anthropology of technology. She is a research collaborator at the Smithsonian Institution and a research associate at the R. S. Peabody Museum in Andover, Massachusetts. She has many articles in scientific journals and edited volumes, including one on African archaeology and technology.

Augustin F. C. Holl is a professor at the University of California, San Diego, after having taught at the University of Paris X for several years. He has carried on fieldwork in the southwestern Sahara at Dhar Tichitt (Mauritania), northern Cameroon in the Houlouf region, and the northern Negev Desert in Israel (Shiqmim, Gilat, and Abu Hof). He is currently engaged in a new regional archaeological project in the Mouhoun Bend in western Burkina Faso.

Joseph O. Vogel is professor emeritus in Anthropology at the University of Alabama and for many years was the keeper of prehistory in the Livingstone Museum, National Museums of Zambia. During his time in Central Africa, he studied Early Iron Age settlements in the Victoria Falls region and the upper Zambezi valley in buLozi as well as cave sites in the Mumbwa district.